PENGUIN

PARTY OF ONE

MICHAEL HARRIS began his award-winning career in journalism at CBC Television, where he became the host of *The Harris Report*, an investigative and current affairs show. He worked for *The Globe and Mail* as Atlantic bureau chief and in Ottawa. Harris was the founding publisher and editor-in-chief of *The Sunday Express*, the St. John's newspaper that broke the story of the abuse of boys at the Mount Cashel Orphanage. His bestselling book, *Unholy Orders: Tragedy at Mount Cashel*, became a prize-winning documentary. His journalistic work has sparked four separate commissions of inquiry, including one on the wrongful conviction of an Aboriginal man, Donald Marshall. Harris is the author of nine books, three of which have been made into movies. He currently writes for ipolitics.ca.

ALSO BY MICHAEL HARRIS

ADULT BOOKS

Justice Denied: The Law Versus Donald Marshall

Unholy Orders: Tragedy at Mount Cashel

Rare Ambition: The Crosbies of Newfoundland

The Prodigal Husband:
The Tragedy of Helmuth and Hanna Buxbaum

The Judas Kiss: The Undercover Life of Patrick Kelly

Lament for an Ocean: The Collapse of the Atlantic Cod Fishery

Con Game: The Truth About Canada's Prisons

CHILDREN'S BOOKS

A Forest for Christmas

STEPHEN HARPER AND
CANADA'S RADICAL MAKEOVER

PARTY OF
ONE

MICHAEL HARRIS

PENGUIN
an imprint of Penguin Canada Books Inc., a Penguin Random House Company

Published by the Penguin Group
Penguin Canada Books Inc., 320 Front Street West, Suite 1400, Toronto, Ontario M5V 3B6, Canada

Penguin Group (USA) LLC, 375 Hudson Street, New York, New York 10014, U.S.A.
Penguin Books Ltd, 80 Strand, London WC2R 0RL, England
Penguin Ireland, 25 St Stephen's Green, Dublin 2, Ireland (a division of Penguin Books Ltd)
Penguin Group (Australia), 707 Collins Street, Melbourne, Victoria 3008, Australia
(a division of Pearson Australia Group Pty Ltd)
Penguin Books India Pvt Ltd, 11 Community Centre, Panchsheel Park, New Delhi – 110 017, India
Penguin Group (NZ), 67 Apollo Drive, Rosedale, Auckland 0632, New Zealand
(a division of Pearson New Zealand Ltd)
Penguin Books (South Africa) (Pty) Ltd, 24 Sturdee Avenue, Rosebank, Johannesburg 2196, South Africa

Penguin Books Ltd, Registered Offices: 80 Strand, London WC2R 0RL, England

First published in Viking hardcover by Penguin Canada Books Inc., 2014
Published in this edition, 2015

1 2 3 4 5 6 7 8 9 10 (RRD)

Manufactured in the U.S.A.

LIBRARY AND ARCHIVES CANADA CATALOGUING IN PUBLICATION

Harris, Michael, 1948-, author
Party of one : Stephen Harper and Canada's radical makeover / Michael Harris.

Originally published: Toronto, Ontario, Canada : Viking, 2014.
Includes bibliographical references and index.
ISBN 978-0-14-318705-9 (pbk.).

1. Harper, Stephen, 1959-. 2. Conservative Party of Canada.
3. Conservatism—Canada. 4. Canada—Politics and government—
2006-. I. Title.

FC640.H39 2015   971.07'3   C2015-900621-X

eBook ISBN 978-0-14-319305-0

Visit the Penguin Canada website at **www.penguin.ca**

Special and corporate bulk purchase rates available; please see
www.penguin.ca/corporatesales or call 1-800-810-3104.

For James Baxter

Parliament can hardly be weakened any more than it already is. Harper can't go much further without making the institution dysfunctional. He is trying to control every aspect of House business. In fact, it will have to be returned to its former state by someone if we are to have a democracy.

—*Peter Milliken*, July 7, 2012, interview with the author, Hurds Lake, Greater Madawaska, Ontario

CONTENTS

one

SIGN OF THE TIMES

On the night that Stephen Harper won the May 2, 2011, federal election, one of the most famous pollsters in Canada found himself in the company of very senior Conservatives at what should have been a victory party. It felt more like a wake. When the pollster asked why everyone was so glum, one of them replied, "This is still a Liberal country, and a Liberal public service and we have to get everything done in one term."

The pollster was later approached by a client who was anxious to do business with the new Conservative government. He had a practical question for the pollster, who knew Ottawa inside out. Who was in Harper's inner circle? the man wanted to know. The pollster replied, "There is no inner circle. Just a dot." It was a brilliant description of what the country had glimpsed through two Harper-led minority governments—the Conservative Party of Canada under Stephen Harper appeared to be a one-man band. Would that change after the Tories had a safe majority government, having won 166 of 308 seats in the House of Commons?

A few formalities remained before Stephen Harper would assume total control of the country and begin to provide the answer. Two weeks after winning the election, the Harper cabinet was sworn in at Rideau Hall. It featured veterans such as Jim Flaherty, Tony Clement, and John Baird, as well as nine newcomers, including Peter Penashue, Alice Wong, and Joe Oliver. Harper promised that his team would hit the road running on its key priority: the economy. All that was left now was to work out the government's legislative agenda and then have it delivered in early June in the Speech from the Throne.

On the morning of the Speech, June 3, 2011, Brigette DePape felt very tired. The previous night, there had been a lot to do and she had stayed up late to make sure everything was ready. Friends had briefed her on her legal rights in the event she was detained or arrested; a press release had to be prepared; and of course she had to buy the red construction paper for her sign and then hand-paint it. She barely made it to Wallack's, an Ottawa art supply store, before it closed. Using the iconic octagonal shape that guards intersections across the land, her red stop sign featured two words in white letters: "Stop Harper."

DePape stowed her sign in her backpack in the downstairs change room of the Senate, where she worked as a page. An hour before the governor general delivered the Speech from the Throne, she retrieved the sign and tucked it into her skirt, under her blazer. She told me that her greatest fear was that before she could carry out her silent protest, someone might spot the sign. "I was very nervous when seating the governor general's family that they would see the red of the sign poking out from my blazer, or that it would fall out."

With her heart racing, the determined protester joined the black-clad and bow-tied pages as they took their places. DePape, her long brown hair tied off in a braid hanging over her right shoulder, was stationed at the southwest wing of the Senate chamber. Time slowed to a crawl. Although she was comforted by the knowledge that her friends were waiting at a nearby coffee shop, the twenty-two-year-old was distressed. She was afraid of what her parents would say, of being arrested, and even of being spied on later by the political establishment whose pomp and circumstance she was about to upstage. The lawyer she had consulted told her that the worst that could happen to her under an archaic law was being sentenced to decades in jail for the high crime of "frightening the Queen." More likely she would get a ticket for trespassing and a small fine, and would perhaps be banned from Parliament Hill.

DePape became even more nervous when Stephen Harper strode into the chamber and took his seat to the right of the governor general. Paralyzing fear that could freeze the will to act battled other thoughts that spurred her on. She was divided. "My gut told me that I had to do it. Part of me was saying—'don't do it,' but my gut knew I was in exactly the right spot, doing exactly what I needed to do," she recalled. "It was when I thought about the people who have been attacked by Harper's agenda that it gave me the strength to act."

With the assembled might of the Canadian government—the prime minister, cabinet ministers, justices of the Supreme Court, privy councillors, senators, and MPs—listening with rapt attention, Governor General David Johnston began the Speech from the Throne. Two minutes later, Brigette DePape made her move. "I walked down the aisle to the middle of the Senate floor where the pages are not supposed to walk, carrying my 'Stop Harper' sign. I stand there for about ten seconds, then turn around for ten seconds to show my sign to Harper. Whereas the last time I saw him at the movie theatre, I was too afraid to say hello, never mind to tell him how I felt about the completely wrong direction in

which he has taken us—but in that moment, I silently spoke out."
In just twenty seconds, the public spectacle was over. With cries
of "Shame" ringing in her ears, the petite page was escorted out of
the Senate chamber by the sergeant-at-arms wearing his cocked
hat and chain of office. "I looked like a criminal being pulled away
like that," she told me. "It felt so backwards to me. The people
doing the real damage to real people were sitting in the chamber."

People who dismissed DePape as a showboating schoolgirl
forgot one important thing. They may not have liked her politics
or what she had done, but it was not the stunt of a publicity-
seeking know-nothing. Brigette DePape had been engaged in
public issues since she was a teenager. In 2007, she won a coveted Loran Scholar Award for her work with Students Without
Borders: Afrique, in a field of 2000 candidates. But it was only
when she became involved in the page program that she suddenly
realized how overwhelming the power of governments could be.
"While working as a page in the Senate, I felt alone, afraid, and
hopeless in the face of the Harper agenda set on attacking people
and the environment that sustains us. I witnessed Harper cutting
social services we value, and handing money over to rich oil and
gas companies. I saw the rejection of the Kyoto Protocol and the
expansion of the tar sands."

While her friends were issuing the press release written the
night before, DePape was taken to the basement of the Senate
building. There, she was questioned by people she believed to be
the RCMP. The grilling went on for two hours. She knew from her
preparations for this day that she was only obligated to tell them
her name, address, and telephone number. None of her inquisitors
mentioned her right to have a lawyer present. She remembered the
eyes of one interrogator "burning" to get answers beyond the ones
she was willing to give. "Who had put Brigette up to her stunt?
'Was it a particular political party? Was it the NDP? Was it the

Liberals? Was it a union? Was it Greenpeace?' He asked me why I did it." Finally, DePape was released, but not before signing a piece of paper confirming that she understood that her contract as a page had been terminated. One of the guards leaned over to her and whispered that he didn't like Harper either. As she was leaving, they seized the sign that had stolen the show at the 2011 Speech from the Throne—her one regret looking back on what happened that day.

The coverage of DePape was predictable in a country dedicated to peace, order, and good government—shrill, near-unanimous, and denunciatory. One major exception was American filmmaker Michael Moore, who offered DePape a job. The media was brutal. DePape's silent protest was roundly denounced, much as Chief Theresa Spence's hunger strike would be a year and a half later. One journalist described the former page's protest as a "swing and a miss." Tory bloggers raged that it was a mere "tantrum"—an odd description given that the page never uttered a word.

The Harper government dismissed DePape as a professional protester, a reference to the fact that she had taken part in the 2010 G20 protests in Toronto. Both main opposition leaders, Bob Rae and the late Jack Layton, joined in the general condemnation of DePape, describing her action as indecorous. The Speaker of the Senate harrumphed about the implications for Senate security. Somehow, an idea had slipped into the chamber that spoiled the peacock moment for the political establishment. There were even charges that what she had done amounted to contempt of Parliament. That was a line of attack that wasn't pursued very far. Just two months earlier, 156 MPs had voted that Stephen Harper was in actual contempt of the House of Commons, causing his government to fall. The indignation directed at the page was best exemplified by the Senate's principal clerk, Blair Armitage: "The role of the staff of a parliamentary administration is to support the parliamentarians in doing their work. It takes an incredible amount of hubris to substitute one's personal opinion on any matter for that of the hundreds of parliamentarians chosen to represent the country and to subvert them from within."

In what must surely be one of the all-time ironies of Canadian politics, the very institutional representatives in the Senate chamber that day who denounced Brigette DePape for subverting the system "from within" would soon, one-by-one, become the victims of a prime minister who would subvert the system from within far more profoundly than the page with the pigtail.

The governor general, who read the 2011 Speech from the Throne, would one day soon see his constitutional duties usurped by Stephen Harper when the prime minister, not the commander-in-chief, received the last flag that had flown in Afghanistan. Few knew that as Harper received that flag, he had ordered government lawyers to oppose the claim by Afghanistan veterans that the government had a social contract to take care of wounded soldiers returning from the wars.

The Privy Council Office would continue to see its duties to the country's public service abandoned by a near-total submission to the political demands of the Prime Minister's Office. It had already stood idly by while the careers of top bureaucrats such as Linda Keen were unjustly destroyed, and there were more victims to come—public servants such as Kevin Page and Munir Sheikh. And when things went wrong, as they would in the looming Senate expenses scandal, it would be the PCO that would take the blame for missing documents.

The Senate itself, which felt violated by Brigette DePape's symbolic intervention in the high affairs of state, would be undermined by the PMO in the matter of an independent Senate audit and the approaching Wright/Duffy scandal. The prime minister's chief of staff and a dozen others in the PMO would do to the

Senate what they had already done to the PCO—bend it to the will of the highest political office in the land.

Harper cabinet ministers, who traduced Brigette DePape on that June day when they assumed control of Canada, were quickly reduced to puppets reacting to every pull on the strings from the prime minister. They did not speak for themselves and their departments, but relayed the speaking points sent their way from the PMO. Nattering among themselves as they rode the green shuttle buses on Parliament Hill, they referred to Harper as the "Chairman." Majority government notwithstanding, their muzzles were tightened rather than removed.

The leaders of the opposition, who stood on the side of decorum in their denunciation of Brigette DePape, quickly came to see the point she was trying to make. After Jack Layton's untimely death, Thomas Mulcair spoke for the NDP, and his words actually supported the point of DePape's protest. "The Tories are smug, smart-ass and full of half lies," he told me. "Harper has no confidence in the process. The contempt of parliament finding led to absolutely no changes in his approach. Harper didn't do anything." Despite disapproving of DePape's actions, the then interim Liberal leader, Bob Rae, came to this conclusion about Stephen Harper a year after his majority government took office: "He can be nasty, cynical and has a deep authoritarian streak. If there is something these guys don't like, they must pass a law to stop it. He destroys the freedom people should have to express themselves."

As for ordinary MPs, who had been upset that a mere page had spoiled the ceremonies of power that day in the Senate, they would see their own roles reduced to mere shadows on the backbench. Committee meetings were moved behind closed doors, Tory MPs' mouths were wired shut, and government MPs soon found themselves in a battle with the PMO and their own House Leader over their right to even ask questions in the House of Commons.

The one group represented in the Senate chamber that day that might well have been most offended by DePape's unorthodox action were the justices of the Supreme Court of Canada—resplendent in their red gowns with white ermine trim. After all, theirs was the deepest commitment in the land to the law and the constitution, to propriety and process. But Harper's actions would prove even more unorthodox and disruptive. After the Supreme Court ruled against Stephen Harper's choice to fill a vacant Quebec seat on the high court, the prime minister would publicly attack Canada's first female chief justice with a vengeance. Harper accused Chief Justice Beverley McLachlin of acting in a way that was "inadvisable and inappropriate" when she contacted his office in an attempt to advise the government about eligibility requirements before filling the Quebec vacancy on the Supreme Court.

The PMO even attempted to retroactively amend the Supreme Court Act in an omnibus budget bill to make the appointment of Marc Nadon legitimate. Legal scholars immediately saw this as an attempt to override the fundamental supremacy of the Canadian constitution and Quebec's unique place in the country. The response from 650 lawyers and law professors was like the blowback from a blast furnace. They wrote an open letter to Stephen Harper deploring his unprecedented attack on the chief justice. A group of blue-ribbon academics even asked the International Commission of Jurists (ICJ) in Geneva to investigate. They alleged that Harper was attacking the independence of the high court, and that his remarks could be construed as intimidation. The international jurists agreed. It is interesting to note that most of the ICJ's investigations are in Africa, Asia, and Russia.[1]

Even retired Quebec Superior Court judge John Gomery added his criticism to the torrent of reaction triggered by the prime minister's smear of Justice McLachlin. The comments were ironic coming from him, since his inquiry into the Liberal sponsorship scandal had figured prominently in Stephen Harper's rise to power: "I think it's appalling that the judiciary should be used for political purposes in this way and I'm puzzled as to the motivation of the prime minister and his office as to why they would take on the chief justice."

A few years after a twenty-two-year-old Senate page held up a sign in front of the cameras imploring Canadians to "Stop Harper," the very people who had denounced her would feel the sting of Stephen Harper's contempt for the Canadian system of government. The question wasn't whether the country had a rogue page. The question was whether it had a rogue prime minister. The beginnings of an answer to that question were buried in the silt of Stephen Harper's political past.

two

THE GENESIS OF STEVE

While some Canadian political careers have ended in snowstorms, Stephen Harper's began in one. Harper and his best friend, John Weissenberger, jumped into a Volkswagen Jetta and headed to the founding convention of the Reform Party in Winnipeg on Halloween 1987. The early storm slowed but did not stop the excited, young politicos.

Harper had worked hard for a year in federal politics as legislative assistant to Alberta MP Jim Hawkes, the PC party whip. But, lonely and out of place in Brian Mulroney's Ottawa, he moved back to Alberta in 1986. Both Harper and Weissenberger resigned from the Progressive Conservative Party in the summer of 1987. They were appalled by Prime Minister Mulroney's unwillingness to tackle the deficit, and by what they saw as the federal government's shameless pandering to ethnic nationalism in Quebec.

The last straw was Mulroney's decision to award the maintenance contract for Canada's fleet of 138 CF-18 fighter jets to Canadair in Montreal, even though Bristol Aerospace in Winnipeg had the superior bid. It was time to reclaim the conservative brand that Mulroney had besmirched. They wanted to be there when the new party that proposed to do just that announced its name, defined a set of principles, and chose a leader. Harper had another reason to attend. He had met Preston Manning earlier that summer and the two men had hit it off. Manning had asked the bright young man to address the convention.

At lunch on Saturday, October 31, Harper and his friend sat at a table with David Somerville, president of the National Citizens Coalition (NCC) and former *Toronto Sun* reporter. Somerville polled the table and discovered that all eight people sitting there were members of the NCC. The right-wing advocacy group would be profoundly important throughout Harper's political career. It gave him a place to work between elected offices, an opportunity to hone his political marketing skills, and a ready-made agenda. The NCC was anti–public health insurance, anti-union, anti–Wheat Board, and pro–corporate governance and control.[1] The coalition's favourite weapon was advertising, and its advertisement of choice, the attack ad. (Sooner than he could have known, Stephen Harper would be meeting the man who perfected the attack ad and helped send Richard Nixon, Ronald Reagan, and both Bushes to the White House.)

Like the right-wing Fraser Institute, the NCC was founded in 1974, just after the October 1973 oil crisis. Oil rose from $3 to $12 per barrel overnight, doubling gasoline prices. Governments around the world made draconian adjustments to this unforeseen disaster. Downing Street asked Britons to heat only one room in their homes over the winter. The state of Oregon banned Christmas lights. Most shocking of all, the nation famous for seeing the "USA in their Chevrolets"[2] drove into service stations that had run out gas. Financial markets were rattled by a series of recessions and high inflation. Within months of the oil price shock, the US government took action. On February 11, 1974, the then US secretary of state, Henry Kissinger, unveiled Project Independence, a plan to make the US self-supporting in the energy sector. It was like divine intervention, conferring as it did a golden future on Alberta.

In 1974, seven of the top fifteen Fortune 500 companies were oil companies. Having experienced the deprivation of the Middle East's vast supply of cheap, light sweet crude, the companies aggressively pursued new ways to develop oil that, although dirtier and more expensive, was closer to home. Blessed with the world's third-largest reserves of alternative oil, Alberta was about to be transformed into the richest—and most aggrieved—province in Canada. The only thing heavier than the oil beneath Alberta's prairie was the hand of Ottawa trying to control and capitalize on it. The creation of Petro-Canada and the National Energy Program infuriated the West.

Next to money, the mother's milk of politics, anger is the most important resource of political parties, especially an opposition party, let alone a protest party like Reform. The West had always resented freight rates that were 20 percent higher for them than for eastern Canadians. Now, in a country where the provinces own natural resources under the constitution, oil-rich Alberta saw the federal government conniving ways to horn in on its staggering prosperity.

Although he was a transplanted Easterner, Harper quickly grafted Alberta's sense of grievance to his own restless search for identity. After dropping out of the University of Toronto just two months into his studies, the young Harper headed west, taking a job at Imperial Oil. He liked the place and stayed. His father had worked for the firm as an accountant in Toronto, and in 1958 led the team that assembled one of the first commercial mainframes in North America. Later, while a student at the University of Calgary, Harper became a devotee of the "Calgary School" of

economics, which argued that Ottawa and Liberal elites had dis-
criminated against Alberta.

At the founding convention of the Reform Party, Harper
skilfully tapped into the sense of Western alienation that would
quickly make the new party a serious force in Canadian politics.
Titling his speech "Achieving Economic Justice in Confederation,"
the expatriate Ontarian began with a quote from an unnamed
"Western Canadian": "I am not advocating separation, but if we
were separate, I would not advocate joining." It was red meat for
lions, and Harper kept serving it up. "In fact, a lot of economic
evidence, including the MacDonald Royal Commission, suggests
that the West would be better off outside of Canada," he said. It
was a typical and telling analysis. For Harper, only one measure of
being "better off" mattered, and that was economic. To him, that
meant corporate balance sheets and the GDP, not the day-to-day
situation of average people. There was no concept of social security, no passion for equalization of the country's unevenly divided
treasure, and no doubt that anything governments could do, private enterprise could do better—including delivering health care.
It was a philosophical tunnel vision Harper would never lose.

The study that he mentioned, ponderously christened the
MacDonald Royal Commission on the Economic Union and
Development Prospects for Canada, had in fact recommended
in 1985 that Canada take "a leap of faith" and enter a free trade
agreement with the United States, a move that was certainly in the
interests of the West. Harper's speech was detailed, well-written,
and consistently critical of what he called the "welfare state" that
had sprung up in Canada run by powerful and distant federal
bureaucrats. Funding for that welfare state, he claimed, had come
from tax grabs, the windfall profits of Western resource industries,
particularly oil. As for Atlantic Canada, Harper declared that it
had been reduced to a state of permanent dependency by transfer

payments. It was grandiosity as only a young man can be grandiose. In one fell swoop, a man not yet thirty ascribed a loser mentality to an entire region of the country he knew little or nothing about, beyond what his father had told him. Harper's father, Joseph, had grown up in New Brunswick and moved to Toronto in 1951 after qualifying as a chartered accountant.

After ridiculing Pierre Trudeau's "Just Society," Harper ended his speech with Reform's vision for Canada: "What Canada really requires is the sweeping winds of change. For the vested interests of the National Policy, the Welfare State, and the Quebec question, this will be a challenge they will resist." The country could "no longer be built on the economic exploitation and political disenfranchisement of Western Canada," he declared. "In the meantime, we require a political party to put the pursuit of the West's agenda at the top of its list." It was the first open declaration of Harper's long-term intentions: the reverse takeover of a country from the home base of a province that looked south for its prosperity and inspiration.

The speech also marked Harper's first public success with exploiting a grievance for political gain. When he finished speaking, the audience gave the twenty-eight-year-old a standing ovation, the reward for both championing their cause and identifying the culprit who was keeping the West down: Central Canada and the Eastern Establishment. Although Preston Manning, the soft-spoken, professorial man who had studied physics in university, became the party's first leader, *Alberta Report* called Harper's speech the "highlight" of the Convention.

Shortly after the Halloween Convention, Preston Manning laid the foundations of Stephen Harper's political career. Fiscal policies were central to Reform, deploring as the party did the debt and deficit run up by the Mulroney Progressive Conservatives. In Manning's mind, Mulroney's profligacy merely exacerbated debts accumulated under the Trudeau government. A bright—and very affordable—economics student fit the bill to become the impecunious party's chief policy advisor. "We asked Bob Mansell at the University of Calgary for the name of his smartest grad student," Manning recalled, "and he told us Stephen Harper."

Harper worked hard developing policy but threw his hat into the electoral ring at the first opportunity, running for Reform in what became the free trade election of 1988. It must have been an odd experience. He ran against his old boss, Progressive Conservative Jim Hawkes, in Calgary West. In those days, he called himself "Steve Harper" and ran on the slogan "The West Wants In." Possibly, but it didn't want "Steve," at least not yet.

Although he lost his first attempt at elected politics, Harper was soon on his way to Ottawa anyway. His ticket was punched by another Reformer, Deborah Grey, who had won a by-election in March 1989. Grey needed a legislative assistant and Stephen Harper drew the assignment. They were the original political odd couple, as Preston Manning told me: "That was a case of two opposite personalities."

As a politician trying to grow a political party, Manning paid more attention to ability than to personality. He told me that in the ten years Stephen Harper had been with him, he really didn't know the stranger at his elbow: "I did not have a close relationship with Stephen Harper—especially after 1997. On a personal level, he keeps it close to the vest. When he first joined us, he was not married. I do remember that he didn't care if you were married or had a wife and kids to think about."

At first, Harper thrived on hard, purpose-driven work. While serving as the party's chief policy advisor, he finished his master's degree, gave a speech at a memorial event for the founder of the NCC, served as national spokesperson for the "No" campaign in the 1992 Quebec constitutional referendum, and found time to marry Laureen Tesky. And then in the early nineties, Preston Manning decided to hire a new political strategist for Reform. Rick Anderson was a proven organizer and a former manager of Hill & Knowlton in Ottawa. He was experienced, personable, and diligent. He was also very much resented by Stephen Harper.

Harper was already having policy disagreements with his leader by this time, over matters such as the Charlottetown Accord constitutional issue and Reform's focus for the next election. Manning wanted to run a national campaign in 1993; Harper believed the party should invest its resources in Alberta. Although Harper himself had quit the position of chief policy officer in 1992, the idea of being replaced by a Trudeau Liberal was especially galling. "Stephen was quite suspicious of Rick Anderson when he joined Reform because he had been a Liberal. The chemistry was not great," Manning recalled. "Since those days, Rick and Stephen Harper have come to a greater mutual respect. When Rick's daughter passed away from brain cancer [in January 2010], Stephen Harper was very deeply moved emotionally."

Harper's next run at federal politics came in 1993, when he again ran against his old boss, PC MP Jim Hawkes. In a moody display of his unhappiness with Reform, Harper withdrew from the party's national campaign and concentrated exclusively on his own attempt to get elected. This time the winds of change Harper had talked about in his 1987 speech were howling. The Progressive Conservative Party was blown into political oblivion like tumbleweed. When the gales subsided, the PCs' representation had been reduced to two seats, and Stephen Harper was the new member for Calgary West in a caucus of fifty-two Reform MPs.

Although Jim Hawkes may not have known it, he was not defeated by the rebranded "Stephen" Harper alone. Working behind the scenes was the NCC and legendary American pollster and strategist Arthur Finkelstein, who had worked for the NCC since the early 1980s. Hawkes had raised the ire of the NCC on the subject dearest to its political heart: third-party funding during elections. The far-right organization portrayed legislation limiting the amount of money third parties could spend during elections as "gag laws" rather than a sensible attempt to make sure these contests didn't come down to who could buy the most advertising. Finkelstein saw Jim Hawkes as Brian Mulroney's point man against third-party spending. The NCC was locked and loaded. Careful not to say it was supporting Stephen Harper, the organization spent $50,000 to get "Hawkes's head on a platter," as the American pollster described his goal.

Like its founder, Colin M. Brown, members of the NCC vigorously resisted any limits on their "freedom." Brown was a millionaire life insurance salesman from London, Ontario, who didn't approve of medicare. The motto of the NCC was "More freedom through less government." Brown had adamantly opposed hospital insurance, medicare, and the expansion of social welfare during the Pearson and Diefenbaker years. Both Preston Manning and his father, Ernest, were ardent supporters of the NCC, sharing its values and vision. Brown himself quit the PC party in 1975 to personally fight the National Energy Program and the so-called gag laws. He assisted the pro–free trade campaign by the business coalition in the 1988 election, which outspent its opponents four to one. At its peak, the NCC took in $2.8 million per year in donations. The organization fervently believed that citizens and organizations should be able to spend as much of their own money as they wanted in election campaigns—a right in the United States that has turned politics into the sport of kings and wealthy kingmakers.

Arthur Finkelstein was crucial to the NCC's plan to turn Canada blue. In 1982, the lobbying group hired this brilliant and secretive political consultant who had perfected the political attack ad. His job was to teach the NCC the art of commando politics as practised in the United States and several other countries where Finkelstein operated. Finkelstein, who knocked down incumbents like bowling pins in US politics, was the most sought-after neo-conservative political strategist in the world. A Libertarian in his personal politics, his first success came in the 1970 Senate race in the US, in which he got James L. Buckley, brother of William F. Buckley, elected. As a member of the Republican caucus, Buckley became the lead petitioner in the Supreme Court decision that shaped new campaign finance law in the United States, striking down limits on spending in Congressional races. (On behalf of the NCC, Stephen Harper took the same issue all the way to the Supreme Court of Canada, where he ultimately lost in 2004.)

In 1988, Finkelstein did a poll that alarmed the far right, suggesting that Canadians might be on the brink of electing NDP leader Ed Broadbent as prime minister. Broadbent stood at 40 percent in the polls—majority government territory if the numbers held until the federal election looming in the fall. Since there were difficulties driving a scandal-ridden Brian Mulroney's numbers up, the NCC decided to bring Ed Broadbent's down. They spent half a million dollars doing it. Under Finkelstein's guidance, the message was simple and deadly: Broadbent the socialist, who wanted to take Canada out of NATO and who opposed Senate reform, was "Scary, very, very, scary."

The campaign virtually sidelined Broadbent, and free trade, not leadership, became the key issue in the 1988 election. But there was still a problem with promoting free trade, because the man who was advocating it, Brian Mulroney, was not popular. Arthur Finkelstein was not deterred, as Gerry Nicholls reported in his book *Loyal to the Core*. Finkelstein told his colleagues at the NCC, "We have to convince Canadians to drink pig piss." They did. Brian Mulroney won a second majority government on the issue of free trade, despite serious doubts about his government's integrity.

Finkelstein would have an enormous influence on Stephen Harper's political career. He worked only for conservative candidates and always tried to get a benefit for Israel out of any of his campaigns.[3] But, according to his associate Gerry Nicholls, he was not a mercenary and wouldn't work with a candidate he didn't agree with, or for the biggest paycheque. But there was a striking exception to that practice. Although gay, Finkelstein helped to elect Republican candidates all over the United States who thought homosexuality was immoral and who opposed gay marriage. He managed to keep the contradiction between his professional and private life secret until 2005. Meanwhile, according to a CNN report on Finkelstein in 1996, his abilities were almost magical: "He is the stuff of Hollywood, a man who can topple even the most powerful foes, yet so secretive that few have ever heard of him."

Executives at the NCC tended to see elections as wars, as did Stephen Harper. Finkelstein had honed the art of third-party advertising to a razor's edge. The strategic use of attack ads could elect or destroy a candidate for public office in a heartbeat. Donors to the NCC not only got to support or attack a candidate; they also received a tax deduction. Finkelstein's modus operandi was always the same: pinpoint polling aimed at exposing a weakness in an opponent; then use a trenchant, repetitive advertisement to exploit the candidate's Achilles' heel. The right fifteen-second spot on TV or radio could end an opponent's career when the attack ad followed the formula of Arthur Finkelstein, nicknamed the "Merchant of Venom." His specialties were upset victories and close races. According to "Finkel-Think," 80 percent of the vote in the US is decided before parties even begin to campaign—evenly split at 40:40. The election is taken by the party that wins the close races in the remaining 20 percent of the swing vote.

Not much is known about Arthur Finkelstein—by design. He almost never grants interviews, and he never appears as a talking head on any of the network gabfests. His advice to clients is almost always delivered face to face—as it would be to Stephen Harper in 1998. But while speaking to a private university in Prague in May 2011, Finkelstein was recorded, and the audio ended up on YouTube. It was an *ex gratia* lesson from the master strategist about how to win in modern politics and about where the world was headed. In a smooth, calm, intelligent voice, he talked about his work in the United States, Canada, Israel, and Eastern Europe, and about the nature of politics. Sounding a little bit like a political reincarnation of philosopher George Berkeley, Finkelstein told his audience that what they perceived to be true was true—as distinct from the objective truth.

An old philosophical chestnut: perception as reality. Good politicians will first tell you things that are true and only later begin to mislead you, Finkelstein said. If they tell lies to you first and get caught out, they will always be disbelieved. Money is important because it determines who gets to hear what, he continued. As for political candidates, apparently looks and size matter. Finkelstein offered his audience an interesting statistic: the taller candidate wins 75 percent of the time. "An ugly person could not be elected now," he said. And if you were female and wanted to get into politics, Finkelstein had some advice: look mannish, strong, and wear a pantsuit. If the economy is a mess, he pointed out, the electorate looks to business people as leaders. The most important resource for any politician is time, both to raise money and to build an identity and image. He noted that 60 to 90 percent of the vote in every election is decided before a candidate ever hits the hustings.

He also talked about different types of campaigns, including ones in which the goal is to get people *not* to vote for a candidate, just as Finkelstein and the NCC had done in the contest between Jim Hawkes and Stephen Harper in 1993. The trick is to create a totally negative vote against an opponent while not showing your own candidate. Surprisingly, Finkelstein said that issues don't matter—people will vote for you if they like you, the way Americans liked John Kennedy and Ronald Reagan.

Finkelstein explained that the current world economic crisis is worse than it feels, claiming anger is rife at the base level of society. Young people will take to the streets when the realization sinks in that their future holds not fame and fortune, but penury. As a result, nervous societies will rely more and more on authoritarian regimes led by people who are capable of ruling with an iron fist. Finkelstein also thought that the future could include the rise of another Hitler if unemployment got any worse. Scapegoating would take place around the world as sovereign nations looked for someone to blame for their reversal of fortune. In Hungary, it's the fault of the Roma, he noted, in France the Muslims are to blame, in the United States, it's Mexicans. These groups will be accused of taking jobs from native citizens and destroying their way of life.

But every crisis has a political silver lining for strategic thinkers. Finkelstein advised that the riots in Greece—the economic basket case of the European Union—could be used to discredit the socialist campaign against austerity. Fear is a political superweapon in the power wars. "Politics is a three-dimensional game of chess," he said in Prague. There is you and the other candidate, and then God steps in: Bin Laden is captured; there is an earthquake or a tidal wave, an ever-changing backdrop that affects the game on the board. In chess as in politics, a good player is always ready to react with the right move.

Finkelstein told his audience that humour is important, especially in advertising. If you make the advertisement amusing, everyone will want to see it, creating resonance. And the medium is the message. He reminded his listeners that in the 1960 presidential debate, those who saw it on television thought Kennedy won; people who listened on the radio gave the nod to Nixon.

Finkelstein pointed out that politics had changed drastically since his days with Nixon, largely because of what he called "fragmentation of information." Today, more information is available about smaller things. People are capable of knowing more and more about less and less. They have turned away from the big things and immersed themselves in the distracting diversity of information on the internet purely of interest to themselves. They are not wired in, but wired out.

The political strategist who had turned the word *liberal* into an epithet of abuse in the United States told his audience that 60 percent of people have no interest in news. In Finkelstein's opinion, content has become the victim of the speed of communication. The day was coming when there would be no breadth of information. The news would be purely episodic and the audience's critical faculty weakened. It was good news for marketers and nirvana for political strategists riding herd on the suggestible masses.

Technology has also made political manipulation frighteningly less difficult, Finkelstein noted. While acknowledging that freedom of speech was sacrosanct, he observed that it was hard to clarify the truth on the internet. Although he said that lying about people had never been his specialty, discrediting them was—as John Kerry learned after he was "swift-boated" in the presidential election against George W. Bush. Finkelstein was widely suspected of having organized the attack ads. "I do not slander someone without proof, but with proof, I am happy to," he said, pointing out that if Kerry had responded more quickly to the attacks against him, he would have become president.

To Finkelstein, a negative campaign is legitimate as long as it's not patently untrue. It comes down to casting the appropriate lights and shadows over your opponent; you are relentless in highlighting his failings and you never mention his strengths. Because most people water-ski over the surface of events, they don't want deep content or even to know what a politician thinks.' They want to know who he is sleeping with and how many of the good human vices he has. Finkelstein said it came from watching "nonsense programs" on TV. With the right information, you can cut somebody off at the neck instantly. It was, he told his audience, "a dangerous world we live in."

It would be four more years before Stephen Harper commissioned a poll by Arthur Finkelstein in 1998 to test the waters for making a run at political leadership in Canada. But what Harper had to offer was on display at the ninth annual memorial dinner for the founder of the NCC, Colin M. Brown. Speaking in Ancaster, Ontario, as a Reform MP, Harper delivered the same message in 1994 he had delivered to the same group in 1989—that there was a "crisis in the welfare state." Harper argued that Western countries were suffering from high unemployment, low economic growth, and very high government expenditures. The choice was either a major reform of government programs or "the state as we know it will experience a financial collapse."

In the public question period after the speech, Harper was asked what he thought of Premier Ralph Klein's slash-and-burn approach to reducing the deficit in Alberta. Harper heartily endorsed Klein and offered a prediction: "If Premier Klein can carry off his program in Alberta, it will lead to a revolution, a very quick political revolution across the country." But as one of his audience members, NCC president David Somerville, noted, getting rid of the deficit would be meaningful only if the system itself were changed in such a way that successor governments and the bureaucracy would be unable to undo the reforms. Stephen Harper was clearly listening.

Despite his hard work and speeches promoting a competitive international market economy for Canada, Harper was growing less and less comfortable in the Reform Party. Preston Manning told me that he thought that part of the explanation for Harper's restlessness was that he had turned against a fundamental principle of Reform: freedom of expression for its MPs. "What soured Stephen early on with Reform was that if a member's constituents differed from the Party's position, we allowed the member to represent the constituents," Manning recalled. "It bothered Stephen that one rogue member could undermine all our work. While the Conservatives and Liberals appeared united, we sometimes got hammered by our own people, and that soured Stephen Harper. Personally, I would prefer the benefits of freedom even at the cost of flack."

Stephen Harper's instinct to control the message and muzzle others took root as he lived through several media meltdowns triggered by bizarre ideas or extremist outbursts from Reformers on the fringe. But another anxiety was eating away at Harper—the sinking feeling that as the election of 1997 approached, Reform was stagnant. He resigned his seat six months before the June 1997 election. "When Stephen left Reform, it was because he thought we were going to lose. In his view, we had made no progress east of Ontario. He was disappointed and discouraged," Manning said. "I had more faith than Stephen did and we pulled it off. We had 150,000 members. This was a blow to Stephen; it tarnished him."

On the same January day that Harper resigned his seat in Parliament, he introduced himself to the staff at his new place of employment, the National Citizens Coalition. Although the lobby group claimed to be independent of political parties, they had hired a politician to become their vice-president. As for Stephen Harper, he ruled out a future run for the leadership of the Reform Party. Resorting to the cliché of frustrated politicians everywhere, he said he wanted to spend more time with his family. He also told reporters that he no longer wanted to be bound by party politics. Instead, he would push for public policies that were important to him. The NCC was the perfect vehicle to practise the wicked game of wedge politics.

Prime Minister Jean Chrétien had called a federal election for June 2, 1997. Stephen Harper and the NCC jumped into the fray, targeting MPs' gold-plated pensions. Two Liberal MPs, Anne McLellan and Judy Bethal, were presented in ads as "pension porkers," their heads placed on a pair of pigs guzzling champagne while wallowing in a trough filled with tax dollars. Pure Finkelstein. Bethel was defeated and McLellan won in a cliffhanger. The Liberals won a solid majority government and Reform became the Official Opposition, winning sixty seats.

After the election, the only politics in Stephen Harper's life took place at the office. As vice-president of the NCC, he shared an office in Calgary with the organization's president, David Somerville. According to long-time NCC employee Gerry Nicholls, it was a case of two type-A personalities unable to play well together. Whether by design or disenchantment, Somerville presided over his last staff meeting as president on December 12, 1997, less than a year after the arrival of Stephen Harper. A pattern was beginning to emerge. Harper had a habit of undermining or replacing the people he had once worked for or supported: Jim Hawkes, Brian Mulroney, Preston Manning, and David Somerville. Now that he was his own man, fully in charge of an influential lobby group, the methodical autocrat popped out of the smooth-talking, unflappable media personality that Harper projected after joining the NCC. The new president didn't like his authority challenged, and according to Nicholls, referred to the NCC as "a dictatorship fighting for democracy."

STEPHEN HARPER'S DIRECT connection to Republican Party political values and strategy was far deeper than the NCC and Arthur Finkelstein. Just after the Chrétien victory in June 1997, he gave a speech to the Council for National Policy (CNP). *The New York Times* described the CNP as "a little known group of a few hundred of the most influential conservative leaders in business, government politics, academia and religion in the United States." The CNP meet three times a year behind closed doors at various locations—a sort of Bilderberg Group of the continental United States. Wealthy right-wing donors use the meetings to network with top conservative operatives to plan long-term strategy.

The CNP was co-founded in 1981 in Dallas, Texas, by Baptist pastor Reverend Tim LaHaye, who was head of the Moral Majority, a group made up of conservative Christians who wanted to assist the political right in the United States. Political success on the right in the US existed at the confluence of social and economic conservatism—and Stephen Harper immediately grasped the potential for similar alliance-building in Canada. Reverend LaHaye was a true believer who enjoyed spreading the word. He claimed that his books about Armageddon and the Rapture had sold fifty-five million copies. He believed that there would be a mass conversion of Jews to Christianity during the "end times." LaHaye was so certain of the gospel that he even tried to convert the Dalai Lama when he bumped into him in a hotel corridor in Israel.

When the CNP meets, a lot of money is on the table. One of the original directors of the organization gave $4.5 million to Swift Boat Veterans for Truth, the group that played a key role in sinking the presidential ambitions of John Kerry. The same director donated $3 million to the Progress for America Voter Fund, which backed President George W. Bush's attempt to privatize Social Security. Seed money was also given by Nelson Baker Hunt, the billionaire son of oilman Howard L. Hunt. Ronald Reagan addressed the CNP's tenth anniversary celebration and had this to say: "A handful of men and women, individuals of character, had a vision. A vision to see the return of righteousness, justice, and truth to our great nation." Besides the vision, the CNP also had tax-exempt status.

Past members of the group include Pat Robertson and Jerry Falwell, former US attorneys general Ed Meese and John Ashcroft, gun rights activist Colonel Oliver North, and the mother of Erik Princep, founder of the private security company Blackwater, which later ran amok in the Iraq War. Their common enemy was political and philosophical liberalism. Their agenda was cleaving to Christian heritage, unqualified support of Israel, a strong military, gun rights, traditional values, and small government—things Canada's NCC would not find objectionable.

The CNP commands the elite of US Republican potentates. Vice-President Dick Cheney flew in on Air Force 2 to address the group at one of their meetings. Mitt Romney gave an address to the CNP in Salt Lake City, Utah. When he made his first run for president, George W. Bush gave a speech to the CNP in San Antonio, Texas, that helped him gain the support of the conservatives in the 2000 presidential election. In accordance with CNP practice, Bush's speech was never released. In the same year that the future president addressed the group, the CNP gave Charles G. Koch the Free Enterprise Award. Koch and his brother preside over the second-largest private company in the United States, Koch Industries, based in Wichita, Kansas. Oil is the basis of their enormous wealth, and the family has been involved in the Alberta tar sands for over fifty years. As reported in *The Washington Post*, the Koch brothers are one of the biggest leaseholders in the enormous development, controlling over half a million hectares. Koch Industries also concentrates on shipping and refining heavy oil. The company has upgraded its Corpus Christi refinery to handle heavy bitumen.

"Canada is one of the cheapest places in the world for Big Oil to do business," according to Mitchell Anderson, who is writing a book, *The Oil Vikings*, about Norway's wise resource use. In

2012, Canada produced over two billion barrels of oil equivalent (BOE, which includes crude oil, natural gas, and other petroleum liquids) and collected $18 billion in provincial and federal taxes, and royalties. Taxpayers realized a benefit of $9 per BOE. Of that total, Alberta produced 1.5 billion BOE in 2012 and collected $6.13 billion in non-renewable royalties. By charging the oil companies higher taxes and investing equity ownership in production, the Norwegian government paid $46.29 BOE to their taxpayers for their oil in 2012—over five times what Canadians received. Norway has an $ 850-billion sovereign wealth fund for its population of about five million people.[4]

So when Stephen Harper gave a speech to what was essentially a secret society of wealthy, hard-right Republicans, it was odd for a few reasons. After all, the members of the CNP are in the business of scrutinizing potential Republican leadership candidates. For example, after listening to Senator John McCain of Arizona speak, they decided that he wasn't conservative enough. The group also vowed to run a third-party candidate if the Republican Party chose Rudy Giuliani as its leader because of his pro-choice position on abortion. Stephen Harper wasn't even a politician anymore and he also happened to be a Canadian. So what was behind the invitation? Whatever the reason, there was no mystery about why he jumped at a chance to speak to them. The CNP had enormous influence on the US government.

In 2003, Alberta's economic development minister, Mark Norris, attended a three-day session of the CNP in a Virginia suburb close to Washington. Norris went to promote the tar sands, but also, as the *Calgary Herald* reported at the time, to mend fences because Canada had not participated in the Iraq War. Donald Rumsfeld was the keynote speaker at the event.

Beyond the appeal of the CNP's great power, the council also shared Stephen Harper's values. For one thing, Harper disliked the governance model in Canada, preferring Congress over Parliament. As he would later tell *The Globe and Mail*, the difference between the calibre and experience of the Bush cabinet and any Canadian equivalent was embarrassing to Canada. President Bush got to recruit "top people" from private industry into his inner political circle, while Canadian prime ministers were stuck with a cabinet stocked from the relatively feeble pool of elected MPs.

Like Harper, the CNP was highly secretive. Its membership and donor list are private. Its events are closed to the public. It has been alleged that members are told not to use the name of the organization in emails to protect against leaks. For Harper, one of the most attractive aspects of speaking to the council was that the event would remain secret. CNP by-laws both blocked the media from attending and prevented the release of a transcript of what had been said unless all speakers agreed. Thinking that he could say whatever he wanted without media coverage, Harper gave quite a speech that June night in 1997.[5]

His American audience must have felt as though they were in Utah listening to a well-scrubbed Republican candidate for the US Senate. The speech was a perfect blend of neo-con and theo-con, which was predictable enough. But what was unexpected was how Harper derided his own country to a foreign audience as "a Northern European welfare state in the worst sense of the word." By comparison, Harper was effusive in his praise of the United States and its Republican politics: "Your country and, particularly, your conservative movement, is a light and inspiration to people in this country and across the world."

He then gave a shorthand civics lesson about governance in Canada, in which his disdain for parliamentary institutions was stunning: "Our executive is the Queen, who doesn't live here. Her representative is the Governor-General, who is an appointed buddy of the Prime Minister. Of our two legislative houses, the

Senate, our upper House, is also appointed, also by the Prime Minister, where he puts his buddies, fundraisers and the like. So the Senate is not very important in our political system. And we have a Supreme Court, like yours, which, since we put a Charter of Rights in our Constitution in 1982, is becoming increasingly arbitrary and important. It is also appointed by the Prime Minister. Unlike your Supreme Court, we have no ratification process." Stephen Harper was essentially describing the Canadian system of government as a dictatorship run by the Prime Minister of Canada: "So if you sort of remove three of the four elements, what you see is a system that's described as unpaid checks and political imbalances. The House of Commons, the bastion of the Prime Minister's power, the body that selects the prime minister, is an elected body."

But Harper warned his audience not to be fooled. Even though voters selected the members of the House of Commons, it was not like the US House of Representatives. What was it like, then? Harper asked his audience to think of the Commons in terms of the US Electoral College. In the United States, the Electoral College chooses the president and then disappears. But the Commons continues sitting for the next four years, having the power to vote on every issue. To Stephen Harper, Canadian parliamentary democracy was the political version of the movie *Groundhog Day*. It was an extraordinary description. Harper reduced the work of Parliament to being simply a rubber stamp of the prime minister's legislative agenda: "The important thing to know is that this is how it will be until the Prime Minister calls the next election. The same majority vote on every issue. So if you ask me 'What's the vote going to be on gun control?' or on the budget, we know that already."

In strikingly simple words, Stephen Harper again declared to his American audience his personal view of Canadian governance.

Between elections, the House of Commons was the property of the prime minister. If you were a member of the opposition, your business was restricted to going through a token exercise of voting on outcomes that were inevitable—the government always winning, the opposition always losing. Missing from his analysis was the opposition's role in bringing out public information in Question Period, and the work of all-party committees in amending legislation and holding the government to account when it breaks its promises or misleads the people.

If Harper's view of how Canada's parliamentary system works was inept, his view of the country's other political parties was grossly dismissive. He described the NDP as a socialist party, "proof that the Devil lives and interferes in the affairs of men." It was only partly an attempt at humour. He was hitting the perfect tone with his audience, just as he had done ten years earlier at the Reform Party's founding convention. He articulated what they despised. The NDP, in effect, represented the opposite of what everyone in the room believed with regard to social value issues. Having dismissed the NDP with the perfect Finkelstein word "socialist," Harper added the other hot-button epithet of abuse—"radical." The NDP was a branch of the Canadian Labour Congress (CLC), which was "explicitly radical."

His description of the Liberal Party was carefully designed to stir just as much revulsion in his audience but in a different way. To Christian-right American conservatives, Bill Clinton, the sexual libertine and great deceiver, was the devil incarnate. So when Harper described Canadian Liberals as a type of "Clinton pragmatic Democrat," it was the end of the conversation: the Liberals were a degenerate political party, full stop.

That left just two other parties to describe. Harper damned the Progressive Conservatives by calling them "liberal" Republicans, which meant to this audience that they weren't Republican at all.

Only the Reformers qualified as conservative Republicans. Preston Manning was populist in the same, leader-driven way that Ross Perot had been. And then Harper's final sales pitch on behalf of Reform: "It's the closest thing we have to a neo-conservative party."

Harper could not finish his Montreal speech without offering his audience a précis of the Quebec separatist movement, and what he called "the appeasement of ethnic nationalism." For a moment, he was back in that Volkswagen ten years earlier heading for Winnipeg, full of anger at Brian Mulroney's catering to Quebec. In making a passing reference to the referendum that included distinct society status for Quebec, he frightened his audience by talking about other changes on the table that "would just horrify you," such as "putting universal Medicare in our Constitution, and feminist rights and a whole bunch of other things." Harper ended by telling his American audience that the trouble with Canada was political, not social. Arthur Finkelstein had taught the NCC the value of humour in spreading one's message, and Harper ended with a very clever line, especially given that the audience was the inner sanctum of the Christian right: "As long as there are exams, there will always be prayer in schools."

Though Harper had protested that he was happy to be free of the constraints of party politics, another possibility was more plausible. He simply wanted to be party leader—partly because he didn't like having to live with other people's compromises, as his former boss Jim Hawkes had noted. So when Jean Charest resigned the leadership of the Progressive Conservative Party in the spring of 1998, Harper listened when he was approached by party members to run for the top job. He was young and spoke French, and since he had once been a member of the Progressive Conservatives, his bid could be presented as a homecoming of sorts.

Harper mentor Tom Flanagan told *The Globe and Mail* what he thought it would take to get the lapsed Reformer to run: "Harper could be persuaded to run on a platform of bringing together under one umbrella, the two right-of-centre parties." Interestingly, when that idea was floated at the Winds of Change conference in 1996, Harper himself thought it would never happen because of deep-seated differences between Canada's main strains of conservatism.

On April 7, 1998, Harper called Gerry Nicholls, a senior staffer at the NCC, to say he would be giving an important speech in Calgary to the Home and Mortgage Loan Association. Although he wanted a media advisory flagging the event, no interviews would be given until the speech was delivered. Senior CBC journalists including Don Newman, Jason Moscovitz, and Julie Van Dusen bombarded the NCC with calls, suspecting that Harper intended to use his Calgary speech to announce that he was running for the Tory leadership.

The day after the speech, Harper was featured in a front-page story in the *Globe*, in which he said that he would not be a candidate for the leadership because his candidacy "would burn bridges to those Reformers with whom I have worked for many years." But just ten days later, Harper was back in Toronto planning to attend a very important meeting. A group of PC party activists was looking to Harper to become the Blue Tory candidate they wanted to run for the leadership against Red Tory Hugh Segal.

For a man who supposedly wanted to spend more time with his family and enjoyed the freedom of being a lobbyist for right-wing causes, Harper spent a lot of time politicking behind the scenes. He asked American pollster and political consultant John McLaughlin to attend the meeting with him. McLaughlin, who worked at the NCC, was one of Finkelstein's "boys." His clients included Governor Arnold Schwarzenegger; Iain Duncan Smith, the leader of the Conservative Party in the UK; multiple incumbent US senators and members of Congress; governors and mayors; and the Republican National Committee itself. Despite Harper's coy public denials, McLaughlin knew from previous conversations that Harper wanted to be prime minister.

The meeting took place on April 21, 1998, at the Toronto law office of Bob Dechert, who headed up the so-called "Blue Committee," composed of Ontario backroom boys looking to make peace between Reform and the Progressive Conservatives so that the Liberals would not be in power forever. Conservative MP Jim Jones also attended. The committee laboured to convince Harper to enter the leadership race, impressed with his demeanour and his ability to speak French. McLaughlin was enthusiastic about the prospects of a Harper candidacy—Harper, less so. During the three-hour meeting, no one had asked him any questions about policy.

The team around Ontario premier Mike Harris was also talking to Harper, promising that the Harris machine would be there to help his campaign if he decided to run. But Harper knew that he couldn't pull off the kind of victory he needed without the help of Reformers, who were now the Official Opposition nationally. Harper began to make discreet calls to members of Manning's caucus, mindful of the fact that a lot of the financial support for the NCC came from Reformers. If Harper upset Manning any more than he already had by abandoning the party before the 1997 federal election, the NCC's finances could take a hit. Manning might even undermine Harper with the NCC board.

One of the more startling revelations made by Gerry Nicholls about his NCC years with Harper was the way Stephen Harper's political mind worked. Fearing that Manning might work against him, Harper decided to make a proactive strike. Nicholls was asked to write a memo to his boss, Harper, which would then be leaked, claiming that Manning was undermining Harper. Nicholls refused to take part in the subterfuge and came to the conclusion that the enmity Harper bore Manning was not just based on disagreement over conservative principles. It was personal, as he recorded in his diary: "Captain Ahab hunting the white whale."

The seduction song to lure Stephen Harper back to the Progressive Conservative Party came to an end in Toronto on June 16, 1998. The formidable Arthur Finkelstein himself had been asked to conduct a special poll to assess Harper's chances in such a race, and on that day he came to Toronto to deliver the results in person, as he almost always did. The ambitious politician must have been crestfallen. Finkelstein found that although Harper was a star in media and political circles, he had no name recognition with the vast majority of voters. Name recognition was critical to winning. The disappointing poll, combined with the lack of hoped-for support from Reform members, convinced Stephen Harper that this was not the time to run.

Instead, he took the NCC into his hands like a lump of clay and made a statue of himself. He *was* the NCC. From now on, there would be more policy delineation and more court battles, like the one to have spending limits for third parties during an election declared unconstitutional. He began criticizing the Canadian Wheat Board with even greater fervour than the NCC had shown before. As for Elections Canada, those "jackasses" were "out of control," as Harper put it in an NCC fundraising letter. He continued to war with the media, particularly the CBC. NCC news releases were sent to select journalists only, and a trusted few would be contacted directly by Harper himself if he wanted to get a particular story out. As for the NCC itself, he wanted it leaner and meaner, even cancelling the Christmas bonus to set an example of frugality.

FROM HIS PERCH at the NCC, Harper kept a watchful eye on the national conservative scene over the next two years. In July 2000, Stockwell Day bested Preston Manning as leader of the Canadian

Alliance, a new party made up of the old Reform Party and a few provincial PC organizations. By April 2001, Harper could see that Day was in trouble. Despite bursting onto the national scene in a wetsuit aboard a Sea-Doo, Day never did get his bat going in what Mike Duffy liked to call "the big leagues." Day's Christian fundamentalism was a problem, as was his awkward relationship with the media. Ottawa was foreign territory: the man who was a star as Alberta's treasurer just wasn't a movable feast.

Harper was furious when he learned that pollster and strategist Arthur Finkelstein was talking to Day about helping him, a move that Harper viewed as a betrayal. Finkelstein called his trusted acolyte at the NCC, Gerry Nicholls, and asked if he should go to work for Day. Nicholls responded that if the American became involved in the race, the Harper team would be overwhelmed. Finkelstein eventually declined Day's offer, and Stephen Harper and his team, with the help of the NCC, went to war against Day.

In March 2002, Stephen Harper deposed Day and found himself astride a political party of his own at last. With a hostile Joe Clark still at the helm of the Progressive Conservative Party, it was not the united right that Harper had once held out for when the PCs came calling. But even if the Canadian Alliance was what Brian Mulroney said it was—"Reform in pantyhose," it was bigger than Preston Manning's old party. Better still, there was now just one obstacle to full unification: the party of John A. Macdonald. The consummate political tactician was a dangerous commodity once he had a clear target in his sights. As one-time mentor Tom Flanagan put it, Stephen Harper was a "predator."

Canadian politics on the right was about to go through volcanic changes. As long as Joe Clark was in charge, his PCs would never join forces with the Canadian Alliance because the former prime minister thought it would pull his party too far to the right. But five months after Harper captured the Alliance leadership, opportunity knocked. Joe Clark resigned. Tories chose popular Nova Scotia MP Peter MacKay to replace Clark on May 31, 2003. Alberta MP Jim Prentice finished second to MacKay on the last ballot, largely because of a backroom deal between MacKay and fellow leadership candidate David Orchard. In exchange for MacKay's promise to review the North American Free Trade Agreement and not to merge the PCs with the Canadian Alliance, Orchard played the kingmaker and delivered his support to MacKay. Five months later, MacKay reneged on the deal. By the end of 2003, the merger with the Canadian Alliance was approved by Progressive Conservative Party members. A few months later, Stephen Harper easily dispatched Belinda Stronach and Tony Clement at the Conservative Party of Canada's first leadership convention. MacKay got to date Stronach, but Stephen Harper got the party.

One of the reasons Stephen Harper was able to wipe out his opposition on the first ballot in the Conservative Party leadership, gaining nearly 70 percent of the vote, was that he had made himself into a thoroughly modern, professional politician. His years at the NCC had taught him that polling, marketing, and money were the holy trinity of the new politics.[6] Seeking power was no longer a matter of debating with honourable gentlemen over great issues, but a gruesome fight to the finish with no holds barred. Ross Perot made an observation that nicely captured Stephen Harper's quest for power in the new techno-democracy the Republicans had forged, and which Harper embraced: war has rules, mud-wrestling has rules, but politics has no rules.

One of the problems conservatives have always complained about in Canada is the media. Whether it was the Progressive Conservatives, Reform, or the Canadian Alliance, they all believed that there was a left-wing bias in the news. Reflective conservatives such as Preston Manning thought it through more carefully. Manning concluded that the bias wasn't just in the media but in other major institutions in society like the university. Small "l" liberalism permeated society, from the politics of professors, to the interpretations of Canadian history, to the image of the military. If conservatives wanted to operate on a level playing field, they would have to come up with a way to institutionalize their own message the way liberals had so successfully done.

In the United States, think-tanks such as the American Enterprise Institute, the Heritage Foundation, and the Cato Institute performed that function for the Republican Party. They began by offering counter-facts to the ones presented in the "liberal" news, which then became news. They created the impression that journalism was as partisan as politics. Such institutes could be just as potent in Canada, and nobody knew that better than Stephen Harper. These organizations take in approximately $26 million per year in Canada, with the Fraser Institute—a Harper favourite—commanding roughly a third of the market. Think-tanks here receive 30 percent of their income from corporations. By comparison, their counterparts in the United States draw just 10 percent of their budget from that source.

It is the ultimate "You scratch my back, I'll scratch yours" relationship. The corporations donate money in the expectation that their interests will be promoted. The "think-tanks" are set up as non-profit "research institutes" with no obligation to publish their list of donors or members. The US-based Donner Foundation gives money to the Macdonald-Laurier, Fraser, and C.D. Howe institutes in Canada, as well as to a group called the Frontier Centre. The Montreal Economics Institute, which pushed to make unions open their books to the public, receives 42 percent of its income from businesses. When the reports and studies of these think-tanks are made public, news organizations such as Sun Media, *The Globe and Mail*, and CanWest featured their work as hard news. It is a little like Noam Chomsky's notion of manufacturing consent.

The stories go mainstream, but the institutions remain hidden behind their undisclosed donor lists.

Both the Fraser and C.D. Howe institutes have campaigned against the Canada Health Act, which was music to Stephen Harper's ears. (In 2001, he had proposed to Alberta's premier Ralph Klein that he get rid of medicare, the RCMP, and the Canada Pension Plan.) Almost all of these think-tanks on the right stand broadly for the same things: unencumbered operation of free markets, lower taxes on corporations, and privatized health care. Many of their donors are Canadian—people such as gold entrepreneur Peter Munk and the Weston family. But they are not the only source of corporate money.

The Fraser Institute also receives money from the ultra-right-wing Koch brothers of Wichita, Kansas, who run the second-largest private company in the United States, with annual revenues of over $100 billion.[7] The Kochs and their Conservative friends spent more than $383 million in the run-up to the 2012 US election. Non-profit organizations set up as trusts reduce public reporting requirements and disguise the flow of money from one group to another, creating layers of anonymity. These entities operate without the public knowing who is actually in charge. All told, the Fraser Institute has received over $600,000 from these politically active American neo-conservatives. Despite the source of their donations, all of these institutes don the same camouflage—the cloak of fierce independence.

The fountainhead of Canada's right-leaning think-tanks (which also have their progressive equivalents now) was the fertile brain of Friedrich Hayek, an Austrian free-market thinker who won the Nobel Prize for economics in 1974. Hayek came up with the idea of setting up organizations like the Fraser Institute to supply a steady stream of studies to demonstrate the superiority of free markets over governments when it comes to solving society's problems.

Despite the fact that these organizations inspired by Hayek often serve the interests of business people and political parties, they register as charities and are permitted tax-free fundraising.

Stephen Harper addressed the thirtieth anniversary celebration of the Fraser Institute in 2004, sporting his silk Adam Smith tie. He liked the organization and came by his enthusiasm honestly. At the University of Calgary, he had studied the free-market philosophy of Hayek, the man widely credited with weaving economic and social conservatism together. Like Margaret Thatcher, Harper was a follower of Hayek and the Austrian school of economics—the supply side rules, interest rates have to be high enough to control the money supply, and debt is death. Hayek opposed the planned economy, both as a threat to freedom and an unworkable proposition.

Any attempt by the Canadian government to plan the economy was doomed to failure according to Hayek's followers. Pierre Trudeau had created the Foreign Investment Review Agency, established Petro-Canada, and attempted to fix the price of oil with the National Energy Program. The result, Harper believed, had been stagflation and 20 percent interest rates. (Less ideological analysts might also have included in the list of causes a severe recession that hit the United States in the summer of 1981, provoked by the Federal Reserve's restriction of the money supply to combat inflation, sending shock waves around the world.)

With no other rival for power inside the party, Stephen Harper began the work of transforming the Conservative Party of Canada into his own image, just as he had done with the National Citizens Coalition. In a speech to Civitas, a collection of conservative journalists, politicians, and intellectuals that was created after the 1996 Winds of Change conference in Calgary, he outlined how he would forge a new coalition of social and economic Conservatives:

Rebalancing the conservative agenda will require careful political judgment. First, the issues must be chosen carefully. For example, the social conservative issues we choose should not be denominational, but should unite social conservatives of different denominations and even different faiths. It also helps when social conservative concerns overlap those of people with a more libertarian orientation. . . . We must realize that real gains are inevitably incremental. This, in my experience, is harder for social conservatives than for economic conservatives. The explicitly moral orientation of social conservatives makes it difficult for many to accept the incremental approach. Yet, in democratic politics, any other approach will certainly fail.

Harper noted that changes to the conservative coalition risked the loss of some Red Tories, such as David Orchard or Joe Clark, but that it really didn't matter: "This is not all bad. A more coherent coalition can take strong positions it wouldn't otherwise be able to make—as the Alliance alone was able to do during the Iraq War. More important, a new approach can draw in new people. Many traditional Liberal voters, especially those from key ethnic and immigrant communities, will be attracted to a party with strong traditional views of values and family. This is similar to the phenomenon of the 'Reagan democrats' in the United States, who were so important in the development of that conservative coalition." Family, crime, defence, even foreign policy driven by religious conviction were all theo-con weapons Harper would store in his arsenal for the looming battle to dislodge the Liberal hegemony. He was playing to the suburbs around big cities such as Toronto and Vancouver, which he believed were full of people whose social values made them natural Conservatives: Chinese, Koreans, Jews, Italians, Vietnamese, and Somalis.

Harper was set to recalibrate the conservative movement with a direct voter campaign that, if successful, would replace the Liberals as the voice of these ethnic communities, particularly around the Greater Toronto Area. His general in this critical battle was Jason Kenney, who, like Harper, had been president of a third-party lobby group—the Canadian Taxpayers Federation. Kenney backed the Iraq War and once compared Hezbollah to the Nazi Party. Harper's most important focus, lifted directly from the Republican playbook of President George W. Bush, was on forming an alliance between Canada's Jewish community and the country's 3.5 million evangelical Christians. A strange alliance indeed, because evangelicals believe that only those who have accepted Christ will be raptured up in the Second Coming, which, unless they convert, does not include Jews.

After taking over the Canadian Alliance, Harper's views were reportedly influenced by neo-conservatives such as David Frum, then a speech writer for President Bush. Born Canadian, Frum emigrated to the United States and became a naturalized citizen. He was a member of the Canada Israel Committee and a board member of the Republican Jewish Coalition. Frum, like Harper, was a staunch supporter of the Iraq War, and believed with Donald Rumsfeld that the invading Americans would be welcomed by the Iraqis as liberators. He was a fellow of the American Enterprise Institute from 2003 to 2010. He co-authored a book with neo-conservative Richard Perle, *An End to Evil*, in which the authors defended the Iraq War and argued for similar attacks on Iran, Syria, and North Korea. They also wanted to completely abandon the Israeli–Palestinian peace process and have all Americans carry biometric identity cards.

When Harper went looking for help in writing his speech for the first Conservative Party of Canada convention on March 17, 2005, he called on David Frum. The carefully crafted speech was a hit. Although Harper promised not to bring in legislation on abortion if elected, he added a crucial qualifier for the party's social conservatives: "I will always allow all your MPs to vote freely on matters of conscience." He denied Joe Clark's statement that the Harpercons had a hidden agenda, and used humour, short sentences, and a teleprompter to get his points across smoothly. Arthur Finkelstein would have approved.

As foreign affairs critic, the born-again Christian Stockwell Day played a crucial role for the new party in building the relationship between the Christian and Jewish vote. Just as Reverend Tim LaHaye had helped Republicans, Charles McVety, the president of the Canadian Christian College, assisted the Conservative Party. Also linked with Frank Dimant, the executive vice-president of B'nai Brith Canada, Stephen Harper had two solid power bases for money, votes, and workers. Churchgoers were the strongest supporters of Israel. The Conservative Party caucus boasted a healthy contingent of evangelical Christians, including Stephen Harper, who is a member of East Gate Alliance Church.

Harper's Republican-style coalition building began to bear fruit. Billionaire Gerald Schwartz, a respected leader in the Jewish community, shifted his allegiance from the Liberals to the new Conservatives. Schwartz had previously been an important advisor of Paul Martin, and a valuable fundraiser. In exchange for Harper's unqualified support for Israel, a number of high-powered members of the Jewish community followed Schwartz's lead, including his wife, Heather Reisman, and legendary film producer Robert Lantos.

Finally, in 2006, it all came together for Harper. Though personally above reproach, Liberal Paul Martin was caught in the undertow of the sponsorship scandal and the inquiry he had called to get to the bottom of it. Stephen Harper won a minority government with his new coalition. According to an Ipsos Reid poll done in April 2006, 64 percent of Protestant churchgoers, the majority of them evangelical, voted Conservative in the January federal election of that year. It was a 24 percent jump over the numbers from 2004, when Paul Martin had eked out a minority government.

The Conservative victory was in every way a remarkable turn of events, not the least of which was the NDP's joining with Harper to bring down the Martin government on a budget with much social spending in it. Until that moment, Canada had been a secular and progressive nation that believed in transfer payments to better distribute the country's wealth, the Westminster model of governance, a national medicare program, a peacekeeping role for the armed forces, an arm's-length public service, the separation of church and state, and solid support for the United Nations. Stephen Harper believed in none of these things.

Using Republican policies and strategies, and taking his advice from American super-consultants like Arthur Finkelstein and policy advisors such as transplanted American Tom Flanagan, Harper managed to ride to power on a base that he himself had earlier told *The Globe and Mail* was "similar to what George Bush has tapped." Harper had shed his skin three times politically: Progressive Conservative to Reform, Reform to Canadian Alliance, and Canadian Alliance to Conservative Party of Canada. He had made clear along the way that he didn't much like the Canada built by generations of politicians and public servants before him. In particular, he had no time for the country's parliamentary democracy, much preferring the US system.

This perspective didn't take long to show. On the day his government was sworn in, Prime Minister Stephen Harper appointed Michael Fortier, who did not even run in the 2006 election, to his cabinet—just the way a US president does in the American system Harper so admired.

It was only the beginning.

three

THE DEMOCRACY
BANDITS

It's so strange. Where did everything go wrong for a government that came into town on accountability? When the Conservatives were elected, many in the base wanted massive changes to government, but the raison d'être was "incrementalism." I can't tell you the amount of times I had to use that line in unofficial communications. I believed it too! I guess corruption happens the same way. It doesn't just swoop in and take over everything. It starts as a little action, a little boundary pushing, a little rule-breaking. And before you know it, your incrementalism on breaking the rules has led to entire elections being tainted.

—Michael Sona, June 25, 2013, to the author

Like Watergate, Canada's worst election scandal went almost unnoticed at the time. On May 2, 2011, election day, at 10 a.m., Guelph resident Susan Campbell received an automated message telling her that her polling station had been moved.

Her caller ID told her that the sixty-three-second message was coming from telephone number 450-760-7746. The scratchy female voice said, "This is an automated message from Elections Canada. Due to a projected increase in poll turnout, your voting location has changed. Your new voting location is at the Old Quebec Street Mall at 55 Wyndham Street North." The voice repeated the message and gave a toll-free number to call if the voter had any questions. An apology was also offered for "any inconvenience that this may cause." It sounded official, especially when the entire message was repeated in French. There was just one problem. Campbell had already voted and no change had been made to her polling location. After dialling the toll-free number given in the automated message, only to find that it was out of service, she smelled a rat. Campbell copied down the number of the automated call from her caller ID and reported it to Elections Canada.

On that spring Monday, Susan Campbell had no way of knowing that what had happened to her was happening to thousands of other people in Guelph. Ben Grossman told authorities that he voted at 9:30 a.m. and returned home just after 10:00 a.m. to find a voice message from a blocked number telling him his polling station had been moved across the city. He too forwarded the information to Elections Canada.

At 11:06 a.m., elections officer Anita Hawdur sent an email to legal counsel Karen McNeil: "URGENT Conservative campaign office communications with electors." Returning officers were calling Elections Canada to ask about fraudulent phone calls, and not just in Guelph. Similar calls were being reported from other locations in Ontario, and in Manitoba and British Columbia. An alert was sent to the deputy chief electoral officer for electoral events at Elections Canada, Rennie Molnar, who then emailed senior director Michel Roussel: "This one is far more serious. They have actually disrupted the voting process." Meanwhile, the Liberal candidate in Guelph, MP Frank Valeriote, issued a statement saying his campaign office had received complaints about the misleading calls. He passed on the evidence to Elections Canada and the Guelph police.

Other irregularities occurred as well. In Montreal, residents of an apartment complex showed up to vote and found that their names were already crossed off the voters list. In Etobicoke Centre, reports came in that Conservative officials had disrupted voting at a polling station. Radio stations began broadcasting warnings about the misleading automated phone calls. In Guelph, where nearly seven thousand calls were made, the university put out a campus-wide email warning that the message about polling location changes was false.

At first, Valeriote thought he was dealing with a few nuisance calls, but he quickly realized it was nothing less than an orchestrated effort to discourage his supporters from voting. In Guelph at least, someone was trying to steal the election. Voter suppression, a well-known campaign tactic in US politics, was virtually unknown in Canada. Valeriote sent a campaign worker to the mall with a binder of polling maps to redirect Liberal supporters to the correct polls. Within an hour, one hundred misdirected voters had turned up at the false location. They were angry and frustrated. Parking was hard to find at the Old Quebec Street Mall, and some of the adjacent streets were under construction. The crowd soon doubled. When they realized that they'd been duped, some people hurried to vote at the correct location. But several voters tore up their voter information cards on the spot. The would-be voters included disabled people using walkers and mothers with strollers, and some had been dropped off by friends because of the difficulty with finding parking. Now they were stranded. The level of "inconvenience" was significant.

The returning officer for Guelph was deluged with calls from voters who had received the same misleading call as Susan Campbell and Ben Grossman. The phony calls were also causing problems at the campaign headquarters of Conservative candidate Marty Burke, or at least they appeared to be. At 10:13 a.m., just ten minutes after the misleading calls began, Michael Sona, Burke's communications director, put out a press release condemning the scam: "Today, many of our supporters have received misleading phone calls regarding voting in the General election," the twenty-two-year-old said. "This group is telling them that their polling location has changed. This is absolutely false, and has no place in the democratic process."

Sona's expeditious action would seem to warrant praise. Instead, his press release elicited what he described as a "furious" call from national Conservative Party headquarters. They wanted to know "what the hell was going on in Guelph." When Sona answered his cellphone, he found Fred DeLorey on the line. Normally even-keeled, the Conservative Party's spokesperson was angry. Sona recalled, "I started to explain the calls that had been going out mis-directing people, but that's not what they were mad about. They wanted to know why I had issued a press release. They ordered me to make no further comments that day. That's the way it was, very rough, tons of stress. HQ wanted to control everything. . . ."

The voter suppression scandal actually began before election day, and it wasn't confined to Guelph. Three days before the general election, complaints began arriving at Elections Canada. People reported "robocalls" in Guelph, and "live" calls in other places where someone allegedly impersonating a representative of Elections Canada was redirecting voters to the wrong polls. As emails to Elections Canada later indicated, Canadians across the country believed they had been targeted by people calling on behalf of the Conservative Party of Canada. This was days before

Michael Sona's press release focused the national media's attention on Guelph as the epicentre of what would eventually become the robocalls scandal, and months before a fellow called "Pierre Poutine" emerged as the mysterious villain of the piece.

On April 29 at 8:16 p.m., Sylvie Jacmain, the director of field programs and services for Elections Canada, sent an email to agency lawyer Ageliki Apostolakos, reporting problems in the ridings of Saint Boniface, Manitoba, and Kitchener-Conestoga, Ontario: "It seems representatives of Mr. Harper's campaign communicated with voters to inform them that their polling station had changed, and the directions offered to one would lead her more than an hour and a half from her real voting place. . . ." The Conservative campaign in Saint Boniface itself got in touch with party headquarters "who were doing the calls," a reference to the party's legitimate automated messaging. Then Elections Canada's lawyer emailed Conservative Party lawyer Arthur Hamilton, informing him of what was happening. The elections watchdog wanted some answers.

It took Hamilton twenty-seven hours to respond. When he did, he told Elections Canada that Conservative campaign workers had simply been contacting voters to ensure they were going to the right polling stations. Just after midnight on May 1, Hamilton replied to Apostolakos's email, stating that "a number of our candidates have had to confirm the proper location of polling stations to a number of supporters during their respective get-out-the-vote efforts. The calls being made by our candidates request the voter to confirm his or her polling stations. There is no indication by the caller that the location may have changed, or words to that effect. And no voter is being directed to a polling location one and a half hours away from the correct polling location." Three years later, we would learn from the commissioner of Elections Canada's report that the Conservative Party provided a script to Responsive

Marketing Group (RMG) for a national campaign that included this line to be used by its callers: "Elections Canada has changed some voting locations at the last moment. To be sure, could you tell me the address of where you're voting?"

But in his response to Elections Canada, Hamilton flatly denied that a voter had been misdirected to a polling station far from her correct poll—at least by the Conservatives. Within hours of Hamilton's denial, Elections Canada had received reports of misleading calls from eleven different ridings. Another email was sent to Hamilton, with the information that some voters had recorded the originating phone numbers of the robocalls, which led back to the Conservative Party. The calls were being received from as far east as Avalon, in Newfoundland and Labrador, and as far west as Prince George–Peace River, in British Columbia. Dismissing the evidence, Hamilton stuck to the party line in a reply to Elections Canada officials at 10:45 a.m. on election day, and re-sent his email. If someone was playing dirty politics, he stated firmly, it wasn't the Conservative Party of Canada.

What looked like a bizarre national scam now had Elections Canada buzzing. According to an internal email, "It's right across the country except Saskatchewan; a lot of the calls are from electoral districts in Ontario. It appears it's getting worse. Some returning officers reported that the calls are allegedly identifying Elections Canada." From party headquarters, Fred DeLorey also denied that the Conservative Party was trying to mislead anyone; it was just calling supporters to get out the vote. His explanation was strange. Why would there be so many protests if the Conservatives were merely calling their own supporters? It appeared that some-one had a list of non-Conservative supporters and was using it to send out misdirections to people who would not be voting for Stephen Harper's party. Still, top Tories kept to their speaking points. Conservative campaign co-chair Guy Giorno told CTV

News that voter suppression was "a despicable, reprehensible practice and everybody ought to condemn it." Giorno denied any party involvement, as did the man who won all the marbles in the controversial election, Stephen Harper.

Meanwhile, in the riding of Guelph, those involved in making the fraudulent calls had gone to a lot of trouble to make them difficult to trace. The callers had paid in cash for a "burner" cellphone, prepaid for the service time, and used two false names: "Pierre Poutine" and "Pierre Jones." The credit cards used to pay for the robocalls were prepaid, and were purchased from two different Shoppers Drug Marts in Guelph. As NDP MP Pat Martin said after the story broke, "Who the hell uses a burner cellphone and is not trying to hide something? Only dope dealers and Hells Angels and Tony Soprano use burner cell phones." A burner phone is perfect for both privacy and anonymity. Since users pay in advance for service use and can pay in cash, they are not required to sign a service plan, and no payment record exists that can establish the identity of the user.

The trail that investigators would later begin to follow backtracked to a point just before election day on May 2. On April 30, 2011, Ken Morgan, the campaign manager for Conservative candidate Marty Burke, sent an email to campaign worker Andrew Prescott. Prescott was contacted because he was responsible for "voice drops," or automated calls to select groups of electors. Morgan, and another member of the campaign, Michael Sona, asked Prescott for the contact information for the company he used for that purpose, RackNine Inc. In the 2011 election, Matt Meier, the owner of RackNine, worked only for Conservative clients and did not advertise. In order to engage his services, you had to be introduced by a current client or be someone he knew, at least according to what he later told Elections Canada investigators. Andrew Prescott was the perfect person to make the introduction because he had worked with RackNine on other political campaigns since 2010, knew Meier, and had the number for his direct line.

That same April night, at 6:49 p.m., someone purchased a $75 prepaid Visa card at Shoppers Drug Mart on Scottsdale Drive in Guelph. Fifteen minutes later, just over a kilometre away, a person walked into Future Shop on Stone Road West in Guelph and bought a prepaid Virgin Mobile cellphone. The buyer later activated the phone under the name "Pierre Poutine," ostensibly a resident of Joliette, Quebec.

According to an Information to Obtain (ITO), a court document sworn and filed by Elections Canada investigator Al Mathews, at 7:19 p.m., an unknown person created an email account—pierres1630@gmail.com—using an IP address at the Burke campaign headquarters. An hour and a half later, the burner cellphone was activated through a cell tower 1.6 kilometres from the Burke campaign office. Then, shortly after 9 p.m., someone using the name "Pierre Jones" called Matt Meier's direct line and set up a new RackNine account. That call was placed just three and a half hours after Andrew Prescott had provided Meier's personal contact information to Morgan and Sona.

The next day, May 1, 2011, three more prepaid gift cards were purchased at a different Shoppers Drug Mart—a MasterCard for $200, a Visa for $150, and a second Visa loaded with $35. At 9:19 p.m. on election eve, "Pierre Jones" logged on to RackNine. A minute later, "Pierre Jones" accessed RackNine again. His IP address was noteworthy: it was the address used by the Burke campaign. The gift cards were used to transfer money to a PayPal account, and that account was used to reimburse RackNine. By design, the payment email was sent through a proxy server that hides the originating IP access location. Someone was doing his best to make sure that the payments to RackNine couldn't be linked back to the Burke campaign.

"Pierre" then called the RackNine phone system, logged in to his newly created account, and uploaded a file containing 6,737 phone numbers of Liberal supporters. He then loaded a nearly identical list, except for a single added phone number, the number of his own burner phone. (That way, he would know when the calls began, and could check his voice mail for public reaction.) "Pierre" uploaded two voice recordings: one purporting to be a call from the Liberal campaign of Frank Valeriote, and the other a fake Elections Canada call telling voters that their polling location had been changed. For unknown reasons, only the fake Elections Canada calls were eventually made.

"Pierre Jones" was up early on election day. Shortly after 4 a.m., he logged on to RackNine from the Burke campaign IP address. Three minutes later, the account assigned to Andrew Prescott logged on to RackNine from the same IP address. Everything was finally in place. A little after 10 a.m., on May 2, 2011, thousands of misleading automated calls claiming to be from Elections Canada directed Guelph area voters to the wrong polling station. Although the number on voters' call displays was a Quebec number, the calls were actually coming from RackNine, the Conservative voice-broadcasting vendor thousands of kilometres away in Edmonton, Alberta. The technique of masking the origin of such calls is known as "spoofing." Account holders can enter any ID number they wish to be displayed for their calling campaign. The Conservatives used an American firm, Front Porch Strategies, for their town hall calls in ten campaigns in the 2011 election. Those calls looked like they were coming from local numbers, but they were actually being dialled from Ohio.

Telephone records from Bell would later show that number 450-760-7746 called only two phone numbers, other than its own voice mail. The phone number 866-467-2259 was called three times on April 30 from "Pierre's" burner cellphone; and 877-841-3511 was called seven times in the late evening, May 1, 2011, by the same cellphone. Both numbers belonged to RackNine, and an automated message welcomed the callers to the service. The second number asked the caller to log in with a customer number. All told, there were thirty-seven other calls made from Guelph to the RackNine numbers between March 26 and May 5, 2011. As the Burke campaign's RackNine contact, most of Andrew Prescott's calls went to the customer login number. RackNine later issued a statement: "The individuals who abused RackNine's services attempted to hide their identity from RackNine itself."

Although hundreds of Liberal voters turned up at the wrong location to cast ballots, the Conservatives lost the seat in Guelph, a riding they had targeted. But that disappointment paled beside the euphoria in the Conservative camp: Stephen Harper had pulled off his first majority government. The story of dirty tricks in the 2011 election died down, eclipsed as it was by the new political reality in Canada. The Conservatives now had a majority, and the Liberal Party had been reduced to third-party status. Its leader, Michael Ignatieff, had been destroyed by the tried-and-true methods of Arthur Finkelstein. This time the deadly slogan seemed innocuous: "Just Visiting," a derogatory reference to Ignatieff's return to Canada after decades of working abroad. But like smoke from an unseen fire, the robocalls scandal continued to smoulder.

Three months after the election, Chief Electoral Officer Marc Mayrand mentioned the "crank calls" to voters in his election report tabled in Parliament in August 2011. Mayrand, a bankruptcy expert until his appointment as chief electoral officer of Canada in 2007, reported in August 2012 that Elections Canada had received 1,394 complaints about misleading or harassing calls in 234 of 308 ridings across the country. Once voters understood what had happened, the number of complaints had skyrocketed.

Only 473 out of 20,000 polling locations had actually changed location during the 2011 federal election—and in the last week of the campaign, when it was too late to send out a revised voter information card by mail, just 61. (The percentage of voting stations across Canada that changed location in the final week of the federal election was just 0.003.) In the forty-first general election "a party" asked Elections Canada for polling site information, which Elections Canada then provided to all registered political parties. In the restrictions accompanying the data, Elections Canada told campaigns not to provide poll site information to voters, specifying that "the database was for internal purposes only, and was not to be 'used to inform voters of their voting locations via mail-outs or other forms of communication.'" Despite the "warning," in 2011, the Conservative national campaign did place calls with poll information. Had someone cleverly realized that those last-minute location changes provided the perfect cover to use calls to suppress the vote?

The investigation into the 2011 election scandal started quietly, just two days after Stephen Harper's victory. The implications were momentous. Had the Conservatives stolen the election, the way many Liberals believed they had in 2006, by illegally spending a million dollars more on advertising than campaign spending limits allowed? Al Mathews, a seasoned investigator and former RCMP officer, began by filing a series of court orders for telephone records. The Conservative Party's main phone bank company was RMG. The Marty Burke campaign in Guelph listed both RMG ($15,000) and another firm, Campaign Research, ($6,215) as campaign expenses. On its website, RMG said it worked exclusively with right-of-centre campaigns to develop fundraising and voter contact strategies. In 2011, RMG provided live calling services for the Conservative Party's national campaign as well as eighty local campaigns using data from the Conservative Constituent Information Management System (CIMS), provided by the party or local candidates.[1] CIMS was the party's voter-tracking database, and kept track of all voters nationwide. Live calls for political campaigns cost about $30 per hour.

But Elections Canada investigators also traced calls from Burke's campaign office to RackNine, the Conservative voter contact firm in Edmonton, Alberta. Inexplicably, the Burke campaign did not include any payment to the Alberta company in its election expenses. That mystery was solved when Andrew Prescott later explained that he had paid for the robocalls himself and been reimbursed through his $1,100 honorarium. His invoice had apparently not been forwarded to Marty Burke's official agent by campaign manager Ken Morgan, nor did it appear on Burke's declaration of election expenses. On June 8, 2011, investigator Al Mathews filed a request seeking Bell Canada records for the "burner" cellphone he believed had been used to make the deceitful calls.

On November 23, 2011, Mathews served a court order on RackNine seeking records related to the Conservative campaign in Guelph, including calls from the burner phone used by "Pierre." RackNine had thirty days to produce the data and documents. The production order specified that RackNine itself was not under investigation for the offences outlined in the official request for information. According to Mathews and Conservative Party records, the Guelph campaign IP address was used by five of Marty Burke's campaign volunteers to access the party database. Mathews alleged that "RackNine client #45, whom RackNine believed to be Andrew Prescott . . . logged into RackNine as client #45 in a single web session along with client #93 using the same IP address." Client #93 was "Pierre Jones."

The call logs showed that the burner phone used by "Pierre Poutine" was contacted multiple times from locations in the United States, including six text messages from numbers in Anaheim and Pasadena, California. There was also an incoming voice call to "Poutine's" burner phone from a number in the area code for Fairport, New York. The call lasted twenty-one seconds. When Mathews tried these numbers, they were perpetually busy or out of service. The US calls and texts baffled investigators.

Mathews found that RackNine received thirty-three calls from phones at Marty Burke's campaign headquarters and the Guelph Conservative Electoral District Association, from March 26, 2011, through to election day. The contact person was Andrew Prescott. Burke's deputy campaign manager, he had used his account at RackNine to send out a mass warning to the public late on election day about the bogus robocalls—long after Burke communications officer Michael Sona issued his press release doing the same thing.

In a sworn statement, investigator Mathews laid out his conclusion about the considerable stealth used by whoever had made the calls: "I believe that the individual(s) behind the misleading calls which are the subject of this investigation would not want a local campaign to be identified with the calls, as they amount to improper activity, and consequently, I believe that any expense would likely be omitted to a campaign return."

Marty Burke's campaign office wasn't the only group calling RackNine. According to investigator Mathews, records of incoming contacts to the Edmonton firm showed forty calls from the Ottawa and eastern Ontario area code 613. Nine of those calls were traced back to voice recordings for Rebecca Rogers, a contact person for local media during Harper's campaign stops, and Chris Rougier, the party's manager of voter relation programs. Both worked at headquarters with Jenni Byrne, who ran the 2011 national campaign.[2] Rogers made eight calls to RackNine on April 30, 2011, and Rougier made one call on May 1, 2011. A Conservative official maintained that the party's central campaign merely used RackNine to promote Harper's events, and that Rebecca Rogers arranged these legitimate calls. The one call to

RackNine that HQ never explained was Chris Rougier's, the day before the election.

RackNine's service worked as follows: The customer would provide three things: a recording of a voice message; an electronic file of phone numbers to be called; and finally, automated scheduling instructions, including what caller ID number they wanted displayed. The firm's automated process would then call the numbers on the list with the recorded message according to the client's scheduling. RackNine could place 200,000 calls an hour at only 1.9 cents a call. Meier said he did not listen to the messages and that his clients normally settled their accounts using PayPal, an internet payment service. He estimated that RackNine placed ten million calls from about two hundred accounts during the 2011 election campaign. At a price of just under 2 cents per call, the robocalls could be considered a bargain: the whole operation cost about $200,000. The high-tech system was capable of doing "serious damage." In 2010, Meier had also described his system as a "political superweapon."

Meier was able to locate a digital copy of the fake election message that "Pierre" had sent to Guelph residents, and played it for Mathews. He also located a second message the same client had uploaded but later deleted, which was never sent. Although technically deleted, the message was embedded within RackNine's sophisticated logging system. As a matter of policy, the firm retained a record of all transactions with clients, including deleted material. It was the best way to deal with any dispute that might arise with a client. When Mathews listened to the second message, he noted that it appeared to support the Liberal Party in Guelph. According to the original customer instructions, the same list of non-supporters used for the fake Elections Canada message was to be called, with two major differences: the calls were to go out to Liberal supporters between 2:00 a.m. and

4:45 a.m. Guelph time on election day, and the calling number to be displayed was that of the Liberal campaign office. The calls were designed to irritate potential Liberal voters by rousing them in the middle of the night, which would hopefully make them less inclined to vote.

Meier said he had identified the client who requested the misleading election messages as RackNine client #93. He located a brief email thread with the client between April 30 and May 2, 2011, which he said was the only record he had of the client's identity. The emails had been preceded by a phone conversation. Meier had asked his new client for contact information, including his name, address, phone number, and affiliated organization. The client replied that he was Pierre S. Jones, a University of Ottawa correspondence student residing in Joliette, Quebec. He gave his burner phone as his contact number—450-760-7746—and signed his emails "Pierre." Meier gave a copy of the emails sent from pierres1630@gmail.com to investigator Mathews.

The more Mathews talked to Matt Meier, the bigger the elephant in the room must have become. As recorded in court documents, Mathews said he was advised by Meier in emails on December 1, 2011, and February 27, 2012, and in person on May 9, 2012, "that all his clients know him or are recommended to him through political candidates, campaign managers, political party staff or party activists/organizers." If that were true, it meant that the proprietor of RackNine could hold the key to the identity of "Pierre." Meier may not have known client #93, but according to his business practice, he should know the person who had recommended him and given out his private contact information. The shortest route to unmasking "Pierre" seemed to be finding the intermediary who had introduced him to RackNine.

But here the story went out of focus. "Pierre" had originally called Meier on his "unlisted extension directly and asked for him by name."[3] Since Meier claimed he didn't know who had referred "Pierre" to him, his services were apparently not quite as exclusive as his company policy would lead an investigator to believe. Either that, or Meier was not telling everything he knew about his mysterious client. The obvious next step in the investigation was to find the IP address "Pierre" had used. When Mathews met with him in November 2011, Meier had not been able to provide an IP address for the logins. For the moment, not only "Pierre's" identity but also the location of the computer he had used remained unknown.

On May 2, client #93 was called at 10:03 a.m. and recorded by RackNine as an early hangup. The first "test call" would have alerted "Pierre Jones" that the calls to voters had begun. (Test calls are a client option on the RackNine database.) The robocalls went out between 10:03 and 10:14 a.m., at a cost of just $162.10.[4] The IP address used to pay RackNine turned out to be a proxy server that investigators traced back to a Marc Norris in Conquest, Saskatchewan—the only province that didn't have complaints about robocalls. Proxy servers are intermediary websites that make internet queries anonymous. Mathews formally requested information from Norris in Saskatchewan on April 16, 2012, and Norris contacted his hosting site, ServInt. Based in McLean, Virginia, the company was founded in 1995 and is a provider of managed virtual private servers (VPS) and open proxies. Their records are retained for twenty-four hours, and then deleted. "Pierre" had clearly wanted to remain anonymous.

When investigator Mathews had initially served the production order on RackNine on November 23, 2011, Meier had told him that because of upgrades to his computer system, he probably couldn't locate the IP address attached to the "Pierre Jones" account as requested. Mathews met briefly with Meier on March 4, 2012, and he had still not been able to locate the information. But on March 6, 2012, Meier emailed Mathews to say he had just found the IP address related to "Pierre Jones" by reviewing session logs generated by the client's contact with RackNine. Meier emailed the investigators three session log spreadsheets that detailed contact with RackNine by client #45 and client #93.

Mathews spoke with Meier on March 6 and 8, and again on May 9, 2012. Meier told him that Andrew Prescott was client #45 and had arranged the legitimate voice message broadcasts for the Burke campaign. He was the only person Meier dealt with from the campaign—and the person whom Morgan and Sona had asked for Meier's personal contact information. Prescott had logged into his account using a number of different IP addresses during the writ period, including five times from the Cayman Islands, where he had gone on a pre-planned vacation. Work was obviously on his mind. On April 19, he logged in from Toronto's Pearson airport. On April 20 and 21, he logged in to RackNine from Herndon, Virginia, and then again on his way home from the Caymans, in Virginia on April 27. On April 30, Prescott was back in the Guelph office, and as Michael Sona observed, things began to happen.

Mathews learned a complex but fascinating detail about how RackNine's service worked. During a single session, once the client logs in, individual clients can log out as a particular client number, and other clients can log in with their unique user name and password. In the Guelph case, since there was only one uninterrupted session, the original IP address remained the same. A session will only close if it times out, or if the browser window is closed by the end user. This raised an interesting possibility. Could someone other than client #93 log in during a session without the Guelph IP address changing?

Meier told Mathews that he had given no training to the person who identified himself as "Pierre Jones." "He [Pierre Jones] used the RackNine database completely on his own," once the account had been established—a not unimportant detail since it suggested that client #93 was either familiar with the system or working with someone who was.[5] "Pierre Jones" accessed RackNine on May 1, 2011 at 11:19 p.m. via the proxy server. But then a minute later, he accessed RackNine in a new session through the Guelph campaign account. The investigator wanted to know what that meant. On May 9, 2012, Meier told Mathews that the most likely explanation was that client #93 inadvertently closed the first session and then immediately returned to the site, either forgetting to use the proxy server, or thinking he was still logged in to RackNine.

If it had been a careless mistake on the part of client #93, he repeated it. On election day, in two separate sessions, both clients #45 and #93 communicated with RackNine using the Burke campaign IP, just minutes apart. At 4:12 a.m. "Pierre Jones" logged in from the Burke campaign address, and at 4:15 a.m. the account assigned to Andrew Prescott logged in from the same IP address. This coincidence raised a tantalizing question: were client #45 and client #93 together in the early hours of election day? Meanwhile, a piece of unsurprising news was obtained by the RCMP. No student named "Pierre Jones" was registered at the University of Ottawa. When an RCMP constable checked out the address, like "Pierre Jones" himself, it didn't exist. The closest the officer could come was 56 Lajoie Nord, the site of the local Royal Canadian Legion in Joliette, Quebec.

On November 29, 2011, after receiving documentation for the ten official campaigns the Burke team ran through RackNine, Elections Canada investigator Al Mathews decided it was time to talk to Andrew Prescott. He left a voice message for the person who was known to RackNine as client #45, asking to talk. Instead of replying to Mathews, Prescott sought advice from a local Conservative in Guelph. Elections Canada's request to Prescott was then forwarded to Jenni Byrne, director of political operations at Conservative headquarters. Byrne's advice to Prescott was to remain silent while she sought legal counsel.[6] When reporters later questioned Andrew Prescott about the robocall scandal during their investigation, he replied via email, "I was not involved in the illegal phone calls. I am a legitimate user of RackNine's services, and have been for several years. I am a devoted believer in free and fair elections. I would never partake in ANY illegal activities, and openly advocate for everyone to play by the rules."

Meanwhile, the connection between Jenni Byrne and Andrew Prescott seemed odd. If Prescott had nothing to do with illicit robocalls, why would he refer an investigator's request to Conservative Party headquarters? And since HQ professed that the party was involved only in legitimate robocalls, and that it was assisting the Elections Canada investigation, why would the party need months to arrange the Elections Canada interview? How does telling someone not to talk to an investigator qualify as cooperating?

Although Prescott spoke in December 2011 with Conservative Party lawyer Arthur Hamilton about Elections Canada's request for an interview, it took Hamilton three months to arrange a date. The timing was noteworthy: the day after the robocalls story became public. A week after Valentine's Day, a scandal that had been quietly developing behind the scenes exploded in the media. The story was written by the formidable odd couple of Canadian journalism, Postmedia's Stephen Maher and the *Ottawa Citizen*'s Glen McGregor. Through their work, the country learned that Elections Canada, with the help of the RCMP's commercial crime unit, had traced fraudulent robocalls made during the 2011 election to RackNine Inc., a small voice-broadcast company in Edmonton that worked exclusively for the Conservative Party of Canada's national campaign and several Conservative candidates, including Stephen Harper.[7]

The robocall story soon dominated the news. Stephen Maher's first big story in Ottawa was a combination of serendipity and steely nerves, a trait that served him well as the robocall scandal developed. An aide to cabinet minister Lisa Raitt, Jasmine MacDonnell, had left her tape recorder in a washroom on Parliament Hill. The first interview on it was with Stephen Maher, so the female colleague who found the tape recorder gave it to him. Maher offered to return the tape recorder to its rightful owner, but MacDonnell never came by to pick it up. Six months later, Jasmine MacDonnell left a sheaf of secret files at CTV's studio. Maher remembered the tape recorder and succumbed to a reporter's best friend—curiosity. "I decided to listen to the files on the tape recorder," Maher told me. "There was an inadvertently recorded conversation between Raitt and her aide, in which she [the minister] said that cancer was a 'sexy' story." It was a reference to the impact of a medical isotope shortage that was affecting cancer treatments in Canada and around the world after the Chalk River reactor was shut down.

When Maher contacted the aide to advise her that he planned to run the story, she sought an injunction to block publication. (Some speculated that the Conservative Party was behind the lawsuit.) After listening to five hours of material on the tape recorder, a Halifax judge denied the injunction. In the wake of publication of the tape's contents, Raitt, choking back tears, apologized for her insensitive remarks. She offered her resignation to the prime minister, but Stephen Harper refused it.

Maher showed the same determination not to back down as the robocall story unfolded. His first inkling of the robocalls story came before the election on April 16, 2011. He had been in Halifax covering the federal election, and noticed a story from CBC's Dave Seglins reporting on mysterious, fake Liberal phone calls in Eglinton-Lawrence, the Ontario riding represented by Liberal MP Joe Volpe. The calls were not coming from Toronto but from an area code in North Dakota. The scent of a scoop was in the air. "It seemed clear to me that some unknown person had hired a call bank to suppress the Liberal vote through deception," recalled Maher. "This struck me as criminal behaviour and I started asking questions, turning it over in my mind."

As with all speculative stories, the usual hot tips and cold trails ensued. Someone even told Maher that a Liberal campaign worker had actually given the Tories the lists of Grit supporters that were used to suppress the vote. After hitting a dead end or two, but still convinced he had something, the reporter made a crucially important move. He convinced Glen McGregor of the *Ottawa Citizen* to work with him on a spreadsheet of the instances of misleading automated calls in the 2011 election. It was a brilliant combination. As McGregor put it, "We're sort of an Oscar and Felix Odd Couple. Steve is more likely to theorize and chase down tips that seem like long shots. I'm more about figuring out how to prove things with documentation."[8]

It was McGregor's work with Hill legend Tim Naumetz that broke the in-and-out scandal, a story that uncovered the dishonesty of the Conservative Party of Canada during the federal election of 2006. "With in-and-out, we had a confession of wrongdoing by the Conservative Party in a deliberate attempt to stealthily violate the election rules to their advantage," McGregor told me. "This scheme involved some of the highest officials in the party—Finley, Gerstein, and Donison. I believe it changed the course of the [2006] election."

At first, McGregor was a reluctant partner in Stephen Maher's big robocalls story, which he thought was, at best, a "pattern" story. In fact, soon after McGregor joined the project in January 2012, he was "looking for ways to gracefully withdraw." He just couldn't see how the two journalists could ever prove what Maher believed had happened. But then came two eureka moments in their investigation. Maher connected with a source who had intimate knowledge of misleading calls in Guelph, and McGregor dug up a cellphone bill that connected the Conservative campaign in Guelph to RackNine. The stars were now aligned for publication. "We broke the story during Question Period," Maher told me. "I was sitting in the [Press] Gallery. I saw Peter Van Loan pass his BlackBerry to Prime Minister Harper so he could read it. That's a once-in-a-lifetime thrill for a journalist to see a big story break like that."

According to the reporters, illicit robocalls were widespread in the 2011 election. Though the estimates varied, at least eighteen ridings had been targeted and had experienced harassing or deceptive calls. Conservative spokesperson Fred DeLorey would not say how much business the party did with RackNine, and insisted they did not know who was behind the fake calls.

After stonewalling investigators for three months, Andrew Prescott granted an interview to Al Mathews—the day after Maher and McGregor broke their story. With Arthur Hamilton listening in on the conference call, Prescott told the investigator that he knew nothing about any wrongdoing in the campaign, the same thing he had told Matt Meier. However, Prescott mentioned that he had passed on the personal contact information for RackNine's Matt Meier to fellow campaign workers Ken Morgan and Michael Sona, later providing a copy of the emails to Mathews. After initially agreeing to a second, formal interview set for March 8, 2012, Andrew Prescott hired Guelph lawyer Mathew Stanley. His change of heart occurred after March 6, 2012, when Matt Meier of RackNine found the session logs linking client #45, Prescott, with the still unknown client #93, "Pierre Jones." With only a day's notice, Prescott's lawyer cancelled the March 8 interview and recommended to his client that he remain silent.

A few days after their original story was published, Maher and McGregor widened the lens. They filed a piece about systematic voter suppression beyond Guelph, in which misleading calls had gone out to Liberal voters in many tightly contested ridings. Interim Liberal leader Bob Rae said that he believed those calls helped defeat his party in the 2011 election. It was a theory not without evidence. The margin of victory in fourteen of the tightest ridings that went to the Conservatives was just 6,201 votes. Rae asked for an emergency debate in the House of Commons on February 27, 2012.

Prime Minister Stephen Harper found himself in the increasingly familiar position of having to deny that the Conservatives were involved in sleazy electoral tactics. At a photo op in Iqaluit on February 23, 2012, Harper said, "I have absolutely no knowledge on anything about these calls, but obviously if there's anyone who has done anything wrong, we will expect they will face the full consequences of the law." It was the standard boilerplate statement used by the prime minister to respond to anything that looked remotely like a scandal for the party or government. Harper left the more practical damage control to the director of political operations for the party, Jenni Byrne.

The day after the story broke, Byrne entered the full "not guilty" plea with the CBC: "The party was not involved with these calls and if anyone on a local campaign was involved they will not play a role in a future campaign." Byrne said voter suppression was "extremely serious." She explained, "We spent the entire campaign identifying supporters and we worked hard to get them out to vote. Our job is to get votes out; we do not engage in voter suppression."

Byrne joined the Reform Party at the age of sixteen and was president of the campus Reform Club at the University of Ottawa, coincidentally the school "Pierre Jones" pretended to be attending. Byrne was a sound political organizer, and famously partisan. Through hard work, she moved her way up in the Conservative hierarchy. As Doug Finley's deputy, Byrne learned the ropes assisting in the party's early campaigns. She went on to manage day-to-day crises in the PMO when Ian Brodie was Harper's chief of staff. Later, after Prime Minister Harper appointed Finley to the Senate while he was under investigation by Elections Canada during the in-and-out scandal, Byrne filled the void. She took over as the Conservative Party's director of political operations in 2009. In a rare profile of her published in *Maclean's* on April 4, 2011, one Conservative anonymously described her as a "hard-ass with a temper."

Beginning with Byrne's damage control on the CBC, the air was suddenly full of suggestions about robocalls from a normally ultra-secretive, media-averse party. Reaching out to select reporters, the Conservatives quietly put out the story that a "rogue operator" was behind the electoral fraud being investigated by Elections Canada and that the party knew who that person was. Brian Lilley at Sun News Network named Michael Sona as the key suspect on February 23, 2012—a remarkable turn of events since the allegation was criminal and it was made without interviewing the subject of the story.

With the government under pressure, senior Conservatives began piling on the outed party worker. Peter MacKay became the first Harper cabinet minister to publicly suggest that Sona was responsible for the false calls. (Now justice minister, MacKay's words may come back to haunt him. Michael Sona had not been charged with anything, let alone convicted, when MacKay prejudged the matter.) In Question Period on Monday, March 5, 2012, the Conservatives rolled out their diversion-and-deflection strategy, repeatedly demanding that the Liberals release their automated call records. Conservative campaign chair Guy Giorno told CTV, "I wish Godspeed to Elections Canada and the RCMP investigators." Where Giorno's wishes fit on the sincerity scale was hard to know. It appeared that the Tories had offered up their rogue operator, to the surprise of everyone, including Elections

Canada investigator Al Mathews. Sona had not been interviewed by Elections Canada, and had not even appeared to be a person of interest to investigators before his name suddenly appeared in the press.[9]

But the most surprised person was the one who had been named as the villain of the piece in the Guelph robocall caper, Michael Sona. He believed that he had been thrown under the bus by someone very senior in the Conservative Party. One thing that should not have come as a surprise to him was the news agency that broke the story. The vice-president of Sun News Network was Kory Teneycke, Stephen Harper's former director of communications, and an associate of Jenni Byrne. Sona tried calling people at party headquarters. No one would take his calls. Finally, lawyer Arthur Hamilton contacted him, bluntly asking Sona, "Did you do it? Do you know who did?"

Sona told me that although he was still reeling from the shock of being described as the bad apple "without even receiving a phone call from the reporter," his answer to Hamilton was unequivocal. "I told him flat out that I was not responsible or involved in what I'd been accused of and also said that I didn't know who had done it. He asked me several questions about my thoughts on other members of the campaign team, as well as several voter contact firms the party uses, but I wasn't able to tell him one way or the other if they were guilty because I frankly don't know." For whatever reason, and despite his denials, Michael Sona received very different treatment from Conservative headquarters than his co-worker in the Guelph election, Andrew Prescott. When Prescott had called HQ to say Elections Canada investigators wanted to talk to him, Jenni Byrne had sent him an email saying, "Please hold off doing anything until I consult with a lawyer."

Byrne had also copied Ken Morgan, Marty Burke's campaign manager, and Chris Rougier, the director of voter contact for the

Conservatives at party headquarters. Rougier was responsible for CIMS, the party's voter tracking database that investigators believed was the source of phone numbers used in the fake robo-calls. As the party's central voter contact manager, Rougier was the key coordinator of mail and phone services during the 2011 campaign. He was responsible to the director of political operations, Jenni Byrne, and also liaised with the PMO and various ministers and staff. According to his résumé, Rougier "developed and oversaw mission critical projects from genesis to completion." Where Prescott got assistance from the Conservative Party's director of political operations and party lawyer Arthur Hamilton, Michael Sona got the cold shoulder. Maher and McGregor reported that Byrne also ordered the young man's employer, Conservative MP Eve Adams, to get rid of him. Reluctantly, the member from Mississauga–Brampton South complied. Michael Sona "resigned."

The fingering of Michael Sona by Sun News triggered a flurry of activity in the investigation into the fraudulent robocalls in Guelph. According to a sworn statement released by investigator Mathews on May 4, 2012, Chris Rougier was twice interviewed by Elections Canada in the presence of Arthur Hamilton. Rougier told investigators that Andrew Prescott, among several others, had access to elector data for Guelph from CIMS. The investigators had asked Hamilton to obtain CIMS records for them on March 5, 2012, and Rougier had subsequently reviewed them. They indicated that on April 30, 2011, Andrew Prescott had apparently downloaded three "Daemon Dialer" reports for Guelph—lists of phone numbers with voters identified as supporters and non-supporters. It was two days before the fake calls went out. Mathews later learned that the third Daemon Dialer download was "cancelled by Prescott and so was never 'exported.'" Rougier provided the "targeting information," which described the criteria "Prescott" used to request the material from CIMS.

(This information would later change in a very important way. On April 3, 2014, Maher and McGregor published an article with information based on what Andrew Prescott had told investigators in March 2014: that Guelph campaign manager Ken Morgan had asked him to log on to a robocall account on his computer, a computer he later destroyed.)

The CIMS data was compared to listings of the outgoing robocalls provided by RackNine under a court order. The lists matched. Investigators were now certain that the list used to make the fraudulent robocalls came from the data bank of the Conservative Party of Canada. Mathews also asked Rougier for the IP addresses that five Marty Burke volunteers had used to access CIMS between April 23 and May 2, 2011. Access is limited by the party, and each person is given a unique password. Rougier told Mathews that thirty-two of the forty-one "access events" were through the Burke campaign IP address. Investigators found puzzling blanks[10] between one person's logon and logoff of CIMS at headquarters on the day the Guelph data was accessed. On May 1, 2011, the day before the vote, a call was made from the Conservative Party war room in Ottawa to RackNine. The number was listed as belonging to Chris Rougier.[11]

On February 28, 2012, and again on April 19, 2012, Elections Canada investigators Ron Lamothe and Al Mathews met with another important player in the puzzle of robocalls, Matthew McBain—and once again the ubiquitous Arthur Hamilton. Lamothe, a seasoned veteran, was the assistant chief investigator in the office of the Commissioner of Elections Canada. In 2008, the former Ottawa police officer's affidavit had laid out the elaborate scheme to move Conservative Party money from national coffers into and then out of the accounts of local Conservative campaigns to skirt national spending limits for the 2006 election. It was brilliant and brave police work. Conservative Party of Canada headquarters was raided as part of the investigation's effort to acquire evidence in the in-and-out scandal.

One of the big unanswered questions of the robocall investigation was why investigators allowed the party to provide the information from CIMS, rather than seizing the computers with a warrant and investigating the downloads themselves. Lamothe was interested in talking to Matthew McBain, a party worker who was in the central war room during the 2011 election. Sona had left voice messages for him during the campaign, but McBain didn't know him. So instead of answering, he sent an email to John White, whom he did know, to see if he should talk to his unknown caller. White was one of five workers on the Guelph campaign who had access to the CIMS list.[12] When Andrew Prescott lost his computer job at a Guelph hospital, John White had helped find the young man a job in Calgary.[13] He vouched for Sona in a return email, explaining to McBain that his colleague on the Burke campaign needed some advice: "His name is Mike Sona . . . and he's good. He has [sic] some advice that you may be well qualified to give." (Later, at Sona's trial, White would testify he meant to say that McBain had advice for Sona.)

Through Arthur Hamilton, a copy of the email exchanges of April 26 and 27 between the two Conservative workers was given to investigators. According to McBain, Sona wanted to know how to make untraceable phone calls. Mathews initially recorded in his account of this interview that McBain claimed that Sona asked about "a campaign of disinformation such as making misleading poll moving calls." But that astonishing assertion was amended in a subsequent affidavit from Mathews dated May 25, 2012. Now McBain "did not recall Sona as relating the call to 'misinformation' or a misleading poll moving call. . . . Sona spoke to McBain about wanting to set up an auto-dial call so that the payment for the calls would not track back to the campaign." After featuring the incorrect information prominently in a brief ITO, Mathews buried the correction deep in a lengthy affidavit and printed it as a tiny footnote.[14] McBain claimed that he warned Sona off any misconduct as the party would not stand for it—a story Sona disputed. According to him, McBain said he would look into it but never called back.

Before talking to the person who had put Michael Sona and Matt McBain together, Mathews called Chris Crawford for an interview. Crawford was a junior staffer who worked as a voter contact person on the Guelph campaign, entering data in CIMS. He was responsible for organizing the door-to-door campaign for Burke. Each morning, he would download "walk sheets" from CIMS grouped by individual polls, using the campaign computer. The names, addresses, and phone numbers of voters were recorded, as well as whether the voter was a Conservative Party supporter or contributor. Canvassers would record the response they received at the door, whether supporter or non-supporter, and note the presence of lawn signs. Crawford would scan the new material into CIMS using a barcode reader, and CIMS was updated nightly with the latest data from the ridings.

The investigators had a good reason for wanting to talk to Chris Crawford. He and Sona had been friends at the University of Guelph, where they had both been members of the campus Conservative club. Crawford and Sona had also been roommates when they were interns for the Conservative Party in 2009. Crawford told investigators that one evening while he was inputting CIMS data during the Guelph campaign, he overheard Sona talking to campaign manager Ken Morgan about "how the Americans do politics." The conversation included fake calls about polling station changes, and the strategy of calling non-supporters late at night pretending to be your opponent. Crawford told investigators he "did not think Sona was serious," but claimed he warned his co-worker that such talk was inappropriate. Interestingly, Crawford, like Matt McBain, did not come forward with his information about Sona and alleged dirty tricks in Guelph until he was contacted by investigators. And even then he didn't go to Elections Canada, but rather to Conservative Party headquarters. From Fred DeLorey, he quickly followed the familiar path to Arthur Hamilton.

Shortly after the interview with Mathews on March 6, 2012, Crawford was promoted from special assistant to director of parliamentary affairs in the office of intergovernmental affairs minister Peter Penashue. Crawford received a $15,000 pay raise. (Penashue himself was forced to resign March 14, 2013, when it became public that he had accepted improper donations to his 2011 campaign. He ran in the subsequent by-election but lost.) Jenni Byrne denied a connection between Crawford's statement and his promotion. She sent an email to Maher and McGregor, who were doing a one-year review of the robocalls story: "Mr. Crawford relayed to Elections Canada information he thought they should know and he is comfortable with the accuracy of what he conveyed. No promotion or raise for Mr. Crawford was in any way related to the assistance he provided to Elections Canada. The Conservative Party has always assisted Elections Canada in this matter, and has always called upon anyone with anything that might be relevant to convey it to Elections Canada."

Next on the investigators' list was John White, who was the Get Out the Vote chair for the Burke campaign in Guelph, and the person who vouched for Michael Sona with Matt McBain. On April 3, 2012, Mathews interviewed White, who claimed that Sona had approached him during the election "about doing some stuff that might not be okay and I told him, go talk to Matt." According to White, Sona wanted to put out a call to electors that couldn't be traced back to the campaign. White claimed he referred Sona to McBain because Sona would not take no from him "and . . . assumed McBain would shoot the idea down." That, he claimed, was the extent of his knowledge about the embryonic dirty tricks of the Guelph campaign.

Oddly, White told investigators that he did not check back with McBain in the war room to ensure that Sona got the right message; nor did he tell campaign manager Ken Morgan about the incident. Even after it was known that misleading calls to electors had in fact been made in Guelph on election day, White told investigators that he never raised the matter of Sona's allegedly shady plans with anyone.

The way the Conservative Party of Canada told it, it all came down to Michael Sona, party loyalist, indefatigable foot soldier, and devout Christian—the most unlikely person to join the crowd under the CPC's bus.

four

UNDER THE BUS

I t's a long way from Hackensack, New Jersey, where he was
born on October 6, 1988, to the media spotlight in a Canadian
political scandal, and it wasn't supposed to end this way for
Michael Sona, who went from being a legislative assistant for a
Conservative MP to being the only person charged in the robocall scandal.

When the tall, gangly, young man who likes to bake his own
bread decided to enter the world of federal politics, it had never
been anything more than a short-term plan. He would immerse
himself in government for a few years, and then use the experience
to enter the private sector, either as a lobbyist or a communications
specialist—a common goal of many young interns who staff the
offices of Conservative cabinet ministers and MPs in Ottawa.

Sona bought his membership in the Conservative Party of
Canada in 2007. Over the next few years, he earned his spurs
on a variety of campaigns, including a provincial leadership race
in Ontario. He also gained experience in nomination races and
party-executive elections. "Pretty much since the day I joined, it

[was] one campaign after another in some capacity or other," he told me.

Then came Ottawa. In Stephen Harper's shop, Sona's biggest task was to master the unique way this government wanted to "communicate." Although Sona was never a staffer in either the PMO or party headquarters (HQ), he worked for cabinet minister James Moore. He also helped cabinet ministers and MPs on numerous campaigns to carry out the Harper government's media strategy. It came down to three words: less is more. "No comment" was often a winning strategy. The cardinal rule was not to turn one bad story into two by advancing it with a comment or reaction. Without the oxygen of fresh information, the theory went, the story would usually die.

Communications in the Harper government was not about passing along facts but often about advancing politically useful narratives while withholding real information. The government tried that tactic during the Afghanistan and F-35 Lightning II fighter jet debates, and would try it again during the robocalls and Senate scandals. On one occasion, Harper even earned a citation for contempt of Parliament for withholding details of proposed bills and cost estimates from Parliament.[1] Public apathy was the government's greatest ally in this dubious policy, and it didn't take Michael Sona long to figure that out. "In my experience, most voters are apathetic to the goings-on in Ottawa unless it involves one of two things: their wallets or their rights," said Sona. "Mess with either of those things, and the voters will care and the story will not die."

The second pillar of the Harper communications strategy was refraining from committing to anything, an approach that allowed the government to mould its message on the fly as new facts emerged. Sona noted that this method was often employed in Question Period, where opposition queries are virtually never answered, and in some cases, not even acknowledged. It left the opposition shadow-boxing most days, and reduced the government's front bench to a platitude-with-attitude brigade.

Sona soon discovered that the Harper government was not a place for creative or independent thinkers. It was a party of one— Harper's way or the highway. "We couldn't even sneeze without calling HQ first," Sona told me. "It wasn't about the content, as I found out many times throughout that 2011 campaign: it was about control. HQ simply wanted everything to be run through them."

The final training project HQ assigned to interns like Sona in the summer of 2009 was a presentation explaining how they would win the federal riding of St. John's South–Mount Pearl in Newfoundland and Labrador then held by Liberal Siobhan Coady. Sona remembered his fellow interns being petrified at the prospect of presenting in front of HQ staff, including Jenni Byrne, Patrick Muttart, and Fred DeLorey. After the presentations, the director of political operations and her colleagues critiqued the presentations, often harshly according to Sona.

Observing how wooden some of the other interns looked who spoke from notes, Sona was glad that he had memorized his speech. The goal was now to look as though he were speaking extempore about his plan to win the riding. The talk went smoothly and he felt confident he had passed muster.

Prior to the election, the local Guelph campaign team had a "fairly vibrant website which was constantly being updated," Sona recalled. But after the writ dropped, HQ micro-managed everything. All posts and photos had to go through Ottawa, and workers in the field could not upload content to the local site directly. Sona heard the same complaints from other ridings, but it didn't pay to buck head office. People grumbled but crumbled when HQ cracked the whip.

According to Sona, the most remarkable thing he learned during his internship was that the Harper government didn't care about the veracity of its pronouncements, just their effect. "It's not the facts of situations that are important to this government; it is the perception of the facts. That is why this government spends so much time driving a simple narrative as opposed to actually fixing problems," says Sona. "When they make mistakes at the top, they try to cover themselves by withholding the facts. . . . When you rode into town on that white horse of transparency and openness, that's a very dangerous electoral position to be in."

Sona, the "son of a preacher man," had been well grounded since childhood in religious morality; his father ministered to his flock at the North River Road Gospel Hall in Guelph, where the family moved when Sona was five. His education in political morality was delivered during the 2011 campaign. "We were told that they weren't telling us to go out and destroy the other guys' signs," Sona recounted, "but if we did, the best thing to use was oven cleaner. The guy said acetone would work just as well and we could get plenty of that from the printing company we were using. Then one of the top guys [deceased senator Doug Finley, allegedly] told us how to get around spending limits, which I thought was funny, since they were still tangled up in the in-and-out thing."

So why, I asked Sona, did he get mixed up in unethical things, assuming it were true he was not "Pierre Poutine"? There were two parts to his answer. The first had to do with a rationalization he and some of his colleagues on the campaign had made: the Conservatives might be bad, but the alternative was so much worse that it justified their tactics. And then there were those dirty tricks the opposition was resorting to in Guelph. "We were getting hit by unidentified robocalls, very, very negative stuff. We wanted to mount a robocall campaign against Frank Valeriote that couldn't be traced back to us—Frank the Flip-Flopper. But none of us knew how to do it. So I asked John White and he told me to contact Matt McBain [at Conservative headquarters] to find out. McBain emailed White to see if I was okay. White said I was on the team and a good guy and to go ahead and talk to me. We talked. I later texted McBain but never heard back." The anonymous robocall campaign Sona was prepared to launch was to have referred to Valeriote's history of alleged political hypocrisy on a range of issues, including his attendance at both Catholic and evangelical churches in Guelph. Sona explained that this robocall campaign never went forward because no one ever showed him how to make the required untraceable call.

Training their political operatives is a priority of the "modernized" Conservative Party of Canada and one of the secrets to the party's success. Sona knew of operatives who were sent to the United States in election years to see how the Republican machine operated. The Conservatives also use the resources of the International Democrat Union (IDU), a global organization of centre-right political parties. Founded in 1983 by the Konrad Adenauer Foundation and US vice-president George H.W. Bush, the IDU's membership includes the US Republican Party, Conservative parties in the UK and Canada, and the centre-right Liberals in Australia. Other founding members included Margaret Thatcher, Jacques Chirac, and Helmut Kohl.

Today the IDU has seventy member parties from fifty-six countries. Based in Norway, the organization's current chair is former Australian prime minister John Howard. An IDU Future Leaders Forum met in Washington in October 2013. The meeting was organized by the Young Republicans and aimed at drawing young representatives from IDU parties and their associated networks around the world. The program included senior speakers from the Republican Party, campaign experts, members of think-tanks, and representatives from the right-wing media. The gathering promised "high-level training and policy discussions." The IDU executive has met in Canada, including a February 2009 gathering in Toronto. In 2012, the campaign directors from member parties in eleven different countries took part in the meeting of the IDU's Standing Committee on Elections and Campaigns. The meeting was hosted by the Conservative Party of Canada in Ottawa on March 29 and 30, 2012. The IDU also regularly holds election technology seminars. The elected officers of the IDU for 2011–2014 included Tony Clement as a vice-chair, and Senator Doug Finley was an assistant chair until his death.

Former Harper chief of staff Patrick Muttart adopted his voter identification techniques from John Howard. Muttart, who was brought back from the United States to work for Harper as a key strategist in the 2011 campaign, was described by Henry Olsen of the American Enterprise Institute as "the world's leading expert on working-class voters in English-speaking countries."[2] Former NDP leadership candidate Brian Topp described work like Muttart's as trying "to manipulate" blue-collar voters into "voting against their own interests."

The idea of organized voter suppression to win an election is new in Canada, but the Republicans have used it effectively in the United States for several years. Americans for Prosperity (AFP) was founded in 2003 by billionaires Charles and David Koch. AFP president Tim Phillips said the group was focused on voter turnout—and, some would say, on suppressing it.[3]

The American Legislative Exchange Council (ALEC), funded in part by the Koch brothers, has put up the money for a drive to require photo ID to vote in the United States. Under the guise of preventing voter fraud, which is largely non-existent, the campaign actually disenfranchises the poor, students who move away to school, young voters, African Americans, and seniors who may not have a driver's licence. That list is primarily made up of people likely not to vote Republican. ALEC was founded by Paul Weyrich, who co-founded the Moral Majority with Jerry Falwell.

(It was Weyrich who actually coined the term "moral majority.")
Weyrich was also a co-founder of the Council for National Policy
(CNP), headquartered in Fairfax, Virginia, the secretive, ultra-
conservative organization Stephen Harper spoke to in Montreal
in 1997 about the shortcomings of Canadian governance. Weyrich
famously said, "I don't want everybody to vote. Elections are not
won by a majority of people. They never have been from the beginning of the country and they are not now. As a matter of fact,
our leverage in the elections quite candidly goes up as the voting
populace goes down."

Not everyone thinks training people how to manipulate elections is an improvement over winning them the old fashioned
way—by information, persuasion, and debate. On September 5,
2012, Preston Manning gave an interview to the CBC in which
he condemned the idea of using robocalls to harass voters or divert
them to the wrong polls. Manning said that workers needed better ethical training and that it was a mistake to link political dirty
tricks to a single party. He believed that part of the problem is
that all parties now send young Canadians to political training
schools in the United States, where politics is practised with far
fewer scruples. The founder of the Reform Party declared that
Canadian politics had to be insulated from US-style tactics. Part
of the answer was stricter oversight by campaign managers and
Elections Canada, but Manning proposed a more fundamental
solution: "I actually think the more effective thing is preventing it
in the first place and that involves ethical training."

The robocalls scandal dominated federal politics in 2012, and
its ripple effect spread from the House of Commons and the daily
Question Period straight across the country. Reports were heard
of harassing and misleading calls to Liberal and NDP supporters
in several ridings, including Eglinton-Lawrence in Toronto, a seat
won for the Conservatives by Joe Oliver, now finance minister.

Oliver beat incumbent Liberal Joe Volpe by more than four thousand votes. As reported by Postmedia, Jewish voters were called repeatedly on the Sabbath. Early-morning and late-night calls were also made, supposedly by Volpe's campaign. This was a tactic remarkably similar to the dead-of-night calls that were planned but not carried out in Guelph with the second CIMS list. There were also allegations of a late influx into polling stations of unregistered voters without addresses, or who provided fake addresses.

In Thunder Bay, Ontario, a worker at the Conservative Party's main call company swore in an affidavit[4] she had been told to direct voters to the wrong polling stations in the final days of the campaign. Annette Desgagné said she and her co-workers had been instructed to identify themselves as calling from the "Voter Outreach Centre." Desgagné swore that at least one of her colleagues had identified himself as calling from Elections Canada when misdirecting voters: "I became very concerned that I was participating in something that involved giving voters wrong information. My internal radar went off. I wrote down what I could recall from the script I was asked to read about Change of Address calls and I arranged for the information to go to the RCMP." Desgagné also reported her concerns to Elections Canada.

Predictably, both Responsive Marketing Group (RMG) and the Conservative Party rejected Desgagné's sworn affidavit as unreliable. And in his robocall report, elections commissioner Yves Côté said he had found no evidence to corroborate reports that callers posed as Elections Canada employees. However, some electors were told to vote at a specific poll, and the poll location indicated was incorrect.[5] According to Elections Canada records, RMG worked on ninety-seven Conservative campaigns across the country, as well as the national campaign, billing them $1.4 million. The company had worked with CIMS as it was developed in 2003, and it was "the best in the business" according to Senator

Doug Finley. The Conservatives won Nipissing-Timiskaming, one of the ridings called by RMG, by eighteen votes.

In its investigation of robocalls outside of Guelph, Elections Canada requested phone records from Shaw, Vidéotron, and Rogers. Elections Canada investigator John Dickson, who was conducting the national investigation, received records of incoming and outgoing calls of forty-five Rogers customers complaining of calls about poll location changes in the week before the 2011 election. NDP MP Pat Martin claimed that thirty-four federal ridings received fraudulent calls telling people that their voting station had changed. Prime Minister Harper responded by challenging the Opposition to "prove" that the Conservatives had made the calls.

After Postmedia journalists Stephen Maher and Glen McGregor broke the robocalls story on February 23, 2012, country-wide demonstrations erupted demanding a public inquiry to reveal the identity of the alleged election cheaters. Stephen Harper steadfastly refused to call an inquiry, practising instead his government's 3-D approach to damage control: deny, deflect, and delay—and, if possible, catch the next plane out of town for important international work.

Part of the effort was public relations on the ground. Senator Mike Duffy was dispatched to downplay the scandal in the media. On February 27, 2012, Duffy appeared on Jordi Morgan's Halifax radio show on News 95.7, claiming that it wasn't "us doing it" and that the Conservatives welcomed the investigation. Duffy then offered an intriguing conjecture: the calls could have been made by what he called unnamed "third parties." "I don't believe it was the Conservative Party," he said. "But if something is going on, don't forget, we have all these other groups. . . . People have to remember that it's not just political parties that are operating during a federal election campaign. Under the law, we have all kinds of interested third parties that are operating in election campaigns, and I think that's where we have to be careful."

Duffy didn't say who these "third parties" were. It was enough to merely suggest a mysterious culprit to draw attention away from the Conservatives. Besides, as the senator made clear, "This isn't the end of the world here. But it is something that needs to be investigated and frankly it burns my butt, because the dirty tricksters are at it and I don't think anybody in politics likes this." Duffy ended the interview by telling Morgan's radio audience that in his forty years covering politics, Stephen Harper was "the straightest politician [he had] ever covered." In less than a year, mired in the Senate expenses scandal, Duffy would offer a very different appraisal of how things were done in Stephen Harper's PMO.

Although the Harper government and Conservative Party headquarters continued to protest their innocence in the robocall affair, the party's credibility suffered a serious reversal. In late January 2013, Saskatchewan residents began receiving an interactive push poll, a robocall critical of draft changes to the boundaries of federal ridings in the province proposed by the Federal Electoral Boundaries Commission for Saskatchewan. With thirty new seats up for grabs across the country in the 2015 election, the new riding boundaries were crucially important public issues. The push poll asked residents if they agreed with a plan that would damage "Saskatchewan values" by pitting rural and urban voters against each other. No message accompanied the robocall to say who had commissioned it.

Saskatchewan Conservative MP Tom Lukiwski and Conservative Party spokesperson Fred DeLorey denied that the party was doing the polling, but the reporting team of Maher and McGregor weren't buying it. Maher thought he recognized the voice on the recording from their previous robocall stories. To test their theory, the reporters hired an American forensic audio analyst to study the voice. It turned out to belong to Matt Meier of RackNine, the same firm used by the Conservatives—and "Pierre Poutine"—to make robocalls in the 2011 election. This time, Meier couldn't claim he didn't know the content of the message going out, because he himself had recorded it. Glen McGregor, who had reported Fred DeLorey's denial that Conservatives were behind the poll, was shocked. "The Saskatchewan riding boundary robocalls story was utterly astounding to me," said McGregor. "The idea that the Tories would be so brazen as to hire RackNine in the midst of the Poutine case, to make such dirty tricks calls, then to cover it up, lie to me about it—Just wow. . . . Providing patently false information, on the record, to a reporter is the worst thing a spokesman can do. Because of this, he [DeLorey] has very little credibility in my view."

The Harper government's deputy House leader, Tom Lukiwski, was livid. Blindsided by the illegal push poll in his own province, he immediately told Saskatoon radio station CKOM that the calls were "deceptive." He went further on a CBC radio call-in show, declaring that Jenni Byrne, the party's most senior official, should be held responsible: "I don't know which party official it would be, but I know that Jenni Byrne, who is executive direc-tor, said, well, ultimately the buck stops with her. She should take full responsibility."

Opposition leader Thomas Mulcair accused the Conservatives of lying about the call. After denying the story, Fred DeLorey now said that there had been an "internal miscommunication." The prime minister insisted, "The party has already explained that it has followed all the rules and the law in this situation." But the CRTC requires that all robocalls identify their sponsor. The Saskatchewan push poll did not declare that it was being paid for by the Conservative Party, and for that reason it was illegal.

After some serious bumps, things began shifting the govern-ment's way in the robocalls affair. Matt Meier threatened to sue

NDP MP Pat Martin unless he apologized for remarks he had made about RackNine's involvement in the Guelph robocalls. Martin obliged, but Meier sued him for $5 million anyway. The case was eventually settled out of court. Ironically, in late May 2013, the CRTC announced that RackNine had agreed to pay $60,000 in fines for fifteen illegal robocalls campaigns sent out on behalf of political parties from March 2011 to February 2013. These included six campaigns for the Wildrose Party and two for the Ontario Progressive Conservatives, all made without identifying who was behind the messages. The "Pierre Poutine" calls from Guelph were not part of the CRTC penalties. However, the federal Conservatives were fined $78,000 for doing the Saskatchewan boundary push poll without a declaration of origin.

The best break the Harper government got in the robocalls affair came at the expense of the Liberals. The riding association of the Liberal MP from Guelph, Frank Valeriote, was fined $4,900 for making illegal robocalls two days before the 2011 election. The anonymous calls attacked the Conservative candidate's position on abortion. (This was the phone campaign against Marty Burke that Michael Sona wanted to counter with a barrage of calls aimed at Frank the Flip-Flopper.) Valeriote cooperated fully with the CRTC when he learned the call did not include identifying information, and told reporters, "I take full responsibility and apologize for the infringement." After the CRTC levied the fine in August 2012, Harper never missed an opportunity of mentioning that the only person convicted in the robocalls affair was a Liberal—MP Frank Valeriote. It was a clever attempt at shifting the focus.

Maude Barlow and the Council of Canadians (COC) had earlier called the prime minister's bluff. Just a month after the robocalls story broke, the COC began filing court applications on behalf of nine voters seeking to overturn election results in seven ridings won by the Conservatives because of alleged cheating. One challenge was later dropped. Reflecting the view of thousands of Canadians, the COC believed the case was of "fundamental importance to our democracy" and was "both critical and unprecedented." The COC observed that although the Conservatives claimed they wanted to get to the bottom of the robocalls affair, "They seem to be doing whatever they can to prevent this case from being heard by a judge." The COC was referring to the fact that the Conservatives had filed a 750-page legal brief asking the Federal Court to dismiss the challenges by Maude Barlow and her organization. Lawyers for the Conservatives argued that no evidence showed that anyone had actually been denied the right to vote. Strangely, those same lawyers seemed uninterested in the fact that if the Conservative Party had nothing to do with deceptive robocalls, the party's database had been hacked, pilfered, and used to break the law.

Despite efforts by the lawyers for the Conservatives, the Federal Court ruled that the Council of Canadians' suit could proceed. The council's lawyer, Steven Shrybman, asked Elections Canada to provide the COC with details of complaints from voters in two hundred ridings. Ultimately, the results in six ridings in the 2011 election were challenged by voters in Federal Court, who were supported by the Council of Canadians. The case wrapped up in mid-December 2012. Although the Conservatives would claim victory when the judgment came down in May, it was in fact a stunning confirmation of electoral fraud in Canada—driven by Conservative voter information buried deep inside the electronic fortress of CIMS.

Federal Court justice Richard Mosley ruled that widespread telephone fraud targeting non-Conservative voters had taken place, likely based on CIMS, but not enough evidence had been presented to overturn the voting results in the six electoral districts. In an indictment of what went on, Mosley wrote, "There was an orchestrated effort to suppress votes during the 2011 election campaign by a person or persons with access to the CIMS database." The COC had brought to light evidence of fraud in multiple ridings outside Guelph but no proof of the fraudster: "There is no evidence to indicate that the use of the CIMS database in this manner was approved or condoned by the CPC," the judge wrote. "Rather the evidence points to elaborate efforts to conceal the identity of those accessing the database and arranging for the calls to be made."

In a rebuke of the Conservative Party's claim that it had always cooperated with investigations into robocalls, the judge also noted that the Conservatives had actually engaged in "trench warfare" to prevent the civil case from coming to a hearing on the merits. If Canadians believed the party line, either someone was trying to frame the Conservatives, or the party had been the victim of an elaborate theft without their knowledge. As Andrew Coyne pointed out in his column,[6] someone had committed massive electoral fraud that could only benefit the Conservative Party, but apparently had done it without the party's involvement.

The two seminal scandals of the Harper years intersected on what must have been a bad day in the PMO. On the same day as the Mosley decision, May 23, 2013, Senator Mike Duffy spoke to reporters for the first time since the bombshell report by CTV's Bob Fife charging that the prime minister's chief of staff had given the senator $90,000 to pay off improper expenses. Duffy said he wanted a "full and open inquiry" and promised to reveal what had happened: "I think Canadians have a right to know all the facts and I'm quite prepared, in the right place and time, to give them the whole story."

After eight months of living under a cloud of suspicion created by senior members of his own party, Michael Sona made a fateful decision. Once he heard elections commissioner Yves Côté recommend charges in the Guelph robocalls case after a twenty-one-month investigation, Sona went public. The figure at the eye of the storm gave an interview to the *Huffington Post* and later to the *Ottawa Citizen*, making the point to anyone who would listen that many of the alleged facts about him in the affidavit of Elections Canada investigator Al Mathews were wrong. With the prime minister refusing demands for a judicial inquiry, and frustrated by the fact that he had been fingered by anonymous senior Conservatives in the Guelph case, Michael Sona reached for the ultimate megaphone: network television.

In an attempt to clear his name, Sona appeared on CBC's *Power & Politics* on October 31, 2012. He told host Evan Solomon that his name had been leaked to the media by anonymous party sources and that he was not going to "take the fall" for something he didn't do. On the main point—who was responsible for the deceitful Guelph robocalls—he categorically denied that he was "Pierre Poutine"; nor did he know who was. Sona's suggestion seemed to be that important players in Ottawa had been deeply engaged in the Marty Burke attack campaign. Guelph was a targeted riding for the Conservatives, and HQ was "very involved" in trying to take it from the Liberals.

Sona told Solomon that Nick Kouvalis, a principal partner of Campaign Research, a company used by the Conservative Party in the 2011 election, was in the Guelph riding between eight and twelve times doing voter outreach. (Kouvalis countered by tweeting that he was in the riding twice.) Kouvalis had been campaign manager for Rob Ford in 2010, and worked for thirty-nine campaigns in the 2011 election, most of them in Ontario. The company was hard-nosed in its approach to politics. A formal complaint was lodged against Campaign Research for suggesting to voters in Liberal MP Irwin Cotler's riding of Mount Royal that Cotler was about to retire, which was untrue. When Cotler complained to the Speaker of the House that his privileges as an MP had been breached by the false campaign, Speaker Andrew Scheer investigated. Though he did not make a finding that Campaign Research had breached Cotler's privilege, Scheer called the deceptive phone campaign "reprehensible." Kouvalis did not seem to be overly concerned. As he told Postmedia, "We're in the business of getting Conservatives elected and ending Liberal careers. We're good at it."[7]

As for Sona, he wanted people to consider how credible it was that one person in a notoriously top-down operation could be responsible for the complex and nationwide voter deception caper that was robocalls. As he put it to me, had a "twenty-two-year-old guy managed to coordinate this entire massive scheme when he didn't even have access to the data to be able to do this?" In fact, there were five workers on the Guelph campaign who did have access to the CIMS database during the election: Andrew Prescott, John White, Ken Morgan, Trent Blanchette, and Chris Crawford. Crawford, White, and Sona gave evidence to investigators. Prescott initially refused, then granted a telephone conversation, and finally cancelled a subsequent formal interview with Elections Canada investigators.

Morgan and Blanchette refused outright to speak to Elections Canada, Morgan by email in April 2012. Four months later, he moved to Kuwait. Not even the dogged reporters who had broken the robocalls story could get to him, as Glen McGregor told me. "Did everything we could to contact him," said McGregor. "I even spoke to the father of his American girlfriend in Kuwait City. He would never talk to us. Still won't. He's a huge open question in robocalls." Though Morgan remained incommunicado, he revealed glimpses of a lonely man on Twitter between November 7, 2012, and June 7, 2013: "Missing Canada today. Family, food, smells . . . even politics." Even the name of his blog site—"The Captain's

Quarters 10,410 kilometres from home"—showed the depth of the isolation he felt.

Given that Sona did not have access to CIMS during the writ period, which would be necessary to obtain the list of non-supporters used in the fraudulent calls, the most likely alternative to the "rogue operator" theory was that robocalls was a highly coordinated deception by skilled and knowledgeable people. There were individuals at HQ, at the automated calling companies, and on the Guelph campaign team who had those technical skills.

Sona had barely washed off his TV makeup before Conservative Party headquarters fired back. Fred DeLorey responded to the claims Sona made on *Power & Politics* in an email, stating that the party "ran a clean and ethical campaign and was not involved in voter suppression." Andrew Prescott, the Burke campaign's official contact with RackNine, again denied he had anything to do with misleading calls. Jenni Byrne also denied that the party was involved in dirty tricks. The narrative was that someone had acted alone, and the party let out the word that that someone was Michael Sona.

Although media critics were impressed by Michael Sona's aplomb during his television appearance, Elections Canada had come to its own conclusions. Five months after his interview with Evan Solomon, Sona was informed of pending charges against him. As a devout Christian, the timing could not have been worse—just prior to the Easter weekend. On April 2, 2013, in the Ontario Court of Justice in Guelph, Michael Sona was charged with having willfully prevented an elector from voting, contrary to paragraph 281(g) of the Canada Elections Act. Yves Côté, who became Elections Canada commissioner after incumbent William Corbett's surprise retirement in June 2012, said, "The strong public reaction to the fraudulent telephone calls made to electors in Guelph during the May 2011 general election shows how deeply disturbed Canadians were by what happened. I hope that the charge we filed today will send a strong message that such abuses under the Canada Elections Act will not be tolerated."

The Crown decided to proceed by indictment, which meant that if Sona were convicted, he would be going to jail. The justice department assigned one of its top guns, Croft Michaelson, to the case. He had participated in the prosecution of the so-called Toronto 18. Sona, who believed the government was out to get him, was not comforted when he allegedly found a tweet from Michaelson to Treasury Board president Tony Clement inviting the minister for drinks when he came to Toronto. In the accused's favour, silence would no longer be an option for witnesses such as Ken Morgan and Trent Blanchette, who had declined to be interviewed by Elections Canada investigators. They and others, along with their documents, would be subject to subpoena if the matter came to trial.

The Conservative Party communications operation blundered in its response to news of the charge against Sona. Even though the former Tory worker was still clothed in the presumption of innocence, Conservative spokesperson Fred DeLorey emailed that the party was "pleased" with the development, commenting, "In 2011 we reached out to Elections Canada when we heard of wrongdoing in Guelph and did all we could to assist them." Not only was DeLorey's statement Disneyesque, it certainly didn't represent what a lot of Conservatives were thinking. Both Marty Burke and his wife left the Conservative riding association in Guelph, allegedly over the treatment HQ had meted out to Michael Sona and the party's apparent gloating over his being charged. Harold Albrecht, the Conservative MP for Kitchener-Conestoga, raised his objections to the Sona affair in caucus. Even the prime minister's former parliamentary secretary, Dean Del Mastro, offered Sona support and disagreed with what had been done to him. Finally, the patron saint of anyone thrown under the bus, long-time Conservative Hill staffer Chris Froggatt, extended his sympathy and support to Sona.

Sona's lawyer, Norman Boxall, issued a statement on behalf of his client: although the charge was disappointing, "If the government was interested in the public being fully informed, and the issue of robocalls being properly addressed, a full public inquiry would be called. . . ." On May 3, 2013, Michael Sona made his first court appearance in Guelph. Boxall indicated that his client would be fighting the charge, a not unexpected plea given that the penalty for his alleged offence carried a maximum penalty of five years in prison and a $5,000 fine.

A pretrial conference was held at the Guelph courthouse on August 29, 2013. The judge seemed to suggest that the case might not go to trial. Justice Norman Douglas said the lawyers would meet again on September 25, 2013, for another pretrial conference: "If there needs to be a trial, we'll set the date at that time."

Court documents made public in August 2013 claimed that Michael Sona admitted to involvement in the scheme, but Elections Canada investigator Al Mathews "suspected that others were involved as well." According to Information to Obtain (ITO) documents that Mathews filed in May, Conservative officials finally acknowledged that the party's database had been used to create the list of non-supporters who received the calls.

The charge against Sona was based on evidence from six current or former Conservative Party staffers who had been named in May 2013 by Mathews. Oddly, Mathews had not found the witnesses himself. With one exception, the five others—Rebecca Dockstaeder, John Schudlo, Tyler Barker, Mitchell Messom, and Conrad Johnson—were all produced by Conservative Party lawyer Arthur Hamilton. Immediately after RackNine was served with a court order for its records in November 2011, Hamilton had embarked on his own internal investigation into the robocalls affair. He interviewed key party workers and asked them not to discuss the robocalls publicly.

It is not known if Hamilton had access to all the data RackNine provided to Elections Canada investigators under court order. Meier would later admit that he had contacted Chris Rougier at party headquarters after the initial visit from Mathews seeking records from Guelph. It was presumably during that three-month period before the story became public that Hamilton learned about the witnesses against Sona. Exactly when he received that information, and what he did with it, is not known. What is known is that before Maher and McGregor published their first story in February 2012, it had taken Hamilton three months to respond to Elections Canada's request that he arrange interviews for them with party officials. After the story was published, the Conservative Party immediately leaked Sona's name as the rogue operative, and Hamilton quickly supplied witnesses against the party worker. Most of them were junior staffers who worked for Conservative members on the Hill. Investigator Mathews admitted in court documents that Rebecca Dockstaeder, John Schudlo, and Mitchell Messom "were strangers to me, and I had no reason to anticipate what evidence [they] could provide or not provide." Hamilton had simply called Mathews and told him he had three relevant witnesses whom he thought the investigator should talk to.

Arthur Hamilton was present for interviews with five of the witnesses as counsel for the Conservative Party of Canada. Witness Benjamin Hicks, who came forward at the request of Elections Canada, provided his information in the form of a written statement. One after another, the witnesses produced by Hamilton told investigators that Sona had bragged to them about his role in the robocalls scheme after the election. In an ITO dated September 2013, Mathews described what he and

Ronald Lamothe learned from interviewing two of the witnesses in an MP's office on March 21, 2012: "Both witnesses said that one afternoon, about a week to ten days after the May 2, 2011, election, Michael Sona visited the office." It was a social visit that allowed party workers to catch up—nothing unusual. Both people knew Sona and described him as someone given to exaggeration and telling tall tales. Two other witnesses interviewed the same day also talked about Sona's tendency to mythologize the facts. Mathews wrote, "Both witnesses knew Michael Sona and both described him as someone given to exaggeration." They also told investigators Sona admitted to them that he had been involved in the false calls that went out to Guelph voters.

Rebecca Dockstaeder told Mathews that Sona had described "what sounded very, very similar to the story that we'd been hearing about these robocalls." She claimed Sona told her he paid cash for the disposable phone and Visa card, and obtained a list of Liberal voters from a friend who owed him a favour. Sona then proceeded to record a message impersonating Elections Canada, according to Dockstaeder. The witness told investigators that it was only after she heard about the robocalls investigation in the media that she reported the alleged conversation she had had with Sona to her boss, MP Chris Warkentin. The Conservative MP for Peace River did not contact Elections Canada with the information but called Jenni Byrne at Conservative Party headquarters. HQ then contacted Arthur Hamilton. If the Conservative Party was reaching out to investigators, as Jenni Byrne and others constantly claimed, several group huddles took place before the information was passed on—and only after the story broke.

The investigation had taken a strange turn. Rather than serving the Conservative Party of Canada with search warrants, Elections Canada investigators relied on Conservative Party lawyer Arthur Hamilton to obtain emails and documents and set up meetings.

Since the Conservative Party itself was to some extent a participant in the investigation, this was unsettling. Ottawa defence lawyer Lawrence Greenspon thought the party's involvement cast a shadow over the investigation. "The presence of a Conservative party lawyer during interviews being conducted by Elections Canada investigators takes away from the appearance of an independent investigation and therefore takes away from the appearance of justice," said Greenspon.[8] Ottawa defence lawyer Michael Spratt agreed, calling Hamilton's presence at the interviews "highly unusual." Spratt said, "That's almost never seen. Normally witnesses aren't interviewed in the presence of their lawyer for the very reason that it potentially could contaminate the evidence."

Both of the reporters who broke the story found it hard to believe that Elections Canada investigators had relied so heavily on the Conservative Party and Arthur Hamilton to filter so much of the evidence. "I think there are very serious questions about EC's approach to the investigation," Stephen Maher told me. "Why didn't they get production orders? . . . Why did they let Hamilton sit in on interviews with the witnesses? I suppose they didn't have much choice. Still, it raises big questions about the contamination of evidence, particularly given the authoritarian culture of the party."

There were more problems with the interviews. Some of the details gleaned from the Hamilton-supplied witnesses were later proven to be incorrect. Investigators knew that the list of Conservative non-supporters in Guelph came from CIMS, yet the witnesses reported that Sona had suggested that a Liberal friend had been the source. More embarrassing, author and *Globe and Mail* journalist Lawrence Martin reported that Michael Sona had actually been holidaying in Aruba on the dates some witnesses said he was with them in Ottawa bragging about his role in the Guelph robocalls. But the most potentially damaging aspect of Hamilton's presence during the interviews of witnesses such as Conrad Tigger Johnson was the allegation of interference in the process.[9]

Documents obtained by the *Huffington Post* and Global News showed that during the interviews with Elections Canada investigators attended by Arthur Hamilton, the Conservative Party lawyer interrupted the investigators, directed questions to the witnesses, and at times appeared to tell them what to say. What made that more astonishing was that Hamilton wasn't representing the witnesses he appeared to be directing. Laura Stone of Global News obtained an email from one of the witnesses, saying, "Well, I said I didn't need a lawyer, wasn't commenting. I don't suppose the Conservative Party lawyer counts, because my choice in the matter wasn't exercised."

The question was this: since Conservative lawyer Arthur Hamilton had breached the appearance of an independent Elections Canada investigation by taking part in these Elections Canada interviews, and had played a role in eliciting information from witnesses, would the witnesses' evidence be discounted in court as tainted?

five

THE UNFAIR
ELECTIONS ACT

B eyond the particulars of the robocalls affair, Canada faced
a huge problem. The way the country elected its federal
government was hopelessly antiquated. Election rules had been
made before the internet age, and the old Elections Act included
no provisions for governing the huge databases of political parties. The system was so outdated that Canada's chief electoral
officer, Mark Mayrand, declared that new rules had to be in
place before the next election if another robocalls debacle was
to be avoided.[1]

Elections Canada received a total of 2,448 complaints arising
out of the 2011 election, from 1,726 voters resident in 261 ridings
across the country.[2] Two types of complaints were recorded: 1,207
related to calls allegedly providing electors with the wrong poll
location, and 1,241 complaining about nuisance calls. (Some voters reported both incorrect poll location calls and nuisance calls.)
Since most of the calls had been received nine months prior to the

investigation, few people could be specific about a time or date of a call, or had proof of the content of the call.

It was important to get the new electoral legislation right. On October 15, 2013, Elections Canada announced it had appointed a non-partisan advisory board, co-chaired by former auditor general Sheila Fraser and former Supreme Court justice Ian Binnie. The thirteen-member board included former premiers Bob Rae and Roy Romanow, former Reform Party leader Preston Manning, and other blue-ribbon members. Elections Canada stated that the purpose of the board was to advise Mayrand "on matters relating to Canada's electoral system, its voting processes, and support for a vigorous democracy."

As a result of the group's deliberations, and Elections Canada's own experience, Mayrand tabled a report in Parliament recommending changes to the law to keep up with new technologies. He was looking for three key changes: greater investigative powers, including the power of subpoena; supporting documents for the expenses of political parties, which, unbelievably, are not required under the old act; and the protection of voter data from political parties with respect to who voted and who did not. Mayrand also wanted calling companies to retain the phone numbers of the people they actually dialled during an election campaign. Finally, the chief electoral officer wanted to make it a crime to impersonate an Elections Canada official, punishable by a fine of up to $250,000. Under current case law it is not an offence to impersonate an Elections Canada official.

The government appeared to be listening. On February 2, 2014, the Conservatives announced they would introduce the Fair Elections Act (Bill C-23), which would reorganize how electoral fraud was investigated and prosecuted. When the opposition and the public actually saw the piece of legislation, it was quickly dubbed the "Unfair Elections Act." The minister responsible for democratic reform, Pierre Poilievre, tweeted repeatedly about the program, promising to give law enforcement "sharper teeth, longer reach and a freer hand." Arthur Finkelstein would have approved. Poilievre repeated the bumper-sticker phrase three times in his announcement. The bill had initially been promised at the height of the robocalls scandal in March 2012. It was to have been tabled in April 2013, but was withdrawn after being presented to the Conservative caucus in a closed-door meeting.

The legislation did anything but what the minister had promised. Elections Canada was stunned by the provisions of Bill C-23. Instead of gaining new powers, Canada's chief electoral officer saw his authority seriously diminished. Not only was there no new power of subpoena to assist Elections Canada investigators, but Mark Mayrand was muzzled under the proposed legislation. He would henceforth be prevented from communicating anything but the most fundamental voting information to Canadians. Whether he wanted to advertise a campaign to promote greater election turn-out, or, remarkably, even issue a warning to the public about a fraud like robocalls, he was silenced under the provisions of Bill C-23.

The bill also cut off Elections Canada's investigative arm, which would now report straight to the director of public prosecutions (DPP) instead of the chief electoral officer. While it is true that both the commissioner of Elections Canada and the DPP are cabinet appointments, many experts saw the change as damaging. Steven Shrybman, the lawyer who handled the Council of Canadians case on robocalls, said that the legislation would move Elections Canada investigations from a position of neutrality to one under political control. It was only after the news stories about alleged voter fraud broke that people realized that what had happened to them were not innocent mistakes. Shrybman pointed out, "What you [have to] remember is no one knew this had happened in May 2011."

According to Harry Neufeld, British Columbia's former chief electoral officer, section 44 of the government's new legislation would actually increase the potential for partisan abuse at polling stations. In an interview with the CBC's Rosemary Barton, Neufeld criticized the provision allowing a riding's incumbent candidate or the candidate's party to appoint all central polling supervisors. Currently, Elections Canada appoints the polling supervisors. By essentially making the positions party appointments, Neufeld warned, officials would be given greater scope for making mistakes at polling stations for partisan reasons.

Postmedia reporter Stephen Maher raised another serious weakness related to a clause in the new bill. Elections Canada could, according to one of its former lawyers, be prevented from reporting on the outcome of its investigation into robocalls. Previously Marc Mayrand provided information about Elections Canada's investigations in three ways: at parliamentary committees, in a public report, and to the news media. That line of reporting would be closed once the new bill passed. And unless an investigation resulted in charges, absolutely no reporting would be done by the elections commissioner under the new legislation.

According to Elections Canada officials, Bill C-23 would diminish rather than enhance voter participation by ending vouching as a means of legitimizing a citizen not on the voters list, and by refusing to accept voter information cards as a legitimate form of identification. The Harper government was following the lead of Republican politicians in the United States who tried to make voter suppression palatable by dressing it up as anti-voting fraud measures. As in the United States, Harper government claims of massive vote fraud were false, just like the reports from Tory MPs and a senator that they had actually witnessed cheaters in action.

The Conservatives' bill also included a self-serving change to the financial rules. An exemption would be built in for fundraising costs associated with previous donors who had contributed at least $20 in the last five years to a party association, nomination contestant, or candidate. Elections Canada would now have no practical way of distinguishing a fundraising mail-out from advertising. The exemption was simply a way of expanding spending limits during an election, which Stephen Harper had religiously advocated for since his days at the NCC and his doomed trip to the Supreme Court of Canada.

The bill also allowed for an increase in the personal donation limit to $1,500, which would benefit wealthier people since those with more disposable income will not experience financial strain by contributing extra money. Assuming wealthier people contribute to the Conservatives, this gives the party a fundraising edge over people with lower wages who may want to contribute to the NDP, Liberals, or Greens. The bill increased the overall campaign spending limit for national parties by about $1 million. Parties will be able to spend $22 million in 2015, an increase that could change the way elections are waged. Further, instead of relying on volunteers, parties flush with cash could hire professional companies to reach voters by micro-targeting. Unlimited third-party spending, long a goal of Stephen Harper both in and out of politics, is bound to become an issue both before and during the 2015 election. The Conservatives will have the clear financial advantage. As former Harper mentor Tom Flanagan told the *Hill Times* on March 3, 2014, "All this legislation . . . probably gives the Conservatives a relative advantage in this election cycle. The Conservatives are going to be extremely well funded in this election campaign. They have far more money than they could ever spend in the writ period, so they will be able to have a very well-funded pre-writ campaign."

On March 6, 2014, an embattled Marc Mayrand addressed Parliament, laying out how measures in the new elections act undermined its stated purpose. He said election day "may be the only time, when all Canadians can claim to be perfectly equal in power and influence, regardless of their income, health or social circumstances." By creating an exception for certain fundraising expenses, the proposed legislation could compromise that level playing field. A case could be made that a vindictive Stephen Harper was merely trying to even the score with an old adversary. After he become prime minister, his Conservative Party of Canada and Elections Canada had had a momentous clash.

The Tories objected to the in-and-out investigation by Elections Canada into illegal campaign spending. They liked it even less in February 2011 when the director of public prosecutions, Brian Saunders, recommended that charges under the Elections Act be laid against the Conservative Party of Canada and four senior officials—Senator Doug Finley, former national party director Michael Donison, former interim executive director Susan Kehoe, and Senator Irving Gerstein. After a six-year legal marathon, the charges were ultimately withdrawn on November 10, 2011, following a plea bargain agreement. The Conservative Party agreed to plead guilty to exceeding spending limits in the 2006 election, and to pay the maximum fine of $52,000 and repay a further $230,198.

The settlement came just as the robocalls investigation was about to heat up. In November 2011, Matt Meier, the proprietor of RackNine, was given thirty days to produce his telephone data and documents. The Conservative guilty plea came six months after the May 2011 election, and the agreement netted out in the party's favour. Even taking into account the fines and paybacks, the party had spent $700,000 more than it was allowed in the 2006 election—and right at the end of a tight election, when it meant the most.

The Harper government had ridden roughshod over the opposition and experts on many occasions, earning the reputation as champions of policy-based facts rather than fact-based policies.

As dictatorial as the government had been on issues such as the closure of scientific facilities, the pursuit of the F-35 fighter jet, and democracy-busting omnibus legislation, the Fair Elections Act was a new low-watermark—and an example of utter hypocrisy. In the mid-nineties, when the Liberals made changes to the Elections Canada Act, Reform Party MP Stephen Harper preached about the need to build a consensus to make such important changes to legislation. He also expressed his abhorrence at the government using time allocation to force its reforms through. At the time, he said that the government's tactics better suited a "third world" country than they did Canada.

Once in power, Harper and his government went much further than slamming their critics. Pierre Poilievre flatly misrepresented research used to support Bill C-23. When he was rebuked over the misuse of information by the author of a report he was citing, the minister continued to insist he was right and the author was wrong. Facing a wall of opposition, Minister Poilievre ignored all expert advice, jeered at the opposition's demands for amendments, and didn't bother to even consult with Elections Canada about the profound and highly dubious changes the government was proposing to how Canadians elect their parliament.

Without either reason or evidence on his side, Poilievre resorted to the one thing he indisputably possessed: power. Instead of answering Marc Mayrand's points, he attacked his reputation. The Harper government even tried smearing former auditor general Sheila Fraser, suggesting she was criticizing Bill C-23 because she was in the pay of Elections Canada. (She was paid $2,450 for her role as an advisor.) The allegation was ludicrous and shabby. As *National Post* columnist Andrew Coyne put it, ". . . when you start to believe your own rhetoric, your brains turn to mush."

The spectacle of the government's effort to ram through a seriously flawed piece of legislation led to a remarkable occurrence

at the 2014 Manning Networking Conference. Prominent
Conservatives used the event to speak out against the PM's political judgment, issues management, and style. Preston Manning, the
man who laid the foundations for Harper's political career, urged
the PM to restore democracy and amend the Fair Elections Act.
In his keynote speech, Manning called on ". . . Conservative governments, Conservative opposition parties, and the Conservative
Movement . . . to constantly affirm and reaffirm their commitment to extending rather than limiting democratic expression."
Manning, like virtually everyone else outside Stephen Harper's
caucus, wanted to see the new legislation amended "to strengthen,
rather than reducing, the role of Elections Canada and the chief
electoral officer with respect to promotional and educational
activities designed to increase voter participation in Canada's elections." As Sheila Fraser told me, "This bill is so bad, I haven't seen
anyone support it yet."

On April 15, 2014, a Senate committee proposed amendments
to the government's controversial election legislation. The Senate
was the "last chance" for opponents to voice their concerns before
the legislation passed. Despite attacking Marc Mayrand during
an appearance at the Senate hearings, given the near-unanimous
opposition to the bill across the country, Poilievre finally backed
down and said he was open to "ways we can make a great bill even
better." The decision to amend the bill was understood to have
come from Harper himself.[3] It was one thing to pass legislation
disenfranchising students and people living on reserves, but the
party was beginning to hear from its rural voters that they could
be disenfranchised because their driver's licence had a post-office-
box address rather than a street address, and identification with a
street address was necessary to vote.

On June 12, 2014, after four months of controversy, Bill C-23,
which is at the core of our democratic system, passed the third and

final reading in the Senate. The bill eliminates vouching, but if a voter with ID has insufficient proof of address, the amended bill allows another voter to vouch for his or her residency.[4] Elections Canada is now banned from campaigning to boost voter turnout. The position of elections commissioner has been moved from Elections Canada to the office of Canada's director of public prosecutions. Tellingly, the new law does not change the rules to ensure that people are required to cooperate with Elections Canada investigations. With royal assent, the bill is now law.

WHILE THE SYSTEM was grappling with the impact of technology on electoral politics and what to do about it, a startling development occurred in the Guelph robocalls case. On January 15, 2014, Stephen Maher reported that former Guelph Conservative campaign worker Andrew Prescott had been granted immunity and had agreed to give evidence to Elections Canada. Prescott,[5] who for two years had insisted he knew nothing about dirty tricks in the Burke campaign, agreed to give "full and complete testimony" about what he knew. Prescott, like Sona a born-again Christian, added another name to the mix—the campaign manager in Guelph, Ken Morgan.[6] Michael Sona continued to deny Prescott's allegations against him and to assert his innocence. "I don't know what's going to happen to me, Michael," he confided to me. "But I think this situation is bigger than me and my troubles."

According to Elections Canada, it wasn't. On April 24, 2014, elections commissioner Yves Côté published his summary investigation report on robocalls. After a three-year investigation, no charges would be laid outside the electoral district of Guelph, and according to the report, no proof could be found of a conspiracy to steal the election. Elections Canada's investigation was doomed from the very beginning not to get to the bottom of robocalls. In normal criminal investigations, officers conduct their inquiries on an independent basis. In the national robocalls investigation done by Elections Canada, investigators had to rely on the cooperation of the Conservative Party and its telemarketers, even though both were potential subjects of the investigation. As Côté reported, some telemarketers and telephone service providers simply refused to cooperate. Why? Because they don't have to; Elections Canada has no power to compel evidence. Conservative Party officials were also not particularly forthcoming. According to Côté, it sometimes took several months for investigators to gain access to their information or for interviews to be arranged. "In one instance," Côté reported, "a person who investigators believed could have provided very relevant information declined to be interviewed."

The Honourable Louise Charron, a former justice of the Supreme Court of Canada, reviewed the Elections Canada investigation. She agreed with the findings, but noted that the conclusions might surprise some, given the forty thousand people who had written to Elections Canada to express their concern about the misleading calls during an election. She wrote,

> There is no question that some inappropriate calls were made to electors in electoral districts other than Guelph during the 41st general election. The evidence revealed that some electors were indeed misdirected to a poll other than the one indicated on their voter information card. However, giving incorrect or false information does not constitute an offence. Without evidence of an intention to prevent an elector from voting, or to induce the elector by some pretence or contrivance to vote or not to vote, there are no grounds to believe that an offence has been committed.

The report by Elections Canada came down to a lack of evidence and a lack of the power to obtain it. Like Judge Richard Mosley in the Council of Canadians case, Elections Canada investigators found ample evidence of misleading calls to voters—just not the identity of the perpetrator behind the calls. The puzzle of robocalls had not been solved. If investigators had obtained lists of non–Conservative Party supporters in targeted ridings that were downloaded from CIMS in the final days of the election campaign, and had known by whom they were downloaded, perhaps they would have found the answer.[7] Who had ordered calls to non-supporters across the country about poll changes, even in ridings where no poll changes had occurred?

Michael Sona's trial began on June 2, 2014, in Guelph. On the opening day, Chris Crawford, a ministerial staffer for the minister of state for science and technology in the Harper government, was the first Crown witness. He testified that only campaign manager Ken Morgan and Michael Sona were in the office when Crawford overheard Sona discuss voter suppression tactics with Morgan: "He was talking about how he might be able to win an election based on something like that." Crawford said the conversation took place a couple of weeks before the election. He agreed with Sona's lawyer, Norm Boxall, that it would not be unusual for campaign staff to discuss the tactics of US campaigns. "People have these conversations. At the time I didn't think anything of it." Crawford further agreed that many Canadian Conservatives look to the United States for strategies. He himself had attended the Conservative Political Action Conference, which had featured speakers such as Ronald Reagan, George W. Bush, Karl Rove, Glenn Beck, Rush Limbaugh, and Ann Coulter.[8]

John White, another member of the Burke campaign team, was asked if he had downloaded the list of non-supporters. "I don't recall specifically doing that," he told the court, "but it's quite possible I could have." (Evidence was submitted that White generated two constituent reports on April 30, 2011, at 12:39 p.m. and 9:17 p.m. No other member of the Burke team generated constituent reports from April 1 to May 2, 2011.)

Shielded by his immunity deal with the Crown, Prescott told the Court a different story than he had told Elections Canada investigators. Prescott admitted that on election day he had accessed two RackNine accounts: his own, and the one used to send out the misleading robocalls. According to his testimony, shortly after 4 a.m. a number of workers were in the office talking about the day ahead of them. The subject of robocalls came up. Prescott stated that Sona paid attention when it was mentioned that it was possible to manipulate caller ID details: "Sona expressed a little bit of surprise and said, 'Let me understand this: you can make it appear to be coming from anywhere?'" Prescott claimed that, hours later, he saw Sona emerge from his cubicle "almost euphoric" as he said, "It's working." Strangely, Prescott did not ask Sona to elaborate on his comment. He also testified that he saw a cheap red cellphone on Sona's desk, and discarded Future Shop cellphone packaging in the trash. These were details Prescott had not mentioned in his first interview with the Crown, even after he had been granted immunity. Apparently his memory continued to improve.

Prescott testified that on election day, after the "Pierre Poutine" call had gone out, campaign manager Ken Morgan grabbed him and sat him down in front of his laptop computer and said, "I need you to stop the dialling." Morgan gave him a piece of paper with a scrawled name and password. Prescott stated that he did what he was asked to do without looking to see what the scheduled call was, ". . . knowing what was going on was something I didn't want to get involved in." For the first time in the trial, it had been alleged that someone other than Sona was involved as RackNine client "Pierre Jones."

On election day, following Morgan's instructions, Prescott opened his browser and went to RackNine, where his client account opened automatically. He then logged in to the other account with the information given to him by Morgan. Knowing the system, he knew where to go, and immediately cancelled the pending calls before logging out. "I was extremely hesitant because obviously I caught wind there was stuff going on that day; we started receiving media reports of fake calls that were going around." Prescott further testified that at the celebration on election night, Michael Sona had toasted Stephen Harper's majority win with the words "Thanks to Pierre," while smoking a cigar. (This seemed odd to many in the courtroom because neither "Pierre" nor the Conservatives had won in Guelph.) Boxall was able to point out several inconsistencies in Prescott's testimony, including the fact that Sona's supposed toast to "Pierre" wasn't reported by Prescott until April 2014. Notes from Prescott's first interview with Elections Canada in 2012 had him saying that he did not recognize the name Pierre Jones.

If Prescott's new testimony was supposed to be the smoking gun to unravel the robocalls affair, the judge, for one, didn't seem to be impressed. According to a tweet from the trial by Laura Stone of Global News, the judge asked the Crown about Sona's toast to "Pierre": "How would that make sense to anyone? Do you think that's damning evidence?" Norm Boxall had the feeling that the Crown's star witness had in fact been a dud on the stand. To highlight the issue of Prescott's dubious credibility, Boxall asked Prescott to read a stunning statement into the record at the trial, a Facebook message he had written to Sona in July 2013:

It's now crystal clear to all but the most rabid partisans that something amiss occurred during the 2011 election. It's also patently obvious that what went on across the country was definitely not the work of a 'lone staffer' on a single campaign as we have heard repeatedly from Conservative spokespersons. . . . This scheme was clearly widespread, national and well organized. It required access, and ultimately complicity from someone higher up in the campaign in order to accomplish. While I don't for a moment believe such actions were condoned by the national campaign, it's painfully clear to all now that the Party is seeking to misdirect Canadians by accusing 'local staffers' of what was a national crime.

Sitting on the stand, and forced to read his own words into the record, all Prescott could do was declare that he didn't really believe what he had written. So why had he written it? Prescott explained that at the time he had posted that message on Facebook, he had been upset because he was having a problem getting accreditation from the Conservative Party to attend the national convention in Calgary in November 2013. It was a damaging admission. During his closing arguments, even Crown attorney Croft Michaelson said Prescott's testimony "should probably be approached with caution." Michaelson also admitted the evidence "points to more than one person" being involved.

As the trial progressed, the Crown's theory about Michael Sona changed in a way the judge could not have missed. At the outset, prosecutor Croft Michaelson painted Michael Sona as the mastermind behind the Guelph robocalls caper. By trial's end, the Crown's theory was that Sona was a person who was in some way involved. The Crown also made the decision not to call Elections Canada's lead investigator, Al Mathews, to the stand—preventing Norm Boxall from raising potentially damaging details about how reliant Mathews had been on getting his facts from the Conservative Party of Canada, by effectively partnering with their lawyer, Arthur Hamilton.

After watching the Crown call a dozen witnesses and rest its case without producing any physical evidence linking Sona to the cellphone, computers, or RackNine, or any evidence of how Sona learned to do the nefarious deed he was accused of masterminding, Boxall huddled with his client. "We had a witness list of our own," Michael Sona told me. "But Norm took me into a backroom at the courthouse and told me that they hadn't proven their case. That's when he decided not to call our witnesses or put me on the stand. He's a pessimistic guy by nature, but he thought we'd won." There was one big advantage to not calling witnesses: Michael Sona's lawyer got to have the last word in court. In his summation, Norm Boxall homed in on the central weakness of the Crown's case. "I think there's more unanswered questions than answered questions," he told the Court.

With Judge Gary Hearn reserving his judgment until mid-August 2014,[9] Michael Sona would have to wait a little longer for justice. On August 14, 2014, Michael Sona became the only person in Canada to be convicted in the robocalls affair. The court and the Crown clearly believed Sona did not act alone in arranging the calls, but the judge concluded that Sona was "actively involved." Judge Hearn dismissed the evidence from star witness Andrew Prescott implicating Sona as "self-serving." Despite inconsistencies, Hearn found the testimony of the young Conservative staffers assembled by Arthur Hamilton reliable. The Crown never explained who purchased the burner cellphone and registered it in the name of Pierre Poutine or how the list of non-supporters from the CIMS database was transferred to Poutine. A second judge had now pointed to CIMS as the source for misleading calls during the 2011 election and referenced the involvement of others. The robocalls case has not been solved. As for electoral fraud in Canada, the only certain thing is that the Fair Elections Act has made it even harder to prosecute. As long as the only evidence it is empowered to gather remains voluntary, Elections Canada will never catch up to the greyhounds of technology in pursuit of political power.[10]

six

THE BIG LIE

On April 3, 2012, after nearly six years of the Harper government misleading Parliament and the public, the much-vaunted F-35 program crash-landed at centre stage in Canadian politics. The engine-trouble had begun nearly a year earlier, just before the general election that gave Stephen Harper his majority government.[1] The Liberals had tried to make the record-breaking acquisition a major election issue, but the smooth-talking prime minister allayed all fears about the government's choice of fighter jet. The strong, stable government had everything under control. Canadians agreed.

Opposition leader Michael Ignatieff's concerns centred on how much it would cost to acquire Lockheed Martin's high-tech aircraft, known as the Joint Strike Fighter (JSF) Lightning II, or F-35, to replace Canada's aging fleet of F-18s. The government set the price at $15 billion for sixty-five of the experimental aircraft. That figure included the acquisition and supporting infrastructure of the jets, or so the government claimed. The Opposition wasn't buying it.

After decimating the Liberals and driving Michael Ignatieff from the field of Canadian politics in May 2011, the Conservatives defended their costing by releasing next to nothing about the aircraft procurement to the political opposition, and merely repeating the talking points to support their disputed figure. Ironically, their accounting for the F-35 acquisition began to crumble when a man the Harper government had hired, Kevin Page, challenged the government's costing. Page was appointed as the parliamentary budget officer under the Accountability Act in 2008. He was to be an independent watchdog, paid for by citizens to provide nonpartisan analysis of the nation's finances and government spending.

Page claimed that the real price tag of the program was $29 billion, nearly double the figure cited by the prime minister and the minister of defence. He also accused the Department of National Defence (DND) of keeping two sets of books for the F-35 program: one for departmental and cabinet use, the other for public and parliamentary consumption. The DND's defence was that there was only one set of books—with two columns.

The extent to which the Harper government badmouthed Page as an incompetent busybody was malicious and disingenuous. The denunciations had nothing to do with the elite civil servant's competence. The reason Page had been appointed by the Conservatives as the inaugural head of the Parliamentary Budget Office (PBO) in the first place was his sterling record in the public service—including a stint with two prime ministers, Paul Martin and Stephen Harper, "as the sort of chief economist for the Privy Council."[2]

During the transition between the Martin and Harper governments—a process smoothly facilitated by seasoned professionals such as Derek Burney and Ian Brodie—Page worked from a third-floor office in the Langevin Block under the then clerk of the Privy Council, Alex Himelfarb. Page attended some cabinet meetings as a key official involved in getting the prime minister and finance minister to sign off on the budget. On a personal level, the Harpers had sent Page and his family a condolence note in 2006, after they lost a child in a tragic accident.

Page was impressed with the way Stephen Harper conducted cabinet, telling me, "PM Harper ran the meetings efficiently. He was a fan of Chrétien that way and followed his cabinet style. The difference between the two governments was that while Chrétien had a lot of experience around his cabinet table—including many people who had been on the planning and priorities committee and had run departments—Harper did not have a lot of experience to draw on. When they appointed me, they saw me as a fiscal conservative. What am I really? A nerdy guy who doesn't like wasting money."

And what is Stephen Harper? A nerdy guy who doesn't like being questioned, much less contradicted. It seemed as if Harper's favourable impressions of Page, including the ones that underpinned his appointment to the PBO, were now water under the bridge. The government was not only defending a hugely expensive and controversial acquisition, but its credibility was squarely on the line.

If the PBO chief had it right, voters had been purposely misled during the 2011 election about the biggest planned expenditure of the Harper government—the fleet of F-35s. And that would mean that Michael Ignatieff, the Cassandra-like Liberal leader of the day, had been right when he claimed the government was lowballing the numbers for the acquisition. Not surprisingly, the Harper government turned on Page like a junkyard dog.

Finance minister Jim Flaherty accused the PBO chief of incompetence. According to Page, Flaherty had "taken PBO criticisms personally" and stopped inviting the parliamentary budget officer to Finance meetings. The prime minister and the

Department of National Defence rejected Page's numbers, insisting that Canada would get the F-35 for $70 million to $75 million apiece. Furthermore, defence minister MacKay said the annual service bill for the new fighter jets would be approximately the same as for the F-18s. Both statements were pure fantasy. The price of the F-35 was at least $20 million more per plane than the government's number, and maintenance costs were 42 percent higher than claimed.

Behind the government's categorical denials of the PBO's much higher cost estimates, and the vicious personal attacks on Page, a whiff of nervousness hovered in the air. Stubbornly maintaining that the F-35 was "the only option available," the prime minister failed to provide any evidence for that statement other than the usual variety—his own pronouncement. Perhaps that's why he told a Toronto news conference in the run-up to the 2011 election, "I'm not going to get into a lengthy debate on numbers."

The controversy over numbers and facts surrounding the F-35 simmered for nearly a year until the spring of 2012. Despite the government's constant cheerleading for the project, the issue wouldn't go away. This was partly because of ominous news about the F-35 coming out of the United States, and partly because the government was persisting in the very behaviour that had triggered a contempt-of-Parliament finding against the previous Harper minority. The issue then had been the government's refusal to give financial information about the cost of government initiatives to Parliament, including the F-35 project—a practice it was still pursuing, according to Kevin Page. But whether you believed the government's numbers or the PBO's, buying the stealth jet would be the single most expensive acquisition in Canadian military history—in other words, a major test of the government's claim to be sound financial managers.

ON THAT SCORE, April proved to be the cruellest month—
at least April 2012. On April 3, Canada's auditor general (AG)
released his report into the F-35 program. Michael Ferguson, new
to the job, took over his post on November 28, 2011, under circumstances that didn't have the high-altitude controversy of the
F-35 but were nonetheless bumpy enough.

Although the Harper government had advertised the AG's
position as bilingual, it chose Ferguson, a unilingual anglophone
from New Brunswick, where he had served as deputy minister of
finance. The selection of a unilingual candidate prompted Michel
Dorais, an official in the Auditor General's Office, to resign as a
matter of principle: his position was that the auditor general had to
be able to speak both official languages or the working atmosphere
in this important institution would be damaged. Treasury Board
president Tony Clement responded in the House of Commons
by tabling a previous political donation by Dorais to the Liberal
Party—the usual government tactic of returning all things to
politics. That contretemps quickly receded in the blowback from
Ferguson's findings. In either language, his scathing report was a
heat-seeking missile into the government's undocumented claim
that the F-35 was the right aircraft at the right price.

The new auditor general revealed that the Harper government's costing for the F-35 was astronomically and deliberately
out of whack. The cost of acquiring and maintaining sixty-five
F-35s over twenty years was not the $15 billion the government
claimed, but $25 billion—and even that number might be low. The
proof cited by the AG for his astonishing finding came in the form
of incontrovertible evidence: the DND's own internal estimates.

The AG also pointed out that the DND's secret costing had
been done in 2010. The revelation of the timing was explosive.
It was in 2010 that the DND had made the internal decision to
select the F-35. The $10-billion discrepancy between the AG's

number and the government's was bad enough—a difference of 40 percent. But there was now another elephant in the room that could not be blanketed by speaking points. Why had senior officials in the DND told Parliamentary Budget Officer Kevin Page in 2011, nearly a year after they had set the real cost of the F-35 fleet at $25 billion, that the bill to taxpayers was only $14.7 billion? An officer of Parliament had ordered the DND to produce public information of the highest importance and the department had failed to do so.

There was worse news in Ferguson's report. The AG said that the Harper cabinet would have known that the government's public number had been off by $10 billion. In addition to the mismanagement represented by that order of miscalculation, there was the issue of garden-variety dishonesty. This revelation also meant that while Harper ministers and DND bureaucrats were castigating Kevin Page for getting the costs wrong for the F-35, they were perfectly aware that his numbers were far more accurate than their own. A good public servant had been trashed for getting it right by the very people who, as it turned out, had covered up the true costs.

Speaking to reporters in a scrum after an appearance at the public accounts committee on April 5, Ferguson said, "I can't speak to individuals who knew, but it was information that was prepared within National Defence, and it's certainly my understanding that that would have been information that, yes, that the government would have had . . ."

If the F-35 debacle didn't reflect well on the government's ability to manage huge sums of money, it did afford an excellent glimpse into the heart of its modus operandi: the notion that the incumbent gets to mint his own facts, the penchant for secrecy at the public's expense, the reflexive blame-shifting. Looked at over the six years the project was in the Harper government's hands, the F-35 is a story of hoodwinking the public, misleading

Parliament, and risking billions of taxpayers' dollars—all that without the federal government having the foggiest idea of what Canadians were getting for their money. As a saga of institutional manipulation and political mendacity, it is unparalleled in modern Canadian politics.

One of the oddities of the F-35 debacle is that the Conservatives inherited the whole mess from a previous Liberal government. It was an orphan they didn't have to take in. As avowed reformers eager to change the way Ottawa did business, the Harper government should have seen the inherently flawed F-35 program as a golden opportunity to show both fiscal prudence and a commitment to getting value for the potentially massive public expenditure involved. It showed neither. And not because, as a participant in the nine-member consortium developing the aircraft, Canada was under any obligation to buy the F-35. It wasn't. Instead, when Gordon O'Connor became minister of defence in 2006, he stayed with, and his successors perpetuated, a procurement process that was a stunning example of "worst practices" public policy.

The F-35 was chosen by the Department of National Defence without a competitive bidding process, an approach that federal procurement experts such as Alan Williams point out adds at least 20 percent to the fly-away price. In fact, the June 1, 2010, letter sent by DND assistant deputy minister Dan Ross to Public Works to justify sole-sourcing the mammoth contract was just 150 words long! The DND tried to justify its approach with the claim that it had done its own review in which the F-35 bested the competition: Boeing's F-18 Super Hornet; the Swedish-built Saab Gripen; the Dassault Rafale from France; and the Eurofighter Typhoon, built by a consortium led by Britain.

In fact, the Harper government and the DND ceded due diligence to third parties, and very strange ones at that—the US Air Force, the principal client for the jet, and Lockheed Martin, its manufacturer. Even more inexplicably, the official in the DND whose job it was to issue the Statement of Requirements (SOR) for this massive acquisition ignored the established process, which is to first produce a formal statement of the military's requirements, and then have the civilian side choose the best equipment at the best price. "That was the responsibility of Assistant Deputy Minister-Materiel Dan Ross. But Ross did exactly what bureaucrats are not supposed to do. He committed to the F-35 and recommended to then defence minister Gordon O'Connor that this was the choice," Alan Williams, former DND procurement chief, told me.

Ross, who retired as the DND's procurement boss in January 2013, admitted that Canada's procurement system was "broken," partly as a result of split ministerial responsibilities for military acquisitions, and partly because of a lack of audits and reviews, and a too-distant working relationship with the auditor general. Above all, Ross told the *Hill Times* newspaper, procurement has to be somebody's full-time job: "Right now . . . you have requests for lunch, juice, and sandwiches sitting on Minister MacKay's desk [along] with Fixed Wing Search and Rescue budgets."

Whatever the cause, something had gone terribly wrong with the jet-fighter program. The Statement of Requirements for the F-35 was issued four years after the decision had been made by the DND to acquire it without competitive bidding—an absurd reversal of how sound procurement unfolds. When the equipment is chosen before the SOR is issued, you may be sure that when it is issued, only one aircraft will qualify—the one already chosen. It is not a rational process, but an exercise in "wiring" the specifications to get what you want.

Think of it as brochure fever, followed by a few whoppers to get the bank loan.

At one level, the military simply wanted the F-35 the way a teenager might eschew a Malibu and lust after a Corvette: DND bureaucrats enabled the acquisitive instincts of the generals by making unsubstantiated recommendations to the political side, all the while ignoring the well-known and agreed-upon rules. As one general told me, "The chief of the defence staff should be at the bottom of the Ottawa River over this. I know for a fact the prime minister is furious over this."

But it was not, as some have argued, entirely a case of the government being asleep at the switch. Far from it. Successive ministers in the Harper government lent the full weight of their uncritical support to a project headed in the direction of the disastrous F-22 Raptor, a US fighter jet so over-budget that the production line was shut down by former secretary of defense Robert Gates after the assembly of just 187 aircraft.

The F-22 bill to American taxpayers was $65 billion. For that, they got a stealth "hangar queen" or "maintenance hog" that never saw combat in Iraq or Afghanistan, a disastrous fate for a piece of equipment that came in at 400 percent over budget. One of the reasons stealth aircraft like the F-35 need more maintenance is that aero-systems that feature low observable (LO) or radar absorbing materials (RAM) rely on plastic as an important element of construction. Metal or even ceramics can't be employed because they reflect electromagnetic waves, which show up on radar. That was the main reason the US Navy never bought the F-22: stealth materials require enormous maintenance and do not hold up well in adverse weather or at Mach speeds—conditions otherwise known as combat.

Nevertheless, the busiest promoter for Canada's acquisition of the F-35 "stealth" fighter was Peter MacKay. During his five years as minister of defence, MacKay earned his keep by posing with the F-35, including one shot in the cockpit of a plywood mock-up of the fighter jet that was trucked to Ottawa all the way from Lockheed Martin headquarters in Fort Worth, Texas. Though

the wooden aircraft was shipped free of charge by the manufacturer, the photo shoot of MacKay at the plastic controls cost
Canadian taxpayers $47,000. MacKay's claims about the stealth
fighter, taken straight from the company's talking points, ran the
gamut from the confusing to the contradictory, from the absurd
to the downright deceitful. The F-35 was not, as MaKay claimed,
the only stealth fighter in the world. Canada's new chief of the
defence staff, General Tom Lawson, told the Commons defence
committee, "There are countries around the world flying [other
aircraft with stealth capabilities] to great success these days."

THE HARPER GOVERNMENT announced its intention to buy
the F-35 on July 16, 2010. In the 2011 election, Harper spoke of
the "contract" to make the unprecedented purchase, complained it
shouldn't be an election issue, and implied that political opponents
who criticized the F-35 were unpatriotic deadbeats. Tellingly, he
insisted the price he was quoting for the so-called "fifth generation fighter" was accurate, despite directly contrary evidence from
the United States. "A lot of the development costs you're reading
[about] in the United States, the contract we've signed, shelters
us from any increase in those kinds of costs. We're very confident of our estimates and we have built in some latitude, some
contingency in any case. So we are very confident we are within
those measures," the prime minister told the *Waterloo Record* on
April 9, 2011.

While both the prime minister and his defence minister were
cheerleading for Lockheed Martin, it was becoming evident from
more forthright sources that no one could make any solid claims
about the F-35. The simple reason for this lack of certitude was
that the F-35 went into production before it was ever flight-tested.
It was an experimental aircraft. The manufacturer never built a
combat-ready prototype that could engage in a fly-off against

competitors so that the best plane could be determined based on merit. In the case of the F-35, it was "buy before you fly."

This perverse procurement model had long since set off alarm bells with American government officials and even with the US military, who were learning that there was a terrible price to be paid for the practice of "concurrency"—of producing and testing the F-35 in parallel rather than in sequence. The evidence from the Congressional Budget Office (CBO) and the US Senate armed services committee revealed that the F-35 program was in deep trouble at every level—from poor production quality on the aircraft's electronic warfare capability to obscene cost overruns and hugely expensive delays. Even the pilots' headrests were too big, limiting aft vision in combat with potentially fatal results.

The Government Accountability Office (GAO), the agency charged with catching government waste in the United States, pointed out that the program was veering off course because the Pentagon had committed to final production before testing and development were complete. Frank Kendall, the Pentagon's chief weapons buyer, offered a scathing assessment of how the US military acquired the F-35. On April 24, 2012, he told ABC.com, "Putting the F-35 in production years before the first test flight was acquisition malpractice. OK? It should not have been done. OK? But we did it."

This was the heart of the matter. The same month that Canada's auditor general revealed that the Harper government had grossly understated the cost of the F-35, the GAO was reporting in the United States that the Pentagon was buying its weapons systems backwards—squandering billions in taxpayers' dollars on sophisticated equipment by "spending first and asking questions later." It was a practice the Congressional Budget Office had been warning about since 1988 in a study called "The Effects of Concurrency," which looked at fourteen major weapons system programs acquired by the Pentagon. Each of them featured a parallel process of production and testing. All of the programs experienced cost increases ranging from 33 to 527 percent, and schedule delays of up to 139 percent.

In other words, the US F-35 program followed a procurement process that the Congressional Budget Office had deemed to be a bad idea twenty-five years ago. Although the aircraft went into production in 2003, the first "test flight" didn't take place until three years later. As long as things went without a hitch—i.e., when flight simulators and computer models correctly predicted how the aircraft would perform—savings on testing costs were realized. But when difficulties arose, it meant the public was stuck not only with expensive upgrades to fix the immediate problem, but also with a huge bill for retrofitting all the planes built to that point. From that perspective, the F-35 was a manufacturer's dream and a buyer's nightmare.

"The F-35 saga shows an essential part of a broken military procurement process in the United States," Winslow Wheeler told me. Wheeler spent thirty years as a national security advisor on Capitol Hill, and is the director of the Straus Military Reform Project at the Centre for Defense Information in Washington. "The heart of the broken process is 'setting the hook,'" Wheeler noted. "The manufacturer over-estimates the performance and underestimates the cost and offers 'fantasies' about the scheduling. The F-35 is classic. The key to 'setting the hook' is making sure that production starts before you begin testing. Contractors like Lockheed Martin say testing can't take place first because it would waste a lot of money. Once a lot of public money is spent, the argument used is that you can't waste all that money that has already been invested. At that point, you have entered the 'buy-in' stage."

In the movies, they called it "the sting." More than one high-ranking US military officer has felt it during the painful course of procuring the F-35. Air Force Lieutenant General Christopher Bogden put it like this in *American Spectator* magazine in May 2013: "What I see Lockheed Martin and Pratt & Whitney doing today is behaving like they are getting ready to sell me the very last F-35 and the very last engine and are trying to squeeze every nickel out of that last F-35 and that last engine."

There was another big problem with the F-35. If a camel is a horse designed by a committee, the Joint Strike Fighter is an aircraft designed by clueless politicians, Star Wars–struck Pentagon planners, and opportunistic contractors. From the late 1980s, when its design first emerged from the Pentagon's Defense Advanced Research Projects Agency, the F-35 was burdened with contradictory demands. It was supposed to be both a short takeoff and vertical-landing aircraft, and a supersonic fighter jet. "This required an airframe that—simultaneously—wanted to be short, even stumpy, and single-engine, and also sleek, long, and with lots of excess power, usually with twin engines," Winslow Wheeler wrote.

Politicians added more humps to the "flying camel" during the Clinton administration, including the demand that the F-35 be multi-service. Consequently, it had to meet the differing needs of the Air Force, the Marine Corps, and the Navy. In reality, three planes in one were being developed simultaneously—with an astonishing twenty-four million lines of computer code in the electronics of each F-35.

The president's officials also imposed the new requirement that the high-tech aircraft be multi-purpose—both an air-to-air fighter and a bomber. That meant that the F-35's already compromised design would be further burdened by adding weight to the airframe to manage heavy bomb loads. Something had to give, and that something was the agility embodied in the F-16, a single-purpose pure fighter jet. The F-35 ended up with the worst of all worlds—not as agile a fighter as the F-16, not as capable a bomber as the F-15E, and nowhere near as effective at low altitudes (in close air support for ground forces) as the A-10.

And then there was the part of the sales pitch the generals couldn't resist. Clinton administration officials imposed the "stealth" requirement, which meant additional tweaks of the aerodynamics of the already guppy-like F-35, and what experts have called "maintenance-intensive skin coatings" required to reduce radar reflections. But as many experts have pointed out, "stealth" doesn't mean invisibility, but merely limited detection ranges against some radar types at certain angles.

Even then, there are no guarantees. This is what retired general Lewis MacKenzie, the commander of NATO forces in the Bosnian War, told me about the sexiest selling point in the F-35 brochure: "In the Bosnian War, the Serbs shot down a 'stealth' F-117 bomber. Posters went up around Belgrade, 'Sorry Bill, we didn't know it was invisible.' They were using old Soviet radar and missiles. The F-35 is really not relevant as an initial-strike fighter because initial strikes these days are not done by fighters, but by Cruise missiles."

More than a decade into the project, what was supposed to have been a low-cost solution to the US forces' need for a new-generation fighter jet has became a procurement nightmare, gobbling up 38 percent of the Pentagon's budget. In 2001, the Pentagon planned to buy 2,866 F-35s at $79 million per plane for a grand total of $226.5 billion. By 2010, the plan was altered. The buy was reduced to 2,456 jets at $298.8 billion—a 14 percent reduction in the number of F-35s against a 32 percent price increase.

By 2012, the cost of the fleet ballooned to $395.7 billion and climbing. Since development began in 2001, unit costs per aircraft have doubled—from $81 million to $161 million. The full life-cycle cost of operating and supporting a reduced US fleet of 2,457 F-35s is now estimated to be $1.5 trillion—a sum, as reported in

Foreign Policy magazine, greater than the annual gross domestic product of Spain.

Even more daunting for potential buyers, the new jet is years behind schedule. The first batch of F-35s was slated for combat use in 2010, but since less than 20 percent of the flight testing on the aircraft has been completed, and just 4 percent of the mission systems verified, the US military now says the deployment date is "to be determined." It could be as far off as 2019 or 2020. Added to an escalating price, the production delay is almost certain to lead to reduced or cancelled orders. And that means just one thing: a much higher sticker price for buyers who proceed with the acquisition.

Production has slowed to such a crawl that the US Department of Defense (DOD) has for three straight years reduced near-term orders, deferring aircraft and costs to future years. Since 2002, total orders through 2017 by the DOD have been reduced by three-quarters, from 1,591 aircraft to just 365.

After a dozen years of development at a cost of $64 billion to US taxpayers, the F-35 project hasn't produced an aircraft that can be mass-manufactured. So how can any country's military even operate training squadrons with F-35s? Since the aircraft is still an "experiment," the answer is that they can't. In fact, the operational limitations are laughable. The F-35 is prohibited from flying at night or in instrument weather conditions, including clouds. Test pilots have complained that the plane's radar often doesn't work. And on days when the temperature dips below 15 degrees Celsius, the fifth-generation aircraft is a little like an old British sports car—hard to start. That is bad news for the F-35s Peter MacKay has said will be stationed in Cold Lake, Alberta. Final flight testing for the F-35 is now slated to be completed in 2017, which means that everyone who flies the aircraft before that date is effectively a test pilot.

While the Harper government stuck with the sales pitch, the Americans weren't the only ones getting nervous about the cost or performance of the warplane that is supposed to give them tactical superiority in the air for the next half century. JSF partners Britain, Italy, the Netherlands, and Turkey were all so "dismayed" about the performance and cost of the F-35, they delayed or downsized their own orders for the troubled aircraft. Israel, which has actually signed a Letter of Order and Acceptance for the purchase of nineteen F-35s, with fifty-five others to come later, was worried enough to send a high-level defence delegation to Washington for a first-hand look at the JSF project. The Israelis were not impressed with the Americans' refusal to share computer codes, or with the state of the project. One of the members of the Israeli team subsequently told the *World Tribune*, "We knew there were problems with the airplane, but things are much worse than we had been told."

There was also the issue of obsolescence. The US military is already talking about a sixth-generation fighter jet. Others[3] who watch the defence industry are beginning to question the wisdom of investing vast amounts of money in fighter jets piloted by humans, when the future of air warfare may well belong to cheap drones that can outfly any manned aircraft because their design doesn't have to take into account the level of G-force a human pilot can withstand. As one pro-drone F-35 skeptic put it in response to an online defence of the F-35, "Building F-35s today is as stupid as fielding horse cavalry was at the beginning of World War I."

GIVEN ALL THE evidence to the contrary, most of it coming from the very country that was actually building the aircraft, Stephen Harper's insistence that the costs of the F-35 were fixed was peculiar to say the least. But his government's uncritical assumption that it was the right aircraft—in fact, the "only" one—for the RCAF was, if anything, even stranger. Associate Minister of Defence Julian Fantino rhapsodized that the acquisition of the F-35 was a "holy" undertaking, and Peter MacKay warned that if the purchase was cancelled, Canadian pilots would "die" and national sovereignty would be at risk.

The government preferred to talk about anything but what the country actually needed from a new fighter. For Canada, where the main roles for fighter aircraft are airspace defence and sovereignty, the F-35 is a poor fit. As the aircraft now stands, it can't communicate by satellite while on reconnaissance missions in the High Arctic—a flaw Lockheed Martin promises to fix by 2019. There is trouble with the weapons systems, trouble with the cockpit, and trouble with the special helmet test pilots say gives them blurred or double vision. As a single-engine jet, the F-35 is less than ideal for long-range reconnaissance flights over remote areas. In the jargon of the industry to describe an aircraft's range, Canada requires a "long-legged" jet fighter—one that can patrol over great distances. The F-35 is "remarkably short-legged," according to expert Winslow Wheeler. "Its short range is an oddity because the F-35 has an enormous 'fuel fraction' rating, able to carry 18,000 pounds of fuel. But to make room for the external tanks, all of the aircraft's weapons systems have to be stored inside. Viewed from the nose, the plane looks rather pregnant. Worse, the huge external tanks are a permanent weight and performance drag," said Wheeler. Retired Colonel Paul Maillet, former manager of Canada's fleet of twin-engine CF-18s, also puzzled over the choice of the F-35: "How do you get a single-engine, low-range, low payload, low maneuverability aircraft that is being optimized for close air support to operate efficiently in the North?"

Although they didn't much like conversations about the cost of the F-35, there was one number the Harper government loved to talk about—the much-ballyhooed windfall of contracts to the Canadian aerospace industry for JSF-related work. As reported by Murray Brewster of the Canadian Press, the government marketing machine had initially pegged the industrial benefits of the F-35 to Canada at US$12 billion. It was a Pollyanna figure that high-balled the potential benefits, just as the government had low-balled the F-35's true costs.

There was one fact that the government's rose-coloured glasses couldn't change. No one knows how much business Canada's $25-billion-a-year aerospace industry will receive. It is true that as a member of the JSF consortium, Canadian industry can bid on work. But as the auditor general reported, there is no guarantee of contracts for the F-35 because Lockheed Martin puts all work out to competitive bid. Even if a Canadian company wins a contract—as seventy of them have at a value of just under $500 million—it would have to have that contract constantly renewed over the fifty years the F-35 is slated to operate in order to realize the maximum economic benefit.

So where did Ottawa come up with the $12-billion figure for economic benefits? From the same place they got their plywood F-35: Lockheed Martin. In the wake of the auditor general's skeptical report, Industry Canada lopped off US$2 billion from the value of the government's contract estimate that had come straight out of a Lockheed Martin database. Perhaps they had taken to heart Michael Ferguson's observation that "only the most optimistic projections" on economic benefits were given by the Harper government.

That is the opposite, for example, of what happens when the finance minister produces a budget. The FM makes his financial "targets" realistic by basing them on an average of forecasts by economists, not on the rosiest projections. Overestimating the economic benefits of the F-35 may be good salesmanship, but it is bad practice, especially at a time when the US military is facing deep budget cuts in a period of austerity. Prudent planners always consider the "what if" question. If the US government seriously cut back its own order of F-35s, there would be no "sweet spot" where Canada could make its purchase when the price for the stealth fighter would be at its lowest during so-called "maximum production." Even worse, Congress could cancel the F-35 program as simply unaffordable, the same way another Lockheed Martin product, the F-22, had been shuttered over rising costs and insoluble problems.

But changing warplanes in mid-jetstream is fraught with complications for the Harper government. Canadian industry and the military are deeply embedded in the F-35 program. It is worth noting that two of the Canadian companies that won F-35 contracts also have direct ties to the prime minister. It was announced at the Paris Air Show on June 17, 2013, that Magellan Aerospace signed a potentially billion-dollar deal to produce over a thousand tail assemblies for the Conventional Take-Off and Landing variant of the F-35. Magellan is owned by N. Murray Edwards, the chair of Canadian Natural Resources.[4]

Edwards was one of the key figures outside of cabinet who had the prime minister's ear in December 2012, when Stephen Harper was formulating Canada's new policy on foreign takeovers. It was the Calgary billionaire who warned the prime minister that the $15-billion Nexen takeover by China's state-controlled CNOCC Ltd., a controversial deal that the Harper government approved, would be "the first of many" if Ottawa didn't move to put conditions on state-owned entities buying into the Canadian resource sector. As reported by Shawn McCarthy in *The Globe and Mail*, the prime minister's ultimate policy decision on foreign investment "closely mirrored" the tycoon's views.

And then there was Nigel Wright. Before becoming Stephen Harper's chief of staff on January 1, 2011, Wright had been a high-powered executive with Onex Corporation, dealing specifically with the aerospace industry. Wright was the face of Onex in Wichita, Kansas, when the company purchased Boeing's commercial aircraft division in 2005. Renamed Spirit Aerosystems, the company is now run by Larry Lawson, former program manager of the F-35 at Lockheed Martin, and chief executive of the company's aeronautics division.

Wright had also worked with investment bankers Goldman Sachs in the purchase of Raytheon aircraft for $3.3 billion in 2006. The company was renamed Hawker Beechcraft Corporation, and has partnered with Lockheed Martin on projects for the F-35. After a few corporate transformations, including a bankruptcy and a failed attempt to sell itself to the Chinese, the company re-emerged as Beechcraft Corporation. Its senior vice-president of military programs is Jim Grant, who spent the last seventeen years at Lockheed Martin as vice-president of new business.

Nigel Wright's answer to the built-in conflict of interest of having worked for Canada's largest private equity company with a finger in many pots, including the F-35, was to erect a self-imposed "ethical wall." This wall would theoretically prevent him from participating in any discussions touching the procurement of the F-35 by the Harper government, an important assurance since the PM's chief of staff was merely on leave from Onex Corporation and intended to return to the private sector. The then industry minister, Tony Clement, came up with an even better defence against allegations about Wright regarding the F-35. "That's baloney," Clement told *The Globe and Mail*. "He's never been involved and he's not involved in this. There's nothing to influence. We've already made the decision."

Giving out contracts to foreign companies whose governments were potential buyers has become a key part of the sales pitch for the F-35. Lockheed Martin held out the allure of becoming part of the supply chain as a way of cushioning the disappointing performance of the JSF, its runaway costs, and chronic scheduling delays. Former DND procurement chief Alan Williams believes that the main reason Stephen Harper supports the F-35 is not the requirement of the military for a stealth fighter but the possible bonanza of contracts for Canadian industry.

There was money to be made by sticking with the program, as Norway learned. In return for placing an order for just two F-35As, the same variant of the aircraft Canada decided on, Norway got a letter from US secretary of defense Leon Panetta, agreeing to integrate Norway's so-called "Joint Strike Missile" into the JSF design. It was a deal that could be worth as much as US$4 billion to Oslo.

But what was an effective marketing tool for the F-35 did not necessarily mean good things for the overall program. With the aircraft being manufactured by Lockheed Martin, the engines being produced by Pratt & Whitney, and some weapons systems coming from foreign countries in order to get those countries to invest, critics fear that it could leave the development process more unstable than ever. And Lockheed Martin is worried about consortium partners getting cold feet. Although industrial partners in the joint effort, such as Canada, paid $100 million for the right to bid on F-35 work, the reality is that only countries who fly the jet can reasonably expect to cash in on contracts. "If in fact the Canadian government were to decide not to select the F-35, we will certainly honor the contracts that we have here with the Canadian industry," Lockheed Martin's executive vice-president, Orlando Carvalho, told reporters in Montreal. "But our approach in the future would be to try to do business with the industries that are in countries that are buying the plane."

Though an albatross for the Harper government, the troubled F-35 program has been blood in the water for Canada's opposition parties, who for years have been unable to penetrate "Teflon Steve's" political coating. Harper's choreographed brush-off of Parliamentary Budget Officer Kevin Page, and his rhetorical acceptance of the auditor general's damning report, merely sharpened their attack. Two senior parliamentary watchdogs—the auditor general and the parliamentary budget officer—had made clear that the government had not just bungled the F-35 program, it had put out deceitful numbers to cover it up. Both the NDP and the Liberals accused the Harper government of misleading Canadians about the true cost of acquiring the F-35.

Short of admitting gross incompetence, defence minister Peter MacKay had no option but to confirm the government's connivance in fudging the numbers on the F-35. As reported by Lee Berthiaume of Postmedia, MacKay eventually admitted that the Harper cabinet had signed off on the $25-billion cost of the F-35 but had kept the information secret. On April 30, 2012, he told the Senate defence committtee, "It ultimately goes to cabinet." There were instant demands for the prime minister and his defence minister to resign for misleading Parliament, and a myriad of questions that the government had no stomach to answer. The biggest question was whether the Conservatives had committed political fraud by misleading Canadian voters in the 2011 election about the cost of the F-35.

One politician had no doubt about the answer. After Thomas Mulcair gave a speech in Ottawa to the Economic Club, the leader of the Opposition had this to say: "We have clear and convincing evidence that the government intentionally provided false information to Parliament and that's serious. This is a basic question of respect for our institutions."

Nor were the Liberals mollified by Stephen Harper's obvious reversal on his previous statements touching the F-35. After listening to him evading the crucial issue of when he became aware of the true costs of the F-35, and then watching him cover his pivot during Question Period by promising more "supervision" of furtive bureaucrats in the DND, interim Liberal leader Bob Rae remembered how Harper had treated critics of the F-35 in the 2011 election: "The numbers did not add up. The numbers were not real numbers. We knew it, we said it. What was Mr. Harper's answer then? He called us liars. He said we were unpatriotic. . . . He cannot now pretend that he was just the piano player in the brothel who didn't have a clue as to what was really going on upstairs."[5]

With his credibility in tatters, defence minister Peter MacKay took no questions on the day the auditor general's report was released. Effectively cutting loose a department that was now humiliated, he confined his remarks to a lame promise: the government would "move forward" with a proper acquisition process to replace the aging CF-18s. MacKay's parliamentary secretary (now immigration minister), Chris Alexander, came up with the stinker of the day in the aftermath of the AG's report. He blamed the media for misleading the public on the F-35, claiming that the government had yet to spend a nickel on a replacement for the CF-18s.

It was an embarrassing moment for the ambitious Alexander. He was pleading innocent to a charge that had never been made, in order to sidestep the real offence: barefaced and repeated duplicity from the government of Canada. Both the prime minister and his minister of defence had talked about a signed "contract" to acquire the F-35 and a total commitment to the project. It was the government, not the media, that had put out the false cost of doing that, as the auditor general reported. Alexander's bloviating aside, the point wasn't that Canada's cheque for the F-35s hadn't been cashed; it was that the government had committed to writing it, and had lied about the amount. The only saving grace between Canadians and a duplicitous mega-procurement was the work of parliamentary watchdogs Page and Ferguson.

A revealing fact was buried in Chris Alexander's attempt to pretend the Harper government had not already chosen the F-35. He referred to the government's seven-point plan as having an "options analysis" component—clearly stating that more than one aircraft was being considered to replace Canada's F-18s. His statement clashed with the parliamentary record. The year before, the DND had reported to Parliament that the F-35 program had entered the "definition" phase, which comes after the "options analysis" phase. So how could Alexander now claim that the choice hadn't been made?

History had simply been rewritten. Two weeks after Auditor General Michael Ferguson released his report, DND officials retroactively amended the department's report to Parliament from the previous year. Where it had once reported the status of the F-35 program as in the "definition" phase, it changed that designation to the "options analysis" phase. Either the DND was assisting the Harper government or someone in the DND had apparently checked the wrong box on a purchase worth $25 billion.

In addition to the political consequences for the government of being outed by the auditor general, there was also a constitutional implication. Under the Westminster model of parliamentary democracy, which Canada ostensibly follows, the practice has been that if waste, corruption, or gross mismanagement in a government department becomes public, the minister himself is responsible—whether or not he was aware of the particulars of the case.

Under the doctrine of ministerial responsibility, Peter MacKay should have resigned as the Opposition demanded. Instead, Stephen Harper followed what would become a pattern for his leadership. The minister was left in place, bureaucrats were blamed, and the prime minister refused to answer any questions about his knowledge of the program.

Claiming to embrace the recommendations of the auditor general, Stephen Harper was left with only one course of action: to smother further debate about the disgraced program before it began to resonate with voters and the party base. The Conservatives moved swiftly to shut down hearings by the public accounts committee into the auditor general's findings.[6] They did this before the committee had heard from ministers and defence department officials who disputed the auditor general's findings—though, paradoxically, they accepted his recommendations. Gerry Byrne, a Liberal MP on the committee, excoriated committee chair NDP MP David Christopherson for letting the government members move the motion: "This is outrageous. We can't shut this committee down. To shut this committee down is a scandal. It means the government is desperate to hide something."

Suddenly, government communications officers began in earnest to spin a whole new narrative for the F-35. The government now insisted that the decision to buy the F-35 had not been made—a breathless reversal given that the prime minister himself was on record multiple times extolling the purchase and arguing that the F-35 was the "only" fighter that met Canada's requirements. The government's position had been best articulated in November 2011 by former associate minister of defence Julian Fantino on CTV's *Power Play*: "Yes, there's a plan A, there's a plan B, there's a plan C, and there's a plan Z; and they're all F-35s."

Suddenly, there was no commitment, and there was no signed contract, despite Peter MacKay having said in the House of Commons on December 13, 2010, "Mr. Speaker, let us look at the actual contract. What the Canadian government has committed to is a $9-billion contract for the acquisition of sixty-five fifth-generation aircraft. This includes not just the aircraft, but also includes the on-board systems, supporting infrastructure, initial spares, training simulators, contingency funds. This is a terrific investment for the Canadian Forces."

As if that weren't enough, this is what Julian Fantino added for good measure in Fort Worth, Texas, in the early days of the Harper majority on November 8, 2011: "We will purchase the F-35. We're on record. We're part of the crusade. We're not backing down."

The Harper government was apparently going to hit the "reset" button and begin the process all over again in the proper way—slinking away in political bedroom slippers from any responsibility for the brewing procurement fiasco and the cover-up. Canadians would finally find out the real costs of putting the maple leaf on Lockheed Martin's fifth-generation fighter, and program funds would be frozen until they did—or such was the latest messaging from the political wizards in the Land of Oz.

Besides the historical revisionism on the F-35 program, the government's damage control had a second feature. The prime minister, his minister of defence, and senior bureaucrats at the DND moved heaven and earth to turn the F-35 affair into a difference of opinion on accounting methods, an honest disagreement between the government and the auditor general over interpreting the rules—the same defence the Conservatives resorted to when they were caught cheating on election expenses in the "in-and-out" scandal.

It was the lowest point in the F-35's ongoing saga of deceit. The obligation to supply the "full life-cycle cost estimates" was not an optional requirement. It was and is a central plank of Treasury Board guidelines. It is also a well-known and accepted principle of cost-estimating inside the DND. Neither the military nor the Harper government abided by the rules of the Treasury Board, or of the Department of National Defence itself, which had agreed in writing with a previous auditor general that full life-cycle costs would and should be factored into the department's procurement process. After all, that's how it worked in every other NATO country. As former auditor general Sheila Fraser, the federal bureaucrat most trusted by Canadians during her tenure, told me, "The truth is, this mess was self-inflicted. All the policy and systems were there. They just weren't respected. It's a bit like the sponsorship scandal."

Despite the well-established rules, neither the government nor Peter MacKay's department initially included "operational costs" in their public estimates. When they finally did, they shortened the base number of years in service for the aircraft to reduce, at least optically, the actual costs. In the United States, the F-35 was supposed to take care of the military's needs for fifty-five years. The Harper government worked out its operational cost numbers for the JSF acquisition based on twenty years of service.

Hopelessly entangled in a web of contradiction and conniving, the government shunted the F-35 issue into a fog of shifting bureaucratic responsibilities, independent outside audits, expert panels, seven-point plans, and token questionnaires to other companies in the fighter-jet business. Soon, some in the media were talking about the F-35 being cancelled and about competition for Canada's new jet heating up. Meanwhile, as the belated audits ordered by Stephen Harper came in, the government's number-fudging became a national embarrassment.

According to accounting firm KPMG, the cost of the F-35 was $45.8 billion over forty-two years—not even in the same postal zone as the government's $15-billion figure. As for the PM's original claim that the aircraft would cost Canada $70 million to $75 million apiece, the accounting firm Raymond Chabot Grant Thornton reported in August 2013 that the number was closer to $95 million. But according to a DND internal report obtained by the *Hill Times*, the worst-case scenario was that the cost for the F-35 fleet could top $70 billion. It was clear why the PM had said that he didn't want to get into a long debate on the numbers for the F-35 during the 2011 election: he was out to lunch—and dinner—on the facts.

But there was one thing the government's ever-whirring public relations machine—a tool calibrated for optics rather than accuracy—couldn't hide: despite a freeze on F-35 program spending, the DND would still not be going to a competitive bidding process to replace the aging F-18s—the only course correction that could turn a procurement travesty into a rational process. Doomed Liberal leader Michael Ignatieff's comment during the 2011 election was true: the program was a sham, the government's numbers were false, and the whole thing should have been cancelled in favour of the established process for making such huge acquisitions.

For self-styled masters of financial management and champions of transparency, the Harper government received a bleak report card. The government had decided to make the most expensive military acquisition in Canadian history without a competitive bidding process, had misled an officer of Parliament, and had concealed the true cost of the F-35 program from Canadians during an election. On top of that, a federal minister, Peter MacKay, walked away from his ministerial responsibility with barely a blink, enjoying the full support of a complicit prime minister. Now that the facts were at last in plain sight, the F-35 fiasco was not so much about the Harper government anymore, but about the people of Canada. Were they watching? Had they noticed? Did they care? The Harper government wasn't sure. It is unlikely a decision about the F-35s will be made before the 2015 election.

"It is about whether ministers speak for their departments, or can disown them when it suits them," columnist Andrew Coyne wrote in the *National Post*. "And it is about whether we, as citizens, are prepared to pay attention, and hold people in power to account when they lie to us."

While the country may have been dazzled into indifference or confusion over the true costs of the F-35, one group of Canadians stood up firmly against the government's attempt to invent the facts. Canada's scientists publicly opposed Stephen Harper's attempt to muzzle them and to dismiss independent information that might form an obstacle to the government's agenda.

seven

THE DEATH
OF EVIDENCE

It was a perfect July day. Tourists milled around Confederation Flame in front of the Parliament buildings, snapping each other's pictures and tilting their faces upward to take the sun. Office workers spread out picnic blankets on the wide lawns, oblivious to the seagulls patrolling overhead. The Peace Tower climbed into a cornflower sky. At its pinnacle, the Maple Leaf rippled in the breeze. It was a quintessentially Canadian moment in high summer in the nation's capital.

And then they came into sight. They advanced west along Wellington Street like a sea of Halloween ghosts dressed in white. They filled the broad avenue with signs and banners still too far away to read. At first, the tourists on the Hill didn't know what to make of the procession. But as the line of marchers wearing white lab coats reached the main gate to Parliament Hill, where an RCMP cruiser was parked broadside across the entrance, the spectators finally saw the coffin. Behind it, a banner read: "No

Science, No Evidence, No Truth, No Democracy." The pallbearers were preceded by a hooded figure in black holding a scythe across its chest. With a deft change in costume, the figure transformed itself into a young woman in a black dress and dark glasses; the Grim Reaper had become the grieving widow. There had been a death in the national family: they called it the Death of Evidence.

The event that triggered this theatrical protest by Canadian scientists, a profession not known for taking to the barricades over public policy, began two months earlier at Winnipeg's Freshwater Institute. The regional director of science, Michelle Wheatley, had called an emergency meeting to deliver some bad news. The Harper government had decided to close the research facility at the Experimental Lakes Area (ELA), a system of fifty-eight lakes in northwestern Ontario, where some of the most important freshwater research in the world has been conducted.

Wheatley's message was as bleak as the first road that was slashed into the remote site outside Kenora back in the winter of 1968. The ELA would be shut down by March 2013, and no further research would be permitted—even though that would mean the loss of invaluable scientific data from ongoing experiments that could not now be completed. It was hardly a theoretical problem. One group of university researchers was deeply involved in examining the environmental impact of silver nanoparticles, which, because they kill disease-causing bacteria, enjoy widespread use in everyday products such as toys and clothing. But engineered silver nanoparticles have also been found in waterways, where they can be toxic to ryegrass, algae, and fathead minnows.

When word of the closure came, the investigation of silver nanoparticles at the Experimental Lakes Area was well under-way—financed, ironically, by an $800,000 research grant from the federal government. Gary Goodyear,[1] the coy creationist Stephen Harper had chosen as his science and technology minister, was dismissive. He advised the Trent University team to complete their research at another facility—even though it might mean losing a year of research. There was just one problem. No other whole-lake facility remotely like the ELA existed.

As for the seventeen scientists working at the ELA, they were told to clear out their personal belongings and remove their scientific gear from the labs at the remote site as soon as possible. If a new operator could not be found in the next ten months, the entire operation would be mothballed. In the long term, if no takers for the ELA came forward, the lake system would have to be "remediated"—put back into pristine condition at a cost to taxpayers of as much as $50 million.

Forty-four years of scientific accomplishment, much of it achieved under renowned Canadian freshwater scientist David Schindler, were coming to what the Harper government hoped would be a quiet end. Few Canadians knew that the ELA, a vast outdoor laboratory created out of a pristine lake system, was a scientific enterprise on the magnitude of the Hubble Telescope. Where else could scientists perform whole-lake experiments? Investigating subjects ranging from the deadly impact on freshwater of phosphorus in detergents to the effects of artificial estrogen on fish populations, the ELA had blazed a trail of scientific glory—which explains, perhaps, why the facility received the First Stockholm Water Prize and the Gerhard Herzberg Canada Gold Medal for Science and Engineering.

Schindler and his fellow scientists also came up with irrefutable proof that industrial pollutants from the United States were killing Canadian lakes. Their evidence ultimately resulted in regulatory changes in the US to control atmospheric emissions from coal plants. It was a long journey from an American president's statement that trees caused more pollution than cars, to the Acid Rain Treaty between Canada and the United States: the immense gulf between Ronald Reagan's credulity and the facts was bridged by ELA science.

The Metallicus Experiment at the ELA also produced remarkable data, establishing a link between atmospheric mercury deposits and mercury in fish—a deadly threat to human health. So why would any government want to close the facility, particularly when just three years before, Ottawa had spent a million dollars on a new fish lab and the local Conservative MP, Greg Rickford, had lauded the ELA as "extraordinary"? Now he was calling the facility "passé." The excellence of the ELA's research had not changed, just the Harper MP's marching orders.

An official reason for the closure was on offer, but no one was buying it. It was left to an acting Department of Fisheries and Oceans (DFO) regional director, David Burden, to supply the flapdoodle. In a letter classified as "Protected," and sent on May 17, 2012, to federal scientists at the Freshwater Institute, Burden wrote that the decision "was part of the government's efforts to reduce the deficit, aimed to modernize government, to make it easier for Canadians to deal with government, and to right-size the costs of operations and program delivery."

This was worse than the usual departmental gibberish, coming as it did from a science ministry. The emptiness of the explanation was not lost on anyone, federal scientists least of all: the ELA had a meagre budget of $2 million a year. The Harper government spent nearly fifteen times that amount to commemorate the War of 1812, and twenty-five times as much beautifying the Muskoka riding of Treasury Board president Tony Clement. Apart from the private pleasures of patronage, there is no study, scientific or otherwise, establishing a public benefit from the proliferation of government-supplied gazebos in cottage country.

This was not about austerity; this was about information control and employer thuggishness—and the scientists knew it. Nor had the DFO itself made the decision. In fact, the department had been busily handing out science grants for the ELA when the shocking news came from on high that the Harper government was closing the facility. The question was whether Ottawa would be able to overrule scientists on a matter of science without an outcry from the scientific community or the public. It all depended on closing a lot of potentially damaging mouths.

How else could the directives from the DFO be interpreted? ELA scientists were strictly forbidden to speak to the media about the closure. The DFO "communications" branch would take all questions, and information officers would supply all answers. As it turned out, the DFO turned down all media requests to interview federal scientists, and denied permission to all federal scientists to speak to their fellow citizens directly. After some budget information relating to the ELA leaked into the media, the reaction from the DFO was swift, as an insider's email to me made clear:

> When a DFO employee questioned [director general] Dave Gillis about why they have not received some promised correspondence about the ELA, he responded that all communication about anything to do with Budget 2012 must be spoken, not written in an email. This is a blatant and despicable strategy by Harper to avoid accountability. No email correspondence equals no tracking record, making access to information requests, audits, and other means of holding government transparent and accountable for decisions completely useless.

Meanwhile, behind the scenes, the DFO was busily at work advancing the government's damage control operation. In a series of by-invitation-only conference calls accessed by a pass code, the DFO reached out to three groups of potential critics: university vice-presidents and the Friends of the Experimental Lakes Area; internal scientific staff at the DFO and Environment Canada; and university-based scientists who worked at the ELA. Those three calls, one on June 25 and two on June 27, 2012, were arranged by the director general of the Ecosystem Science Directorate, David Gillis.

The VPs of the five universities—Alberta, Manitoba, Waterloo, Trent, and Lakehead—were advised that the Harper government was closing the ELA. The good news, however, was that the Conservatives were nevertheless "eager" to find a new operator for the facility. How eager? When the representative from Lakehead University asked about federal resources to run the new ELA, Gillis replied that neither the DFO nor Environment Canada would contribute any staff or budget to a new operator. The Government of Canada was washing its hands of the freshwater research business—divorce, with the very warmest of wishes.

Next came the "So-long-it's-been-good-to-know-you" call to employees. It was made to scientific staff in the two federal departments affected by the closure. The call was preceded by an email inviting employees at the DFO and Environment Canada to participate in the conference call. The message made the usual declarations of appreciation for a job well done while at the same time kicking bodies out the door. (It could have been worse. When sixty-five staff at the National Research Council got the axe a week later, included in their termination letter was a $3 gift card for a coffee and a doughnut at Tim Hortons.) The ELA scientists were told that there would be no federal funds to operate the facility in 2013, and that if no private operator was found by April 1, 2013, it would be mothballed—or, in the incomparable bureaucratese of the moment, would "transition into cold lay-up." As for terminations, the scientists would likely be gone before the facility itself was closed.

The final call, the one to external and university scientists working at the ELA, followed the same government talking points, but this time the director general's message was more rigorously challenged. This group had greater independence and posed questions David Gillis couldn't readily answer. How could the government claim that other freshwater facilities could do the research of the ELA, when everyone on the conference call knew it was a one-of-a-kind facility? How could a new operator be found in a few months with no funding from Ottawa—especially with Natural Sciences and Engineering Research Council (NSERC) funds already frozen by the Harper government? Since universities had short-term funding for their research programs, and the work at the ELA often unfolded over decades, it was ludicrous to think that academic institutions could operate the facility. Finally, the scientists wanted to know the DFO's mandate. If it had changed, and that was why the ELA was being closed, exactly what was the department's new mission? And if it hadn't, which Gillis seemed to imply, why was the ELA being closed?

One of the scientists on the call remembered Gillis interjecting that the purpose of the discussion was to implement the decision, not to question it. If anyone wanted the ELA closure reversed, they were advised to express their preference in the traditional way—at the ballot box. It was pointless to appeal to the DFO because the department was obliged to carry out the government's wishes, a decision that had been made by what Gillis referred to as the "federal family."

The scientists who followed the coffin to Parliament Hill with their signs and their megaphones under the brilliant July sun were not part of that family. They had come to defend their métier, their colleagues who worked for government, and the country's intellectual honesty. And there was one other thing on their minds: the desire to defy the Harper government's assault on their fundamental right to free speech. One protester showed up with a telescope taped to his bicycle helmet and a sign that read "Looking for signs of intelligent life on Parliament Hill."

The prohibition against speaking freely, including about research on climate change, the tar sands, and the protection of wildlife, had already garnered worldwide disapproval. *The Economist* described the Harper government's muzzling as "comical excesses in communication control." Others were less amused. Both *The New York Times* and the prestigious British science journal *Nature* slammed Canada's government. The *Times* called Harper's suppression of federal scientists "an attempt to guarantee ignorance."

By April 2013, Canada's information commissioner, Suzanne Legault, opened an investigation into complaints that departmental officials were silencing Canadian scientists. Six months later, the Professional Institute of the Public Service of Canada released a survey done by the Environics Research Group in which 90 percent of four thousand federal scientists who responded said they were being muzzled.

NOT EVEN MEMBERS of Parliament could find out what was really behind the decision to close the ELA. When Thunder Bay–Superior North Independent MP Bruce Hyer[2] requested permission to tour the site with an ELA scientist, he was turned down by a department clearly marching to the PMO's drum. Internationally acclaimed scientist Ragnar Elmgren noted that closing the ELA was the kind of knowledge-killing decision you would expect from the Taliban, not the government of a Western democracy.

So that summer day in front of Parliament—Tuesday, July 10, 2012—two things were on the agenda for the two thousand people who listened to the speeches under the watchful eye of the RCMP. They were protesting the shuttering of a unique facility for research into freshwater, the world's most important resource. They were also rejecting the notion that any federal government could reduce its scientists to compliant and wordless serfs, even under the provocation of a decision as absurd as this one.

Defend and defy they did, but with an appeal to reason that might have impressed the minister of science and technology, Gary Goodyear—if only he had shown up to listen to his own scientists. Dr. Vance Trudeau, professor of biology at Ottawa University, told the sea of white coats and an ever-growing band of curious onlookers that aspects of the Harper government's social and environmental policies reminded him of the Duplessis era in Quebec. How, for example, could you plan the economic, educational, and social programs for a nation of thirty-five million without the data provided by a detailed census?

Dr. Trudeau had no partisan axe to grind. He praised the Harper government for promoting some aspects of applied science as a "very good thing." But neither was he there to have politicians tell him that pure and applied science was an either/or proposition. It was, he said, a fundamental misunderstanding of science to promote applied science "at the expense" of pure scientific inquiry, which actually drives applied research. In the real world of science, the two go hand in hand, with pure science leading the way.

The enthusiastic crowd liked the sound of rational defiance. They shouted their responses to Dr. Trudeau's litany of questions. "Would a physician tell you that you have cancer without a test?" he asked, waiting for the response. "No!" the crowd roared. "Would you even accept the diagnosis based on one test?" he continued. "No!" they shouted. "Do you demand that Parliament revisit their ill-intentioned and ill-advised decisions about science cuts?" he teasingly asked. "Yeeesss!" the audience thundered. "Yes," he repeated. "Evidence can be resurrected."

There would soon be more to get them applauding—fighting words from water activist Maude Barlow, and an appeal for the freedom of scientists by young Ph.D. students Katy Gibbs and Adam Houben. Then there was Dr. Arne Mooers from Simon Fraser University, a professor of biodiversity who noted that evidence is how adults navigate reality. People were bound to lose their way in the fantasy world of the Harper government where propaganda was substituted for fact. "This sounds alarmist, even to me, and I am saying it," Professor Mooers said. "But we should call a spade a spade."

When it came to calling a spade a spade, few scientists in the country could match the person who spoke next. Jeff Hutchings has been acknowledged as something of a rare breed in his chosen profession—a gifted biologist and an indefatigable champion of the independence of science in the public domain. "This is like an inquisition," Hutchings told me. "Who did you speak to, what did you say? And I can tell you that the international community, Norway, the UK, Sweden, the US, our colleagues are in a state of disbelief over what is happening here. The Soviet-style of information suppression—in Canada? If you disagree, you are shut out—it's not careful thinking, it's ideology."

Hutchings, the former head of the Royal Society of Canada, was not supposed to be at the Death of Evidence rally. He was actually in Ottawa attending the First Joint Congress on Evolutionary Biology, an event with more than 2,400 registrants—nearly two thousand of them from around the world. When he found out about the rally, he used his lunch break at the convention to join the marchers and to speak about the "death of evidence." Hundreds of his colleagues followed him from the Westin Hotel to Parliament Hill: international scientists found it incomprehensible that Canada, once in the vanguard of evidence-based policy, was stifling its science and scientists.

There was a buzz in the crowd as the bespectacled Killam Professor of Science from Dalhousie University made his way to centre stage. Canada's science community had already been alarmed by Harper's steady assault on their budgets and research since coming to power. But they were stunned by the government's demolition of an environmental regulatory system that many of them had spent their careers building.

The March 2012 federal budget eliminated nearly three thousand environmental assessments, including scores of projects dealing with fossil fuels and pipelines. Was the government clearing the legislative deck to smooth the way for speedy and untrammeled resource development, including the construction of pipelines? That had certainly been the impression created six months prior to the Death of Evidence rally, when Reuters quoted from a policy paper generated by bureaucrats in Harper's International Trade Ministry. In the paper, the bureaucrats described the National Energy Board (NEB) as an "ally" of the Harper government's resource development plans. The government promptly disavowed the story, but it was not a confidence builder for the government's critics. The NEB was, after all, holding hearings into the controversial Northern Gateway Pipeline, and would be advising the government on whether the project should proceed. It is a dark road from advisor to ally. On December 19, 2013, the NEB recommended federal approval of the pipeline.

Hutchings saw the death warrant for the ELA as part of a sinister pattern, an anti-knowledge, anti-science animus in the Harper government that had killed the long-form census, cut science funding, closed research installations, reduced atmospheric studies to 70 percent of their 2006 levels, and gutted critical fisheries legislation that left species at risk. Remarkably, the then DFO minister, Keith Ashfield, made the changes to the Fisheries Act contained in Bill C-38 without consulting his scientific staff—which might explain why the controversial omnibus legislation was leaked by someone in the DFO.

One of the most outrageous cuts was made in the autumn of 2013, with the decision to close seven of nine world-famous DFO libraries across the country. According to a leaked secret document, the Harper government's decision would save $443,000 a year, less than half of what Ottawa pays China for Canada's rented panda bears every year.

Some of the closures were inexplicable. The government had spent millions of dollars modernizing the St. Andrews Biological Station in New Brunswick, only to close the famous library there, where environmental scientist Rachel Carson did research for her seminal book *Silent Spring*. Dalhousie University biologist Jeff Hutchings called the closures "an assault on civil society." He said that "losing libraries is not a neutral act. It must be about ideology. Nothing else fits."

While the Harper government poured $24.6 million into the new Canadian International Institute for Extractive Industry Development at the University of British Columbia, rare collections from the country's marine science libraries, including fifty volumes produced by the HMS *Challenger* scientific expedition of 1872 to 1876, were being dumped in landfills.

Hutchings got backing from an unlikely source—former Conservative fisheries minister Tom Siddon. Siddon told CBC the move was "Orwellian because some might suspect it is driven by a notion to exterminate all unpopular scientific findings that interfere with the government's economic objectives." A research scientist who worked for the federal government for thirty years was quoted in *The Tyee* as saying, "All that intellectual capital is now gone. It's like a book burning. It's the destruction of our cultural heritage. It just makes us poorer as a nation."

AS CATASTROPHIC AS the changes to Canada's fisheries legislation were, they also placed a political dunce cap on the Harper government—or at least they did in the opinion of a strange trio of experts. Three former federal fisheries ministers came together in a non-partisan effort to steer the government away from making what they viewed as a huge policy and political blunder. Liberal David Anderson and Conservatives John Fraser and Tom Siddon came out with a joint statement. As Anderson told me, he wrote the original draft, which was then sharpened by his Conservative colleagues. "I did a draft which I purposely softened so that I wouldn't be seen as putting my colleagues into an uncomfortable partisan position as Conservatives . . . they actually took what I wrote and toughened it up. The reaction was very positive, lots of emails. People were very glad we had done it. There was an even greater level of unease out there over what they were doing to the fisheries and environment than I had imagined."

Tom Siddon, the only former fisheries minister who was also a qualified scientist, said that Bill C-38 was an "appalling" attempt "to gut" the Fisheries Act. John Fraser, who in addition to having held the fisheries portfolio had also been Speaker of the House of Commons, declared that the politics of the omnibus legislation were "dumb" and that it was a mistake to portray critics as "left-wing radicals." David Anderson, who was "surprised" at the level of cooperation from his former political opponents, said that greater fines by the Harper government for companies who despoil the environment wouldn't accomplish anything. "Their incoming penalties, which they use to justify what they've done, amount to phony toughening. Bigger fines don't mean anything in major projects. No one will be deterred."

In addition to the critique, the triumvirate also offered to share their expertise with the federal government before the legislative plans were finalized. Anderson described the response from the Harper government as "a puerile put down." The trio were not only ignored, they were ridiculed: in dismissing their advice, the then environment minister, Peter Kent, accused the former federal fisheries ministers of not having read the government's bill. "That really did annoy me," David Anderson told me. "I was expecting something like 'Interesting take, we'll take a look at what you've said.' Instead, we were insulted. It was demeaning of our intelligence and experience. We are not just a bunch of fuddy-duddies. And I can tell you that their attack line is not selling in BC."

Another thing on offer from the Harper government that wasn't selling was the suppression of significant studies by federal scientists. Jeff Hutchings was disgusted by the way in which researchers Kristina Miller and David Tarasick had been silenced. The prime minister's own department, the Privy Council Office, had stopped Miller from being interviewed about a study she had done showing that a virus might be responsible for the alarming decline of sockeye salmon in British Columbia's Fraser River.

Even though her study had been published in *Science* magazine, the DFO's west coast chief of molecular genetics was forbidden to talk about it—possibly because it might cast an emerging industry in a bad light. Had fish farming produced the deadly virus that nearly wiped out the sockeye run in 2009? If so, Ottawa didn't want Miller talking about it, any more than it was anxious to halt the growth of salmon farming, even though that had been recommended by BC Supreme Court Justice Bruce Cohen in his three-volume, $26-million report into the decline of the sockeye. A year after the completion of Justice Cohen's federal inquiry, not a single major recommendation had been adopted by the Harper government to protect wild salmon.

Just as the PCO silenced Miller, Environment Canada had likewise forbidden climate scientist Tarasick from giving interviews about his work. He had been part of a team that had discovered a gigantic hole in the ozone layer over the Arctic. Tarasick later published a paper in *Nature*. Every federal scientist knew that the Harper government didn't like reminders of its do-nothing policies on climate change. (The standing joke was: Why send environment minister Peter Kent to international climate conferences?

Just mail him the Fossil Award and save the airfare.) The prime minister had been so successful in keeping journalists out of the loop on the work of federal scientists that there had been a two-thirds drop in stories dealing with global warming since Harper began restricting scientific information about climate change, wildlife, and the Arctic—all subjects with profound implications for resource development.

The government had gone so far as to send official "minders" with Canadian scientists attending a Polar Year Conference in Montreal in April 2012. The idea was to make sure Canadian federal scientists did not speak to any journalists without a set of eyes and ears from the "Politburo"—the name some scientists privately used to refer to their department's communications operation. The derisive nickname was wickedly accurate. This is essentially how Environment Canada described its communications ideal in a 2007 media protocol that applied to all federal scientists—and which was tightened up even further by the Harper government in 2012: "Just as we have 'one department, one website' we should have 'one department, one voice.'"

Jeff Hutchings had more reason than most for picking up on the Orwellian resonance in the government edict. Twenty years earlier, he had witnessed what happens when an organization decides to speak with one voice to sustain the unsustainable and its own reputation by smothering the facts. In 1992, Hutchings joined the federal fisheries department as a Natural Sciences and Research Council fellow just as the curtain rose on the greatest ecological disaster in Canadian history—the destruction of the Great Northern Cod stocks off Newfoundland.

A Conservative government, backed by a compliant science branch, in a *Yes Minister*[3] department, had been instrumental in wiping out the third-largest biomass in the world. The department had failed to detect deadly flaws in the computer model it used for setting cod quotas, not realizing it was killing far more fish than its annual mortality rates suggested. But there was an industry to sustain, votes to be jigged, and fish-plant operators to satisfy, so the hefty cod quotas kept coming from Ottawa—right to the day the trawls from deep-sea fishing companies like National Sea were winched in empty from what had once been the richest fishing grounds in the world.

Tragically, going back as far as 1986, scientific studies had been suggesting a disaster was brewing in the water. But the studies had not been widely shared among DFO scientists. As a fish biologist, Hutchings could find "no evidence" for the abundance of cod allegedly found in DFO surveys. He and a colleague, the late Ransom Myers, were bitterly attacked by senior DFO managers for questioning departmental stock assessments, quotas, and the selective use of scientific studies. But by the summer of 1992, the scurrilous attacks on Hutchings and Myers came to an abrupt halt. There was no more room for empty ego, for sucking up to politicians, for self-interested denial. The fish were gone.

It fell to the then fisheries minister, John Crosbie, to deliver the devastating news. There was only one place on earth to do it—his home province of Newfoundland. On a July day in St. John's, I stood in a room in the Radisson Hotel while Crosbie formally closed a stock that had been fished consecutively for four hundred years by as many as sixty nations. Along with the closure, the minister announced a relief program for the thirty-one thousand fishermen who were instantly thrown out of work. You could hear the groans through the wall from the adjacent room. That's where they put the overflow of fishermen who came in from around the bay that day to watch their fate unfold on closed-circuit TV.

The bad news struck Newfoundland like a bolt of lightning. For safety reasons, Crosbie's staff wanted him to leave through the hotel kitchen when the event ended. Instead, the minister went through the front door and parted the angry mob as he strode out. After all, he was Ches Crosbie's son, and the family was not known for shying away from a battle. He found himself on the receiving end of an abusive blast from fiery Fisheries Union president Richard Cashin and catcalls from enraged fishermen. The bear-like Crosbie gave as good as he got. Despite the theatrics on all sides, a pall descended over Newfoundland with the realization that something sacred had been lost—perhaps forever.

The price to Canadian taxpayers of their politicians and bureaucrats manipulating science for political and commercial gain was dizzying: all told, nearly $4 billion was spent under The Atlantic Groundfish Strategy (TAGS), which forty thousand fishermen received—ten thousand more than federal bureaucrats had foreseen. To this day, the spawning biomass of the northern cod remains too small to support a commercial cod fishery. Politics had overridden science, with terrible consequences for all concerned.

The passion in Jeff Hutchings's voice at the Death of Evidence rally was an echo of the sheer dimension of the cod collapse—an event that might very well have been avoided had available scientific data been acted on instead of suppressed, ignored, or misunderstood for seven, deadly years. The crowd pumped their signs up and down as Hutchings spoke. He criticized the Harper government for "weakening national fisheries and environmental legislation" and talked about how scientific advice had been "trivialized" by a government that thought so little of the profession that the PM had gotten rid of his science advisor in 2008.

As a fish biologist, Jeff Hutchings knew that the last official Stephen Harper should have dumped was his science advisor. Under the UN Fish Stocks Agreement, Canada is supposed to have 10 percent of its waters designated as "marine protected"; the actual number achieved thus far is 0.5 percent. Although Canada has sixty-one so-called "marine protected areas," fishing is allowed in sixty of them. And Canada's ability to live up to its national and international obligations to protect species at risk was further compromised by Bill C-38, which removed key protective legislation. Hutchings thought it was inexcusable that Ottawa had eliminated the Experimental Lakes Area and government scientific research of "fundamental importance" to the health of the Canadian people and the environment. "After the ELA decision," he said, "all Canadian scientists now have a tougher job. ELA led the way on issues like marine pollutants, including oil spills. Instead of celebrating our finest minds, we devalue science and call it an economizing measure."

The crowd gasped when Hutchings came to the heart of his address. Why, he asked, were such harmful actions being taken against science and the country? His answer was that the Harper government had prioritized economic development "at any cost." Hutchings offered proof. Quoting from a June 14, 2012, letter written by the then fisheries minister, Keith Ashfield, Hutchings said that the minister had complained that the existing Fisheries Act offered "few tools to authorize pollution," but that new legislation in Bill C-38 would "establish new tools to authorize deposits of deleterious substances." The crowd fell silent as Hutchings paused for maximum impact. "In other words, changes to the Fisheries Act will make it easier to authorize the pollution of Canada's waters. . . . An iron curtain is being drawn by government between science and society. Closed curtains, especially those made of iron, make for very dark rooms."

Indeed. In early February 2013 I had come into possession of documents showing how government intended to make those rooms even darker. The documents laid out a new publishing policy for DFO scientists. In the past, the department had only had a say in the publication of papers prepared by its own staff. Now, when government scientists teamed up with non-DFO scientists on a joint paper, publishing approval had to be obtained from the DFO. Even after a manuscript had been peer-reviewed and accepted for publication by a scientific journal, a divisional manager would now sign off on the copyright—an official who had nothing to do with either the research or the science. The implication was clear. DFO managers had been given a previously unavailable hammer to wield: the withholding of copyright permission to block any publication they wanted to suppress that might compromise an existing departmental policy—without the obligation of ever explaining a rejection.

I published the story on February 7, 2013, in iPolitics, an online newspaper, and my editor received this brief note the same day from DFO communications officer Melanie Carkner: "The iPolitics story by Michael Harris . . . is untrue. There have been no changes to the Department's publication policy." The minister repeated the same declaration in the House of Commons. Then I published a second column, which included this excerpt from a DFO employee: "Here is the email I got from my division manager. . . . 'Subject: New Publication Review Committee (PRC) Procedures. . . . This message is regarding the new Publication Review Committee procedures. . . .'" The email noted that the new policy would take effect on February 1, 2013.

This time there was no denial of the story—a good decision, as it turned out, since a DFO scientist posted departmental documents outlining the new policy, complete with an administrative chart showing the changes that would kick in after February 1. The communications Batmobile was quickly thrown into reverse. There had been changes to the policy, the minister confirmed, but they had been made unilaterally by departmental officials without his knowledge.

Back at the rally, it was the turn of the "grieving widow" mourning the death of evidence to have her say. I had known

Diane Orihel for a few months in her offstage, real life as a young aquatic scientist three months away from finishing her Ph.D., who was married to an ELA scientist. For ten years, the rugged camp between Kenora and Dryden had been their home in the summers. They had paddled its lakes, walked its woods, and had a small cabin on the site where the science was done. What Jeff Hutchings told me about Ph.D. candidates—that they spend fifteen years at university and do post-doctoral research because they love knowledge—is part of what Orihel is all about. Hutchings also said that for people engaged in the search, "Suppression snuffs the initiative out of you. There is the intimidation factor."

As the Harper government would learn, you could pick an easier task than "suppressing the initiative" out of Diane Orihel. After the personally devastating news that the ELA was closing, every government scientist who worked there found themselves in a delicate position. All of them were hoping for new assignments, and everyone knew that openly criticizing the Harper government would reduce that possibility to near zero. So while people like her husband, Paul, had to remain prudently silent, hoping there would be a new assignment, Diane Orihel was free to speak.

Her remarkable journey, which would eventually be featured in *Nature* magazine, began the day after the closure was announced. Orihel purchased the domain name www.saveela.org and opened a bank account for the newly minted Coalition to Save ELA. She requested leave from her Ph.D. program and, against the advice of her academic advisor, the renowned David Schindler, she plunged into the public battle to save the storied facility. Just five days after the government dropped its bombshell, the Save ELA Parliamentary Petition was posted on the coalition's website.

It would be hard to find someone less likely to become the public face of a movement. Orihel was more comfortable in a canoe than a conference room, more at ease diving to take test samples from the bottom of a lake than debating weighty political issues under the glare of TV lights with glib talking heads. With no experience in the media, no journalistic training, and little help, Orihel, the brilliant winner of the Alexander Graham Bell Science Award, turned a little-known scientific gem, the ELA, into a household word. And she did it all in five months.

Over that period of time, and often spending her own savings, she recruited an astonishing number of supporters to her cause—top scientists from fifty-eight countries; municipal leaders and citizens in Kenora; the former head of Manitoba Hydro; provincial premiers; federal politicians, including Opposition leader Thomas Mulcair (she buttonholed the NDP boss while he was out jogging in Ottawa and she was waiting for a bus); and environmental activists such as Maude Barlow and Elizabeth May. She even caught the ear of Canada's keenest social commentator posing as a comic, Rick Mercer. "My Canada includes weird scientists who are devoted to keeping our water clean," he quipped on his popular broadcast.

Orihel gave speeches in places big and small, never knowing if anyone would show up. She appeared tirelessly on national television, penned editorials in major newspapers, and wrote open letters to the prime minister. She never got the meeting with Stephen Harper that she repeatedly requested. Nor did Kenora MP Greg Rickford agree to publicly debate her. But despite the official wall of opposition to her cause, Orihel succeeded in making the integrity and importance of science a major national issue that the Harper government and all opposition parties will have to deal with in 2015. And as the Alberta election had proven just a month before the Death of Evidence rally, science could be a political giant-killer. When asked to explain the unexpected loss suffered by Danielle Smith and the Wildrose Party, former Alberta premier Ed Stelmach said it was the leader's rejection of the science around climate change.

At the July rally, Orihel began her address slowly. Using a literary conceit, she spoke of the ELA as a child. Born in the 1960s during a decade of hope, it was the offspring of a forward-looking government that recognized that science-based evidence was essential to solving society's problems. As a one-year-old, the facility's first mission was to save a dying Lake Erie. At age eight, the ELA discovered that acid rain was killing the base of aquatic food-webs, causing fish to die of starvation. As a young adult, the research facility helped hydroelectric utilities design more eco-friendly reservoirs. Next came the discovery that hormones in sewage were "feminizing" male fish. And now, Oriel gravely declared, in full maturity, with desperately important work to be done on climate change, on oil spills, and on nanoparticles in freshwater, the Harper government was condemning the ELA to an early death. The tall, slow-speaking woman from Winnipeg delivered her final line in a firm voice full of emotion: "We mourn the blindfold of ignorance imposed upon our once great country."

There was no one present at the rally from the PMO, the DFO, Environment Canada, or Science and Technology to challenge a single word that Orihel, or any of the other speakers, said. Where, everyone wondered, was the Harper government? Faced with Orihel's withering campaign, and polls that showed Canadians overwhelmingly in favour of keeping the ELA open, Ottawa was informally putting the word out that if the facility wanted to find a new operator, the protesting had better stop. Stephen Harper was playing his favourite political role as the Great Divider.

At a 2012 meeting of senior ELA scientists and government representatives in Winnipeg, a number of people in the room made the observation that the "sensitive negotiations" to keep the ELA open were being hampered by the constant criticism of the government's record on the science file. One of the people present was Tim Burt,[4] a Winnipeg-based money manager and the riding president of Joyce Bateman, the Conservative MP for Winnipeg South Centre. Claiming that there was no political motivation behind his actions, Burt wrote to the six major developers of the Alberta tar sands—including Suncor, Cenovus, and Imperial, and asked them to bankroll the ELA. For those scientists who wanted to keep the ELA open at all costs, the suggestion looked like a life-line. Some jumped at it—or at least didn't dismiss it out of hand. Scientists, they rationalized, should deal with science, not politics. It was wrong to take on the government, wrong to go to the media, wrong to conduct an abrasive, no-win war with Stephen Harper. The wiser course was compromise, and private money from the oil industry was better than no money at all, some argued.

In the special myopia of panic-stricken self-interest, these sci-entists did not care to talk about the elephant in the room: if Big Oil, or any other private group, bankrolled the ELA, who would decide the science that was undertaken, and who would own the studies produced? If scientists at a privately operated ELA were to discover that the chemicals creating mutant fish in the Athabaska River come from tar sands sites, would the oil companies make that information public?

In the wake of that meeting, Diane Orihel was eventually asked to "go silent" on her indefatigable campaign to ensure that freshwater research was conducted by the federal govern-ment in the public's interest. The request came from people she greatly respected and who were long-time friends. Exhausted by her exertions on behalf of the ELA, and emotionally drained by the sniping and bitterness of former colleagues and mentors, she resigned her post at Save ELA in early December 2012 to focus on her Ph.D.

Diane Orihel may not have persuaded Stephen Harper to keep the ELA afloat, but she and her colleagues caught the eye of the Ontario and Manitoba governments. With some funding from both, the facility was saved from being shuttered. Under the auspices of the International Institute for Sustainable Development (IISD), three scaled-back, whole-ecosystem experiments would be conducted at the ELA during the 2014 field season.

But even with a leader as accomplished as Scott Vaughan, Canada's former commissioner of the environment and sustainable development, the IISD faces tough negotiations to maintain its independence in the world of privately funded research the ELA now faces. In Orihel's opinion, life at the new ELA will be challenging and difficult without access to federal grants to pay for experiments. As she wrote in *The Globe and Mail* on April 1, 2014, "The Harper government has decided that its environmental policies no longer require the guidance of science, indeed all the signs are that science is unwelcome."

Prime Minister Harper tried to take credit for keeping the doors of the ELA open a crack, at the same time as his government firmly shut it on federal funding. The divisions in the scientific community about scientific activism and advocacy are open and bitter in the wake of all that has happened. I wrote about how the PM had thrown the apple of discord into the scientific community and noted that many scientists who had once advocated standing up for science were now recommending strategic silence. One of the comments I received to that piece came from Thomas Duck, an associate professor in the Department of Physics and Atmospheric Science at Dalhousie University:

> The silence you describe in your article is not limited to the ELA. It is a huge problem across science. Most everyone I know is trying to keep their heads down and not get caught up in this war. Most try to see if there is some way they can work within the system. Most have no idea what is really going on here—that science in Canada is in a fight for its very life.

Democracy too, for that matter. Those of us at the universities who are willing to speak out—the vanishingly few of us—are putting our careers at very real risk in the process.

Fear of speaking out? Careers at risk? Both the minister of the environment and the minister of natural resources unconvinced by climate change science? Canada was becoming the unrecognizable place that Stephen Harper had once talked about.

eight

MELTDOWN

Looking across the table in my Ottawa apartment at Linda Keen, I realize that years after she became front-page news, what happened to her then is even more important now than it was in 2008.

At the time, Keen's case, an egregious violation of the independence of the head of an administrative tribunal, looked like an aberration. It wasn't. The former ranch-girl from Alberta was actually the first senior public servant whose personal experience showed what Stephen Harper really thought of evidence-based decision making, or any form of opposition.

Since those days, the Harper government has attacked, and in some cases destroyed, a number of other senior public servants—Kevin Page, Munir Sheikh, Marc Mayrand, Peter Tinsley, Richard Colvin, and even Sheila Fraser, to name a few. These people were smeared or pushed out not for incompetence or improprieties, but simply for standing fast. They wanted to do their duty and Stephen Harper wanted them to do what they were told. Harper's new normal was submit or be crushed—something arm's-length officers of parliament and heads of tribunals had never seen before.

Not everyone has the spittle to stand up to the prime minister of Canada, especially a PM with a reputation as an authoritarian bully. It is important to note that Keen's battle with the government was not a matter of defiance but a fierce determination to carry out her duties under the act that she was legally obliged to administer.

Stephen Harper's recently well-documented war on science began with an incremental war on Keen that eventually became known as the "Slaughter on Slater"—the street in Ottawa housing Canada's nuclear regulator. His target, who took a year to subdue, could not have been more unlikely. By the time Linda Keen became president of the Canadian Nuclear Safety Commission (CNSC) on January 1, 2001, she was a veteran of fourteen years in the Public Service of Canada. Holding degrees in both chemistry and interdepartmental agricultural sciences, she began her career at Agriculture Canada. From there, Keen moved to Industry Canada before becoming senior assistant deputy minister in Natural Resources Canada. Formally in charge of Minerals and Metals, Linda Keen was the administrative face of government to the mining industry.

The talented manager caught the eye of the Privy Council Office as one of the senior science leaders in the federal public service. Keen participated in the clerk of the Privy Council's committees on assistant deputy minister leadership and risk management. She had no background in politics and no political affiliation, and was selected to head up the Canadian Nuclear Safety Commission after winning a competition run by the PCO.

Her new desk was big and messy. Linda Keen found herself watching over an industry that was a shadow of its former self. In 2000, a lot of bureaucrats thought Atomic Energy Canada Ltd.

(AECL) was a dying industry. Its decline was scarcely believable. In the post-war period, AECL created a world-class nuclear research facility. Its two reactors at Chalk River produced radio-isotopes for the medical industry, and its engineers developed the CANDU brand of nuclear reactors.

In those heady days, the nuclear regulator was the Atomic Energy Control Board (AECB). But the AECB had what Keen described as an "overly cozy" relationship with AECL, acting more as a partner than a regulator. For the industry it was an ideal set-up, one that it had gotten used to and wouldn't give up without a fight.

In the 1980s, AECL enjoyed major success, selling CANDU reactors both at home and abroad. Its overseas customers included China, Romania, and South Korea. Then the federal Crown corporation "got behind the innovation curve." In the nuclear industry, Keen explained to me, a country is either an innovator or an adopter. Through mismanagement and under-funding of research, Canada went from innovator to adopter. Despite work on several new reactor designs over the years, including the CANDU 9 and the ACR 700 and 1000, AECL made no sales. It became a money pit, gobbling up tax dollars without much prospect of returning to the glory days.

The one bright spot was the production of medical isotopes, which accounted for half of the world's supply. But that division had been privatized under the Mulroney government in 1988. The isotope division got a new name—Nordion International Inc.—and was moved into the Canadian Development Investment Corporation. This was not the best of deals for taxpayers. The federal government gave the private company a supply of isotopes at bargain-basement prices, guaranteeing the arrangement for twenty-two years. The public still owned and operated the reactors and extracted the raw isotopes, but the private company,

MDS Health Group, processed, sold and distributed the finished product—and reaped the profits. In 1991, MDS formally acquired Nordion.

With not much but promises coming from AECL on the reactor side, something had to give. It finally did in 2000. After fifty years of the Atomic Energy Control Board acting as Canada's regulator of the nuclear industry, the Chrétien government decided it was time to shake things up. The then natural resources minister, Anne McLellan, updated the regulatory legislation with the Canadian Nuclear Safety Control Act (NSCA). The AECB received a new name: the Canadian Nuclear Safety Commission (CNSC). The legislation was aimed at developing a more independent nuclear regulator and placing greater emphasis on the protection of the environment and people through nuclear safeguards.

Linda Keen was well aware that the nuclear industry had grown accustomed to near-automatic support from Canada's nuclear regulator. Before taking on the presidency of the CNSC, she questioned senior bureaucrats about the independence of the new post. Keen received the assurances she needed from them, or at least thought she had. (Some of them would later deny they gave her any promises of independence.) She took the job.

For six years, things worked as well as could be expected in an industry that wasn't selling any reactors. From 2000 to 2006, through a handful of ministers of natural resources, the CNSC operated independently as quasi-judicial, arm's-length tribunals should. Occasional attempts were made by AECL and other industry players to apply pressure to the regulator, but the ministers' offices of the day refused to intervene or pressure Linda Keen. Then, in 2006, the universe changed for Canadians and Canada's nuclear regulator. Stephen Harper won a minority government and Keen had a new minister at Natural Resources—a man who had practised law for two years before turning to politics, Gary

Lunn. Like a lot of senior civil servants, Keen was uncertain about how the new government would conduct its business.

These were nervous days for the federal public service. Stephen Harper was on the record with his view that he faced daunting obstacles in his pledge to clean up Ottawa—a Liberal-appointed public service, Supreme Court, and Senate. But Linda Keen was encouraged by promises made under the Accountability Act to respect the independence of administrative tribunals across the government. It took just one meeting with the minister to realize that Gary Lunn, like the prime minister, was not interested in independence.

In her first briefing of the new minister, Keen acquainted Lunn with what she described as the "built-in" conflict of interest in Natural Resources Canada. The problem was simple. Both AECL and the regulator reported to Parliament through the minister's office. Keen told the minister "it wasn't IF but WHEN there would be a conflict between AECL and CNSC and that he would need to be prepared for that eventuality." Nor did the minister seem to understand that the nuclear regulator reported *through* him, not *to* him.

Keen got no reaction at the meeting, but it soon became clear that "Lunn's preoccupation was how to make AECL a business success with its new reactors." Although the Harper government talked about "streamlining" the system of approvals, what they wanted was a return to the regulatory values of the 1970s, when the industry and the regulator were kissing cousins and the environment was an afterthought. As Lunn told Keen in a meeting in the presence of his deputy minister, "I don't much like regulators." From the beginning, Linda Keen was rolling down the highway into the future, while the Harper government pressured for a return to the past.

Keen and the CNSC had become more active on the international scene, working with other regulators to come up with common standards for a potential new generation of nuclear reactors. In fact, Keen was elected president of the International Nuclear Regulators Association (INRA) and also president of the International Atomic Energy Agency (IAEA) review of nuclear safety. Through this work, it became clear that Canadian regulators had not kept pace with international standards—which was surely not the way to sell Canadian-made reactors worldwide. With thirty-three reported nuclear accidents since the first one in history at Chalk River in 1952—which sent future US president Jimmy Carter into the reactor to make repairs—regulations out of the 1970s didn't seem to be the best way to market Canadian nuclear reactors. Keen believed that when it came to safety standards, "We should be in the international sphere, focusing on best practices of what is seen as safe internationally."

A collision was coming between Canada's nuclear regulator and AECL, which had powerful allies such as SNC-Lavalin Corporation, and, as it turned out, in the Harper government as well. Keen saw another unsettling development. A big part of her mission was to convince the nuclear industry that it should take responsibility for nuclear safety, and that included paying for it. In her opinion, that was how the industry obtained the "social contract" to do its work. Instead, with a huge staff compared to Keen's tiny band of regulators, AECL was constantly trying to get the CNSC to help with its design projects.

A case in point was the ACR 700 project, a new reactor AECL was hoping to sell both domestically and abroad. The CNSC had been assisting with the work since 2005, but there was little progress because of problems with the physics of the new design. For Keen's operation, their assistance on the ACR 700 project was beginning to eat into the staff time available for regulatory work—an untenable proposition at a time when all Canadian nuclear power reactors were undergoing refurbishment. In itself, that raised another serious issue. Since there were also problems with the new Maple reactors (another AECL project), there was intense competition for nuclear physicists and engineers from the very industry that needed regulatory oversight. Keen noted, "One industry CEO told me that no matter what I paid staff (controlled by Public Service pay levels), he would be able to pay more!"

In September 2006, three critical meetings were held. The president of AECL, Robert Van Adel, asked for a meeting with the nuclear regulator and CNSC executives. Keen and her staff were told that AECL wanted not only to finish the ACR reactor overview but also to add a new design, the ACR 1000, plus work on a revamped old design, dubbed CANDU 6E. "Remembering that the Maple reactors were already five years behind schedule and also requiring regulatory oversight, it was impossible for the CNSC to agree," Keen explained to me.

Keen told Van Adel that their entire agreement was to be cancelled after completion of the ACR 700 review until AECL could sort out its priorities, pointing out that it was not the regulator's role to effectively turn CNSC staff into "quality control experts" for the company. What the legislation required Linda Keen and her staff to do was regulate not collaborate. In fact, the work on the new reactors was not required or covered under the NSCA but was done under a separate agreement with AECL and paid for by the government of Canada. Keen reported to the deputy minister of natural resources, Cassie Doyle, that "there was an issue brewing."

The same day as her meeting with the president of AECL, Linda Keen announced at an industry meeting that international standards were being developed. The work was being conducted by a large group of regulators under the auspices of the Nuclear Energy Agency of UNESCO. Keen pointed out that these standards would help all nuclear reactor companies, including AECL, but also their principal competitors, Areva from France and Westinghouse in the United States. With her announcement, it was now clear to the industry that Linda Keen meant business. From that moment, she was in their sights.

At the end of the meeting with industry stakeholders, Keen and her executive vice-president met with executives of Ontario Power Generation (OPG). The head of OPG said that two new reactors were in the future for the Darlington plant. Jim Hankinson also said that he had been told by Atomic Energy Canada Ltd. that the CNSC had agreed to "grandfather" the old CANDU 6 design and not to require new international standards. Based on that information, Hankinson reportedly said Ontario Power Generation planned to buy the old CANDU 6 design from AECL and that "they were going to pop them in the ground." Keen also recalled that Hankinson told her, "I promised the premier that this was going to happen soon."

The Ontario Power Generation executives were in for a shock. Linda Keen informed them that the Canadian Nuclear Safety Commission she headed had never told AECL that it was possible to "grandfather" the CANDU 6, and that international standards would indeed apply to any "new-build" reactors for a very good reason—they would likely be in the ground for a hundred years. As angry as Atomic Energy Canada Ltd. was at Keen's decision, SNC-Lavalin, the giant engineering firm, was apoplectic. "What they had felt in October 2006 was this CANDU contract is a sure deal; that we're going to get this contract as part of the CANDU Group. . . . They were really upset, because this was money in the bank," Keen told Clean Break Blog.

The relationship between the nuclear regulator and the Harper government deteriorated further when the French nuclear company Areva requested that the CNSC review its designs since it was performing that function for AECL. The purpose of the request was to explore whether or not the French might make reactor sales in Canada. In December 2006, the Harper government answered on behalf of the regulator: a firm no. It also used the occasion to take its first public swipe at Linda Keen. In talking to reporters, Minister Lunn said, "The CNSC may say that they are neutral on reactor designs, but Natural Resources is not. We intend to sell AECL reactors."

In January 2007, Linda Keen wrote to the minister and deputy minister of natural resources, outlining options for resolving the issue of reviews of the AECL reactor designs by the Canadian Nuclear Safety Commission. She agreed that the CNSC would complete the work on the ACR 700 (which AECL wanted in order to test the design), but suggested a new approach on reviewing the ACR 1000 and the enhanced CANDU 6. Following the practice in the United States, the United Kingdom, and France, she proposed that future power operators be involved in assessing designs. This partnership would mean that potential buyers would be involved early on in the assessment of the plan. Keen reported that at least one power operator had indicated interest in the idea.

Linda Keen didn't know it, but with that letter she had entered the Harper government's "deep freeze." She received no response, either formally or informally. From that point on, for a period lasting eleven months, the minister and the deputy minister of natural resources refused to meet with the president of the Canadian Nuclear Safety Commission on any matter—including critical changes to environmental assessments that could impact nuclear facilities.

The pressure began to build on Canada's nuclear regulator. In March 2007, SNC-Lavalin dispatched one of its vice-presidents to a Canadian Nuclear Association meeting, where he claimed Keen's "regulatory uncertainty" was the obstacle preventing the building of new reactors in Canada. It was the engineering firm's reaction to another decision by the regulator that they really opposed. Keen would not promise that no regulatory changes would be effected during the life of the build and operations of reactors—potentially twenty and one hundred years, respectively.

But Keen was sufficiently concerned about SNC-Lavalin's comment that she offered to meet with the board of the company. She explained the Nuclear Safety Commission's viewpoint on international safety standards, and the need for the regulator to spend her scant resources on regulatory oversight, not on helping with reactor design. Nor would she specify that only AECL designs would be regulated, since that was not the role of the regulator. After a few peremptory questions, the session was over.

The board meeting, though void of enthusiasm for Keen's message, went off without incident. The lunch that followed was a different matter. In fact, Keen was reluctant to accept the invitation once her presentation had been given. The Nuclear Safety Commission had a policy of agreeing to lunches only if the commission itself paid. And there was another condition. She insisted that a note be written to file on all discussions that might take place. The lunch conversation went badly, and Keen found that the executives were "super-furious" with her. A top SNC-Lavalin executive made it personal: "You're not being patriotic," he told her. "How could you do this? It's being built in other places."

Keen later learned that the company formally complained about her to the clerk of the Privy Council, repeating their charge that the CNSC was an "obstacle" to new reactor sales at home and abroad. As she told Clean Break, the regulator now found herself in the sights of SNC-Lavalin, with the help of lobbyist Hill & Knowlton. The giant engineering firm wanted her ousted.

Meanwhile, Linda Keen wasn't the only public servant having difficulty with the Harper government's bare-knuckle tactics. Many heads of administrative tribunals across the public service were having similar issues with independence. They asked Keen to present a case to the Privy Council Office on their behalf.

In the summer of 2007, Linda Keen asked for a meeting with the clerk of the Privy Council. She had no reason to expect anything but a timely and professional meeting. She had, after all, known Kevin Lynch since her days at Industry Canada. But Keen didn't get the meeting with her former colleague. After months of delay, she was given a meeting with the chief legal counsel of the PCO and the assistant secretary of machinery of government. To any reader of George Orwell, it would not have been a promising sign. At the meeting, Keen explained the general problem of the administrative tribunals and her own specific problems with her own minister. There were silent nods but no commitment to any course of action. It was the PCO's job to resolve issues between the public service and ministers. In washing its hands of Linda Keen, the Harper PCO was showing signs of a politicization that would deepen over time.

In fact, the end was near for Keen's career in the Public Service of Canada. In early November 2007, her scientific staff at Chalk River reported that AECL was in violation of its licence conditions: specifically, the unfulfilled commitment to install backup power in the event of an incident—either an earthquake or power outage—which might prevent conventional power being available to the aging reactor. Instead of installing the required second backup power pump, AECL staff at Chalk River challenged the validity of the licence condition the company had agreed to and then breached.

Brian McGee, then AECL's vice-president and chief nuclear officer, happened to be on vacation. Ironically, Linda Keen was in Australia as keynote speaker at the inaugural IAEA conference on the safety of researcher reactors, like the ones at Chalk River. After connecting by BlackBerry with Chalk River, Keen was advised that the situation was not critical because AECL was entering a regular maintenance shutdown on November 18. When McGee returned from holidays, Keen said that he promised the Canadian Nuclear Safety Commission in a public meeting that he would not seek to restart the reactors after their maintenance shutdown until the backup power pump was installed. But behind the scenes all hell was breaking loose.

The first tremors of what was to come rumbled through Linda Keen's world. After eleven months of silence, she received a call from Minister Lunn, who started the conversation as if they were old friends: "Well, Linda, I know that those guys at AECL have screwed up," she remembered him saying. "But what can we do?" She replied that staff from AECL and the CNSC were working "non-stop" on the problem, and wouldn't cease until a solution was found. But that was not the answer the minister needed, and now things began to slip out of his control. Although this was a dispute over the National Research Universal (NRU) reactor at Chalk River, and Linda Keen was head of an arm's-length, quasi-judicial tribunal, she discovered that the PCO had become involved. The matter was now clearly political.

After years of successive governments neglecting growing problems at the aging Chalk River facility, it looked like the NRU reactor might be down for a significant period of time. That would mean a gap in the world supply of medical isotopes and possibly major lawsuits. The Harper government opposed the shutdown but needed someone to blame and a reason for blaming that person that would resonate with the public. They chose Linda Keen and used the prospect of a deadly shortage of medical isotopes to bring her down.

The NRU reactor at Chalk River provided 50 percent of the world's medical isotopes. But in order to lay the blame for the loss of this supply on Linda Keen, one major fact had to be obscured:

Linda Keen had never ordered the shutdown of the reactor at Chalk River; that decision was taken by AECL itself.[1] After a shutdown for routine maintenance, the company had agreed, for safety reasons, that it would not restart the reactor before installing a second pump. But in early December, the company flip-flopped. The acting president of AECL contacted the vice-president of operations at the CNSC, informing him that, contrary to the commitment made by the company's chief nuclear officer, AECL now intended to start the reactor with only one of the two licence-mandated, backup pumps in place. He said that the change of plan was the result of pressure from the minister's office, and claimed that he had met with both Lunn and his deputy, Cassie Doyle.

Two days later, on December 8, 2007, the minister himself called Linda Keen. It was a Sunday, and she was at home. In blunt terms, Lunn told her that she must agree to restart the reactor. Keen immediately knew that the minister had "crossed the line with an independent regulator." Then Lunn told the regulator that he needed to go urgently to attend to another matter and abruptly ended the call. Keen later found out he had been summoned by the prime minister to explain the problem with the CNSC.

Shortly afterwards, Keen received a letter from both her own minister and the minister of health demanding that she solve the problem of the shutdown. She told them that the CNSC was working with AECL, "and AECL is aware of what they need to do"—meet their licence conditions by installing the second pump.

Realizing that Keen wouldn't be pushed off the letter and spirit of the Canadian Nuclear Safety Control Act, the Harper government did an end run around her. Lunn and his deputy asked for an independent assessment of the safety of the NRU without the two pumps. The "independent" review of safety issues was carried out by former vice-presidents from Ontario Power Generation. They concluded that the reactor is safer with one pump than no pump.

Keen was now in bureaucratic no man's land. Justice Canada instructed the seconded justice staff who worked with Keen to stop giving legal advice to the CNSC. That was because the government and the regulator were not in agreement. Then, with just two hours' notice, on December 11, 2007, Prime Minister Harper called the House of Commons into a special session, the first time that had happened in thirty years.

The CNSC, AECL, and the "independent" reviewers were questioned. Keen explained the reasons behind the CNSC's position, but also made it clear that she respected the right of Parliament to overrule the regulator—and take responsibility for the results. Though the Chalk River reactor was built on an earthquake fault line, and had partially melted down in 1952 and suffered another nuclear accident in 1958, Stephen Harper gazed into the future and declared, "There will not be an accident."

Minister Lunn and the president of the Canadian Medical Association gravely told the House of Commons that patients "would die without isotopes." The prime minister himself slagged Linda Keen publicly, wondering if she had the "good judgment" to be the nuclear watchdog, and describing her as a "Liberal appointee"[2] who had put tens of thousands of lives at risk. Keen's colleagues in the public service were agog. "I can't believe they named you," one of them told her.

It was not the finest hour for the opposition. Choosing not to defend the regulator, the NDP sided with the government.[3] Though the then Liberal leader, Michael Ignatieff, argued for balance in the government's reaction, it was no match for the prime minister's crystal-ball assurances of an accident-free future at Chalk River and the prospect of dying patients. The House voted to allow AECL to start the reactors at Chalk River without a second pump in place, a decision endorsed by the Senate. Without any debate, the Harper government invoked a clause of the Canadian Nuclear Safety Control Act directing the CNSC to consider the supply of isotopes, as well as health and public safety, in its decisions.

Without the slightest subject knowledge, and against the advice of a science-trained administrator taking scientific advice from a professional staff, politicians reopened the Chalk River reactor on December 18, 2007, twenty-eight days after it was shut down by AECL. There was one fact that even the politicians couldn't change: AECL, the operator of the NRU reactor at Chalk River, was in violation of its licence. Yet it was the regulator who lost the battle in Stephen Harper's Ottawa.

What Linda Keen did not know was that she had lost more than a battle; she was also about to lose her job. On December 27, 2007, Canada's nuclear regulator received a letter from Minister Lunn. The minister informed her that he was considering removing her as president of the CNSC, but he was giving her an opportunity to reply. The letter was drafted by Justice Canada, a requirement before the removal of a governor-in-council appointment. Sources say no Justice Department lawyer wanted to draft the letter, so the work fell to senior departmental personnel. The letter was also anonymously leaked to the press. Linda Keen replied to Minister Lunn in a letter she herself made public at the time.

Then came the Godfather moment. A senior deputy minister of the Harper government called Linda Keen at home and told her a possible deal was still on the table. Keen would not be fired in the short term if she said publicly that the CNSC had made the wrong decision on the Chalk River reactor. In return, the government would allow her to resign in six months instead of being fired immediately. To her caller, it was a good deal. "You get to resign anyway, honey," she recalled being told. Her reply sealed her fate: "So, my professional staff is committed to their professional technical views on the NRU and I accepted their advice.

Your proposal would mean that I would be double-crossing my staff. I can't do that. It would wound the staff permanently in their trust in the president. I depend upon my staff."

It was the end of the conversation and of Linda Keen's career. At midnight, the evening before she was set to testify in front of the Parliamentary Committee on Natural Resources, she received a letter from the PCO removing her from the presidency of the CNSC. The letter stated that she was being removed because of a "lack of leadership," parroting the language used by Stephen Harper and various other ministers when the "Slaughter on Slater" became public. Keen cancelled her appearance before the committee, convinced that the Harper government had used the isotope crisis to set up her firing. When I asked her what her personal experience told her about the Harper government, she replied, "The traditions don't matter at all. In the past, we've had a very competent public service which mostly gave good advice. Now the process has been politicized. How far has it gone? There is no science department in the federal government run by a scientist, not Health, Environment, Natural Resources, Agriculture, or Fisheries and Oceans. That says a lot. A good public service is top-drawer people with good ideas. You risk all that when the new role is 'give the minister what he wants.'"

For a time, AECL got what it wanted. Linda Keen's successor was Mike Binder, a long-term assistant deputy minister at Industry Canada. He immediately reinstated AECL's pre-licence approvals for new reactors. Binder reported to Richard Discerni, one of two deputy ministers who joined AECL's board in May 2008. The old cozy relationship between AECL, the regulator, and the Harper government had been restored. If Linda Keen had really been the problem, AECL should now have been ready to fly.

It never got off the ground. After burning through $820 million of taxpayers' money in 2010, and still without a new reactor order since 1978, AECL spiralled toward a hard landing. It also soon became apparent that Stephen Harper was badly in need of a new crystal ball. The man who said there would be no accident at Chalk River was proven wrong less than a year later.

On December 5, 2008, 47 litres of heavy water containing tritium leaked from the reactor. When the leak stopped on its own, the reactor was restarted by AECL without finding the source, after receiving approval by the new president of the CNSC. The public was informed of the accident but not of the amount of radioactive material that was involved. The same reactor had been leaking 7,001 litres of light water per day from a crack in a weld of the reactor's reflector system. Just five months later, in May 2009, the NRU was shut down yet again. It was discovered that heavy water was leaking from the base of the nuclear reactor vessel. The location of the leak was the same as in 2008, but the flow was greater. Unless one believes that the danger to patients decreases the longer they are deprived of medical isotopes, the shutdown of the NRU reactor at Chalk River laid bare the vicious political assault on Linda Keen and the disingenuous nature of the government's arguments at the time.

This time, no floor show took place in the House of Commons, complete with dire predictions from the Harper government that patients would die if the Chalk River reactor were not restarted. No lone bureaucrat was singled out for blame. Stephen Harper didn't call a special session of Parliament because human lives were on the line. And this time, it was not just a twenty-eight-day shutdown, but closure from May 2009 until August 2010—a staggering sixteen-month interruption in the production of raw medical isotopes.

So what did the prime minister do? He merely sent out his health minister of the day, Lisa Raitt, to say that there was no problem with the lengthy shutdown at Chalk River because there were other sources for the badly needed medical isotopes—the polar opposite of the message that Stephen Harper, Tony Clement, Gary Lunn, and the CMA had delivered in their attempt to discredit Linda Keen.

It is noteworthy to remember the words used by the new president of the Canadian Nuclear Safety Commission, Mike Binder, when he appeared before a parliamentary committee to answer questions about the heavy water leaks from the NRU reactor at Chalk River: "The Commission's (CNSC) decisions are final and binding. They are subject to review only by the Federal Court and not by the government." One can only imagine the wintry smile those words put on Linda Keen's face.

While Keen was accepting the Women in Nuclear Global Award in Marseille, France, AECL was going through the first of a series of painful changes. After spending $680 million on the project, and falling seven years behind schedule, the company cancelled the Maple reactor program. The fact that Maple reactors were owned by Nordion but were being designed and operated by AECL sparked a $1.6 billion lawsuit against the company. No sales of the old CANDU design were recorded, despite years of promises to Parliament from AECL. Finally, little progress had been made in the development of their new ACR reactor design and the potential for sales was limited. Companies in the United States and the United Kingdom had already rejected the new reactor design.

It was atomic sunset in Canada: the nuclear industry was too expensive even for the Canadian government. In the end, Stephen Harper "sold" AECL's reactor business, though the facts of the transaction could bear another interpretation. Since SNC-Lavalin gave Ottawa a cheque for $15 million, and then the Harper government handed Lavalin another one for $75 million, it could be argued that the feds had paid Lavalin $60 million to take a dubious asset off its hands.[4]

The cabal that worked to get rid of Linda Keen did not prosper. Natural resources minister Gary Lunn was demoted in the next cabinet shuffle to a minister of state. He would lose his Saanich-Gulf Islands seat in the next election to the leader of the Green Party, Elizabeth May. SNC-Lavalin has become mired in international fraud and corruption charges after admitting it paid bribes to acquire contracts. The World Bank has banned the company and its affiliates from working on any project financed by the bank for a ten-year period. As for Stephen Harper—the man who accused Linda Keen of putting thousands of lives at risk during the twenty-eight-day shutdown at Chalk River—he announced on June 10, 2009, that Canada would be getting out of the medical isotope business altogether.[5]

When you tangle with Stephen Harper, it is never really over. Although Linda Keen remains one of the leading experts in the world on nuclear safety, she has not worked again in Canada since being legally, but unjustly, dismissed by the Harper government. "To this day, I have not had a dollar's worth of consulting in Canada," says Keen, "and most of my expertise is being contracted to the US. I have been blacklisted completely."

As for the colleagues she left behind in the Public Service of Canada—Harper's most likely whipping boys in the next federal election as they negotiate new contracts—Keen has an important lesson to pass on: "The gentleman's agreement promised in the Accountability Act never happened. We now know all of this was a house of cards. The traditions don't matter at all."

nine

THE EXONERATION BLUES

I had just come from covering the Conservative Party convention in Calgary, an event that gave journalists little information but an excellent idea of what it might be like to take part in a cattle roundup—on the four-legged side of the process. Winter beat me to Edmonton. As I picked my way through the slush on Whyte Street on a raw Alberta afternoon in November 2013, I kept wondering if there was life after the "busty hooker" affair. I would soon find out. I was on my way to the Artisan Café to interview the star player in this tragicomedy: former Conservative cabinet minister Helena Guergis.

She greeted me as I came through the door. It's easy to see why Stephen Harper chose the elegant Guergis to occupy the seat above him and to his right in Question Period. Every time he rose to answer a question, there was the telegenic Helena, a former Miss Huronia, nodding approvingly. "Everyone tried to please him in those days," Guergis recalled. "I admit it, for a time I was one of them. There is so much jealousy amongst caucus—so pathetic—all hoping for some small recognition—recognition meaning favour with the Leader. He is the one who gives things out." Guergis even consented to the party paying for voice lessons to overcome something about her that they didn't like: when speaking naturally, she has a baby voice. "In Question Period rehearsal, Stephen, other cabinet ministers, and Jenni Byrne would sit there watching," Guergis told me. "Sometimes, some of them would coach. When I lapsed into my real voice, because it was hard to project that phony one for too long, Peter Van Loan would urge, 'Helena, big-girl voice, big-girl voice.'"

Since her ejection from cabinet and the Conservative Party, Guergis's life has consisted of a struggle to maintain her dignity, her reputation, and her marriage. She lives in her brother-in-law's house and tells me she has "nothing" and that her husband, Rahim Jaffer, has "very little." Jaffer spends a lot of time out of the country living at a cousin's trailer in Florida. Diagnosed with chronic pain, Guergis is entering her third year of law school at the University of Alberta, but only her second year of required courses because her medical condition has worsened, forcing her to become a part-time student. She now requires a voice-activated system to type.

Much of this woman's story has been mythologized. For one thing, she was not the daughter of rich and doting parents in Angus, Ontario, whom so many people believed her to be. When she became a young woman, her father, who owned a furniture store, advised her to find a husband "because her looks would be gone by age twenty-eight." Although by Angus standards, the family was well-to-do, they were "by no means loaded," as Guergis put it—though they would come to wield considerable political influence in the Simcoe-Grey electoral district.

Nor was life in Angus pastoral perfection. When Helena was a girl, police and provincial revenue officers raided the Guergis home looking for proof of income tax evasion. "I was standing there in my pyjamas and asked if I could put on my robe," she remembered. "They said no." And then there was the racism: "Our skin was too dark for a lot of them," she told me. "And on top of that I had this little, tiny voice that everyone made fun of." One day, a teenager in Angus called her "a dirty, slimy Iraqi who should go back to where she came from." (Guergis actually has Syrian, Jewish, and Swedish roots.)[1] Guergis learned to be tough. When another kid was beating up her sister on an outdoor hockey rink, Helena threw the bully over the boards. Even after she made the long, difficult climb to the federal cabinet, skin colour was occasionally an issue in her hometown. "I was asked by a constituent why I had brought my driver with me to town, the brown man. I told them, 'That's not my driver, that's my husband.'"

For all that troubled past, including a failed first marriage, Helena Guergis was, for a time, half of Ottawa's premier power couple. But that sort of success came only after putting in a grinding fourteen and a half years for the Conservative Party in both Ontario and Ottawa, including a stint working for former Ontario finance minister Janet Ecker. The other half of the power duo was Rahim Jaffer, whose movie-star good looks and easy charm made him a natural for politics and a hit with his colleagues. He was known around town as "the life of the party" and "everyone's best friend."[2]

When Jaffer first asked Guergis along on a young MPs' night out, she turned him down. "What's wrong with her?" she heard him ask a fellow reveller. The truth was that Helena Guergis was not a party animal but a studious loner who preferred staying in to going out—not anti-social, but solitary. Rahim could not have known that she was smitten. "When I looked into those eyes, I knew he was the one for me. I hunted him after that."

Jaffer, whose own family fled Kampala in Uganda to escape the reign of terror of Idi Amin, came to the Conservatives from the Reform Party. When he was just twenty-five, he won the federal riding in Edmonton that included the "cool" area of Old Strathcona. Preston Manning was his leader. He stayed with politics after the merger of the Canadian Alliance and the Progressive Conservatives.[3] At the height of his influence in the new Conservative Party, he became chair of the Conservative caucus. In fact, when Guergis and Jaffer decided to get married in 2007, they announced their engagement in caucus to a thunderous, standing ovation. There was one exception. Stephen Harper remained seated, staring. "I noticed that he was twirling his foot, the way he does when he is angry and thinking of pouncing," Guergis told me.

For a time, the former beauty queen, who unexpectedly won the Ontario riding of Simcoe-Grey for the Conservatives in 2004, enjoyed the prime minister's confidence. After Harper won a minority government in 2006, he called Guergis with some good news and some awkward news. The good news was that he was going to make her a parliamentary secretary—suggesting a possible cabinet post down the road and adding $15,000 to her paycheque. She would have to wait for the official swearing-in for the other news—the person she'd be working for. "He made me parliamentary secretary to David Emerson. [Emerson became minister of international trade the same day he crossed the floor from the Liberals to join Harper.] It put me in a funny spot," recalls Guergis. "For weeks I had been the lead in the House of Commons, criticizing Belinda Stronach for crossing the floor. Now I was working for a floor-crosser." The connection with Emerson broadened her horizons. Back in 2004, she was the one Jason Kenney turned to when he was looking for someone to do some China-bashing. But Emerson's economic rather than ideological analysis of the China relationship gradually persuaded Guergis that engagement was the better path.

Rahim and Helena would soon move into a four-level, $800,000 condominium in Ottawa's trendy Byward Market—close to the

Hill. Helena failed to report the mortgage liability on the property on her declaration of assets, earning her a $100 fine from Ethics Commissioner Mary Dawson—a minor offence in official Ottawa. The couple dined with the Harpers at 24 Sussex and zigzagged through Ottawa traffic in one of the multiple black security SUVs that took them all to the movies. On one occasion, Helena travelled with Harper in the PM's SUV.

Just after New Year's in 2007, Guergis made cabinet with a dual appointment: secretary of state both for Foreign Affairs and International Trade, and for Sport. A big part of her task in Foreign Affairs was to defend the Harper government over the increasingly controversial Afghan detainee affair. Guergis faithfully repeated the government's mantra: no proof existed that prisoners handed over by Canadian forces to Afghanistan's notorious National Directorate of Security had been tortured—a claim the opposition answered by demanding documented evidence. Liberal MP Derek Lee pointed out that "340 years of bedrock constitutional history" gave Parliament the right to look at unredacted documents. The Harper government refused.

Eventually, the Speaker of the House of Commons, Peter Milliken, ruled that Parliament did have the right to the documents, and an all-party committee (less the NDP) set to work on how access might be granted without damaging national security. Three former Supreme Court judges acted as backstop to the committee on sensitive issues. In the end, the committee was shut down, with the bulk of documents never released and both the letter and spirit of the Speaker's ruling disregarded.

The detainee affair exploded onto the front pages in November 2009. After years of denying torture allegations, the then chief of the defence staff, General Walter Natynczyk, told the House of Commons Defence Committee that a prisoner transferred from Canadian custody to the Afghans had indeed been abused. Defence minister Peter MacKay had previously insisted there was no evidence that detainees turned over by Canadian forces to the Afghans had been tortured.

WHILE GUERGIS KEPT a firm grip on the brass ring, it was a different story for Jaffer. The *Hill Times* voted him the "laziest MP in Ottawa." In the 2008 federal election, the unthinkable happened to the popular MP. The New Democrats under Linda Duncan narrowly won Edmonton-Strathcona. Jaffer could now lay dubious claim to being the MP who spoiled the Conservatives' otherwise clean sweep of every federal riding in Alberta.[4] The prime minister was not pleased, and in a subsequent meeting with his defeated candidate he warned Jaffer not to lobby his former colleagues in government—a message repeated to Rahim by his cabinet minister wife. Word filtered back to Guergis that Harper had "dissed Rahim big time" as a "bad" caucus chair. The PM allegedly promised that his replacement would pay attention to all members, not just a few, suggesting that Jaffer played favourites.

It was a strange time for Jaffer after losing in Edmonton. No call came from the prime minister until Jaffer's friends pressed Ray Novak to set up a meeting. "I wish we never had that meeting," Jaffer recalled. "It was just a ten- to twelve-minute meeting, but he left me more crushed than I already was. I left more upset than when I came in, but more determined to succeed. Harper is willing to do anything it takes to keep the job, and people are expendable. The system makes him untouchable and he knew that if he went rogue, there was nothing much people could do about it."

The only silver lining in Jaffer's defeat was what Helena Guergis did next: "I grabbed a flight the day after the election to be with him. We were married in blue jeans in Ian McClelland's backyard. (By Ian!) With Rahim's cousin Alia and James Rajotte. No honeymoon." McClelland, a former MP, was a marriage commissioner, and James Rajotte, the most popular MP in the Conservative caucus.

In the same election in which her husband was defeated, Helena Guergis was returned in Simcoe-Grey with a whopping 55 percent of the vote. Stephen Harper appointed her minister of state for the Status of Women, a junior posting that many observers saw as a demotion. One person who was happy about that was Stéphane Dion. He wanted Harper to fire Guergis over leaking news of his visit to Afghanistan while she was in Foreign Affairs, a breach of practice that Dion said had endangered his life. A letter-writing campaign to newspapers praising the minister's performance in office took place early in 2010, from people in her own circle—who withheld the fact of their relationship to Guergis.[5]

Despite the criticisms against Guergis, and although she still enjoyed the prime minister's confidence, her political capital was diminishing. After hearing unconfirmed stories that Canadian officials had discovered torture paraphernalia in an Afghan prison, she refused to spout the party line on Afghanistan. She also was in open disagreement with the government's handling of Sisters in Spirit, the organization that has done monumental research into the disappearance and deaths of over six hundred Native women. After passionately arguing for the preservation of the group's funding as minister for the Status of Women, Guergis failed to persuade her cabinet colleagues. The Harper government refused to renew the program. Instead, it gave $10 million to the RCMP for a new centre for missing persons and unidentified remains. "I was very angry at him and I know it got back to him. I was not quiet about my dissent. You don't diss Stephen that way."

With people jockeying for the plums of office, government circles could sometimes be hotbeds of jealousy, gossip, and ambition. Stories began to circulate that Guergis was spoiled, prickly, and entitled. They clucked about how many chauffeurs she went through, forgetting to mention that she had actually asked not to be assigned a driver. It was rarely mentioned that her severe allergies were a factor in the high turnover. "In one case," she told me, "the driver was smoking in the car and trying to hide it with air freshener. I am severely allergic to it."

If the knives were starting to come out against Helena Guergis, gossipy barbs were nothing compared to the powerful weapon her detractors were handed on the night of September 11, 2009. Rahim Jaffer, by that time in private business, was stopped for speeding by the OPP in the Ontario village of Palgrave. He was driving Guergis's Ford Escape. After failing a "blow test," the procedure used to determine if a Breathalyzer is required, Jaffer was arrested and taken back to the OPP detachment. Police administered a Breathalyzer, which he failed. The ex-MP was then strip-searched. He was subsequently charged for speeding, impaired driving, and possession of cocaine.

Jaffer had been socializing earlier that night with Nazim Gillani, a self-described Toronto financier who referred to the Club Paradise, a "gentleman's" strip club, as his Bloor Street office. The night before, Helena Guergis had joined her husband and Gillani for dinner at Sassafras, a high-end restaurant in Toronto's Yorkville district. Guergis was devastated when she heard the news of Jaffer's arrest: "When I heard it on the radio, I told one of my assistants, 'There must be another Rahim Jaffer, this can't be him.'" According to Guergis, she experienced immediate consequences from Jaffer's run-in with the law, including a visit to her riding by finance minister Jim Flaherty (now deceased) and Kellie Leitch (who ultimately replaced Guergis as MP for Simcoe-Grey). They were allegedly looking for key Guergis workers to switch to Kellie Leitch. "Yes, even before the boot happened. Jim had power, so they did," Guergis told me.

It was a difficult Christmas that year for Helena Guergis. With her husband in disgrace and facing criminal charges, she decided not to attend the Conservative caucus Christmas party. Instead, Guergis and Jaffer held a small, informal get-together at their downtown condominium for any MPs who wanted to drop in. "A lot of people showed up, including Jason Kenney, an old friend of Rahim's from the early days of Reform. But the big surprise was Justin Trudeau."

Then, on February 19, 2010—another public relations disaster. Arriving late for her flight from Charlottetown to Ottawa, an incident erupted between the flustered minister and airport security. An anonymous letter was sent to Liberal MP Wayne Easter accusing Guergis of screaming at airport staff and petulantly throwing her footwear, which she had been asked to remove before going through the scanner.[6] The story got national attention—all of it bad for Guergis. It was as if all of her alleged personality issues were on display—but only in the anonymous letter, not in the airport video recording of the event. When the CBC's chief correspondent, Peter Mansbridge, viewed the video, here is how he described what happened:

> I watched the security video of that moment when Helena Guergis went through security at Charlottetown Airport. It was shot from five different cameras and from all sorts of different angles. You can see that she did not throw her shoes around, wave her hands around, or yell at anybody. I can tell you I have seen a lot worse on most of my trips through Canadian airports of people being upset about what they were being put through. It was pretty tame stuff.[7]

Sadly for Guergis, she worked for a prime minister who firmly believed that perception was reality. CTV's Robert Fife reported on March 15, 2010, that people in the "highest ranks of the Conservative Party" had asked the prime minister to drop Guergis from cabinet after the alleged incident. They believed Guergis had "offended working-class Canadians by her actions and damaged the party's reputation in Atlantic Canada— especially PEI."[8] The anonymous letter had painted a picture of a rude and condescending Conservative cabinet minister throwing her weight around in a way that damaged the Tory brand. An apology was arranged to dispel the negative image created by what was being widely reported as the minister's tantrum. "I apologized," she told me. "I was made to do and say things I didn't want to."

Guergis texted Peter MacKay to seek his advice about raising the matter in caucus. MacKay, who had been in the House of Commons since 1997, advised her to raise it herself before someone else did, to "get ahead of it." Guergis remembers MacKay texting her "that no matter what happens, he would not forget what I had done for him." It was a reference to her stout defence of MacKay in the House of Commons when he was accused of calling Belinda Stronach a "dog" after the couple's breakup over Stronach's defection to the Liberals.

Helena Guergis caught what should have been a break in early March 2010. The enormous burden of her husband's criminal charges came and went. Rahim Jaffer pleaded guilty to careless driving, was given a $500 fine, and lost six demerit points from his licence. The big story was that Jaffer had escaped the scandal without a criminal record. That was because the more serious criminal charges of drunk driving and possession of cocaine were dropped. Crown prosecutor Marie Balogh explained that there was "no reasonable prospect of a conviction." In the Crown's view, the OPP had made two mistakes: they didn't wait for Jaffer's Calgary lawyers to call back before administering a Breathalyzer; and they strip-searched the former MP after finding cocaine in his clothing. What should have been a measure of vindication for Jaffer, and by implication, Guergis, turned into more public bludgeoning.

Callers to radio talk shows described the outcome as a fix; and letters to the editors sided with the OPP, which wanted the trial to go forward, despite the Crown's misgivings about how the police had handled the incident.

Beyond the hurly-burly of politics, a "miracle" occurred. Helena Guergis who had already had two miscarriages, one known, one unknown to her husband, became pregnant. She badly wanted a child but had trouble staying pregnant. The couple had visited a fertility clinic and been told there was virtually no hope. Guergis was determined to see this pregnancy through to childbirth. As her troubles mounted, she told me they said she was "lying about being pregnant." Nine months later, Helena Guergis delivered a son, Zavier, on his father's birthday—December 15, 2010.

Politics on the Hill was about to go Bollywood, a soap opera driven by the allegations of a private investigator named Derrick Snowdy, who had in turn gathered his information from the shadowy Toronto figure Nazim Gillani. Snowdy was working for a private client, Dennis Garces. He had been conducting an undercover investigation, posing as a potential business partner for Gillani to gather information about Gillani for his client. It was during that charade that Gillani revealed an alleged business connection to Jaffer and Guergis.

At the time, Gillani was the subject of a police fraud investigation. Gillani claimed, "Mr. Jaffer has opened up the Prime Minister's Office to us"—words he committed to an email he would later apologize for writing in front of the Government Operations Committee of Parliament. When asked what Gillani did for a living, Snowdy told the same committee, "Serial fraud." As if that weren't sensational enough, Gillani also claimed that three offshore companies on Belize in the Caribbean had been "reserved" to hold cash for Jaffer and Guergis. Making that particular allegation more tantalizing was the fact that the couple had indeed travelled to

Belize on government business three months before the 2008 election, while Jaffer was still an MP and his wife was a secretary of
state for Foreign Affairs. To complete the tabloid titillation, Gillani
said there were cellphone pictures of Guergis and Jaffer with "busty
hookers" at a party where cocaine was snorted.

On the directions of his client, Snowdy began shopping his
salacious scoop. According to Snowdy, he had already given his
information to the RCMP and the OPP. He tried getting to
Liberal leader Michael Ignatieff but was rebuffed. He was met
with a very different reception when he offered the same information to Conservative Party lawyer Arthur Hamilton. Hamilton
returned Snowdy's call at 11 p.m. on April 8, and listened closely
to every detail of their conversation, which went on for an hour.
Hamilton hung up and then alerted Ottawa immediately. The next
day, he had a face-to-face meeting with Snowdy.

Hamilton was a big player in all things Conservative. He
had participated in the merger of the Canadian Alliance and the
Progressive Conservative Party in 2003. He also signed a retainer
with the Conservative Party of Canada in 2008 to effectively
become its in-house lawyer on three matters: compliance with elections legislation, in which he is reputed to be the country's leading
expert; the Conservative Fund of Canada; and anything involving
individual Conservative MPs that raised legal issues. In the wake of
the sponsorship scandal, Hamilton represented the party superbly
at the Gomery Commission. He also played a role in the secret
payment from the prime minister's former chief of staff, Nigel
Wright, to Senator Mike Duffy. He considered his ultimate client
to be Stephen Harper, as prime minister and head of the party.

Without investigating any of the allegations made by Snowdy,
Arthur Hamilton came to the conclusion that it was his duty
under his retainer with the Conservative Party to pass the third-
party hearsay about Guergis and Jaffer to the highest office in the

land. Although the precise routing that landed Hamilton's discussion with Snowdy on the prime minister's desk is unknown, the information got to Stephen Harper immediately. After going over Hamilton's report, but without looking into any of the hearsay allegations against his minister and his former caucus chair, let alone giving them a chance to respond to Snowdy's accusations, Stephen Harper decided to fire Helena Guergis. He also decided to call in the RCMP and Ethics Commissioner Mary Dawson.

On April 9, 2010, the prime minister placed a call to the Dominican Republic, where Guergis was vacationing, and gave her the news. It was a conversation she would never forget. "He said 'from one friend to another, it's time you knew what your husband has been doing.' I begged him not to fire me. He just laughed, slowly . . . and hung up. I tried to call him back but he wouldn't take the call." Harper announced Guergis's "resignation," with the information that she would sit as an independent pending the outcome of two investigations: one by the RCMP and the other by the ethics commissioner.

Every member of Guergis's family advised her to hire someone who could act as a spokesperson in the coming media firestorm. She had a conversation with an old friend, Jaime Watt, to get some advice. Watt said he had a personal relationship with Arthur Hamilton and would give him a call. He made the call on April 9, but it didn't do any good. The party was not pleased by the ex-minister's contact with Jaime Watt. During Guergis's battle to be readmitted to caucus, the Conservative Party would suggest that the couple tried to hire Watt, and it later asked Guergis in writing, "Why did you believe that you needed a registered lobbyist to represent you in your dealings with the government and the caucus?"

Meanwhile, Mary Dawson's office moved expeditiously to carry out what must have been the shortest investigation on record. At 4 p.m. on Friday, April 9, private investigator Derrick Snowdy returned a call from the Ethics Commissioner's Office. Quoting from the prime minister's letter, a representative of the commissioner asked Snowdy about the allegations against Helena Guergis. "I said to him I had made no allegations against the Member," recalled Snowdy. "He asked if I had spoken with the prime minister's chief of staff. I said 'No.' Did I make any allegations against the member? I said 'No.' And then he stated to me, 'Well, it doesn't seem to me that we have a complaint here. Thank you very much.' Hung up the phone."

April 9, 2010, must have been an interesting day at 1200 Vanier Parkway, the headquarters of the RCMP. Stephen Harper's principal secretary, Raymond Novak, wrote to the then RCMP commissioner, William Elliott, for the prime minister:

> The Prime Minister has asked me to provide the following information on his behalf.
>
> Late last night our office became aware of the specifics of allegations made by Mr. Derrick Snowdy, a private investigator, concerning the conduct of Mr. Rahim Jaffer and the Hon. Helena Guergis. The allegations are numerous and include fraud, extortion, obtaining benefits by false pretences and involvement in prostitution. The extent of the allegations makes it impossible for me to summarize them completely in this short letter.

Novak went on to explain that the PMO had no first-hand knowledge of the allegations, but that the Conservative Party's legal counsel Arthur Hamilton had communicated with Snowdy, who claimed to have collected evidence to corroborate his allegations. Snowdy informed Hamilton that his information had already been shared with the RCMP and the OPP. Novak wrote to the commissioner, "But I want to ensure that you are aware of it." Novak gave him Hamilton's office and cell phone numbers, and told him to let the PMO know if they could provide "any more assistance."

Novak's letter, based on hearsay three times removed from its alleged source, Nazim Gillani, was strange in many ways. The highest office in the land was involving the RCMP in a matter that a single telephone conversation had already persuaded the ethics commissioner was not worth investigating. And the prime minister was doing this without knowledge of either the truth of the allegations or the credibility of the people making them. Even stranger, if, as Novak wrote, Snowdy had already passed on his information to the RCMP and the OPP, why did the prime minister of Canada need to write to the RCMP commissioner? The information could hardly be considered a "tip" if two major police forces already had it. Or was the letter an implicit invitation straight from the top for the RCMP to launch an investigation? If so, it was successful.

Scrawled across the note bearing the prime minister's letterhead, Commissioner Elliott wrote, "Please task 'A' Division with this for follow-up. I'd like regular update please. Thank You." "A" Division certainly got the message, and the biweekly updates started coming. Seven officers, including an inspector, two staff sergeants, a sergeant, a corporal, and a constable, went to work lifting up every conceivable rock on the Guergis/Jaffer affair, while playing coy with the media that an investigation was actually in full swing. They were backed up by a prosecutor in the Ontario Attorney General's Office.

One of the investigators' initial interviews, on April 16, 2010, was with Conservative Party lawyer Arthur Hamilton, who rode the elevator to the fifth floor of the RCMP building at 155 McArthur Street in Ottawa. The interview was conducted by lead investigator Inspector John Keuper and Staff Sergeant Stéphane St-Jacques of the Commercial Crime Section. Hamilton laid out nine different allegations that had been passed to him by Derrick

Snowdy—which the private investigator had already disavowed to the ethics commissioner.

Making clear that he was just a "cut out" and didn't "know anything," Hamilton proceeded to give stunning details of Snowdy's allegations—many of them already published in the *Toronto Star*. Someone was clearly leaking information to the newspaper, and reporter Kevin Donovan was following the story with alacrity. The picture Hamilton drew for the RCMP came down to this: Gillani and Jaffer were passing themselves off as "venture capitalists" who would use Jaffer's political access to the government to draw on the government's Green Fund for possible "bump-and-dump" stock deals in taking companies public. Helena Guergis attended some of the dinners to amplify the appearance of access because she was a federal cabinet minister. Finally, Gillani's business practices included obtaining compromising cellphone shots of clients and even using physical intimidation to get his way.

Staff Sergeant Stéphane St-Jacques then asked Hamilton a question that had nothing to do with Derrick Snowdy or accounts in the media: "And, were you able to back up the story with something else?" "This is going to frustrate you, the answer is yes," Hamilton replied. "Um, but, uh, what I was able to match this up with is privileged, because of previous retainer steps I had taken. Specific to, to the Minister, and um, Mr. Jaffer. And uh, without disclosing anything privileged, if I can, uh, if I can explain it this way. Had a private investigator called me out of the blue and told me that Prime Minister Harper was on the take, I would have kicked the tires. And you know, that, that's one level of an allegation uh, to hear the information that was passed on about Mr. Jaffer and Minister Guergis; um, it did not create a big leap to determine that some of these statements were credible." "Given prior history?" Inspector Keuper asked. "Yes. I'm afraid so," Hamilton replied.[9]

The RCMP investigators also noted in their record of the

interview, "Hamilton is aware of events involving Jaffer and Guergis at the 2008 Winnipeg Conservative Party convention. These events would be consistent with allegations and lend credibility to them." What Hamilton may have been referring to was a "wedding social," a tradition unique to Manitoba,[10] thrown for Rahim and Helena by their friend and political colleague Rod Bruinooge, the Conservative MP for Winnipeg South. It was a Saturday night bash at the Delta Hotel featuring the Boogie Nights Band. There was only one problem, clearly not understood by those not from Manitoba. Attendees were charged admission, and it became an issue that the money may have been going into the pockets of Jaffer and Guergis. "I cringe at the thought of this still today," Guergis told me. "When we figured this out, we insisted that it go to a charity. I never organized it, did not know there were tickets sold—I should have paid closer attention. I just wanted to help Rod. A wedding social with hundreds of my closest friends I never met before is what I called it. I was not keen on it from the start and only agreed because Rod asked me. This had potential in politics to be a big issue."

Though Arthur Hamilton scrupulously avoided divulging any information that was "privileged," about Winnipeg or anything else, he didn't leave much doubt in the investigators' minds as to what he thought about the ethics and judgment of either Guergis or Jaffer. Referring to Helena Guergis, Hamilton told the investigators, "Not only does Helena tolerate Jaffer hanging out with escorts, and prostitutes, but there's apparently video of her snorting cocaine off the breast of a prostitute. I've made no verification of that." (The allegation was not true.) Hamilton even alerted the investigators to a recent story in the press that they might have missed because of the Jaffer/Guergis affair's domination of the news: "Uh, missed last week in the, in all of the press flurry, and I think possibly even before the *Toronto Star* article came out, there was a small little story about Mr. Jaffer potentially stealing money from the CONSERVATIVE caucus fund. You'll remember that he was the chair of the CONSERVATIVE caucus before his defeat in the 2008 election. Um, the allegation in the paper was that Mr. Jaffer had taken an amount of money from that caucus fund."

Though not reported publicly, the amount of money taken from the caucus fund by Jaffer after he lost the election of 2008 was $4,408.50. The Conservative Party said that Jaffer took the money without authority and tried to justify it with receipts submitted in 2009 to cover expenses he claims go back to the period of time when he was caucus chair. Jaffer had a meeting with the PMO's chief of staff, Guy Giorno, over the matter, including the allegation that Rahim had stolen the money. Guergis wrote to the MP making that charge, Guy Lauzon. "I told him he was not the judge and jury and that he should consider what his comments would mean for the government if he were to keep telling people his version." The dispute was never resolved.[11]

Investigators noted in their record of the interview, "Hamilton opines that, in view of the fact that Jaffer has personal business interests and that Guergis uses her office to lobby, both violate the Conflict of Interest Act and the Member's Code." Before Hamilton's interview ended, he had a question of his own for the investigators: "Does the RCMP have any, um, expectation, obviously I've made no comment in the press, the CONSERVATIVE PARTY, the Prime Minister's Office, are not making any comment about my actions. I assume my meeting with you is not going to be disclosed unless there is some extraordinary requirement that the RCMP do so?" "Uh, you're right. Um, all our investigation, we're keeping that for ourselves," Staff Sergeant St-Jacques replied.

And so it went—for three solid months. The RCMP Commercial Crime Section interviewed every staff member, including the many drivers of Helena Guergis, looking for proof she had misused public resources or improperly shared them with her husband, offshored money, or committed fraud. The investigators delved into seven companies involved in the accusations, among them Greenpower Generation, Wright Tech Systems, Green Rite Solutions, and International Strategic Investments. They worked up financial and real estate profiles of both Guergis and Jaffer. They checked the couple out on CPIC, an information database maintained by the RCMP, and FINTRAC, Canada's financial intelligence unit.[12] They even interviewed Ken Murray Cook, the former Canadian ambassador in Guatemala, and also Canada's high commissioner to Belize. They wanted to know if any meetings had taken place on the couple's official trip to Belize in 2008, other than what was on the official program. The ambassador had witnessed none.

And so, on July 2, 2010, the chief superintendent of criminal operations in "A" Division, Serge Therriault, wrote a letter to the PMO staffer who had forwarded Derrick Snowdy's allegations to the RCMP on behalf of the prime minister—Stephen Harper's principal secretary, Ray Novak:

This is further to your correspondence to Commissioner Elliott of April 9th, 2010 pertaining to allegations of fraud, extortion, obtaining benefits by false pretences, and involvement in prostitution against former Conservative MP Helena Guergis and Mr. Rahim Jaffer.

This letter is to inform you that the RCMP has completed its investigation of your complaint of alleged criminal wrongdoing.

The investigation disclosed no evidence to support a charge under the Criminal Code. This determination was made with the benefit of legal advice from the Ministry of the Attorney-General for the Province of Ontario. . . .

After a very thorough, three-month, seven-person investigation by the national police force into the allegations against Guergis and Jaffer, the RCMP had found absolutely nothing to support charges against the couple.

If the PMO had done due diligence, it might not have climbed aboard the hearsay train so quickly. Just the year before making his shocking claims, Derrick Snowdy had declared personal bankruptcy with $13 million in liabilities, including $2 million owed to Revenue Canada. Snowdy's source for the allegations against Guergis and Jaffer—Nazim Gillani—was under police investigation for fraud at the time of Snowdy's discussions with him. He also claimed to have laundered money for the Hells Angels, had been fined for breaking the Income Tax Act in British Columbia, and had been arrested for carrying a concealed weapon— a .22-calibre pistol.

Despite being fully cleared by an exhaustive RCMP criminal investigation, which generated a report more than 2,900 pages long, to Guergis, exoneration felt a lot like guilt. Although the prime minister had said that Guergis would sit as an independent in the House of Commons pending the outcomes of the RCMP investigation, she remained in exile. Harper wouldn't take her back and seemed not to care that he had put two people through public hell for what turned out to be nothing.

Ray Novak had described Snowdy's allegations in his letter to the commissioner of the RCMP this way: "I have been informed that Mr. Snowdy states that he has collected evidence to corroborate his allegations." Compare that to what Derrick Snowdy said in testimony in front of the Government Operations Committee when the matter came before Parliament: "I have no evidence, or no information with respect to the conduct of Ms. Guergis in my possession or knowledge." That is the same answer Snowdy gave to the ethics commissioner on the day Guergis was fired—and why there was no ethics investigation at that time.

It was an embarrassing fiasco. The Harper government had to come up with a justification for its crimeless punishment of Helena Guergis, who was out of cabinet and out of caucus. After all, when foreign affairs minister Maxime Bernier left a briefcase of secret documents at his girlfriend's apartment, he lost his place in cabinet but not in caucus. Stephen Harper couldn't say that Guergis was thrown out because she had broken the law; the RCMP confirmed she hadn't. He couldn't say that she was ejected because she had used her ministerial letterhead to recommend the services of a constituent to another level of government; the late finance minister Jim Flaherty had been cited for exactly the same ethical breach, except that he was writing to a quasi-judicial body, the CRTC. Flaherty remained in cabinet and caucus. And if being under investigation by an officer of Parliament justified dismissal, then why hadn't Lisa Raitt and Dean Del Mastro been thrown out of caucus when they were under investigation?[13]

The question was stubborn and needed answering: why was Helena Guergis cast into the outer darkness? In the end, the Harper government turned to low comedy. "Dean Del Mastro came out of caucus and gave an interview where he said that there was a standard in the Conservative caucus that I didn't meet," Guergis told me. "He knew what was coming down the pike for him [Elections Canada charges]—they knew even before the last election—and he said that. I let him have it."

Helena Guergis isn't shy about saying who she holds responsible for the injustice she has suffered: "I am no angel, but I never used coke and I've never even been in a strip club. Harper and his henchmen used to their advantage sexism and the acceptance of sexism to manipulate. Everyone fell for it. I was not even human, just something to kick around for a couple of years. The media disgust me as much as Harper does—they were stupid. Harper used them to carry out his plan and they still can't see it. Rahim was a private person at the time of his arrest,[14] and the media and Stephen made sure the whole country wanted to attack me for it. And they still think it is for me to answer for another person. Well, it is not."

ten

FAREWELL DIPLOMACY

The elegant Ottawa house on North River Road looks across the street to the river, a fitting view for a man who was immersed in the flow of the world's great events for thirty-eight years as a senior member of Canada's foreign service.

Paul Heinbecker, Canada's former ambassador to the United Nations, answers the door wearing an open-necked shirt and chinos. He leads me into a dining room decorated with treasures from his most important diplomatic posting: Turkey. Most important, yes, for it was in Ankara that he met and married his wife, Ayşe Köymen, who added a new culture and two daughters, Yasemin and Céline, to his life.

We make our way through the house to a deck overlooking the back garden, where anything capable of blooming is gaudily ablaze in the afternoon sun. Sitting around a table of Turkish treats and a cool pitcher of ice tea, I look into the face of benign fatigue belonging to the man who helped end the Kosovo War and kept Canada from blundering into Iraq with President Bush and his coalition of the misguided.

Before speaking, he ponders my question about the state of Canadian diplomacy under Stephen Harper. Heinbecker had grappled with the diplomat's concerns: the burden of talking when others want to fight, of compromising when antagonists prefer to stand fast, and of persevering in these delicate arts when things appear hopeless. In a voice alternately soft and steely, a struggle declares itself. It is an argument between the seasoned diplomat not given to making unflattering judgments about his own government, and the troubled professional who can find no other way.

"Canada's diplomacy is hugely different under Harper," Heinbecker responds. "The neo-conservative idea of foreign policy is about flexing military muscle. It's about free-trade deals. It is a reversal of our history. We used to be advocates of constructive internationalism, we used to work hard to make that work. That's why our advice and our particular insight were so sought after by other countries. Now we are a country with baggage. Those invitations to counsel others and to take part in that international meeting of the minds don't get issued.[1] We have become outliers. We are seen as more American than the Americans, more Israeli than Likud. Given what our foreign policy has become, I would not have joined the service today if I were a young man." It is a surprising declaration only until Heinbecker supplies the context. He judges the prime minister's foreign policy—a kind of international morality play directed by Stephen Harper—through the lens of the diplomatic corps he entered in 1965 and left in 2004. These were not just different times but different planets.

Attracted by the feats of Lester Pearson, who found a way to restrain the dogs of war amidst the powder keg of Suez in 1956, Heinbecker joined the foreign service straight out of what was then called Waterloo Lutheran University, now Wilfrid Laurier University. He was the son of a father who worked in the Dominion Tire Factory, and his mother sold products out of her house to help put him through university. He rose steadily in the department with postings to Stockholm, Paris, Washington, and Ankara. Much later he served as ambassador to Germany and then in 2000, to the United Nations.

The career diplomat's résumé is a blue-ribbon list of the big files. He was the most important policy advisor to Prime Minister Jean Chrétien on the Iraq War, chief negotiator of the Kyoto Protocol to the International Climate Change Convention, and head of the Canadian task force on the conflict in Zaire. Over his career, he served three prime ministers of two different political stripes.

The first was Pierre Trudeau, a man Heinbecker found was not a "people person" —much like Stephen Harper. But there was an enormous difference between the Liberal and Conservative leaders. Trudeau entered discussions and debates with gusto, while Harper rejected, sometimes boorishly, views that didn't square with his own. For Harper, it was a trait that went back to his days as head of the National Citizens Coalition (NCC). After firing a senior member of the NCC for disagreeing with him, Harper told another staffer that they should burn the man's chair—an incident related in the memoir *Loyal to the Core* by former NCC employee and now political consultant Gerry Nicholls.

Trudeau didn't want to burn your chair, just put your ideas through the crucible of that subtle, Jesuitical mind. One day in Trudeau's office, the prime minister made the point that he could get away with lecturing others on international affairs because Canada did not spend big dollars on the military and wasn't a bully. Heinbecker espoused the opposite view. Precisely because Canada didn't invest in its armed forces, it left the country without any clout with those nations that were "doing the heavy lifting." Trudeau debated the issue with his speech writer and concluded that Heinbecker's position was not persuasive. Heinbecker's nerves tingled. "I worried for a bit that I had shit on the prime minister's carpet with what I said. He didn't see it that way. We just had different views and that was fine by him."

Although Trudeau's closest diplomatic confidant in those days was Robert Fowler, he turned to Paul Heinbecker to prepare his last speech on the so-called Peace Initiative in October 1983. It was in the jittery days of the Cold War, with the United States and the Soviet Union involved in an arms race. Disarmament talks in Vienna had broken down and Trudeau, nearing the end of his career, wanted to initiate a "cooling down" period between the world's twitchy superpowers.

The attempt to de-escalate the Russo-American standoff had become urgent on August 30, 1983, when the Soviets shot down a Korean Airlines Boeing 747, killing everyone on board, including ten Canadians. The prime minister chose to see the tragedy as an accident rather than a hostile act demanding a military response. Only through diplomacy, Trudeau believed, could the world shake free of the Cold War and all of its apocalyptic risks. Heinbecker wrote the speech that the PM planned to use "to civilize the dialogue" in an increasingly confrontational world. "Without referring to notes, Trudeau questioned me closely on the content, citing actual pages. You had to know your stuff when you met him because he knew his stuff. And if he could question you without a copy of the speech in front of him, you had better be able to look him in the eye and answer his questions the same way."

Working with Trudeau had its lighter moments. After the two men reworked the speech together, the prime minister continued to press Heinbecker for more words. The speech writer was puzzled. They had covered all the agreed-upon points in detail. Trudeau finally explained the need for prolixity. If he spoke from noon until 1 p.m., there would be a break before Question Period; that way, the PM wouldn't have to listen to the response to his speech from Opposition leader Brian Mulroney, the man soon to become the second prime minister of Paul Heinbecker's career.

Brian Mulroney may not have had Pierre Trudeau's charisma, intellectual gravitas, or string of celebrity girlfriends, but when he went on a charm offensive, there was no public figure quite like him. Heinbecker got to know the Progressive Conservative prime minister much better than he, or anyone else, ever got to know the enigmatic Trudeau. Following the adage that the beginning of wisdom is the suspension of judgment, Heinbecker saw Mulroney's flaws but he also saw through them to a better side: "I liked him. He had all the virtues and vices of a human being. He was personable to an extent that few other politicians are."

Heinbecker was well regarded in the Mulroney administration, though never a member of the inner circle. He lived through four chiefs of staff—Stanley Hart, Norman Spector, Hugh Segal, and David McLaughlin. Even though Heinbecker didn't enjoy the access to Mulroney that was shown to confidants such as Dr. Fred Doucet, the prime minister had an uncanny way of reaching out to staff at moments of personal distress. It made people feel special. It also forged a personal loyalty to Mulroney that a mere working relationship never could—a phenomenon rare in the Harper PMO. There, as an insider told me, everyone serves at, but not necessarily with, pleasure.

Mulroney took an intense interest in his staff. When Heinbecker's daughter Céline had to undergo surgery after she slipped off a slide and fell face-first into a wooden plank, the prime minister called during the child's operation for a report. He called again when Heinbecker's mother was involved in a lengthy cancer surgery; and, finally, when Bob Graver, a fellow PMO staffer, died of a heart attack in the office, Mulroney had Heinbecker paged at Pearson airport. He wanted to break the news personally before Heinbecker heard about his colleague's sudden death in the media.

While Mulroney's well-ploughed sins and misdemeanors in domestic politics eventually destroyed his government, his party, and to some degree his reputation, his contributions internationally were epic and enduring. As for the diplomatic corps, the man who sang "When Irish Eyes Are Smiling" with Ronald Reagan was a dream prime minister to work under.

While many of Mulroney's own citizens disliked what they took to be his obsequious fawning over figures such as the US president, world leaders responded to his personal charm, whereas Pierre Trudeau's relentless rationality had frequently left them cold. One of Trudeau's greatest attractions was that he never held membership in any old boys' club; Mulroney's principal strength was that he did, enjoying a string of corporate connections running back to his days as president of the Iron Ore Company of Canada. In the end, where Trudeau's intellectual rigour and aloofness made tepid friends and passionate enemies, Mulroney's personality and networking got some very big things done.

Under Mulroney, Canada was instrumental in keeping up the economic pressure to end apartheid in South Africa. Canadian businessmen and world leaders alike were pressuring him to ease sanctions in order to do more business with the racist but wealthy state. They argued that the government of Willem de Klerk was making progress on human rights and that sanctions, as Margaret Thatcher a little disingenuously observed, "only hurt the poor."

Mulroney asked Canadian diplomat Lucie Edwards to make contact with the still-imprisoned Nelson Mandela. On behalf of the prime minister, she asked the legendary ANC leader if the sanctions should be lifted. Mandela told her that they were still important and should remain in place. That was enough for Brian Mulroney. As he told Heinbecker, by then his chief foreign policy advisor, "If Mandela thinks the sanctions should remain, our decision is that they remain."

It was easier said than done. Behind the scenes, another Brian Mulroney, unrecognizable as the smarmy schmoozer on the nightly news, went to work against a wall of opposition. He stood up to and eventually won over three powerful world leaders who wanted sanctions against South Africa relaxed—German chancellor Helmut Kohl, US president Ronald Reagan, and the Iron Lady herself, British prime minister Margaret Thatcher. When Thatcher's press secretary later made a public statement at odds with Thatcher's commitment to keeping tough sanctions in place, Mulroney snapped the British delegation back into line with a withering comment: "Where I come from, you don't make a deal at five o'clock and then disavow it at six."

Years later, after Nelson Mandela became president of South Africa, he and Mulroney found themselves visiting Germany at the same time. Paul Heinbecker was Canada's ambassador in Bonn, and Mandela asked him to set up a meeting with his former advocate. The ambassador obliged. At the end of their meeting, Mandela asked Mulroney to lend financial support to the African National Congress. Knowing that the organization had a militant wing, Mulroney was wary of appearing to support terrorism. In the end, he pledged a modest sum of money to his old friend. As Mandela left the room, he turned to Mulroney and said, "And Brian, make sure your donation is in American dollars."

In his two terms in office, successive majorities, Mulroney had a string of foreign policy accomplishments unrivalled in Canadian history: the Acid Rain Treaty with the United States; the Canada–United States Free Trade Agreement; the North American Free Trade Agreement; tough sanctions against apartheid in South Africa; a pivotal role in the reunification of the two Germanys; and foundational work on international responsibility for famine.

As Heinbecker reflected, "Under Mulroney, Canada came down on the right side of history on apartheid and a good many other international issues."

As professionally satisfying as Heinbecker's Mulroney years were, more solid accomplishments lay ahead of him. Canada's diplomats remained busy under the government of Heinbecker's third prime minister, Jean Chrétien. During Chrétien's tenure, Canada was instrumental in bringing forward the international ban on land mines and in creating the International Criminal Court in The Hague. Canadian diplomats were in the vanguard of a UN initiative to impose sanctions against trade in "blood diamonds" (diamonds mined and sold to finance a warlord). When the sanctions were flouted, it was Canadian diplomat Robert Fowler who headed up an investigation into how to put an end to the blood-diamond trade. As a result of his work, countries trading in blood diamonds were "named and shamed," and the Kimberley Process Certification Scheme was put into place. That process prevented blood diamonds from entering the world's rough diamond market, thereby cutting off funds for armed conflicts in war-torn places such as Angola, Côte d'Ivoire, and Sierra Leone.

Heinbecker himself had a defining career moment serving under Chrétien. In the lead-up to the Iraq War, the seasoned diplomat was Canada's ambassador to the United Nations. Every day in the UN, the drumbeat of war came from the US side in the person of John Negroponte, the permanent representative to the United Nations under President George W. Bush.

The more diligently Ambassador Heinbecker worked behind the scenes to gain more time for inspectors from the International Atomic Energy Agency (IAEA) to search for weapons of mass destruction inside Iraq, the angrier Negroponte became. Heinbecker was accused of "obstructing US diplomacy"—code for impeding the Bush administration's march to war. Negroponte summoned Heinbecker and proceeded to dress him down over the Canadian position at the UN. When Heinbecker persisted in his efforts to avert a shooting war, Negroponte expressed his displeasure by asking Canada's ambassador a pointed question: just how big a fight did he want with the US government anyway? "They actually sent me a threatening email," Heinbecker disclosed. "If I'd kept that email, I could have dined out for the rest of my life on that exchange."

After being raked over the coals by Negroponte, Heinbecker alerted Ottawa to what was happening in New York. He told the PMO and the PCO that the Americans were livid that Canadian diplomacy was blocking a more "direct" way of dealing with the regime of Saddam Hussein. The reply from the prime minister was vintage Chrétien: "Paul, you're a big boy; do what big boys do. Tell them to go to hell."

As the geopolitical clock ticked down to the witching hour of war, Prime Minister Chrétien had to decide whether to throw his lot in with President Bush, or to face the consequences of opting out of a dubious and perhaps illegal invasion badly wanted by Washington. It was one of the big decisions that Chrétien's government had to get right. Jim Wright of the Department of Foreign Affairs, Trade and Development played a role in the deliberations, but Chrétien's final decision on the Iraq war—not to get involved—was crafted by three people: foreign policy advisor Claude Laverdure, senior political advisor Eddie Goldenberg, and Ambassador Paul Heinbecker. "Of the three of us," Heinbecker confided in me, "my advice had the biggest influence."[2]

By diplomatic standards, Heinbecker had hit a tape-measure home run: he had kept his country out of a war, and better yet, a war triggered by false intelligence and in violation of international law. The decision to stay on the sidelines of the Iraq War in the absence of approval for the mission from the Security Council remains one of the enduring accomplishments of Jean Chrétien's tenure as prime minister. As a legacy issue it was not inconsequential, given that the Quebec ad sponsorship scandal tarnished Chrétien's record at the end.

Chrétien's respect for the UN, for his own diplomats, and for international law stood in stark contrast to Stephen Harper's mantra of damn the Security Council and full speed ahead. As leader of the Opposition, Harper famously wrote in the *Wall Street Journal* that it was a "serious mistake" for Canada not to have gone to war in Iraq. Much later, during a televised election debate, Harper reluctantly admitted that the serious mistake had been his, not Jean Chrétien's, in accepting the bogus claim that Saddam Hussein had weapons of mass destruction as justification for war.

In Heinbecker's judgment, and seen against the accomplishments of the prime minister's predecessors, Stephen Harper has left fifty years of Canadian diplomacy in tatters, seriously damaging the country's international reputation. As a politician, this prime minister seems to look out from a kind of intellectual suburbia onto a cosmopolitan world that is poorly understood, uninteresting, and perhaps even unimportant to him except in terms of the economic opportunities it provides. It is his instinctive position. When Harper was a Reform Party MP, Preston Manning tried to broaden his acolyte's horizons by introducing him to the virgin territory of foreign affairs. Harper balked. "One thing that did surprise me about Stephen as an MP. He had no interest in international stuff," Manning told me. "We simply couldn't get him to travel."[3]

Perhaps it was Harper's parochial bent; perhaps it was a deeply ingrained mistrust of international politics, diplomacy, or leaders with different views than himself. Whatever the reason, soon after winning his majority government in 2011, Stephen Harper became the proverbial skunk at the diplomatic garden party.

Harper's support for the Likud government of Israeli prime minister Benjamin Netanyahu had always been unconditional. But armed now with his new majority, the prime minister took a deep stride into international isolation in May 2011 at the G8 Summit in Deauville, France. Like many of his fellow veteran diplomats, Heinbecker was stunned by what the prime minister did: "He took the unbelievable decision to block President Obama's statement in the draft communiqué from the G-8 that the starting point for Israeli/Palestinian peace negotiations would be the 1967 borders. We vetoed that. It may have gone down well in Tel Aviv. It didn't go down well in Washington."

Seven months later, the prime minister used the power afforded by his majority to take a contrarian position on what is arguably the greatest issue of the age: global warming and climate change. Despite the scientific evidence calling for a concerted global effort to reduce carbon emissions before planetary warming becomes irreversible, Canada became the first country in the world to withdraw from the Kyoto Protocol. Kyoto was a legally binding international agreement signed and ratified by Canada that committed industrialized countries to reducing their carbon emissions to 1990 levels by 2020. Canadian politicians, NGOs, and diplomats including Heinbecker had been deeply involved in crafting the original agreement. The Harper government left their work in pieces. The entire climate change division within Foreign Affairs was axed. In the words of Green Party leader Elizabeth May, Stephen Harper was turning Canada into "the North Korea of the Environment."

The prime minister's official reason for breaking the treaty was financial. The Harper government claimed it would cost Canada $14 billion in penalties to remain in Kyoto because the country simply could not meet the binding emission targets imposed under the agreement. Rona Ambrose, the first Tory through the revolving door of Harper environment ministers, warned of exactly that in 2006.

But Russia and Japan both showed that the financial penalty could be avoided without withdrawing from the Kyoto Protocol by simply not renewing the treaty. The more likely reason Canada opted out of Kyoto was to avoid the requirement of filing annual reports. Such reports would show the country going the wrong way on greenhouse gas emissions—the inevitable outcome of aggressively expanding Alberta's tar sands, arguably the raison d'être of the Harper government.

The world's reaction was instant and unequivocal: Canada was pilloried by France, India, Japan, China, and South Africa for reneging on the only international agreement that had a hope of reducing carbon emissions. What made Canada's retro-thinking even harder to stomach was that Stephen Harper was pushing tar sands oil onto all and sundry, including emerging economies. At the same time, the prime minister had zero interest in helping emerging economies pay for new, lower-emission technology, as Kyoto required.

Not only had Stephen Harper broken Canada's word, he was adding to the problem of greenhouse gases and actively encouraging others to join this potentially catastrophic enterprise. The Harper government was pressuring European countries not to "discriminate" against measurably and undeniably dirtier tar sands oil in establishing their fuel quality standards. Harper's strategy leaned heavily on Ezra Levant's book *Ethical Oil,* in which Levant imputed an "ethical" component to tar sands oil. The spin played like divine revelation to the hundreds of fans of Sun TV. But it was an absurd proposition that was dead on arrival in any place where citizens still had a critical-thinking capacity and scientists were not under the government's thumb.

But that didn't stop the prime minister from relentlessly lobbying in the United States to force through the Keystone XL

Pipeline project, warning President Obama that Canada "would not take no for an answer." From promises of security of supply to assurances of job creation, hyperbole and bullying were at the core of the Harper government's sales pitch. As former prime minister Joe Clark observed, Canada had adopted an "almost adolescent tone" in dealing with others. Given what Harper had done to the Americans at Deauville, it was a very odd tactic to demand the "right" answer from President Obama.

The new facts on the ground made Harper's tactless hard sell even more objectionable. Oil production was booming in the US, with new technologies such as shale fracking holding out the real possibility that Americans might soon achieve their own security of supply—without having to resort to Canada's tar sands crude. The situation has changed so dramatically in the last few years that legislators such as Senator Lisa Murkowski of Alaska are lobbying the Obama administration to lift the forty-year ban on US exports of crude oil.

However boisterously the prime minister of Canada over-sold his hand, US authorities dismissed his baseless claim that Keystone XL would create "hundreds of thousands of jobs." The State Department set the actual number of jobs at forty-two thousand for the two-year construction period, if you included jobs for suppliers, lodging and food services, and other jobs related to construction. After that, the 2,700-kilometre (1,700-mile) pipeline would virtually run itself, a fact that left President Obama under-whelmed by the Harper hustle. During a jobs speech in Tennessee on July 30, 2013, the president said, "They keep on talking about this—an oil pipeline coming down from Canada that's estimated to create 50 permanent jobs. That's not a jobs plan."[4]

In addition to fictionalizing the benefits of Keystone XL, Harper also played the political skinflint. He offered Obama no assurances on reducing the carbon footprint of the Alberta tar sands. Without such a promise, the US president was left with nothing to mollify the Democratic Party's environmental supporters, even if he were inclined to approve the pipeline. The Harper government has been promising emission controls on the oil and gas sectors for seven years. The regulations were due to be in place in 2013, but just before Christmas of that year, the prime minister made a present to energy industry lobbyists of a further delay in regulating the oil patch.

At every opportunity since it abandoned the Kyoto agreement, the Harper government has undermined any global effort to come up with a new climate accord. Even the alternative pledges on reducing carbon emissions made by Canada at Copenhagen were egregiously broken. In the words of former diplomat Daryl Copeland, the Harper government's botching of the environment file had made Canada the "idiot boy" of the climate change crisis. In this year's report by the Washington-based Centre for Global Development, Canada ranked dead last among twenty-seven wealthy nations in protection of the environment.

In his dealings with President Obama, the prime minister was playing his favourite game—having it all his way. It was an attitude that perfectly suited his world view. At best, the rest of the planet was a collection of potential customers, a grid for working out free-trade deals, and a pool of alliances of doubtful morality but undeniable political benefit. At worst, Harper was simply not interested in the wider world, as Preston Manning observed at an earlier stage of his career. If the PM were concerned about Canada's increasing isolation on the international scene, a condition driven by his obsession with the interests of his corporate constituency, you would never know it from what happened in March 2013.

In the wake of a story from the Canadian Press, the Harper government grudgingly confirmed in Parliament that Canada was also withdrawing from the United Nations convention established to fight drought, principally but not exclusively in Africa. As with many of his decisions, Harper made the move quietly if not surreptitiously, informing neither Parliament nor the UN of Canada's decision to withdraw from the agreement until the story was broken by CP.

The rest of the world saw encroaching deserts as an urgent issue, touching as it did on the problems of famine and poverty. But Canada's foreign minister, John Baird, characterized the global effort as a fruitless "talkfest" that spent too much taxpayers' money on bureaucracy. (Baird was not so concerned about taxpayers' money when he and six friends used Canada's London embassy for a free, eight-day holiday in 2012,[5] prompting the NDP's Paul Dewar to call the foreign affairs minister a "freeloader." The previous New Year's Eve, Baird had holidayed without charge in the Canadian Consul in New York.) The amount in question, required to support the drought convention between 2010 and 2012 was $238,000. Meanwhile, the Harper government spent more than a hundred times that amount commemorating the War of 1812.

In classic Harper-government fashion, Baird refused to take any questions about quitting the drought convention, referring reporters to the Canadian International Development Agency (CIDA). There was irony in his deflection. A week before, Canada's foreign-aid agency had been swallowed up by the Department of Foreign Affairs and International Trade. The loss of its independence conferred a new role on CIDA. It would not be dealing solely with development to alleviate poverty in underdeveloped nations. It would now play a supporting role in international trade deals—and not necessarily in poor countries. Foreign aid, it seemed, was now tied to doing business with your "benefactor."

Another dubious novelty about the Harper government's view of CIDA was that, according to critics such as University of

Ottawa professor Stephen Brown, the agency was being used, in effect, to pay for the social and environmental damage of mining abroad by highly profitable Canadian resource companies. Firms such as Barrick Gold and Rio Tinto Alcan created so-called "corporate social responsibility projects" in tandem with aid agencies, often establishing them near mining projects. Regardless of the spin, the aim was obvious: to have Canadian taxpayers underwrite some of the costs of private Canadian companies operating in foreign countries.

In an interview with the *Ottawa Citizen*, Professor Brown called it "scandalous" that foreign-aid dollars, getting scarcer by the year under Harper, were subsidizing poor Canadian corporate practice. (According to Daryl Copeland, under Harper $377 million in cuts had been made to CIDA and another $314.5 million to DFAIT.) Why shouldn't the companies who were doing all the damage and making all the profits pay for their own misdeeds? It was yet another example of the Harper government allowing big business to socialize its costs and privatize its profits, this time at the expense of Canada's foreign-aid program.

The country's reputation was beginning to take a beating. Canada had been odd man out at the G8 meeting on Middle East peace talks and the first to withdraw from Kyoto. Ottawa had broken its pledge on emission reductions made in Copenhagen, and had become the only state out of 193 countries to quit the UN drought convention. Canada was now using foreign aid to subsidize the damaging consequences of mining[6] abroad by Canadian resource giants. And these weren't the only blemishes on the government's often shabby foreign policy; the list was long and dumbfounding to Ambassador Heinbecker.

In 2009, Canada imposed visa restrictions on visitors from Mexico. "How could we have blundered into the Mexico visa fiasco?" Heinbecker asks. "These are our North American free trade partners. How could we betray people who stood in the immigration line according to our law and then tell them their applications have been erased but they are welcome to start all over again?" He is also aghast at Harper's tactics in the United Arab Emirates:

> We showed tremendous incompetence with the United Arab Emirates. For nine years they allow us to use Camp Mirage as a staging area for our troops going back to Afghanistan. This was no small risk to them, affording a base to people who were going to fly out and go fight Muslims. They ask us for more commercial flights into Canada and we say no. The prime minister goes to Europe and lectures them on their financial crisis. He makes derogatory judgments on the Iranians. He sends the message that it is all right with Canada if those threatening Iran use military force. No other prime minister made those kinds of statements. In my books, that is just irresponsible. Their whole foreign policy comes down to the four 'I's': inexperience, ignorance, incompetence, and ideology.

Even when the issue was literally motherhood, the Harper government dropped the ball with its international partners. Out of the G8 meeting in 2010, Canada spearheaded a worthy effort to improve maternal health and reduce early childhood death in poor countries. The government announced (and re-announced in 2013) a financial commitment of $3 billion over five years to support mothers and children in poor nations. Harper's G8 colleagues liked the idea, until Harper's then foreign affairs minister, Lawrence Cannon (now ambassador to France), told a House of Commons committee that the maternal health initiative "does not deal in any way, shape or form with family planning." Both the United States and Britain rebuked the absurd restriction. In less than a week, Prime Minister Harper had to disavow statements from two of his own cabinet ministers and declared a compromise position that he hoped would satisfy his political base: the maternal and child health initiative would fund contraception but not abortion. He was still not prepared to offer the full spectrum of reproductive health services that Canadian women have enjoyed since the 1988 Supreme Court of Canada decision that struck down the country's abortion law as unconstitutional under Section 7 of the Charter of Rights and Freedoms.

Stephen Harper's knack for upsetting his international colleagues has not gone unnoticed. Four former Canadian prime ministers have openly panned the Harper government's foreign policy, including two Progressive Conservatives, Joe Clark and Kim Campbell. All of them saw more deeply into the consequences of poorly-thought-out foreign policy than Harper or his foreign ministers.

Walking away from the drought convention, for example, was only part of a profoundly more important story: the decision to shift the country's diplomatic and development efforts from Africa to South America. Interestingly, the shift was made just at the time Ottawa was negotiating free-trade deals in South America. A lot of critics, including Paul Heinbecker, saw such a diplomatic realignment as both a short- and long-term disaster in the making. "Leaving Africa is a monumental mistake for Canada," says Heinbecker. "It is no longer the basket case of the planet. Huge strides are being taken there, including education for women and girls on an unprecedented scale. This place is going to be a planetary powerhouse. It will become the world's most populous place. And we will be dealt out."

It was an analysis I had heard before. Former prime minister Paul Martin told me that he found it morally and economically irresponsible to pull back from engagement with Africa as the Harper government was doing. It was undeniably true that Africa would have the largest agglomeration of people on the planet by 2050—a continental population estimated at two billion. Martin also believed that the world has a big stake in the outcomes of national experiments in North and Sub-Saharan Africa. If countries like Canada don't engage in the battle to close the gap between great wealth and crushing poverty in places like the Democratic Republic of the Congo, the result will be heavily armed, failed states foisting junta-governance on their own peoples and presenting a threat to global peace. Martin was appalled.

"The Harper government's African policy is incomprehensible," he told me, ". . . they walked away from decades of Canadian governments building a bridgehead to Africa. . . . Throughout Canada's history, governments of differing political stripes have succeeded each other. The tendency has been to build on the successes of previous governments." Martin believes that in the case of Africa, the Harper government has abandoned the constructive policies of both the Liberal and Progressive Conservative governments before them. "The Canadian perspective has always believed it can be a player in fostering social justice and economic development. That has been Canadian policy since the time of my father, Paul Martin Senior," said Martin. "Now Stephen Harper says we've paid enough attention to Africa and it's time to shift Canada's focus to South America. Why does he think the two are mutually exclusive? Canada has always been involved in both Africa and Latin America, and so we should be. Now the Conservatives have marginalized Canada's reputation in both."

A hint as to what lay behind this remarkable shift in Canadian diplomacy emerged in the fall of 2012. A Foreign Affairs document was leaked to Greg Weston, a CBC journalist. In it, departmental officials urged the government to drop its traditional diplomatic posture and concentrate on economic relations in emerging economic powerhouses. The document contained little mention of human rights, peace and security, international aid, or Canada's long-standing reputation as a once-respected "honest broker."

The Harper government brushed off the well-documented story with the standard lines: it doesn't respond to unauthorized leaks, and the document was not government policy. But just over a year later, international trade minister Ed Fast announced the new thrust of the Canadian foreign service. It aligned perfectly with the leaked document: "economic diplomacy." Canada's foreign service officers were now going to be travelling salespeople pushing economic ties in Asia and South America.

Meanwhile, their colleagues in more traditional postings weren't going to be plying their profession out of the usual addresses. A vast, diplomatic yard sale was in the works, with former finance minister Jim Flaherty the chief auctioneer. Flaherty had pored over a list of the two thousand properties owned by the federal government abroad and realized this was low-hanging fruit in his quest to balance the budget. Priceless assets were being sold off for short-term political gain.

The process had actually begun with the sale of Strathmore, the Canadian ambassador to Ireland's residence on the outskirts of Dublin, a deal done in the second Harper minority against the better judgment of former ambassador to Ireland Michael Phillips. He called the sale "a big mistake." Another former ambassador, Robert Fowler, agreed. "It's a pretty sad statement about Canada's position in the world," he told reporter Randy Boswell in the *Ottawa Citizen*.

Canada's diplomatic downsizing accelerated with the sale of the home of the Canadian high commissioner to the UK at One Grosvenor Square in Mayfair. Steeped in history, Macdonald House was purchased by an Indian real estate developer for $530 million. The Harper government served notice that it will also be selling the Canadian embassy at 35–37 Avenue Montaigne and the Canadian Mission to UNESCO, both addresses in central Paris. Two official residences in Brussels and another in Oslo are also on the block.

It would be easy for the Europeans to see the real estate offload as a sign that Canada wasn't quite as interested in the EU as it once was. In mid-2012, when the EU was struggling with its financial crisis, the majority of G20 countries agreed to contribute money to the International Monetary Fund to prevent a financial collapse in Europe that would have far-reaching implications for the entire world. The Harper government was odd man out again, saying no to any European bailout. "This prime minister will not force hard-working Canadian taxpayers to bail out sumptuous Euro welfare-state countries and the wealthy bankers that lend to them," the ever-diplomatic Conservative MP Pierre Poilievre said in the House of Commons.

All told, as reported by John Ivison in the *National Post*, the Harper government plans to sell forty official residences around the world. The justification was supposed to be a search for efficiencies by putting more Canadian agencies and missions under a single roof. But to diplomats watching their profession being retooled by foreign affairs dilettantes and childish name-callers, it was clear that the Harper government didn't have much respect for the role and traditions of the foreign service.

All doubt was removed when 1,350 foreign service officers went on strike in April 2013 over the revolutionary concept of equal pay for work of equal value. By the numbers, their union, the Professional Association of Foreign Service Officers (PAFSO), had a strong case. In some instances, out-of-country diplomats were being paid as much as $14,000 per year less than colleagues who were doing the same work in Ottawa. PAFSO had been principled but not pushy about its demands. Its members had been without a contract for almost two years, and on April 2, 2013, they resorted to work-to-rule campaigns. The rotating work stoppages turned into the longest strike in federal public service history.

The Harper government did not cover itself in glory in the six-month war of nerves between employer and employee. The Tories got personal, a standard tactic when dealing with opponents. Treasury Board president Tony Clement portrayed Canadian diplomats as the coddled elite of government service, implying that they were perpetually hunched over champagne and caviar, showered with perquisites, and protected into old age with gold-plated pensions.

A lot of serving and former foreign service officers bristled at Clement's pejorative portrayal, seeing it as further proof that the Harper government didn't respect their profession and hadn't noticed that since 9/11, diplomacy wasn't all cummerbunds and canapés. One of them was Ken Taylor, the legendary ambassador to Tehran who in 1979 spirited six American embassy employees out of the country during the Iran hostage crisis. Taylor decried Clement's portrayal of diplomats as lucky to have their cushy jobs, and countered that today's foreign service officers are, if anything, underpaid. As for Clement's tactics in blackening diplomats in the eyes of taxpayers, Taylor was blunt: "I find that a mischievous approach."

Clement was nothing if not full of mischief. Despite the public reproach from Canadian diplomatic royalty, Clement continued to slag Canada's diplomats in the press and the social media. It was, he insisted, all about protecting the taxpayer. That was a tough sell coming from the man whose government broke all the rules in its G8 and G20 spending—according to interim auditor general John Wiersema, a government that may also have broken the law. Perhaps Clement thought that the public had forgotten that the Harper government ignored established protocols for approving infrastructure grants, including $50 million worth of gazebos, public washrooms, and sidewalk upgrades in his Parry Sound–Muskoka riding.

As the auditor general pointed out in his report, he was "very concerned" that there was zero documentation to explain how the Conservatives selected those thirty-two municipal projects in Clement's riding. He was equally troubled by the fact that Parliament approved the spending only after being told by the Harper government that the special infrastructure fund would be used to reduce "border congestion." That at least should have been an easy problem to fix. Parry Sound is 340 kilometres from the border.

With a blatant appeal to the Conservative base, Tony Clement advised the diplomats to go back to work because the government's offer wouldn't be sweetened. It was an uncompromising stance designed to set the tone for the comprehensive negotiations with public servants coming up in 2014—Stephen Harper versus the unions. Clement famously assured the striking diplomats that he was firm in his position and wouldn't "fold like a $3 suitcase."

Predictably, the relationship worsened. During the strike, the government snooped on the email of union members, and even punished temporary workers if they were perceived to be participating in the strike. From the president of the Treasury Board on down the line, government played a vindictive hand to the end, refusing to attend PAFSO's annual awards dinner where outstanding foreign service officers were recognized for their service to the country in a sometimes very dangerous occupation.

In the end, Tony Clement folded like a $10 suitcase. The Harper government gave the striking diplomats roughly half of what they had been holding out for, but not until the Public Service Labour Relations Board found that Minister Clement had bargained in bad faith with the union. The cost to government of fully meeting the union's wage demands was set by Tim Edwards, PAFSO's president, at $4.2 million over three years. The cost to the economy of the six-month labour disruption was estimated at a billion dollars. With no visas being issued, Canadian universities and the tourism industry, both benefiting greatly from foreign clientele, suffered the most. It was a heavy price for the Harper government to inflict on the country in the name of reassuring its base that it hated unions as much they did.

It was the nasty new world of Canadian foreign policy, largely the product of the navel-gazing ruminations of a single man: Prime Minister Stephen Harper. Canada's approach to the world was no longer being driven by a professional diplomatic corps with a depth of experience and knowledge, and a commitment to public diplomacy and soft power. It was in the hands of a quixotic and inexperienced neophyte whose judgments and edicts were often inconsistent and contradictory.

Prime Minister Harper was one of two leaders (the prime minister of Mauritius was the other) to boycott the Commonwealth Conference in Sri Lanka in 2013, ostensibly over a concern for human rights and the unconstitutional manner in which that country's chief justice had been removed from office. Yet Harper attended the Francophonie Summit in the Democratic Republic of the Congo, where horrendous human-rights violations were taking place in a country that has become a stranger to the rule of law. The prime minister claimed that he had not travelled to the DRC to "excuse" the atrocities being committed in that African country but to "spotlight" them. But if that were so, why not attend the Commonwealth Conference in Sri Lanka to "spotlight" his concerns about Colombo's undermining of human rights and democracy?

It all came down to one man's personal judgment of longstanding international conundrums. Not understanding them, and not interested in the advice of his diplomatic corps the way Brian Mulroney and Jean Chrétien had been, he reduced complex international situations to comic-book proportions and Sunday-school solutions. In the case of Sri Lanka, there may also have been a political calculation—as there usually is with this prime minister.

Toronto's sizable Tamil population—between twenty-nine thousand if you believe Statistics Canada and two hundred thousand if you trust expert academics and the *Toronto Star*—was no doubt delighted that the PM refused to go to Sri Lanka, where they had once been persecuted. Their gratitude may well be expressed at the polls in 2015.[7]

Like the Commonwealth Conference, another thing Prime Minister Harper decided he could do without was Ottawa's Canadian studies program abroad. The program had been set up forty years ago as part of a public diplomacy effort to promote Canada's brand abroad. Its $5-million annual budget supported Canada-focused projects by foreign scholars, graduate students, and researchers. The return has been impressive. There are now Canadian studies programs in fifty countries. According to Patrick James, president of the International Council for Canadian Studies, Ottawa's $5-million investment translates into $200 million in spending on Canadian studies globally. Though some found his number high, the Canadian Press obtained a 2010 internal report from Foreign Affairs showing that the government realized a fourteenfold return from its annual $5-million investment.

Still, the bland notice on the program's website that announced its demise was not totally unexpected. In 2008, the Harper government renamed the program "Understanding Canada." It should have been called "Understanding Harper's Canada." From that point forward, foreign applicants with Canadian projects in mind would have to confine their research to priority policy areas established by the Harper government—one of the faster ways to turn off inquiring minds.

WITH ALL THE momentous changes to the country's diplomacy under the Harper government, I asked Paul Heinbecker what has been the greatest difference in the way Canada now meets the world.

"The biggest difference between Harper and his predecessors when it comes to foreign policy is that he believes it should be fought out on moral grounds," Heinbecker replied, referring to a statement Harper made in 2003. "But for some reason, the moral argument did not extend to the Palestinians. We became blind in one eye, a pretty major change when we present ourselves internationally as principled and fair-minded."

"Blind in one eye" is an apt description of much of Stephen Harper's foreign policy, but occasionally the blindness has been total. The Harper government couldn't find its moral compass when Egypt's new democracy was overthrown in a bloody military coup in August 2013. While hundreds of protesters were being shot dead in the same Cairo Square where Hosni Mubarak's police state came to an end, the prime minister of Canada was silent. He was silent when the junta arrested the democratically elected leader of the country, Mohammed Morsi, threw its political opponents in jail, and ultimately declared the Muslim Brotherhood a terrorist organization.[8]

And while the Harper government had nothing to say when a resident of Canada was shot dead while opposing Egypt's violent coup by the military, Canada's foreign affairs minister, John Baird, did condemn the shooting of a Coptic Christian priest—a message he knew would resonate with the Conservative Party's religious political base. As for the religious freedom of hundreds of thousands of Muslim supporters of Mohammed Morsi, again, the Harper government was silent.

When it came to China, it looked at first as if Stephen Harper had his moral compass firmly in hand while framing Canada's relationship with the economic giant. Back in 2006, Harper not only routinely lectured China on its abysmal human-rights record, he pledged that he would never sell out Canadian values for economic returns. Talking to reporters from the Canadian Press en route to the Asia-Pacific talks in Vietnam, Harper said, "I think Canadians want us to promote trade relations worldwide, and we do that, but I don't think Canadians want us to sell out important Canadian values. They don't want us to sell that out to the almighty dollar."

The almighty yuan was another matter. In 2012, Canadians, including the prime minister's bewildered political base, saw a pro–Communist China Harper government make a series of secretive, mega-deals with Beijing. The trend had already begun in 2010 when Sinopec, the giant Chinese petroleum and chemical company, plunked down $4.6 billion to buy a 9 percent stake in Syncrude. There was more to the deal than met the eye, as author Andrew Nikiforuk reported.

Along with a big piece of the tar sands, Asia's largest refiner now had the right to veto whether Syncrude refined bitumen in Canada or shipped it abroad "like a good global coolie." The then industry minister, Tony Clement, who took a rickshaw ride to tour the new $2.5 million Bethune Museum in Gravenhurst, applauded the deal as a "net benefit" to Canada, though just exactly what was in the net he never explained. None of it played well with the Conservative base, from the Chinese national anthem blaring from speakers to the minister's choice of a rickshaw for transportation.[9]

The Sinopec deal paled beside what came next. In December 2012, the Harper government approved the mammoth $15.1-billion takeover of the Calgary-based Canadian resource company Nexen. The buyer was the state-owned China National Offshore Oil Corporation Ltd. (CNOOC). It was easily the biggest overseas purchase ever by a Chinese government—and the most controversial sale approved by a Canadian government. The champions of unrestricted free enterprise had just sold a valuable Canadian asset to a state entity of a totalitarian regime.

Many argued that the Nexen deal was a grave risk to Canadian sovereignty against uncertain returns. It was done against the backdrop of the Canada/China Foreign Investment Protection and Promotion Agreement (FIPPA) personally signed by Stephen Harper in September 2012. FIPPA gives China the right to sue Canada for unlimited damages if domestic laws by any level of government harm the value of Chinese investment.

This special "investor arbitration" provision is conducted in courts outside the country and behind closed doors. Its findings trump Canadian law and the provision is far from theoretical; the Chinese have already used investor arbitration against other "partners" such as Australia to the tune of millions in cash compensation.

The advantage to the Chinese of the Nexen deal was clear: ownership of a resource it would need to power its industrial machine. The advantage to Canada is another story. When the then industry minister, Christian Paradis, was asked about Nexen's "net benefit" to this country, he told reporters it was a matter of corporate confidentiality. Canadians would have to have the benefits of their own government's policies explained to them by the Chinese. Paradis's words were at quite a distance from the Canadian values the prime minister once said he wouldn't sell out.

As for the prime minister, he did what he always does when the facts are not flattering: he makes up new ones. Speaking in the House of Commons under withering cross-examination from Opposition leader Thomas Mulcair, Harper claimed that the "vast majority" of Canadians liked the Nexen deal. The polls told a different story. Just 16 percent of Canadians liked it, according to EKOS, 12 percent by Angus Reid's numbers, and just 8 percent in an Abacus Data survey. Evidence never had much weight with the prime minister once he had made up his mind—one of the reasons few people argued with him.

Setting aside the economic implications of these secretive mega-deals, a fundamental rule of foreign policy had been violated. Once policy is set, Canada's strategy has been to follow the position until changes on the ground require an adjustment to the playbook. The Harper government changed the policy toward China when, if anything, it was plunging ever more deeply into totalitarian darkness. It was not a diplomatic move, rewarding the Chinese leadership for improving its human-rights record, but a nakedly political one ignoring Beijing's transgressions in exchange for cash. And it was plainly laid out in the Foreign Affairs draft document leaked to the CBC. "To succeed," its authors wrote, "we will need to pursue political relationships in tandem with economic interests even where political interests or values may not align."

For Conservative values, China poses the mother of all alignment problems. The authoritarian one-party state has sharp curbs on freedom of speech and association. There is no freedom of religion, no free press, and a blunt rejection of judicial independence. Extra-judicial persecution of anyone seen as "an enemy of the state" is commonplace, as is the brutal repression of ethnic minorities in places such as Inner Mongolia and the Xinjiang Uyghur Autonomous Region in northwestern China. The language and cultural rights of Xinjiang's ten million Uyghurs, who happen to be Muslim, are being stamped out with China's push for cultural "standardization." In other places, it goes by another name, something that NATO went to war over in Kosovo: ethnic cleansing.

In February 2011, the Chinese Communist government began a crackdown on human-rights lawyers, internet activists, and public critics. Beijing rounded up thirty of China's most prominent pro-democracy advocates and simply made them "disappear." Chinese literary critic Liu Xiaobo became a political prisoner in Jinzhou for the high crime of calling for political reforms, including the end of one-party rule. Beijing placed world-renowned artist and pro-democracy activist Ai Weiwei under arrest for eighty-one days without charges.

China's violations of human rights are widespread. It bans unions; women's reproductive rights are trampled with forced abortions; and Chinese citizens (like Canadians under our own government) are under surveillance. Tibet remains under siege and the Falun Gong are brutally repressed. The Chinese government hosted Sudanese president Omar al Bashir, despite a warrant for his arrest by the International Criminal Court for war crimes, crimes against humanity, and genocide. And at the UN, Beijing has used its veto three times to prevent Security Council action against Syrian president Bashar al Assad. This is Stephen Harper's business partner, a country that has been called the largest criminal enterprise on the planet.

As for one of the world's longest-running tragedies, there is no Canadian diplomatic position on the Israeli–Palestinian conflict—just unconditional support for one side, implacable opposition to the other. It is a "moral" judgment with political benefits that ignores the real lives of millions of stateless people. If Canada were the judge in this case, it would have to recuse itself, so unquestioning is the Harper government's support of Netanyahu and Likud. That position doesn't reflect the traditional Canadian approach—two ears, two eyes, and a single goal—to reach a peace deal that will see a viable state for the Palestinians and recognition and security for Israel.[10]

During the Harper years, the honest broker has become the rabid partisan—one of the reasons that for the first time in sixty years the world chose a bankrupt Portugal over an economically strong Canada to sit on the UN Security Council in 2010. Former mentor and Reform Party leader Preston Manning explained to me part of Harper's aversion to diplomacy and his preference for extreme partisanship—a short route to the wrong side of history in this momentous standoff: "I tried to keep a more even hand than Stephen has. I thought that somewhere down the road

Canada would play a broker's role in gaining peace. I think he saw that as weakness or wishy-washy. He said that you can't be friends with everybody and the other side didn't respect us for our middle of the road position. I think Canada's influence internationally has been diminished with Stephen's approach."

ONE OF THE greatest changes Stephen Harper has made to Canada's foreign policy touches the United Nations. Since its creation, the UN has been at the heart of global diplomacy. Canada has been an ardent supporter and crafted its foreign policy around membership in the place it helped to create—until now. Stephen Harper sees the United Nations as the castle of weak nations that turned to multilateralism as a substitute for real national authority. After winning his majority government, Harper couldn't have made his disdain for the UN more obvious.

Three times now he has passed up addressing new sessions of the UN General Assembly, once so that he could attend the return of Tim Hortons corporate headquarters to Canada. On the other occasions he was in New York, but busied himself with other official duties, making his disrespect for the UN perfectly clear. It was all part of the rebranding of the country, Harper-style.

"Stephen Harper doesn't have a clue what the UN is about," Paul Heinbecker told me. "His view tends to be the West is always right, and the UN should always do what the West wants. Harper doesn't understand that this organization is run by its members. The secretary-general can't do a thing when the members disagree."

Prime Minister Harper's bungling in the world of Big League diplomacy was on full display in the tentative yet still historic détente between the United States and Iran in 2013. The interim accord was signed not just by the United States and Iran, but also by Britain, France, Germany, Russia, and China. Instead of joining the plan to draw Tehran back into the world's mainstream economy—in return for no less a prize than getting a verifiable pledge not to develop nuclear weapons—Canada was sidelined by its own policies. The year before, in September 2012, the Harper government had closed the Canadian embassy in Tehran, a move the Iranian government called "hostile, unwise, and unconventional." Parroting the message that was coming out of Tel Aviv, the prime minister and his cabinet ministers were full of skepticism and poisonous portrayals of the Iranian leadership.

It was reminiscent of Stephen Harper's earlier remarks about Iran, in which he said the Iranian government was lying about its nuclear program and wouldn't hesitate to use nuclear weapons if it had them. Mimicking Benjamin Netanyahu, he declared that Iran was the greatest threat to world peace, stopping just short of endorsing a pre-emptive strike on Tehran's nuclear facilities.

Harper's sabre-rattling earned him an oblique reproof from President Obama, who noted that "loose talk" about war was not helpful. In an interview with Peter Mansbridge, Harper even implied that investigators from the IAEA had proof that Iran was developing a bomb—it was just a matter of how long it would take to finish the job. The politician who had rushed to foolhardy misjudgment in the case for war against Iraq was doing it again—and again, the facts were not on the prime minister's side.

The White House, the Pentagon, American and Israeli intelligence, and the IAEA had all come to the same conclusion based on the evidence: Iran does not have a nuclear weapon, is not building one, and has not decided to build one. What it does have is a civilian nuclear program that leaves that possibility open. While Stephen Harper inveighed against the dangerous theocrats running Iran, the chief of the Israeli military, General Benny Gantz, offered a more measured view in April 2012. "Iran is going step by step to the place where it will be able to decide whether to manufacture a nuclear bomb. It hasn't gone that extra mile. I don't think

Iran's Supreme Leader will want to go that extra mile. I think the Iranian leadership is composed of very rational people."

As the shadows get longer in Paul Heinbecker's garden, the talk turns to Stephen Harper's diplomatic legacy. It is a short conversation. "Pearson and Mulroney were giants on the international scene, Heinbecker says. "Trudeau got the world interested in Canada because he was so dynamic. So far there are no big achievements I can think of that the Harper government can claim unless you count war."

These days the prime minister doesn't talk much about his wars—the one he used to call "vital" in Afghanistan, and the other one in Libya. Soldiers who survived Kandahar—158 didn't—are beginning to die by their own hand back home—enough of them to have former chief of the defence staff Rick Hillier demand a public inquiry. In September 2012, less than a year after Peter MacKay defended spending nearly a million dollars flying combat jets over Parliament Hill to celebrate victory in the Libya mission, American ambassador J. Christopher Stevens and three of his staff were murdered in Benghazi. Unknown warring factions who were supported by NATO's bombing campaign against Muammar Gaddafi have since turned the country into something resembling a failed state. Canada led the mission.

Tradition is beginning to fray as the Conservatives "rebrand" Canada. In a country where one hundred thousand members of the armed forces have served in UN missions from Cyprus to the Golan Heights, Canada now has just thirty-two soldiers wearing the blue helmet of the peacekeeper. In 2011, the Harper government tripled the amount of weapons and ammunition licensed for export—$12 billion worth of brute force. In 2010, Canada sold Saudi Arabia $35 million worth of weapons and military equipment. In 2011, the year of the Harper majority, the number was a hundred times higher, at $4 billion.

As reported by Lee Berthiaume of Postmedia News, Canadian-made LAV-3 armoured vehicles showed up on videos of the Saudi/Bahraini crackdown on pro-democracy protesters in Bahrain, where thirty demonstrators were killed and three thousand others arrested. Canada also licensed $44 billion worth of "dual purpose" exports to China, items that can be used for either peaceful or military purposes—including uranium. The biggest customer for Canadian arms is the United States. But since arms companies don't require licences to move their products across the border, no one knows how much weaponry or ammunition Canada sells to the Americans. Since dismantling the Long Gun Registry, the Harper government has four times delayed rules that would assign serial numbers to guns. Without implementing the new rule, Canada can't be in compliance with international conventions on arms smuggling.

It is also an international convention not to spy on your guests. According to top-secret documents released by American whistle-blower Edward Snowden, the Harper government gave the green light for the National Security Agency to spy on heads of state and diplomats at the G8 and G20 Summits hosted by Canada in 2010. Snowden said the Americans were assisted in the surveillance they ran out of the US embassy by the Communications Security Establishment Canada.

Though it caused understandable consternation at the time, it wasn't such a bad idea when foreign affairs minister John Baird demanded, in violation of Treasury Board rules, that the words "Lester B. Pearson Building" and "Canada" be removed from his official business cards—leaving the minister's own name as the largest printed words.

Lester Pearson wouldn't recognize what passes for diplomacy these days in the building that bears his name.

eleven

BAD BOYS

Political parties dream about supporters like Nathan Jacobson. Rich, generous, and very well connected, few businessmen were as close to the Harper government as the man who held dual citizenship in Israel and Canada, and who claimed that he had introduced Jason Kenney to Benjamin Netanyahu. Fewer still could boast of having made a fortune in post-Soviet Russia. When one sups in Vladimir Putin's house, one must have a long spoon.

The kid who had grown up poor in Winnipeg now operated at the highest levels of business and politics. The Mackenzie Institute posted a photo dated 2010 of a kibitzing Jacobson standing between Prime Ministers Harper and Netanyahu. It was posted under the caption "Members in Action." Shortly before I published a piece on Jacobson in iPolitics in September 2012, the Jacobson photo disappeared from the site, although other photos featuring members posing with Stephen Harper remained.[1]

When Jacobson's fortunes sank, the Harper PMO's reaction to the photograph was that the PM met Nathan Jacobson at a "community event" as he meets thousands of ordinary Canadians.

Ordinary is the last thing Nathan Jacobson is—nor is he the kind of man you are likely to meet at a neighbourhood corn roast. Jacobson was a star in a demographic uppermost in Stephen Harper's political mind—Canada's Jewish community. After leaving high school in Winnipeg, Jacobson served six years in the Israeli army during the 1970s, rising to the rank of Captain. Honourably discharged in 1979, he returned to Canada and settled in Toronto, taking a job with a subsidiary of IBM.

Well known for their philanthropy, Jacobson and his wife, Lindi, remained staunch backers of Israel. The couple were major sponsors of an event in September 2007 to celebrate the fortieth anniversary of the "re-unification of Jerusalem." Jacobson was also a sponsor of the Maccabi Tel Aviv football club, a franchise that Gerald Schwartz of Onex Corporation once considered buying. In October 2010, when the Royal Winnipeg Ballet celebrated its seventieth anniversary with performances in Israel, two of the major funders of the tour were Gerald Schwartz and Nathan Jacobson.

Jacobson's business acumen and philanthropy made him legendary in both Canada and Israel. He was honoured at the thirty-eighth Annual Sports Dinner in Winnipeg on June 23, 2010. "Nathan lives in Herzliya, Israel and is the current International Ambassador of Jerusalem," a local paper proudly declared. The Israeli ambassador to Canada attended. Jacobson received glowing profiles in the *Winnipeg Jewish Review*, a favourable notice in the Jewish National Fund of Canada newsletter, and praise in newspapers including the *Jerusalem Post* and *Haaretz* for his entrepreneurial brilliance.

Jacobson was busy in the world of the boardroom, too, holding positions with the Jewish National Fund, Golda Meir Hospital, and the Ukrainian Jewish Congress. He also sat on the board of Tel Aviv University (TAU) and personally funded two faculty recruitment chairs at TAU, bringing over young researchers from

Toronto. Fellow board member Sheldon Adelson is corporate royalty. In 2014, *Forbes* ranked the gambling tycoon as the eighth-
richest man in the world. Earning an average of $32 million a day,
he had a personal net worth last year pegged at $38 billion. Jacobson
and Adelson shared the same working-class roots as descendants
of immigrants from Ukraine, and both were self-made. Both have
given generously to a variety of charitable causes, and have shown
unwavering loyalty to the hard-right policies of Israeli prime minister Benjamin Netanyahu and to neo-conservative causes in their
own countries.

If Mitt Romney and the GOP couldn't imagine a better supporter than Sheldon Adelson, Stephen Harper and the
Conservative Party would have had trouble finding a more dedicated backer than Nathan Jacobson. He not only shared their ideology, he put his money where his political heart was. From 2007 to
2011, he made the maximum donation to the Conservative Party
of Canada, and also gave money to several individual Conservative
MPs and cabinet ministers, including Peter Kent, Lisa Raitt, and
Wajid Khan. The love did not go unrequited. Jacobson was a fixture at major events involving senior Harper cabinet ministers. In
May 2009, Jacobson was master of ceremonies for the sixty-first
anniversary of the founding of Israel, an event that took place in
the West Block of Parliament. He introduced the keynote speaker,
the then minister of citizenship and immigration, Jason Kenney.

The same month, Jacobson and Kenney appeared with Ezra
Levant at a private party, an event attended by the who's who of
conservative journalists, columnists, and bloggers. Guests at the
party included conservative author Mark Steyn; Stephen Taylor,
who would be appointed a director at the National Citizens
Coalition on December 7, 2010; Kevin Libin, who, while at the
Western Standard, published the controversial Danish cartoons
mocking the prophet Muhammed; Sun Media's Brian Lilley, who

would later out Michael Sona in the robocalls affair; and *National Post* columnist Father Raymond de Souza. One of the pictures posted on the internet by an attendee of the event shows Nathan Jacobson with his arm around a smiling Father de Souza.

When the then transport minister, John Baird, travelled to Israel in March 2010 to study airport security methods (principally conducting behavioural analysis to identify human threats), Nathan Jacobson was photographed with Baird at Israel's holiest site, the Western Wall. Baird and Jacobson also attended the annual ACTION party of the Canadian Jewish Political Affairs Committee (CJPAC) together that same month. Jacobson sported a T-shirt bearing the caption "Marxism" with a picture of Groucho Marx. His sense of humour and skills as a raconteur were legendary. CJPAC works to advance the interests of the Canadian Jewish community and claims it does not endorse political parties. But since the powerful committee does not have charitable status, it can be directly involved in political action.

Jacobson moved in the Jewish community's highest social circles. On December 8, 2008, Robert Lantos was honoured with an Award of Merit dinner at the Sheraton Centre in Toronto. It was put on by B'nai Brith Canada. The co-chairs were Peter Munk, chair of Barrick Gold, and Gerald Schwartz, chair of Onex Corporation. Jacobson was on the Tribute Committee, along with such luminaries as former Ontario premier David Peterson and renowned criminal lawyer Eddie Greenspan.

On May 5, 2010, Jacobson and his wife, Lindi, sponsored an event on Parliament Hill to celebrate Canada's partnership with Hebrew University of Jerusalem's Institute for Medical Research Israel–Canada, designed to conduct world-class research into prostate cancer. The event was attended by four hundred people, including MPs, senators, and six Harper cabinet ministers. Peter Kent and Tony Clement both spoke at the gathering.

On November 4, 2012, Nathan Jacobson was to have attended another glitzy event with significant social and political overtones—the Mount Carmel dinner in Toronto's Fairmont Hotel. The event was hosted by the Canadian Friends of the University of Haifa. Immigration minister Jason Kenney was to receive an honorary degree from the university. Senator Irving Gerstein, a man soon to be in the middle of the Senate expenses scandal, was master of ceremonies. The campaign chair for the event was to have been another heavy hitter: Nathan Jacobson.

That was before an extraordinary disclosure by the US Department of Justice put an end to Jacobson's life at the pinnacle of business and political elites in two countries. Though his troubles had been brewing for some time, the official date of his exit from the corridors of business and political power was July 30, 2012. It was on that day that the millionaire-philanthropist was supposed to appear for sentencing in front of a California judge. He had quietly entered a guilty plea on May 7, 2008, to charges of conspiring to commit money laundering, including processing $46 million through his credit card clearing company RX Payments Ltd. US judge Irma Gonzalez issued an arrest warrant for the convicted fugitive and Nathan Jacobson went to ground.

The investigation by US authorities had been painstaking, involving special agents from six federal agencies, including the Drug Enforcement Agency, the Federal Bureau of Investigation, and the Internal Revenue Service. Their work led to a 313-count indictment against 18 people on July 27, 2007. The individuals, including doctors and businessmen, were all involved to varying degrees with a company called Affpower. It was an internet-based prescription pharmaceutical business that generated $126 million in illegal sales of prescription pharmaceuticals before police entered the picture.

The delay in sentencing Jacobson after his guilty plea in 2008— following multiple charges of fraud, money laundering, and the distribution and dispensing of a controlled substance through an online pharmacy—is part routine and part mystery. Jacobson simply made a deal with US prosecutors, just as David Radler did in the Conrad Black case. In exchange for his cooperation in the continuing criminal investigation of Affpower, Jacobson's file was sealed. What is mysterious is that Jacobson's guilty plea was kept under wraps for four years. He had, in fact, been indicted in 2007, charged with ten criminal offences, including racketeering. A year later, he pleaded guilty to conspiracy to launder $46 million. Then due process slipped into the shadows.

Over the next several years he continued his career in the business and political stratosphere. No one apparently knew he had already been fined $4.5 million for his part in the Affpower scheme, or that he was looking at a maximum twenty-year stretch in prison when he finally stood in front of an American judge for sentencing. After his guilty plea was made public, the exits began to clog with friends, contacts, and business partners who claimed they didn't know anything about Jacobson's dealings or history, and who reduced their relationships with him to distant associations, or, as in the case of the PMO, chance acquaintanceship.

According to his office, foreign affairs minister John Baird knew Jacobson but didn't know about his legal transgressions. For some reason, foreign affairs officials neglected to tell the minister that they had stopped the appointment of Jacobson as an honorary consul after a police review of his file, and that his travelling companion had once sued CSIS. Nor, Baird's office said, did the minister meet with Jacobson during an official trip to Myanmar in March 2012. Jacobson was reportedly on a business trip to Asia, in Myanmar, when the indictment against him was unsealed by the Americans.

Jacobson's new company, Myanmar Access, was created in 2012 to develop business opportunities in Myanmar, one of the last frontiers in Asia. The company was based in the same city, Yangon, that Baird travelled to in 2012 after Canada decided to open an embassy in what was considered the third most corrupt nation on earth. Resource rich, but wracked by civil war and military rule, Myanmar was (and continues to be) the site of many human-rights violations, including child labour, human trafficking, and media censorship. (In a list of 182 nations, only North Korea and Somalia were considered more corrupt.) Baird told Myanmar opposition politician Aung San Suu Kyi, "We would love to play a bigger role in development and trade and commerce," an objective Nathan Jacobson shared. Suu Kyi wisely replied that she welcomed development aid "that is used for our people."

Treasury Board president Tony Clement's office said that Clement knew Jacobson but had no idea of his US conviction before July 30, 2012, or the activities that led to it. Former business associate Alan Bell said in a telephone interview from Toronto that he knew nothing about Jacobson's legal problems in the US. Bell and Jacobson were members of the Mackenzie Institute, and did a security evaluation of the oil sands together in 2006. When the institute rebranded its website on January 20, 2014, Alan Bell was the new president. The new site described the Mackenzie Institute as "a globally recognized Canadian-based public policy institute for research and comment on issues impacting political and social stability, specifically terrorism, organized violence, and security." It also announced something not seen on the previous site: "Working with colleagues in Washington DC, Israel, and the UK, we emphasize a world view on the various topics we cover." Canada and Israel had signed a major security agreement in 2008.

When Stephen Maher, who broke the Jacobson money-laundering story, asked the PMO for a comment, the then director of communications, Andrew MacDougall, told him, "I understand the prime minister may have met with Mr. Jacobson at a community event, as he meets thousands of Canadians from all walks of life each year." It was intended to be an official response, but it was more like the PMO's debut in stand-up comedy—unless you believe someone gets their picture taken between the prime ministers of Canada and Israel by running into them at a political barbecue.

When Netanyahu landed in Ottawa on May 30, 2010, he was met personally by Canada's foreign minister, John Baird. No one in the Harper government, including Canada's foreign minister, had apparently read the Israeli newspapers just three days before that power picture with Jacobson standing between two of the most security-conscious prime ministers in the world was taken. If they had, they would have known that *Haaretz* had run a story about a police complaint focusing on PayGea, a Canadian company controlled by Jacobson that entered the Israeli market in 2008.

That was also the year that Nathan Jacobson secretly entered his guilty plea on money-laundering charges, and the year he moved to Israel, which does not extradite its citizens. PayGea provided online services similar to Paypal Inc., but specialized in clearing payments for medicines, soft pornography, and gambling sites. It is astounding that the security forces of both Canada and Israel would have allowed a man with Jacobson's criminal conviction so close to their leaders.

On April 2, 2012, Jacobson's online clearing company abruptly halted its Israeli operations, leaving behind debts running into the millions of shekels. As one of PayGea's creditors told *Globes*,[2] a business paper in Israel, "One morning they were simply gone." So was Nathan Jacobson. A full three months before senior members of the Harper government, including John Baird and Jason Kenney, said they learned of Jacobson's self-admitted crimes with the unsealing of his US indictment, PayGea was an open scandal in Israel—a country in which both ministers had more than a passing interest and excellent contacts.

Even if Conservative cabinet ministers and the PMO didn't read the newspapers, they could have learned a lot about the man posing between the two prime ministers by looking into a lawsuit launched by Jacobson against the attorney general of Canada and various members of the Canadian Security Intelligence Agency (CSIS), Export Development Canada (EDC), and the Canadian Commercial Corporation (CCC) when the Liberals were in power. John Grisham would have found the legal twists and turns inspirational.

It all began in Russia, where Nathan Jacobson embarked on a stunning business career with the establishment of a GM dealership, extending the franchise to Ukraine and Kazakhstan. He also owned the distributorship of Philip Morris for Russia and Kazakhstan. He founded IFG Canada Ltd., an investment and development company with offices in Toronto, Calgary, Tel Aviv, Kiev, Montreal, Panama City, and Costa Rica. The company invested in technology, pharmaceuticals, financial services, real estate, and development projects. Jacobson's company The West Group Inc. built six hundred gas stations, eight fuel terminals, and two oil complexes in Russia and Ukraine. At its peak the company had eighteen hundred employees. The West Group won almost a quarter of the deals signed by a Team Canada trade delegation to Russia in 2002.

Jacobson proposed a partnership with SNC-Lavalin to build pipelines and aluminum smelters in Russia. According to *Canadian Business* magazine, he also consulted for GM, Magna Corporation, and the CIBC. Jacobson was described in the magazine as "a persistent but charming man with a huge repertoire of jokes and amusing stories." The success story changed with a bizarre lawsuit. It is not every day that someone takes Canada's domestic spy agency to court, but that is exactly what Jacobson did in 1998. The case, which dragged on until 2004, laid out serious allegations about several CSIS agents who in the mid-nineties worked on the Russian Desk of the intelligence agency.

In his lawsuit against the attorney general of Canada, which included several amended statements of claim as Jacobson gathered new information, his settlement demand went from $5 million in 1998 to $50 million by 2004, as well as $1 million in punitive damages, plus legal costs. According to Jacobson's statement of claim, a business associate was told by CSIS that "Jacobson is heavily involved in criminal activities, specifically, narcotics, representing the Russian mafia in Canada, bringing over Russian members of the mafia to Canada—and other criminal activities. Jacobson is under close scrutiny by CSIS who are planning to arrest Jacobson in the near future."

There was one other critical component to Jacobson's allegations against the Canadian government when he went to court. He claimed that not only had a false report been entered into the government's computer system by CSIS, but that the report had been shared with the Federal Security Service (FSB). The FSB is the intelligence successor in Russia to the Soviet-era KGB. This in turn led to a major and, according to Jacobson, damaging investigation into his business activities by Russian authorities. The impression was being created—falsely and maliciously, according to Jacobson—that his company, The West Group Inc., was up to no good in Russia. Jacobson alleged that this had also taken a grave toll on his private life.

In his statement of defence, the attorney general of Canada denied virtually all of Jacobson's allegations, with one exception. The AG admitted that his office had not responded to a formal complaint from Jacobson's lawyers in 1997 about the visa refusals and the alleged involvement of CSIS. The government specifically denied that a "false" report had ever been placed on its computer system by an agent, or that the alleged report had been shared with

Russian intelligence. It also denied that two other CSIS agents named in the action had defamed Jacobson to a potential business partner. The AG went on to raise the issue of security certificates, the legal tool of choice in national security matters to withhold or redact documents, in an attempt to block Jacobson's access to information. Jacobson objected to the government's motion and battled on.

The action moved at a snail's pace, with the government opposing Jacobson's multiple amended statements of claim and missing agreed-upon dates for providing documents. Pending the outcome of mediation, the stage was set for a bombshell court case pitting one of Canada's leading businessmen against the domestic spy agency and several Crown corporations—all of it to be played out on the centre stage of the Canadian media universe, Toronto.

And then, nearly six years after it had begun, Jacobson's lawsuit was dismissed without costs on a motion brought by the plaintiff and agreed to by the defendant. The case was settled out of court, though no record of a settlement could be found on the public accounts under either government departments or lawyers of record. Nathan Jacobson's allegations against CSIS, EDB, and CCC were never established in court, nor were the attorney general's blanket denials of any wrongdoing that caused harm to Jacobson's business operations. Since CSIS and the other Crown agencies involved in the action were blameless, Nathan Jacobson wasn't entitled to a dime of damages—or so the government argued.

Former justice minister Rob Nicholson's office declined to comment on the settlement, claiming that inquiries should be directed to the lead agency in the matter, CSIS. CSIS spokesperson Tahera Mufti told me the terms of the settlement were "confidential" and suggested an alternative source: Nathan Jacobson. Of course.

Notwithstanding the murkiness in which the lawsuit was resolved, Jacobson got right back to business before the legal dust settled. By May 2004, newspapers in Israel were reporting about the dynamic businessman's latest venture, an online pharmacy called MagenDavidMeds.com. The idea was to sell drugs manufactured in the United States or Israel to American consumers at prices up to 70 percent lower than at their neighbourhood pharmacy. Jacobson's marketing focused on Jewish community media. He personally regarded the new business as a "social and Zionist mission." Many of his elderly customers faced a choice of buying medication, turning down the heat, or going without a hot meal. The whiz kid from Winnipeg was determined to give them another option by becoming a kind of pharmaceutical Robin Hood.

Not everyone was thrilled with his new business adventure. The US Food and Drug Administration frowned on Jacobson's venture, arguing that his company couldn't guarantee the safety of the imported drugs and charging that the businessman had simply taken advantage of the "Canadian niche"—the price gap between the cost of a particular drug in Canada and in the United States, where pharmaceutical prices are market-driven.

And another new direction appealed to this Canadian entrepreneur: the security business. Jacobson's long-running battle with the attorney general of Canada—which featured a confession that he had made regular payments to a CSIS agent—didn't appear to limit his extraordinary access to some of the most sensitive intelligence issues in Canada. In March 2006, three months after Stephen Harper became prime minister, Jacobson was given permission to do a four-day, independent security assessment of the tar sands with a team of experts paid for and provided by Jacobson himself. The six-member team included Alan Bell, former British SAS officer and president of Toronto-based Globe Risk Holdings; James G. Liddy, the son of Watergate's Gordon Liddy, and a former leader of the US Navy's Antiterrorism Assessment Team; and Alon Moritiz, an Israeli computer expert.

Bell had already designed security protocols and armed tactical teams for Ontario's nuclear reactors. He wasn't impressed with what he saw in Alberta: "You can't have a $9-an-hour security guard protecting this kind of asset," he told the *Edmonton Journal*. With ten Muskoka-sized lakes full of highly corrosive toxic waste at the tar sands, a breach in one of the containment berms could produce what Jacobson told an Alberta cabinet minister would be "an environmental holocaust."

So how did a businessman with no obvious expertise in oil security matters gain access to the Alberta tar sands with a team that included foreign experts? The question is all the more intriguing since Jacobson's serious run-in with CSIS and the Canadian government is so firmly on the record. One potential explanation can be found on Jacobson's own declaration of his board memberships, which included the Mackenzie Institute—one of Stephen Harper's favourite groups. The Mackenzie Institute website features several pictures of the prime minister: Stephen Harper in conversation with Mackenzie Institute officials in 2006; a portrait of a smiling prime minister with the chair of the Mackenzie Institute a month after Harper won his majority government, "subsequent to a briefing to the Prime Minister about the security of Canada's infrastructure"; and that photo dated 2010 of Mackenzie Institute board member Nathan Jacobson, with the caption "Nathan enjoying some levity after a meeting with visiting Israeli prime minister Benjamin Netanyahu and Canadian prime minister Stephen Harper."

After his guilty plea became public in July 2012, Jacobson told the CBC that he had purposely been avoiding his friends in the Harper government: "I myself made the decision that it's best to keep a distance, in order to protect my friends. I would, for the most part, consider them still my friends. But while I'm—for the lack of a better term—radioactive, better let them to continue to run government."

By failing to show up in San Diego for sentencing on July 30, Jacobson had breached his plea deal, and an arrest warrant was issued. Despite that warrant, Jacobson was able to fly from Myanmar or somewhere in Asia home to Canada. US extradition proceedings began against Jacobson while he remained a free man in Toronto. Finally, in October 2012, after an international "red notice" was issued, Jacobson voluntarily surrendered to Canadian authorities and was remanded into custody. Freed on bail, he was finally escorted to San Diego by US Marshals on June 27, 2013. Surprisingly, Jacobson was granted bail again in the United States, even though he had already proven to be a flight risk. There are no other cases on record in which a defendant who had failed to appear for sentencing, and had to be extradited to the US, was subsequently granted bail pending trial or sentencing. Nathan Jacobson was no ordinary felon.

Jacobson had more surprises in his bag of tricks. The disgraced businessman hired a new set of lawyers, including Michael Attanasio, the attorney who represented controversial baseball player Roger Clemens. On August 30, 2013, Jacobson was freed on $1.4 million bail, albeit wearing an ankle bracelet to monitor his whereabouts. Despite pleading guilty to money laundering in 2008, he now wanted to change his plea. Jacobson claimed that his previous lawyer, the highly regarded Steven Skurka, had talked him into a guilty plea in a deal with US authorities. Under the terms of the proposed deal, he would remain free while he cooperated with US investigators. Otherwise, Skurka had allegedly advised, Jacobson was looking at a twenty-seven-year prison sentence.

But Jacobson had serious reservations about doing a plea bargain. He emailed his lawyer to remind him that a criminal conviction would affect his ability to receive diplomatic postings. This was not a theoretical matter. In May 2007, President Oscar Arias of Costa Rica and his acting foreign minister, Edgar

Ugaide, had appointed Jacobson as honorary consul of Costa Rica in Toronto. The prescription drug network Jacobson was involved with also operated out of Costa Rica. In May 2006, Jacobson had visited San José, Costa Rica, and donated $25,000 to the Arias Foundation for Peace and Human Progress, an organization created by the country's former president. The Canadian government twice rejected Jacobson's appointment and asked the Costa Rican authorities to withdraw his name after an RCMP review. In fact, the deputy director of protocol in Foreign Affairs warned that Canada would react negatively if Jacobson's name was not withdrawn. Finally, Costa Rica withdrew the appointment on December 6, 2007.

As for his guilty plea in 2008, Jacobson said that it all came down to paying $3 million for bad advice—a claim that was swiftly answered by Skurka's lawyer, Brian Greenspan. Greenspan replied on behalf of Skurka—who was silenced by his solicitor–client privilege with Jacobson—that "any suggestion of ineffective assistance, coercion and conspiracy with prosecutors has no foundation of fact and is categorically denied."

In supporting documents filed with his December 20, 2013, motion to change his plea, Jacobson further claimed that he and his family "suffer from the fear and for threats against our lives by organized crime directly connected to my plea bargain." He also said that for many years he had "provided services and information, some of it classified, to government agencies in the United States, Canada and Israel." It raised an interesting question. Had Nathan Jacobson been a spy or a double agent during his close relationship with the Harper government? Jacobson claimed that government files, including transcripts of telephone conversations with US agents "were forwarded to foreign companies and international crime syndicates in order to systematically defraud [him] of all [his] business interests." Had anyone in the Harper government bothered to look at Jacobson's lawsuit with CSIS, this claim would have had a familiar ring. He had also accused CSIS of sharing their information about him with Russian intelligence.

In his December 2013 motion to change his plea, Jacobson said a strange thing. He told authorities that a criminal conviction "would prevent [him] from being nominated as a Senator" and would also likely prevent him from receiving the Order of Canada or the Israel Prize. Had these public honours been sought or offered before his legal debacle?

The motion to withdraw his guilty plea continues to work its way through the US courts.

THE WORST APPOINTMENT decision Stephen Harper ever made was placing Dr. Arthur Porter in charge of the Security Intelligence Review Committee (SIRC). In that capacity, the medical doctor with a controversial past had access to all information held by Canada's domestic spy agency, CSIS, "no matter how sensitive and highly classified that information may be." The one thing he couldn't examine was cabinet documents.

SIRC is an independent external review body that reports to Parliament and depends entirely on the integrity of its members. SIRC reviews the past activities of CSIS, and also examines complaints made against it, including those lodged by applicants who are denied a security clearance. It meets once a month and reports to Parliament, and can make recommendations to the minister of public safety. Two years after Porter joined the board, Prime Minister Harper elevated him to chair of SIRC on June 24, 2010.

Dr. Arthur Porter was charming, cherubic, and a brilliant networker. He also had the common touch, being comfortable in conversation with anyone. He was also, like all con men, deceitful to the bone. The committee that chose Porter to become head of the McGill University Health Centre (MUHC) apparently didn't know there were serious clouds over his previous posting, when he was in charge of the Detroit Medical Centre (DMC). Although Porter was never accused of improper activity by the board, there were allegations in the media of overspending and conflict of interest. The place was falling apart under his stewardship, and was near bankruptcy when the board finally pulled the plug on Porter. One board member recalled, "It was my understanding that the DMC board asked him to leave because he really wasn't accomplishing what they had in mind." Yet Porter was headhunted for the Montreal job. He was recruited to oversee an immense project, the building of a super-hospital that would give Montreal a world-class medical institution that would conduct groundbreaking research and provide health care of the highest quality.

Like Jacobson, Dr. Porter had friends in high places. In 2003, Porter donated the maximum, $25,000, to the Republican National Committee, and the maximum to the Bush–Cheney 2004 re-election campaign. As Jacobson did with his picture taken with Harper and Netanyahu, Porter displayed photos in his office of himself with Bush and Cheney. Porter was also ambassador plenipotentiary for his native Sierra Leone, and an advisor to that country's president. The plenipotentiary is authorized to represent the head of state. This was a clear conflict of interest and held obvious potential for foreign influence should he ever be considered for public office. Once he arrived in Montreal, he began donating the maximum to the Conservative Party of Canada.

According to a CBC documentary about Porter that aired on January 28, 2013, David Angus, retired senator and former chair of MUHC's board of directors, introduced Porter to the prime minister. Harper and Porter toured the old Montreal General Hospital together in 2006. The prime minister appointed him to health advisory boards, and on September 4, 2008, the PCO appointed him to the SIRC board, on the express recommendation of the

PMO. Bigger things were just ahead. Porter assumed his new position as head of SIRC the same month he reached an agreement with alleged arms dealer Ari Ben-Menashe about a business transaction in Sierra Leone.

On the same day that the CBC broadcast Terence McKenna's documentary "Porter's Way" on *The National*, the prime minister launched his famous Twitter charm offensive. Most of the media offered banal shots of the PM driving in the limo, working hard at the office, showing off the cat and the family's pet chinchilla. The tweets succeeded in muting response to the documentary, a report that entered far deeper waters.

Porter's appointment was sandwiched between two important events. Two days before he was made chair of SIRC, the director of Canada's civilian spy agency, Richard Fadden, made an extraordinary statement. He said that cabinet ministers in two provinces might be under the control of foreign governments. A CBC interview with Fadden hinted at China and countries in the Middle East, economic espionage, and the sharing or outright theft of state secrets. And two days after Porter's appointment, on June 26, 2010, the G20 Summit began in Toronto. A billion dollars was spent on the event with virtually no oversight, a sum never before paid for these summits. Dr. Porter would now provide the oversight for whatever CSIS did during those meetings. As it would later be revealed, though not by Porter, Canada assisted the US National Security Agency to spy on allies while this country was their host—information that became public through documents leaked by American whistle-blower and fugitive Edward Snowden.

And then there was the matter of Arthur Porter's extracurricular business dealings. The June 2010 contract between Porter and Ari Ben-Menashe to receive $120 million from Russia, and the June 2010 groundbreaking for the Montreal hospital to be built by SNC-Lavalin, gave Porter connections to Russia, Israel, and the security/spy world, where national borders are becoming obsolete. Stephen Harper had created a very powerful subordinate. So powerful that he could intervene in banking matters when his business partner, Ben-Menashe, was under pressure from his bank. The bank had become suspicious because of large money transfers going through Ben-Menashe's account. In October 2010, Porter sent a reference letter to the Bank of Montreal on behalf of Ben-Menashe. Using Privy Council stationery, with the address of SIRC at the bottom, Porter vouched for his partner and told the bank, "In all my dealings with him, I have found him honest and straightforward."

Porter was also appointed to the board of Air Canada, giving him free flights around the world. He was made a member of the Queen's Privy Council, a lifetime position, the day he was appointed to SIRC. Gilles Duceppe, the then Bloc Québécois leader, refused to endorse the SIRC appointment because he said there was "a lack of clarity" about the doctor's departure from Detroit. Duceppe said he was aware of Porter's problems in Detroit from news reports in *L'Actualité Médicale*, and *Le Devoir*. He also worried about Porter's apparently close ties to George Bush and Dick Cheney.

In May 2013, Brian Hutchinson of the *National Post* obtained a letter dated July 6, 2010, showing that Porter was trying to be appointed honorary consul-general to the Bahamas from Côte d'Ivoire just two weeks after Harper made Porter the head of SIRC. Bells should have been going off in the PMO and Foreign Affairs. At the time, the African country was run by unelected strongman Laurent Gbagbo, who a year later was sent to The Hague to face charges of crimes against humanity. The request was denied despite Porter's thirty-three-page résumé and photos of his three luxury cars. Porter apparently had wanted to register a bank in Côte d'Ivoire, as well as open a branch in the Bahamas.

Asked about Porter's attempt to be appointed as a diplomat of a foreign country on May 29, 2013, Andrew MacDougall, the PM's spokesperson, said in an email, "To my knowledge, our office was not aware."

On April 1, 2010, David Angus, chair of MUHC, had announced the winner of the $1.38-billion hospital project: SNC-Lavalin. On April 23, 2010, $10 million was wired to Sierra Asset Management (SAM), a Bahamas-based company incorporated on November 19, 2009. In July 2010, Sierra Asset Management received another $5 million. By August 2011, the SAM company had received $22.5 million of an alleged $30-million kickback to Porter. According to SNC-Lavalin company accounts, the $30 million to Sierra Asset Management Inc. was to be paid in installments disguised as legitimate payouts for a gas project in Algeria. Porter's activities flew under the radar until another of his clandestine deals hit the newspapers.

On November 8, 2011, the *National Post* broke the Porter/Ben-Menashe story. Ari Ben-Menashe alleged that Porter approached him in 2010 with a proposal to hire Ben-Menashe's lobbying company, Dickens & Madson (Canada) Inc., to help raise $120 million for an infrastructure project in Porter's native Sierra Leone. According to Ben-Menashe, Porter made the original proposal through a banker friend in the Bahamas, Hermann-Josef Hermanns. Hermanns was a German-born Montrealer who ran the Bahamas branch of a Swiss-based private bank, Compagnie Bancaire Helvétique (CBH). The money was to be deposited in the Helvétique bank. For his part, Porter would pay Ben-Menashe a $200,000 lobbying fee. Asked about his frequent description as an arms dealer, Ben-Menashe told me, "We are consultants, we consult governments, we do lobbying work for governments." Many of his deals involved acting as go-between in Russia's dealings with developing countries.

Ben-Menashe's bank accounts in Canada have been frozen, and he believes intelligence agents are after him. Journalists are some sort of protection, he told me, because at least the public knows about his situation. When I asked him about Porter's job as chair of the MUHC, he replied, "He shouldn't have gotten the job in the first place. He was working in Detroit, then suddenly he appears in Canada." As reported in the *Post* on November 18, 2011, Ben-Menashe readily accepts he has a reputation: "I'm a liar, I'm crooked, I'm delusional. I've heard and read all of it." But he said it's not true, that "people keep getting it wrong." He has been charged but never convicted of anything. (In 1989, the US government charged him with trying to sell three US-built military transport planes to Iran. His defence was that the deal was officially sanctioned by Israel. He was acquitted.)

Ari Ben-Menashe explained to me on November 18, 2011, why his deal with Arthur Porter fell apart. Porter had initially told him that his Africa Infrastructure Group was a government agency. Ben-Menashe did some investigating. He claimed that he visited the Geneva headquarters of the Helvétique bank, and grew suspicious when he discovered that it was what he called a "rickety bank"—one small office in the Bahamas, one in Geneva. And there was more. Ben-Menashe claimed that he terminated the agreement because it was supposed to be with Africa Infrastructure Group, but this turned out to be a Porter family–owned company registered in Sierra Leone, not a government agency as he had been led to believe. At that point, Ben-Menashe said he returned Porter's money and backed out of the deal. According to the ex-Israeli military intelligence officer, Porter begged him to reconsider, reminding Ben-Menashe, "I'm a very powerful guy."

For his part, Arthur Porter denied that Ben-Menashe had returned the $200,000, telling the *Post* that he, in fact, had asked for his money back. Porter kept to his story, explaining that he was introduced to Ben-Menashe by his friend Hermanns. The idea was to raise money for Sierra Leone. He said he knew nothing about Ben-Menashe's past, his work with Israeli intelligence, or with the infamous leader of Zimbabwe, Robert Mugabe—something a simple Google search would have revealed. Yet Stephen Harper had made Arthur Porter chair of SIRC. As part of his agreement with Ben-Menashe, Porter was to obtain the consent of Sierra Leone's president for the development of new port facilities for use by the Russian Federation for non-military purposes. That consent was not given.

So who was telling the truth, if anyone? Ari Ben-Menashe had made his accusations in the media but was not sued by Porter. And despite his protestations of innocence, on November 9, 2011, Porter decided to leave SIRC. The prime minister accepted his resignation. In a brief statement, Harper thanked Porter "for his service on the Security Intelligence Review Committee and to his country." He didn't specify which one.

After his resignation as chair of SIRC, which Porter attributed to the *National Post*'s "scurrilous portrayal" of him in its November 8, 2011, edition, he offered a final self-serving explanation for his resignation. He was leaving because he did not want the baseless allegations to tarnish SIRC during a period of "significant transition." He offered no explanation of what that meant, stating only, "I am a proud Canadian and a man for whom integrity, honour, and respect hold tremendous meaning." As for his foreign dealings, Porter repeated that his motives were philanthropic: he simply wanted to help rebuild his birthplace, Sierra Leone, which had been devastated during a terrible civil war. Upgrading harbour facilities to accommodate the Russians seemed a strange way of doing that.

Other board members at the MUHC were now in a quandary. They held an emergency, six-hour, Sunday-night, closed-door meeting to discuss Porter's future as head of the hospital network that employed twelve thousand people. The MUHC issued a statement on November 14, 2011, stating its support for Dr. Porter. Yet in the delicious language of euphemism, the board added that it had formed a committee to oversee a smooth transition to his scheduled departure in April 2012. Arthur Porter was now under surveillance.

The PMO trotted out its typical response: the prime minister had no knowledge of the dealings between Porter and Ben-Menashe outlined in the *National Post* story. When asked how such a person could have been recruited for one of the most sensitive positions in Canada's security establishment, the PMO passed the buck: it was not responsible for background checks and financial disclosure, and any questions on those matters should be directed to the Privy Council Office. The PCO would not comment on whether they knew of Porter's business dealings, a stunning abdication of public accountability. As for Porter himself, he claimed that he was interviewed about his résumé in 2008 by PCO staff and that "They know what I do."

During the Quebec anti-corruption investigation, it was discovered that MUHC was on the verge of clinching a medical consulting deal with Kuwait that would see possible infrastructure spending in the kingdom. The letter about the project was signed by Arthur Porter.

Less than a month after Arthur Porter resigned from SIRC, on December 5, 2011, the bow-tied sweet talker stepped down as director of MUHC, four months before his contract was up. MUHC threw two lavish farewell parties for him, and announced that the curved road in front of the hospital would be called Arthur T. Porter Way—a decision that would be revoked on March 20, 2013, with red faces all around. On September 18, 2012, police raided MUHC headquarters. Quebec's task force on corruption had been probing how the contract for the Montreal mega-hospital deal had been "awarded" to SNC-Lavalin Group Inc. Porter had overseen the

deal for the complex, which he considered one of his greatest lega-
cies. Investigators on Project Lauréat were particularly interested in
records related to the awarding of the $1.3-billion hospital contract.
They found crucial information in the fourteenth-floor corner office
of former MUHC director general, Dr. Porter. Framed photographs
of Porter with George W. Bush, Stephen Harper, Dick Cheney, and
Sierra Leone's president had once decorated the suite.

Former Conservative Party senator and fundraiser David
Angus was reportedly questioned on the day of the raid. Angus
was director-at-large of the MUHC board, which had approved
the search committee's recommendation and hired Porter as
director general in 2004—the year the giant hospital project was
conceived. Angus and Porter had co-chaired the seven-person
committee charged with finding a developer for the hospital project, with Porter in the lead position. Bids were received in 2009,
and by early 2010, SNC-Lavalin was chosen by the Quebec government's final selection committee. That decision was ratified by
the MUHC board in April 2010.

Montreal-based SNC-Lavalin, formed in 1991, was one of
the five largest construction firms in the world, and operated in
over one hundred countries. It built the mammoth, gravity-based
Hibernia oil platform, the 407 toll highway north of Toronto,
extensions to the Montreal subway, and light rail systems in
Calgary and Vancouver. In 2011, the company bought the reactor
division of Atomic Energy of Canada for just $15 million. The
firm has also been linked to corruption regarding a bridge project
in Bangladesh, and in Libya over a 4,000-kilometre water pipeline.

After the police raid on MUHC headquarters, Montreal
newspaper *La Presse* reported that SNC-Lavalin had spent
$22.5 million in "agent fees" to obtain the hospital contract. Two
former top executives of SNC-Lavalin were charged with fraud
in November 2012 for allegedly authorizing $22.5 million in

"irregular" payments related to winning the $1.3-billion hospital contract. There have been eight arrests in the case. The money was paid to Sierra Asset Management Inc. The company was registered at the same address in Nassau, Bahamas, as a branch of Compagnie Bancaire Helvétique (CBH)—the Swiss bank run by Porter's business associate Hermann-Josef Hermanns. This was the same bank where the $120 million for Sierra Leone was to have been deposited. According to Porter, Hermanns had introduced him to Ben-Menashe in 2010. Porter denied knowing anything about the $22.5 million or Sierra Asset Management.

According to a past SIRC chair, a person conducting this sort of business would be required to disclose it to the PMO. And according to the Privy Council Office, Porter would have been subject to the Conflict of Interest Act, the Lobbying Act, and the Ethical and Political Activity Guidelines for Public Office Holders. Porter would have also been subject to an RCMP check of police records, a security check by CSIS under section 13 of the CSIS Act, a check with the Canada Revenue Agency, and a check with the Office of the Superintendent of Bankruptcy.

In November 2012, McGill University brought court proceedings against Porter to recover over $300,000 that remained outstanding on a loan, though no one knew where he was. He turned up in the Turks and Caicos Islands offering private cancer treatment with his partner, Dr. Karol Sikora. Sikora was the doctor who had managed to get convicted Lockerbie bomber Abdelbaset al-Megrahi released from prison on the compassionate grounds that he had terminal cancer and had only three months to live. Al-Megrahi was given a hero's welcome when he returned to his native Libya—where he lived for another three years.

On November 28, 2012, Pierre Duhaime, the former president of SNC-Lavalin, was arrested by Quebec's anti-corruption squad on charges of fraud, conspiracy to commit fraud, and using forged documents in connection with the MUHC contract—a public–private partnership. His arrest was based on evidence obtained in the police raid of MUHC offices, where documents from Arthur Porter were seized.

Meanwhile, former SNC-Lavalin executive vice-president Riadh Ben Aissa was in a Swiss jail, facing charges of money laundering and corrupting public officials—part of a separate international probe regarding $56 million in unauthorized payments made by SNC-Lavalin. *La Presse* reported that $22.5 million of this $56 million went to obtain the MUHC contract. Porter was photographed next to Ben Aissa on April 1, 2010, at the groundbreaking ceremony for the hospital.

On January 25, 2013, a Quebec Superior Court judge issued a ruling ordering Porter to pay back McGill University more than $252,000 relating to a low-interest loan and salary overpayments he had received. Just as Nathan Jacobson had not shown up in a San Diego courthouse for sentencing, Porter did not appear in court to defend himself. Looking embarrassed and incompetent, the Harper government announced supposedly strict new vetting procedures for nominees to SIRC. (The greater scandal might be that such procedures were not there in the first place.) Stephen Harper prepared to appoint a new chair of SIRC. On June 19, 2012, former Conservative MP Chuck Strahl was named to succeed Arthur Porter. Strahl said the PMO took charge of the vetting "to make sure [the appointment] was not going to cause a kerfuffle."

Despite the PMO's direct involvement, Strahl barely lasted eighteen months. From the outset, there was a problem with his appointment: the new chair of SIRC was also a lobbyist, and Stephen Harper had known that before he made the appointment. Strahl promised he had a system of what he called "double make-sure" to protect both himself and the public from conflicts of interest. He would continue his consultancy business but promised not to "lobby" governments. If a potential problem did arise, he would consult the ethics commissioner, Mary Dawson.

Things did not go well. By January 2014, Opposition leader Tom Mulcair had joined the growing list of those calling for Strahl's resignation. They got it. On January 24, 2014, Strahl was forced to step down as chair of SIRC when it was revealed he had been lobbying on behalf of Enbridge, the company hoping to build the Northern Gateway pipeline from Alberta to BC. Since CSIS conducts surveillance on First Nations and environmental groups opposed to Enbridge's planned pipeline and the government has openly denounced these groups as "radicals," the conflict of interest was obvious. But not to everyone. Ethics commissioner Mary Dawson found Strahl's activities outside SIRC to be in compliance, a judgment that said more about the ethics commissioner's office than it did about Strahl's fitness for the appointment. Although Strahl had a good reputation, the potential was certainly there for conflict, even if the new chair promised to recuse himself from anything to do with the pipeline that came up at SIRC. CBC's Greg Weston found that two other SIRC members sat on the boards of energy companies. For a government obsessed with perception, the optics were bad.

Meanwhile, the more that was revealed about Arthur Porter, the murkier the picture became. Just two weeks before matters came to a head for Porter, he had met Gerhard Baur at his home in Old Fort Bay, near Nassau in the Bahamas. Baur's company, Canstar Arms Development Corporation, is based in Alfred, Ontario, and manufactures restricted firearms. In the summer of 2010, Porter had driven up Baur's driveway in his Mercedes and started talking about investing in a state-of-the-art weapons manufacturing plant. He picked up the thread of that conversation during their February 2013 meeting in the Bahamas.

Porter said he wanted to build a $100-million plant in Africa that would employ two hundred people. Millions of dollars would be available to produce five types of restricted weapons in large quantities. The global arms industry is a $12-billion business for Canada. Canada sells weapons and military equipment to countries with questionable human-rights records, including Saudi Arabia, Colombia, and, ironically, the former Victor Yanukovych regime in Ukraine.

The gathering storm of Porter's legal problems got in the way of his wheeling and dealing about an African armaments factory. On February 27, 2013, an arrest warrant was issued for Arthur Porter. His former right-hand man, Yanai Elbaz, was arrested on February 28, 2013, on charges of fraud, conspiracy to commit fraud, fraud against the government, embezzlement, secret commissions, and laundering the proceeds of crime. He was freed on $100,000 bail. And the charges facing the man who watched over Canada's spy service were serious: thirteen counts of fraud, accepting a bribe, paying secret commissions, conspiracy to commit breach of trust, and money laundering.

Extradition procedures were started by the Harper justice department. It was a stunning embarrassment for Stephen Harper. The man the prime minister had personally tagged to become the watchdog of CSIS was now a wanted man. Porter denied any wrongdoing, but claimed he was too ill to travel to Canada to face the false charges. He said that he had stage-four liver cancer. For once, even Stephen Harper was nonplussed: "You know, I don't know what to say. This is obviously a matter that's ultimately going to be before the courts. I just point out that none of these matters relate to his work in his former federal responsibilities." The PM offered no basis for that conclusion. In a March 4, 2013, interview with *La Presse*, Porter said: "I don't like to smear people, but if I opened up my papers, I could cause quite a fuss in

Canada." (Porter is reported to be writing a book with freelance journalist Jeff Todd.)

In March 2013, Green Party leader Elizabeth May called for Porter's removal from the Privy Council, calling his appointment to SIRC "perhaps the most shocking failure of judgment and due diligence in Canadian history." Meanwhile, the company that received the MUHC contract from Porter was in as much trouble as the man who had awarded it. On April 25, 2013, the World Bank barred SNC-Lavalin and one hundred of its subsidiaries from bidding on any of the bank's projects for ten years. The harsh penalty was meted out after the company itself admitted to paying bribes to get government contracts. In September 2013, the World Bank updated its catalogue of blacklisted companies. Of the 250 companies and individuals listed, 120 of them were Canadian, with SNC-Lavalin topping the list. By comparison, the United States had 46 blacklisted companies.

After months of saying he was too ill to travel to Canada to face charges, Porter and his wife, Pamela, were apprehended in Panama on an Interpol warrant while en route to the Caribbean on Sunday, May 26, 2013. Although Pamela Porter was arrested immediately, Porter flashed his diplomatic passport and talked his way out of being detained on the spot. But he was taken into custody at his hotel the next day. *The Globe and Mail* reported on June 3, 2013, that oncologist Karol Sikora claimed Porter had terminal cancer that would kill him in six months to a year: "The prognosis is not good. He will never go to trial."[3] Sikora had known Porter for thirty-five years. Porter's lawyer claimed that the doctor and his wife were on their way to Antigua, where Porter said he was scheduled to meet with the prime minister as part of a diplomatic mission for Sierra Leone. The *Montreal Gazette* interviewed a senior official in Antigua who told the paper, "We don't know anything about that. We weren't expecting him." Porter's lawyer said the couple would fight extradition to Canada.

On June 26, 2013, Arthur Porter's status as ambassador-at-large for the Republic of Sierra Leone was revoked, as was his diplomatic passport. Porter remains in a Panamanian jail fighting extradition, while his wife, Pamela Porter, is free on bail in Canada.[4]

Testimony at the Charbonneau commission into corruption in late May 2014 revealed details of how Porter, and the others charged in the conspiracy to defraud taxpayers, allegedly rigged the bidding in favour of SNC-Lavalin. During a second round of submissions, SNC-Lavalin supporters were placed in key positions on the MUHC selection committees. It was also alleged that former MUHC executive Yanai Elbaz warned a member of the selection committee to "remember where [her] paycheque comes from," while pushing for the SNC-Lavalin bid. She testified it was clear to her the message was coming from "the boss," Arthur Porter.

Technical drawings from the rival Spanish consortium were allegedly even slipped to SNC-Lavalin by Elbaz. According to investigator Jean-Frederick Gagnon, this was "the biggest fraud and corruption investigation in Canadian history." The investigator revealed that $22.5 million was allegedly to be split between Porter and Elbaz. After the money went into Sierra Asset Management, Porter's share was directed mostly to Regent Hamilton Lumley Associates, a shell company under his wife's name. A preliminary hearing in the criminal case against Porter and seven others is scheduled for 2015.

As for Porter's former business partner, Ari Ben-Menashe, his home in Montreal burned down December 2, 2012. A man was seen running from the scene. The Montreal arson squad investigated whether a military-grade accelerant was used.

The case remains unsolved.

IT IS NOT every prime minister who hires a convicted man with eighteen months of jail time on his résumé as his senior policy analyst. But when Stephen Harper won the 2006 election, that is exactly what he did. Bruce Carson had served eighteen months in jail for two charges of theft in 1983, and was convicted of fraud in 1990. Carson was part of Stephen Harper's transition team, which also included Chief of Staff Ian Brodie. Carson went on to become Harper's chief policy analyst and troubleshooter from 2006 to 2008. "The Mechanic," as he was known because of his ability to fix tricky problems, also had a top-secret security clearance.

After leaving the PMO in 2008, the personable and outgoing Carson was given a soft landing by Stephen Harper. Carson was appointed the inaugural head of the Canada School of Energy and Environment (CSEE) in Alberta, administered by the Universities of Alberta, Calgary, and Lethbridge. Although he had no science background, Carson found himself astride an institution with 260 researchers and almost 7,000 students. It also had one other thing—$15 million in federal funding at a time when established scientific organizations run by scientists were having their budgets slashed or their doors closed.

Although the stated goal of Carson's new school was to make Canada a clean-energy superpower, it was essentially a platform for the oil industry. Although Carson claimed he wanted it to become the go-to place in North America for research into the development of clean energy and protection of the environment, his closest working associates were conventional energy producers. Carson felt that the oil companies in the tar sands had been unfairly criticized for producing dirty oil. In his speeches, he came across more as a government spokesperson than the head of an independent research facility. He dismissed Kyoto as unrealistic, and defended the Harper government's environmental policy at every opportunity. Carson used the school to fund a series of multi-million-dollar energy exhibits in national museums, which were criticized by environmentalists as a public relations show for the tar sands.

Carson returned briefly to the PMO on January 5, 2009, on unpaid leave from CSEE, and was soon in trouble. Harper's then chief of staff, Guy Giorno, sent two letters to ethics commissioner Mary Dawson in 2009 to say that Carson was being screened out of 2009 budget talks, or talks about his school, while he remained in the PMO. The firewall was triggered when Carson's January 6, 2009, email to government requesting funding for CSEE turned up at the Department of Natural Resources at the same time as he was heavily involved in preparing the 2009 budget. The subject of Carson's email, Carbon Management Canada, which he chaired, later received $25 million in federal funding from the government's Centres of Excellence Program. That program funds research into technology to reduce carbon emissions. Carson was soon replaced as chair because of obvious concerns there could be a conflict of interest. He claimed the email was drafted before he went to the PMO, and mistakenly not sent until after his return to work for the prime minister.

Then, on March 16, 2011, there were new and disturbing allegations against Carson. The allegations were the result of an investigation by the Aboriginal Peoples Television Network (APTN), which reported that Carson had allegedly lobbied Indian and Northern Affairs Canada, including the minister's office, on behalf of an Ottawa-based water filtration company. It is illegal for anyone who once worked in the PMO to lobby government for five years after leaving the office. The company was called H2O Pros and it was trying to sell filtration systems to First Nations reserves with water quality problems—a big market.

APTN reported Carson's alleged activities directly to Dimitri Soudas in the PMO. The prime minister directed Ray Novak, his deputy chief of staff, to hand the material over to the RCMP with this message: "These materials contain troubling details about recent actions and claims made by Mr. Bruce Carson. The materials we have seen may provide evidence of matters inquiring [*sic*] investigation by the RCMP." Then Stephen Harper consigned Bruce Carson to the outer darkness. Privately, some of Carson's friends were upset that the prime minister had banished his longtime advisor without waiting for the results of the RCMP investigation.

Carson had been a senior member of Harper's PMO since the first days of the new government. Active in conservative politics since the early 1990s, he had helped develop the federal Conservative Party election platform in 2004 and was director of policy and research for Harper when he was leader of the Opposition from 2004 to 2006. Left of the prime minister politically, and older, he was also known to have a moderating effect on the PM.

As a result of the allegations, Carson stepped aside from his position as founding executive director of the Canada School of Energy and Environment. In taking a leave of absence, he declared, "Out of respect for this process, the office of the prime minister, and many business and community leaders with whom I work, I will be taking a leave of absence effective immediately from all of my professional responsibilities until the investigation is concluded." CSEE temporarily went offline and secured Carson's laptop.

His personal landscape darkened. On April 3, 2012, APTN reported that the RCMP's Commercial Crime Unit was actively probing the Mechanic regarding his dealings with government on behalf of an Ottawa water filtration company, and the role played in the whole affair by Carson's fiancée, a twenty-two-year-old former escort he involved in the scheme after meeting her as a client. The RCMP had thousands of emails written by Carson, and documents from his computer during the time he headed the school.

In addition to the RCMP, the commissioner of lobbying and the conflict of interest and ethics commissioner were also looking into Carson's alleged dealings.

Bruce Carson was not the only person with some questions to answer. A lot of people wanted to know why Stephen Harper had ever hired the disbarred lawyer in the first place. Why had the convicted fraudster been given top-secret security clearance and become a senior advisor of the prime minister of Canada? Remarkably, an embarrassed prime minister confirmed that he had known about the fraud convictions in the early 1980s before taking Carson into the heart of government power. The prime minister then tried to say that he hadn't known about the second set of fraud convictions against Carson dating from 1990. He sounded a little less than prime ministerial in his explanation: "The fact is I did not know about these revelations that we're finding out today. I don't know why I did not know."

Harper insisted that he would not have hired Carson if he had known about the second set of convictions in 1990, an explanation that raised more questions than it answered. Is the rule really "One criminal conviction is okay, but two is not"? Shifting the blame to others, the prime minister told the CBC in early April 2011 that it was the PCO that was responsible for giving Carson a top-secret security clearance, not him. Carson's lawyer, Patrick McCann, disputed that Carson had disclosed only the first set of convictions. He said his client remembered telling them everything in his security clearance application: "He honestly believes that everything was disclosed in his application for security clearance. All his criminal convictions, in other words."

The affair left many people in a state of breathless incredulity. Former CSIS intelligence officer Michel Juneau-Katsuya told journalist Althia Raj, "Nobody would have recommended to keep that guy. Nobody." According to the former agent, "The issue is that he [could] have used privileged information for his own benefit. These positions are extremely sensitive, you get to know things ahead of time, where the government is going and everything, and you can leverage your access to favour, maybe, some friends." Carson would have been given the security clearance by the PCO after the RCMP made its recommendation. But according to federal government guidelines, Carson's manager in the PMO could overrule the security agency's recommendations and hire him, regardless of any warnings. Ian Brodie, who was Harper's chief of staff from February 2006 to July 2008, declined to be interviewed for this book.

The particulars of the new scandal were straight out of the *National Enquirer*. The water filtration company had signed a deal giving a 20 percent share (later reduced to 15 percent) of the profits on the filtration systems to Carson's fiancée, Michele McPherson. According to the original Information to Obtain a Production Order, McPherson, the former Ottawa escort, had first met Carson around February 2010. Carson allegedly tried to use his federal government connections to get meetings with Aboriginal Affairs officials to promote the product. The First Nations deals could potentially be worth tens of millions of dollars.

Ottawa businessman Patrick Hill was head of the water filtration company H2O Global Group. Hill said Carson advised him on Indian and Northern Affairs (INAC) but they had no contract and Carson did not take any money from him. According to the former co-owner of the company, Nicolas Kaszap, Carson claimed he knew people—the then Assembly of First Nations (AFN) chief, Shawn Atleo, television handyman Mike Holmes, former cabinet minister Jim Prentice, Aboriginal affairs minister John Duncan, and Prime Minister Harper himself. Kaszap told the RCMP he believed Carson had high-powered connections that could help sell the water filters through AFN and Aboriginal Affairs.

Carson had sent Kaszap an email following a meeting with AFN officials, on July 26, 2010: "Thought we did as well as we could today—i [*sic*] told Michele and I will you because it means so much to her and I that we will get this done—the AFN need my help of getting rid of the Indian Act—so all of this will work together—I think six months from now we will be well on our way." Kaszap said it was a message Carson repeated several times in person. Asked if McPherson did any work for the company, Kaszap told investigators she was not paid and did no work for the company. But according to a contract signed in a Chateau Laurier meeting room on August 31, 2010, McPherson would act as an agent of the company for all dealings with First Nations. Kaszap told the RCMP he thought the contract was a legal way for McPherson to get money for nothing. He had misgivings, but signed the contract with McPherson anyway. Carson initialled the document as a witness. No filtration units were sold to First Nations.

When asked how he had met Carson, Kaszap told the RCMP they met through McPherson in June 2010. McPherson had asked Kaszap to pretend to be her brother for the first meeting. The RCMP had an email showing Carson was being sent material from Aboriginal Affairs officials and the AFN that would normally be sent directly to the company. Kaszap told APTN reporters that he felt like he was working for Carson rather than the other way around.

During a series of interviews with APTN in March 2011, Carson said he had regular contact with Harper and several of his ministers. He also claimed to have been friends with the prime minister for nearly two decades. Freelance reporter Kenneth Jackson, who broke the Carson story with his friend APTN reporter Jorge Barrera, had a copy of an email Carson wrote indicating he knew about an August 5, 2010, cabinet shuffle the day before it became public. When Carson realized how much the reporters knew about his activities, he said, "I'm in so much shit," then walked to a window and stood looking down at the street six floors below.

The government fell a few days after the story broke, and an election was called for May 2. During the 2011 federal election campaign, Liberal leader Michael Ignatieff said revelations about Carson's fraud convictions raised the "fundamental question" over whether Canadians could trust Harper: "Can you trust this prime minister with power? Can you trust him to respect our democratic institutions?" In one of his few effective jabs in the election, Ignatieff observed that Stephen Harper "talks tough on crime everywhere but in his own office."

As director of CSEE, Carson had promoted Conservative tar sands policy. He supported the Northern Gateway pipeline to BC, and pushed the tar sands as sustainable oil rather than dirty oil. In April 2011, Carson's interim replacement at CSEE was another energy industry player, Dr. Rick Hyndman. Hyndman was former deputy minister of energy in Alberta and a policy analyst for the Canadian Association of Petroleum Producers (CAPP). After his death in October, Hyndman was succeeded by Dr. Robert Skinner, a former oil industry executive. Funding for the school ended in 2014.

Gordon Lambert, a Suncor executive since 1997, began his career at Imperial Oil around 1982, by coincidence the same period when Harper also worked at the company. (Dropping out of university to join the oil company that employed his father had been his idea of adolescent rebellion. Lambert replaced Bruce Carson at Carbon Management Canada.) In effect, the oil industry had taken over the government's clean energy program.

The man Stephen Harper had once put in charge of developing a national energy strategy was charged with influence peddling on July 27, 2012. Two hours before the charges were laid, Carson sent a text apologizing to family and friends, saying he expected to be charged. It was alleged that Carson "accepted a commission for a third party in connection with a business matter relating to government." He was scheduled to appear in an Ottawa court on September 10, 2012.

Like Porter, Bruce Carson wrote a book, *14 Days*, about his take on the modern Conservative Party. Stephen Harper offered no explanation for Carson's close relationship with his government. Instead, the PM's then spokesperson, Andrew MacDougall, said Carson's activities took place "after he was in our office" and did not affect the image of the Conservative government. "Anyone who violates the law should be punished . . . they should have the book thrown at them if they violated the law." It was getting to be a familiar refrain.

On July 27, 2012, Minister of Foreign Affairs John Baird even tried to find the silver lining in the debacle: "We brought in the Federal Accountability Act to set the bar high, and we hope it's enforced with the full force of the law. We are the ones that raised the bar for accountability and we strongly support people being held accountable." Missing from Baird's bluster was any account of the alarming number of his own colleagues who weren't making the grade.

Even after Carson's charges, NDP ethics critic Charlie Angus still had questions. In a written statement he said, "The prime minister still hasn't explained, or taken any responsibility, for how his inner circle included someone with previous criminal convictions for fraud—who then went on to allegedly use his political connections to take advantage of impoverished First Nations communities for a quick buck." Liberal ethics critic Scott Andrews pointed out that despite being made aware of Carson's fraud convictions, Harper had hired Carson twice to work in the PMO, and given $40 million in grants to two of his projects. Andrews said in a written statement, "If we are the company we keep, I would strongly suggest Mr. Harper re-evaluate who he chooses for his inner circle."

On June 11, 2013, Bruce Carson called in to a special edition of CBC TV's *Power & Politics* about the Senate expenses scandal, to say he was "surprised" Harper had been left in the dark about the secret financial deal between Senator Duffy and Nigel Wright. Carson said that during his tenure in the PMO, the PM would have been briefed "immediately" about something that significant, no matter how bad it was. "I guess I could say I'm surprised by it. But I guess each PMO operates differently . . . but certainly when Ian [Brodie] was there, we tried to, and certainly I did, tried to make him aware of whatever [he] had to be made aware of, immediately."

Two and a half weeks later, on Friday, June 28, 2013, Carson's scheduled July 22, 2013, trial was postponed. Instead, he was scheduled for surgery on July 15 to remove a growth in his lung suspected to be cancerous. Not only were he and Arthur Porter writing books, but they now shared another similarity: they couldn't face justice for health reasons. Carson made an attempt to have his charges thrown out, but finally, on June 2, 2014, a four-day preliminary trial on influence-peddling charges related to the now-bankrupt water company began. Evidence was taken under a publication ban because it was a preliminary trial. Michele McPherson was the first witness, and no witnesses were called in Carson's defence. On June 5, Justice Jonathan Brunet determined there was enough evidence against Carson for the case to proceed to trial. The case is still working its way through the courts.

But Carson had other problems. On March 5, 2014, CBC's Laura Payton learned that the RCMP had seized Carson's banking records. It was an important story. Emails obtained by the

Mounties during the water filtration system investigation showed that Carson had allegedly attempted to lobby very senior members of the government on other matters. These included the clerk of the Privy Council, Wayne Wouters, and the PM's former chief of staff, Nigel Wright. The lobbying was done on behalf of the Energy Policy Institute of Canada (EPIC), for a national energy strategy. Information to Obtain[5] documents filed in court reveal that Constable Marie-Josée Robert alleged Carson's "continuous association" with public officials allowed him to accept money for "consideration for his co-operation, assistance or exercise of influence in connection with business matters with the government on behalf of EPIC." The officer believed Carson was, in fact, lobbying government.

On November 16, 2009, Carson had emailed Wayne Wouters, clerk of the Privy Council, about meeting him the following week: "—will be in Ottawa from monday to wed inclusive next week—you got half an hour for a visit—bc." Wouters replied the same day: "Sure. Set it up with my office." Other email exchanges occurred with top civil servants in Natural Resources and Environment Canada, followed by meetings. On November 26, 2009, Carson emailed the deputy minister of natural resources, Cassie Doyle, telling her he'd had one of his regular meetings with the clerk of the Privy Council and that they had spent most of their time talking about energy: "I brought him up to speed on various initiatives I am involved in—in this area—especially the so-called 'think-tank' one I wrote to you about a month or so ago after a meeting in Winnipeg." The officer noted in her affidavit that although the executive committee of EPIC had decided early in January 2010 not to lobby the federal government, Carson's lobbying activity actually increased after that decision.

In a November 2010 email, Doug Black, one of EPIC's founders, praised Carson's efforts, and said money was "No issue. . . . We are making progress and you are the secret sauce." Carson earned $160,000 between February 2010 and February 2011 for his work with EPIC. Carson was the principal author of the institute's policy, and according to Gerry Protti, now chair of the Alberta Energy Regulator, Carson was "probably seen as one of the most knowledgeable people in the country on how to navigate the federal process." Shortly after Nigel Wright became Harper's chief of staff in January 2011, Carson made contact: "Nigel—I don't think we have ever met—but we have a few mutual friends. . . . thought I would share with you a report I just finished on energy . . . would love to meet with you at your convenience—bc." Wright replied, "I've heard a lot of good things about you. Feel free to give me a call any time. I'll read the report over the weekend." In February, Carson briefed Wright about EPIC and reported to Doug Black that Wright seemed generally supportive. According to the court documents, Black responded to Carson in an email, "Excellent. Need Nigel on side."

Carson's lawyer, Patrick McCann, denied his client was lobbying government or anyone else, and said Carson would fight the new charges if they were laid against him. He emailed CBC: "The initial search for a Canadian energy strategy involved a number of think-tanks and the Energy Policy Institute of Canada all trying to determine what a Canadian energy strategy—in an embryonic way—would look like and what it would do. In pursuing this, Mr. Carson consulted with federal and provincial governments. This did not constitute lobbying." Under the Federal Lobbying Act, Carson was banned from lobbying for five years after he left the PMO on February 4, 2009. He was founding co-chair and then vice-chair of EPIC, as well as head of CSEE. EPIC was created in August 2009 to gain support from industry leaders, academics, and the public before going to government with their ideas for a Canadian energy strategy.

EPIC had big names on board, including former New Brunswick premier Frank McKenna, former president of the Canadian Council of Chief Executives Thomas d'Aquino, and former Harper cabinet minister David Emerson, who became a co-chair. Doug Black had helped to create EPIC in 2009, and became chair of the board on January 1, 2012. Black was appointed to the Senate by Harper on January 25, 2013, and resigned from the EPIC board on June 30, 2013. The Conservative senator from Alberta says he did not lobby any government official following his appointment to the Senate.

After the RCMP seized Carson's emails from his CSEE computer and the University of Alberta servers during the water company investigation, they believed they had found evidence of other alleged crimes. On May 12, 2014, Carson faced new charges: three counts of lobbying while prohibited and one count of influence peddling. It was alleged he used his contacts in Conservative circles to further his work with both EPIC and CSEE. He was scheduled to appear in court in Ottawa on the second set of charges on June 18, 2014.

Daniel Gagnier, the Liberal Party of Canada's national campaign co-chair, now heads the Energy Policy Institute of Canada. Gagnier was chief of staff to Jean Charest when he was Quebec premier, and was also a board member during Carson's time at EPIC. The political winds may be changing and it is possible that the oil patch was beginning to hedge its bets by appointing a powerful Liberal to head the board of EPIC.

In retreat from corruption in his innermost circle, Stephen Harper made the dubious decision to mock Liberal leader Justin Trudeau as a man unfit for leadership and "in over his head." Trudeau responded by listing all the bad appointments Stephen Harper had made: Arthur Porter, Mike Duffy, Pamela Wallin, Patrick Brazeau,

Bruce Carson, and even Nigel Wright. After Question Period, Trudeau observed, "We see this prime minister doesn't have a gift for making good choices when he makes partisan nominations in areas where we shouldn't have partisans." With Harper's record of elevating jailbirds, con men, and fraudsters to positions of influence, his own judgment had been called into question.

twelve

FORKED TONGUE

On July 5, 2013, a report marked "Secret" landed on Prime Minister Stephen Harper's desk. The document was written by his special envoy on West Coast energy infrastructure, Douglas R. Eyford, a Vancouver-based litigation lawyer. Eyford had been sent to find out how the stakeholders, in particular First Nations peoples, viewed Ottawa's push for oil and gas development on their lands. Entitled "Interim Report to the Prime Minister," the document is full of general statements about how Ottawa needed to proceed rapidly on its most urgent initiative—energy and pipeline development in the West. The looming energy bonanza is incomprehensibly huge and the matter had suddenly become urgent.

Canada's energy exports totalled about $110 billion in 2012, roughly 25 percent of the country's total exports. While most Canadian petroleum goes to the United States, the industry is changing rapidly as the US develops its own domestic supplies. The Harper government wants to diversify markets—which makes economic sense. The industry has been developing refinery capacity in Quebec and upgrading existing capacity in New Brunswick at the Irving Oil Refinery.

Both Alberta and BC see energy infrastructure projects as key economic drivers. Canada is the world's fifth-largest producer of crude oil and natural gas, and Alberta has the third-largest crude oil reserves in the world. With approximately 101 tar sands projects in Alberta, the industry generates one in fourteen jobs in the province and provided about $4.5 billion in royalties in 2011–2012. BC had shifted its natural resources focus to natural gas,[1] and the government estimated in 2013 that the liquefied natural gas (LNG) industry could create $1 trillion in economic activity over the next thirty years. BC's goal is to have the first LNG facility in Canada up and running by 2015, with three more in operation by 2020.

With more than six hundred resource projects on the drawing board over the next ten years, time is of the essence. Several projects are in the planning and development stage—two interprovincial oil pipelines; five LNG export facilities; four intraprovincial gas pipelines; and an oil refinery near Kitimat, BC—so the stakes are enormous. The oil pipelines alone would require a direct capital investment of $11 billion, and would result in an estimated $94 billion of additional investment in the oil sands over the next twenty-five years.

The existing Trans Mountain Pipeline has been shipping Alberta oil to the west coast for export for about sixty years, and Kinder Morgan wants to triple capacity with a new, twinned pipeline. The five LNG facilities proposed for the west coast will require a capital investment of $278 billion by 2020. But as Douglas Eyford told the prime minister, because of an abundance of energy from new technologies such as fracking, the clock was ticking: "This opportunity is time-limited due to intensive global competition and changing market dynamics."

Eyford was preaching to the converted on the importance of the developments. Stephen Harper is, first and foremost, a son of the oil patch. He had already done everything in his power to clear the path for the rapid development of Alberta's tar sands, and in particular, to win approval for the controversial $7-billion Northern Gateway Pipeline. After a series of public hearings, from which some environmental groups were barred, the project was approved, as expected, by the National Energy Board (NEB), albeit with 209 conditions. On an internal document from the Department of International Trade and Development that was leaked in January 2012,[2] the NEB was listed as one of the "allies" of the Harper government. "Opponents" of the government listed in the document included "green" groups, which Ottawa had already accused of being "foreign-funded" radicals. Once again, the government's sneaky side was on display.

The Harper government has bent over backwards to accommodate Big Oil. Ottawa gutted seventy environmental laws and regulations in its widely denounced omnibus legislation that would otherwise have set some limits on sustainable development. Harper has lowered corporate tax rates to just 14 percent, and failed for seven straight years to bring in promised emission regulations for the oil sector. The Harper government also spent millions in taxpayers' money portraying Big Oil as the industry that would pay for Canada's future social services. Opponents of the tar sands were spied on by the government and publicly portrayed as dangerous threats. But despite all he had done for the petroleum industry, the massive developments Stephen Harper desired were in jeopardy.

In British Columbia, a giant Douglas fir lay across Stephen Harper's yellow brick road to speedy resource development: Canada's Aboriginals. The natives found themselves facing the usual peril; standing between a white man and his money has always been a dangerous place to be. Historically, Aboriginal Canadians have not benefitted as much as others when natural resources have been developed on their territories, whether for the fur trade, the fishery, or the logging and mining industries—and now oil and gas.

In Alberta, forty-five Indian Act bands are included under three historic treaties: Treaties 2, 7, and 8. In BC, 203 Indian Act bands are represented by 21 tribal associations. The majority of the Aboriginal groups in BC have not negotiated treaties, but over the last decade the government of BC and some Aboriginal communities have established government-to-government frameworks. The parties then work through non-treaty agreements to develop resources. Doug Eyford reported that the Harper government was getting failing grades for its handling of the delicate negotiations with industry stakeholders, the provinces, and, in particular, BC First Nations. Between the lines, his message was clear: it might be time to put away the bulldozer and start listening. "Generally, the messages were respectfully delivered," Eyford told the prime minister, but they were "firm and critical."

The energy industry, meanwhile, was worried that investors, especially in Asia, would look elsewhere if government didn't solve the Aboriginal issues. As an experienced lawyer, Eyford knew that an "effective relationship among federal and provincial governments, industry stakeholders, and First Nations" was critical to future energy developments proceeding. Over 150 Aboriginal communities in Alberta and BC would be affected. It was a matter of settled law by the Supreme Court of Canada that Ottawa had a constitutional obligation to consult First Nations. From a native perspective, it all came down to credibility, something that the Harper government often manufactures with slick ads during hockey games when the facts don't do the job. But the public relations onslaught portraying rapid resource development as a boon for all wasn't working with First Nations peoples.

Eyford noted that television and print advertising was not advancing the discussion, and that it "appears to perpetuate divisions." Harper's envoy noted that it was also not helpful that some in the media relied on "a small group of commentators with narrow perspectives." Commercials were no match for the treaty rights that are affirmed in section 35 of the Constitution Act of 1982. Eyford wrote, "The legal duty to consult is grounded in the core precept of the honour of the Crown and the recognition of the unique relationship that exists between the Crown and Aboriginal people in Canada."

In 1995, Canada recognized that First Nations have an inherent right to self-government under section 35. It was a right that had been smothered in feckless negotiations and broken promises, and a new mood of defiance was awakening in the native community. Eyford warned, "Some First Nations have indicated they will engage in civil disobedience and direct action if the Northern Gateway project is approved." The grand chief of the Assembly of Manitoba Chiefs, Derek Nepinak, seconded that observation: "There is enough momentum, there is enough diversity in the groups and the grassroots movement, there is enough geography covered to put a stop to resources development in Canada until we get what we need to break the chains of poverty."

Generally, First Nations were cautiously supportive of the LNG projects, perceiving natural gas to be more benign than bitumen. What they opposed were the bitumen pipelines and tankers because of the potential for catastrophic damage to the environment, including thousands of streams and rivers and the formidable waters of the Douglas Channel, through which oil tankers would be navigating. Galvanizing their opposition to Northern Gateway was the grossly inadequate response by Enbridge in 2010, when three million litres of tar sands–diluted bitumen were released into a tributary of the Kalamazoo River in Michigan after the company's pipeline ruptured. The heavy, viscous crude is mixed with corrosive chemicals such as benzene to allow it to flow, and benzene is known to cause cancer in humans.

Miles of wetlands and waterways were contaminated, and the cleanup costs topped a billion dollars. Complicating that operation, tar sands oil sinks in water, rather than floating like conventional oil. Investigation of the catastrophe showed that Enbridge had violated several laws involving pipeline management. And even though it had been twenty-five years since the *Exxon Valdez* disaster in Prince William Sound, the damage to the marine environment on the west coast was still visible. People remembered.

With all the risks, First Nations were still willing to support responsible resource development and even become directly involved in sustainable projects, as Eyford reported to the prime minister. But not as coolies. "There is an interest in borrowing capital at preferred rates, backed by a federal government guarantee, for the purpose of obtaining an equity position in partnership with industry stakeholders," Eyford wrote. This was a position that Eyford indicated was supported by industry. But according to First Nations negotiators, it was not supported by the central federal agencies in Ottawa: Finance, the Treasury Board, and the PCO. Eyford would later revise his interim report and say in his final report that Aboriginal communities had not expressed an interest in obtaining a federal loan guarantee to obtain equity interest in pipelines or LNG facilities, although in future Canada might be asked to consider such proposals. For now, this was "a proposal without a project."

Nevertheless, industry stakeholders knew that First Nations could delay or prevent projects without using the courts, and they wanted the Harper government to do more to find an amicable solution. Their own token efforts to involve First Nations had failed. Both the Athabaska Chipewyan and the Fort McKay Nations had pulled out of the Joint Oil Sands Monitoring Program. They had left because the program was mere window dressing. As the Harper government itself had reported to the United Nations, emissions at the tar sands are expected to soar over the next thirty years, so why go through the charade of protecting the environment with scrupulous monitoring?

Simply put, the energy companies didn't think the federal government was reaching out for partners. Nor was industry Harper's only critic. Eyford reported, "Alberta and British Columbia conveyed their views that the Government of Canada does not effectively engage First Nations." They too believed the Harper government should be doing more to identify ways for Aboriginal groups to become partners in the development of oil and gas. Both provinces saw themselves as pursuing "creative, flexible and innovative approaches to improve their relationships with Aboriginal peoples." But according to Eyford, the provinces believed, "Canada is either unable or unwilling to adopt similar approaches." The problem of "limited presence on the ground" was affecting Canada's relationships with Aboriginal groups. Both provinces also wanted more information, earlier, about federal initiatives so they could coordinate activities in support of development.

British Columbia's first priority was to move as quickly as possible with LNG development. Provincial representatives were even worried that the controversy over Northern Gateway could cause First Nations to resist LNG the way they were rejecting bitumen. First Nations were concerned that if energy corridors were constructed for gas pipelines on their territories, oil pipelines would soon be built alongside them. First Nations also felt they had a lot to contribute to pipeline and marine safety initiatives because of their knowledge of and connection to their traditional territories. The chiefs had company in complaining about Stephen Harper's unilateralism. The British Columbia government expressed frustration that it had not been consulted on the announcement of an expert marine safety panel. Eyford suggested that Canada should address First Nations issues through early engagement, to build a relationship between the two parties, as well as reconcile the rights of Aboriginals with the needs of all Canadians. It was good advice but offered late in the day.

One of Eyford's most strategic observations was that Canada approaches resource development from a national or global perspective, but there was no common First Nations perspective because of different cultures and traditions among Aboriginal communities in BC. However, the bands united around the common concern that, in the big picture, the risks of resource development would outweigh the benefits. There was a selling job to be done here, and failing that, a path that would lead straight to the courts. Eyford noted that Aboriginal groups in BC have generated almost all the landmark Aboriginal rights litigation in Canada. Many tribal councils believe that the development of oil pipelines is an opportunity to gain "greater judicial certainty about the nature and content of Aboriginal rights, including title." In other words, they were not going to be induced to support a project simply with the offer of a job. They were looking for linkage to other key issues. Important land claims remained to be settled, nation to nation, and Ottawa was moving at a snail's pace on that front.[3]

Another significant observation made by Eyford was that First Nations were not opposed, per se, to economic development in their traditional territories. But Ottawa had been treating them as an afterthought. In fact, the constitutionally protected Aboriginal and treaty rights required that they be involved at the outset with project planning; that their rights be acknowledged before projects proceed; and that the projects undertaken respect "the long-term sustainability of the environment and their communities." Aboriginal Canadians see themselves as stewards of the environment, a conviction that is integral to their identity. Eyford understood that and recommended to the prime minister cultural sensitivity training "at all levels" of the federal government to improve the negotiation process.

The lack of credibility of the Harper government was a deeply rooted problem. Eyford noted that the First Nations peoples had a deep mistrust of Stephen Harper after the aggressive passage of Bills C-38 and C-45 and the profound legislative change they created. If, for example, the Northern Gateway Pipeline went through a community, community consent was no longer needed, just the consent of the individual people whose property the pipeline traversed. Changes were also made to the Indian Act without proper consultation. The Canada–China Investment Treaty signed in September 2012 was adopted without consulting First Nations, even though it affected their constitutional rights.

Finally, after a promise of greater consultation, Harper made surreptitious, unilateral changes to the contribution agreements with Canada's 630 bands.[4] These contribution agreements were their primary source of income. In the 2013 appendix of conditions attached to the documents, there were a number of provisions never seen before, and the bands were in turmoil about whether to sign. The bottom line was that the conditions in the appendix could be interpreted as requiring bands to support omnibus legislation and proposed resource developments as a condition of accessing their funding. First Nations believed that the federal agenda was designed to develop the projects at the expense of the environment and to find a way to force First Nations to go along. But as Eyford noted in his report, failure to explain the rationale for the legislative changes would only harden attitudes and entrench the positions of the First Nations.

The 2013 federal budget raised more red flags for Canada's Aboriginals. Despite promises, the document included almost nothing new that would alleviate poverty for First Nations. Instead, it introduced "workfare" for native youth. Without prior consultation with native leaders, the government announced $241 million over five years for a native youth job-training program. Bands could only access the money if they made it mandatory for youth on social assistance to participate in the program.

Workfare seemed an odd way to recognize self-determination or mend a broken relationship. The elephant in the room was the fact that there is a third level of government in Canada with constitutional protection, which many have argued should be getting transfer payments not handouts. What this centuries-old injustice requires is a visionary and a peacemaker, not a federal government that perpetually tries to strong-arm opponents into submission. Three former prime ministers—Brian Mulroney, Jean Chrétien, and Paul Martin—all denounced the Harper government's unilateral approach to the First Nations relationship.

KITIMAT, WHICH IS both the intended terminus for the Northern Gateway Pipeline and the proposed location of two LNG plants, is within the traditional territory of the Haisla Nation. In March 2013, the federal government unilaterally announced that Kitimat would become a public port. The chief of the Haisla Nation only learned about the decision when he read about it in the newspaper. It was not a confidence builder.

On April 24, 2013, the chief councillor for the Haisla Nation, Ellis Ross, wrote a zinger to the minister of transport, Denis Lebel, and the then minister of natural resources, Joe Oliver. The Haisla were unpleasantly surprised by the announcement that Kitimat would be designated a public port under the Canada Marine Act, wrote Ross. "Canada had ample opportunity to apprise the Haisla Nation of its intention to establish a public port at Kitimat prior to making its public announcement. Your choice not to do so underlines a profound lack of understanding of the legal relation-ship between your government and the Haisla Nation."

The Haisla Nation had asserted a powerful claim of Aboriginal rights and title to its entire traditional territory. Chief Ross con-tinued, "The new regulatory regime that you are contemplating has the potential to infringe our aboriginal rights and title and, accordingly, cannot lawfully proceed absent appropriate consulta-tion and accommodation." Ross said the Haisla Nation was already working effectively with stakeholders Rio Tinto Alcan and Shell Canada in Kitimat to regulate non-toxic LNG cargoes. The Haisla didn't need the heavy hand of the federal cabinet intervening. He concluded that Canada was advancing the public port proposal to further its tar sands agenda, which would see "pernicious hydro-carbons, in particular diluted bitumen" move through their territo-rial lands and waters.

Ross reminded the cabinet ministers that the Haisla Nation had been instrumental in getting the parties to agree on an appro-priate regulatory framework for the Douglas Channel. Canada had promised that the Haisla would sit on the relevant task force, and had then excluded them. This was "discourteous." Canada had also refused to engage in meaningful consultation on the Northern Gateway Project, a project that, in the Haisla Nation's view, was a threat to them, the more so because the review process on the project was, in their opinion, deeply flawed.

Ross ended his letter with the words "You are, with all respect, not acting in accordance with the honour of the Crown. Please review this matter and re-engage with the Haisla Nation but this time on the footing of equality, legality, and respect." From the Haisla's perspective, and given the Harper government's objectives, Canada should have involved them in the decision. As Eyford put it, "This has undermined relations and created suspicion about the Government of Canada's motives and agenda."

No one knew the territory better than First Nations. They wanted a role in monitoring pipelines and tanker traffic, and in providing emergency response, demands that industry supported. Instead, the Harper government said it would not fund or participate in a proposed working group on that subject. Eyford expressed the bottom line with a flourish of understatement: "Northern Gateway appears to lack a critical mass of support among British Columbia First Nations."

The Carrier Sekani Tribal Council was every bit as forceful as the Haisla's. They thanked Eyford for meeting them in Prince George in May 2013 during an internal planning session on pipelines, but they had a message to deliver. The chiefs wanted to assure Eyford that they were not anti-development. They wanted him to know that they were prepared to work with companies that offered sustainable development. They would also work with the Crown on ensuring their people benefitted equally from development in their territories, but the Crown had walked away, unwilling, in their view, to negotiate a fair deal.

The chiefs were also concerned that loans owed as a result of fruitless negotiations were a burden to the First Nations. They were well aware that their rights and title were enshrined in the constitution, and supported by the United Nations Declaration on the Rights of Indigenous Peoples, which Canada had endorsed. On behalf of the chief, the council wrote, "Governments on countless occasions have broken promises and the level of trust is diminutive." They pointed out that the Conservative government did not implement the Kelowna Accord or keep its promised commitments of $5 billion in extra funds when they took office.

The Carrier Sekani position on the transport of bitumen through their territories by Enbridge was an absolute "no," at any price. That was partly because of their low opinion of the firm: "This company has a terrible safety track record and is one of the most deceitful organizations that we have ever dealt with since the industry entered our territories. We are not holding out for a better deal as some have presumed. In this situation, no means no." In an interview in April 2014, Enbridge CEO Al Monaco observed, "We probably should have spent more time building trust."

According to the chiefs, some industry players had acted in good faith, but others had not. They had watched as industry extracted resources from their lands "and governments continue to accrue benefits while our communities still live in third-world conditions." This time, revenues had to be shared proportionately. The chiefs also noted the 30 percent cuts to band and tribal council funding that the Harper government had made. The Assembly of Manitoba saw its funds cut by 80 percent.

First Nations peoples were "appalled at the comments by Minister Joe Oliver who labelled us as radicals." They found his attitude towards their communities racist. "We cannot understand why we would be considered radicals for standing up and protecting our rights in our own lands. We are protecting our lands, waters and resources for all our children's children." They asked for a public apology from Minister Oliver for his disrespectful comments, and then watched as the Prime Minister Harper promoted him to the post of finance minister after the late Jim Flaherty's retirement.

From the First Nations perspective, the passage of omnibus legislation in bills C-38 and C-45 was a reminder "that colonization is still alive in Canada." The tribal council reminded everyone, "The original practice of colonization was to isolate us on reserves in order for the Crown to extract our resources. The new version of colonization is to change laws without consulting us in order to extract our resources." The tribal chiefs requested that their letter be included in Douglas Eyford's report to Prime Minister Harper. It was.

With Stephen Harper determined to push ahead and First Nations committed to protecting their constitutional rights and the environment, it wasn't hard to predict a collision was coming. That was all the more likely with the Idle No More movement gaining traction in the Aboriginal community—a movement based on a sense that "this is our time" and the status quo is unacceptable. Former prime minister Paul Martin told me he is worried about the deteriorating relationship between the federal government and First Nations people. "The great tragedy of Kelowna is that the fundamental problem has only gotten worse as Harper has gone back to the old way of doing things that has been failing since the 1920s," he said. "There is great tension now because the Harper government has reversed wheels on the issue."

The Kelowna Accord was supposed to lift up the standard of living for Aboriginals and honour treaties. The immediate goal was to fund health and education infrastructure, and give native Canadians a share in the resource developments taking place on their lands. After eighteen months of hard negotiations, a remarkable consensus had been achieved. For the first time, all stakeholders, including the federal government, the provinces, territorial leaders, First Nations, Métis, and non-status Indians, had come to an agreement. There would be $5 billion over five years, and hard performance measurements of the results.

The wisdom of Kelowna was in the approach: "Look, tell us what the issues are." Martin recalled, "They told us what the problems were: education, health care, clean water, housing, economic development, accountability and, of course, resource sharing. Then we asked all of the Aboriginal peoples to tell us what the solutions were and they told us. Once again, we knew imposing solutions doesn't work. So governments were going to be partners in bringing about the conditions that would put the Aboriginal people's own solutions to work." This was a fundamental departure from the usual approach of bureaucratic analysis and unilateral federal action. "Two hundred years of history has shown us that that doesn't work," Martin told me.

Although Stephen Harper promised to support the principles of Kelowna, he never did. In fact, Harper made cuts to health programs such as the Aboriginal Youth Suicide Prevention Strategy and the Maternal and Child Health Program, while committing $3.5 billion to improving maternal health abroad.[5] Many First Nations people do not have equal access to clean drinking water, good education, or adequate housing. Martin believes the Harper government has created the false impression of a crisis of accountability and transparency in the First Nations world. "The fact is," Martin told me, "there are outstanding Aboriginal leaders and in the vast majority of cases, they are both accountable and transparent."

ON NOVEMBER 29, 2013, the day the final Eyford report was presented to the Harper government, the president of the Canadian division of the US company Kinder Morgan[6] told a business forum at Lake Louise, Alberta, that First Nations issues desperately needed to be addressed. Ian Anderson said, "Facing up to our situation . . . is mission critical. It's not someone else's problem to solve. It's our issue to resolve—all of us." Governments, industry, average citizens, members of the public, had to listen and learn, he said. "We've got to help create economic certainty for industry for our country, but only through hard work with our First Nations communities to make them partners in what we're trying to accomplish."

The Harper government was sufficiently concerned about the warnings contained in Eyford's draft report that before receiving the final version in late November, the prime minister dispatched several cabinet ministers and their deputies to a meeting in Vancouver on September 23, 2013. Once again, he misplayed his hand.

The Union of British Columbia Indian Chiefs was invited to attend on very short notice. Harper was ignoring one of the key recommendations of his envoy: respect your negotiating partner. The chiefs were not given a preamble or agenda, or any idea of what was on the table. They had been summoned, not invited. Once again, the odour of paternalism was in the air. Grand Chief Stewart Phillip had a sinking feeling "that perhaps they're covering their backsides in terms of a consultation record"—a reference to Ottawa's largely unfulfilled constitutional obligation to consult. This was the first time that the chiefs had heard from the Harper government in months. Eyford stressed in his report that regular meetings and discussions were critical to building relationships with Aboriginal communities. The Carrier Sekani First Nation had repeatedly asked for such meetings with the prime minister, but the requests had gone unanswered.

The sad truth was that it was all really unfinished business from the historic Crown–First Nations Gathering of January 2012, attended by the prime minister, the governor general, and First Nations chiefs. That had been a meeting that promised hope and re-engagement. But a year later, in January 2013, the reality of life for Canada's Aboriginals was even further behind the rhetoric of the inaugural Crown–First Nations Gathering. The anniversary of the historic 2012 meeting was a dismal affair at the official level. The governor general did not attend the January 11, 2013, meeting—a deep insult to some of the chiefs because he is the head of state and represents the Crown, with whom their treaties were made.

The prime minister and some of his ministers were there, as was AFN National Chief Shawn Atleo. But Atleo's leadership had been deeply wounded by the government's failure to advance the agenda. Many chiefs boycotted the meeting and sided with the hundreds of members of Idle No More, who no longer supported endless talk without palpable outcomes. Instead, they rallied round

a lone, female chief who from her cold teepee on an island in the
Ottawa River would soon steal the show from the politicians—
Theresa Spence.

In his opening remarks, the PM said he understood that as head
of government, the leaders wanted him to hear the dialogue directly.
Harper made reference to commemorations of the War of 1812
that included a tribute to First Nations support and his apology
for the residential schools. This came across as yet another attempt
to substitute ceremony for substance. Some chiefs expressed anxiety over even sitting around the table with Harper. Outside, their
people were calling for real change. The sound of the street protest could be heard in the prime minister's office, where the meeting was taking place. Several Idle No More members had stood
at the door of the Langevin Block and begged their chiefs not to
enter and to hold fast with Chief Spence. Grand Chief Charles
Weaselhead perhaps said it best: "Idle No More and our grassroots
peoples force both of us to take heed and address these issues."

The number one priority for the First Nations was a renewed
relationship and full implementation of treaties. The nations had
very specific demands they wanted met, not interminable negotiations imposed on them for decades. Instead of advancing treaties,
the provisions of Bills C-38 and C-45 had run roughshod over
them. Harper knew Idle No More put pressure on First Nations
leaders, but he offered them nothing they could use to show their
people that dialogue was getting somewhere. He had made the
political judgment that if an Aboriginal Spring were to occur, it
would not be popular with Canadians.

No one should have been surprised that Canada's Aboriginals
had finally lost their patience. First Nations have been waiting
for social justice for 250 years. With the Constitution Act of
1982, Canada's Aboriginals believed their special rights and status
would finally be implemented under section 35(1). But eight years

passed with no real progress on land claims. The Innu occupied the NATO Base at Goose Bay, the Lubicon Cree boycotted the Calgary Winter Olympics, and resource blockades were erected in British Columbia. Then, in July 1990, came the first powder-keg moment: the deadly Oka crisis in Quebec that ended with the tragic death of Corporal Marcel Lemay of the Sûreté du Québec. Five years later, it was Ipperwash, where native protester Dudley George was shot dead by police.

The Royal Commission on Aboriginal Peoples in 1991, called by the federal government in response to Oka, dragged on for five years. Finally, a five-volume, four-thousand-page report was published in 1996. Aboriginals are still waiting for the renewed relationship and the "sharing" promised in the report. And while it was true that the Harper government, inspired by the late NDP leader Jack Layton, made a historic apology in the House of Commons in June 2008 for the criminal abuse of native children at residential schools, even that laudable gesture quickly soured. After creating the Truth and Reconciliation Commission to look into the tragedy of the residential school period, the Harper government then refused to turn over documents requested by the Commission "for privacy reasons." In the end, the Truth and Reconciliation Commission had to take the very body that had created it to court to obtain documents it needed to do its work. Shades of Parliamentary Budget Officer Kevin Page.

Stephen Harper simply didn't grasp the depth of the anguish in the native community. Many Aboriginals carried horrific memories from the days of the residential schools—of sexual and physical abuse, torture, even documented cases of medical experimentation. Former PM Paul Martin told the federal Truth and Reconciliation Commission that it was "cultural genocide." About 150,000 children were taken from their families and sent to church-run schools to "civilize" them.

Facing the combined and often allied power of Big Government and Big Business, Canada's Aboriginals have traditionally fought back in two ways: lawsuits and symbolic statements. Chief Theresa Spence began her now-famous forty-seven-day hunger strike on December 11, 2012—a month before the prime minister met the AFN in his office. She was a single, middle-aged Aboriginal woman with a grade-eight education received at a residential school. She wanted a working rather than a ceremonial meeting with Canada's leaders, including the governor general, to discuss "treaty issues."

Chief Spence was from Attawapiskat, a northern Ontario reserve with third-world conditions situated adjacent to a fabulous diamond field. DeBeers Canada is developing open pit mines there "with a $7 billion footprint." The diamonds are some of the finest quality ever discovered, and the recent find of a thirty-five-carat stone at the site made news around the world. For the use of their traditional lands, the company gives the Attawapiskat Nation $2 million a year. Some natives get a hard hat and short-term jobs. When the company eventually leaves, the band will be left with giant craters on their traditional land.

The Attawapiskat First Nation is part of Treaty 9, known as the James Bay Treaty. It was signed in the summers of 1905 and 1906, with treaty commissioners from Ottawa speaking on behalf of King Edward VII—which was why Spence wanted the governor general included in the meeting she was demanding. For $5 and land for a reserve, the native signatories to the original treaty were told they would receive "benefits that served to balance anything that they were giving up." Chief Spence had a simple condition for ending her fast: a face-to-face meeting with the chiefs, the prime minister, and the governor general. Chief Spence, like the young people thronging the grounds in front of Parliament Hill, had simply come looking for the honour of the Crown.

Instead of hitting the reset button and kick-starting a new era in the relationship as promised at the Crown–First Nations Gathering in 2012, Stephen Harper continued to act like an Indian Agent rather than a partner. Spence experienced the blunt force of the Harper government's power. While she was on Victoria Island in a teepee in 18-degree-below-zero weather, Ottawa released an audit by Deloitte questioning the record keeping of the Attawapiskat band from 2005 to 2011—in other words, Spence's competency, if not honesty. Hundreds of instances of questionable accounting practices were uncovered, and even though Spence had only been elected chief in 2010, the public shaming was all hers. Senator Patrick Brazeau and other Conservatives lined up to take potshots at her.

Brazeau, who would soon be facing criminal charges and expulsion from the Senate, said Spence wasn't a good role model for native children. Some in the media and the general population carried Spence-bashing to the point of racism: Indians were lazy, freeloading drunkards, and their leaders stole from their own people. (The average salary of a First Nations leader is $36,845, about $10,000 below the average Canadian wage.) In its December newsletter, the right-wing Mackenzie Institute even hinted that some Aboriginal people had been "chumming around with some Iranian government officials." At no point in the occasionally racist public dialogue did Stephen Harper intervene with a request for mutual respect.

The poisonous barbs and the Deloitte audit did their work. Chief Spence ended her fast without getting a meeting. According to an Ipsos Reid poll, only 29 percent of Canadians approved of what she had tried to do. But only 27 percent in the same poll believed that the prime minister was treating First Nations peoples fairly. Meanwhile, Chief Spence's popularity grew by leaps and bounds in the native community and in other countries. Round dances and flash mobs occurred in Edmonton and Toronto, and even at the Peter Pond Mall in Fort McMurray, Alberta. Support for Spence and Idle No More came from indigenous people around the world. Te Wharepora Hou, a Maori women's collective in New Zealand, took it as the global call they had been waiting for: "Now we can join together and start looking for solutions."

Stephen Harper had promised a new respectful relationship between Ottawa and First Nations, but instead he set out to vilify an icon of the Idle No More movement. After a year in which he had done nothing to improve the life of Canada's Aboriginals, he reserved his final mockery for his New Year's message, boasting that his government "continued to strengthen First Nations relations in 2012." Joining in Stephen Harper's idea of relationship building, Canada's spy agency, CSIS, kept close watch on Idle No More from December 2012 to February 2013, which included making lists of planned demonstrations.[7] The policy of watching native protesters would soon be expanded to include all public demonstrations in the country by anyone.

Unlike other Canadians, many of whom disagreed with Harper's steamroller politics but felt there was little they could do about it, First Nations employed another powerful tactic to fight back: the law. While Chief Spence was fasting on Victoria Island, two bands, the Mikisew Cree and the Frog Lake First Nation, began legal action against the federal government over Bills C-38 and C-45. The bands believed that the changes brought in by the bills violated their right to be consulted before native lands are affected by development. While both the NDP and the Liberals committed to resolving key native issues within a five-year time frame, the prime minister continued his personal version of the game Cowboys and Indians.

First Nations replied again with the litigation card. On January 30, 2014, it was reported that five more challenges were filed in Federal Court by groups arguing against a green light for the $7-billion Enbridge project. Four environmental groups and three native bands were trying to get the court to set aside the federally appointed review panel's report. They noted that the proposed twin 1,177-kilometre pipelines, one for the bitumen, the other for the toxic product that thins it, would cross more than 360 water courses in Alberta and 850 in BC—some of the least contaminated rivers in the world. A high proportion of the proposed route crosses lands traditionally used by Aboriginals.

Things got even more complicated for the Harper government when, on January 8, 2013, the Federal Court ruled that Métis and non-status Indians living off-reserve were "Indians" under section 91(24) of the Constitution Act of 1867, and that they fell under federal jurisdiction. The *Daniels v. Canada* case had taken fifteen years to work its way through the courts. It was launched in 1999 by the late Harry Daniels and the Congress of Aboriginal Peoples (CAP), the organization former senator Patrick Brazeau once headed. The court decision affected six hundred thousand people. The Harper government appealed, but the Federal Court of Appeal upheld the decision of the lower court on April 17, 2014. An estimated $9 million was spent by the federal government to fight the *Daniels* case. CAP, which had spent $2 million during the court battle, announced that if the Harper government decided to appeal the case to the Supreme Court of Canada, the congress would continue the fight "in order to address the wrongs of the past."

Today, over 75 percent of Aboriginal people in Canada live off-reserve. Paul Martin applauded the Supreme Court of Canada after its historic ruling backing Métis land claims in Manitoba in March 2013.[8] "Thank heaven for the Supreme Court. But I would rather have the government of Canada remember its honour in these matters than have the Supreme Court remind the government of its obligation of honour."

With trust levels for Ottawa at an all-time low, Stephen Harper appeared to blink. With the deadlines closing in for Northern Gateway, and his envoy telling him he needed the First Nations to close the deal, the prime minister offered an olive branch. The new First Nations education bill was announced with great fanfare on February 7, 2014. It had the support of national AFN chief Shawn Atleo, but Harper had hung Atleo out to dry during the Idle No More protests in Ottawa by giving him nothing. Atleo had lost respect and support among his own people. They viewed his endorsement of the new bill with anger rather than appreciation.

Meanwhile, the Harper government repeated a fundamental error in judgment. It had failed to consult First Nations on an earlier draft of the legislation, and then did the same thing again with the new bill. And the legislation had another political aspect that wasn't missed by First Nation chiefs. None of the money attached to it, $1.9 billion over three years, would be spent until 2016—after the next election. Further, the new bill tabled in Parliament as "The First Nations Control of First Nations Education Act" gave only the illusion of native control. The minister of Aboriginal affairs and northern development still had sweeping powers. Manitoba chief Derek Nepinak laid down the cultural reality in an opinion piece for CBC News: "Only through the development of our own education systems based in our indigenous pedagogy and ways of being will our students thrive in a school system." Nepinak emphasized that there had been a long history of colonial lawmakers in Canada "creating laws and policies in the pursuit of making indigenous peoples more like them." That agenda had led by a direct route to the tragedy of the residential schools.

A rarely convened oversight body within the Assembly of First Nations, the Confederacy of Nations, met on May 14, 2014, and resolved to reject the Harper government's native education bill, C-33. On May 27, 2014, First Nations leaders, youth, and elders gathered in Ottawa for an AFN Special Chiefs Assembly. The chiefs debated for several hours whether to kill Bill C-33 or work for amendments. In the end, they voted unanimously to reject the government's education bill. They wanted an honourable process that would lead to "true First Nation Control of education." That could never happen if the minister of Aboriginal affairs still had the power, as he did under the proposed deal, to take control of a community education program based on performance outcomes. Those performance outcomes were in turn developed by provincial governments with no Aboriginal input. As the First Nations had learned on other occasions, you always had to read the fine print when dealing with Stephen Harper.

In an interview with Evan Solomon on CBC radio, Paul Martin said he was "very angry" about the federal government's refusal to talk to First Nations about education on their own terms, and understood why Aboriginals had bristled at the Harper government's plan. Martin believed that, had Stephen Harper invested in the Kelowna Accord, disasters such as the Attawapiskat housing crisis might have been averted and more Aboriginal young people would be in university and the workplace. Instead, ten more years had been wasted.

The Harper government wasn't in an accommodating mood. Aboriginal affairs minister Bernie Valcourt, part of the federal team that travelled to BC to promote resource development, put the education bill, already at second reading in the House, on hold. His bottom line remained unchanged: no bill, no money. The $3,500-per-student gap between off-reserve and on-reserve education grants would remain. At the time this book is being written, the legislation continues to sit on hold in a state of parliamentary limbo.

Shawn Atleo had no choice but to resign as national chief of the Assembly of First Nations. He faced a vote that would likely have ousted him anyway. Many of the chiefs who supported Idle No More thought that Atleo had aligned himself with a government that was working against them. Stephen Harper hadn't even been willing to call an inquiry into hundreds of dead and missing native women. Atleo failed to deliver anything but Harper's warmed-over rhetoric.

In May 2014, a new poll done by Forum Research found that the Prime Minister's Office was one of the least trusted branches of the federal government, rivalled only by the Senate. The Supreme Court, where the First Nations lawsuits may end up, has a trust level four times that of the PMO.

On a chilly March day in Ottawa, with the wind blowing out of the east, the Harper government's reputation sank to a new low among Canada's Aboriginals. A group of Cree youth walked 1,600 kilometres to Parliament Hill from the James Bay Cree community of Whapmagoostui—a fly-in community of about eight hundred people on Hudson Bay—in support of Idle No More. They called the trek "The Journey of Nishiyuu," meaning the journey of the people. They left their community on January 16, arriving more than two months later in Ottawa on March 25, 2013. When they started their walk through a thousand miles of winter, it was minus 54 degrees. Some days their toques froze to their heads like helmets; other days they were up to their knees in slush.

By the time the original six walkers and their guide reached Ottawa, their numbers had swollen to 270 from people who joined in along the way. Indigenous and non-native people thronged to greet the walkers in a crowd of about 4,000 on Parliament Hill. A banner emblazoned with "Keep your word" fluttered in the keen wind. Chief Theresa Spence, who had inspired the walkers, greeted them with a message: the treaties between the Crown and First Nations were not going away, and the meeting she had asked for from Victoria Island had still not happened.

Opposition leader Tom Mulcair had no coat and faced the bitter wind, waiting for hours as the walkers gave their emotional testimonials before he delivered a thirty-second speech. He said simply that he had asked the government why native children receive 30 percent less funding for education than off-reserve students. He declared he would keep on asking the question.

No one from the Harper government welcomed the walkers to Ottawa, and the prime minister was otherwise engaged. Stephen Harper had flown to Toronto to greet a pair of panda bears he had rented from the Chinese government for $10 million, which were arriving that day at Pearson airport.

thirteen

A TANGLED WEB

Like a pinhole breach in a dam, the signature scandal of the Harper years began with a trickle. On November 20, 2012, a media report disclosed that Senator Patrick Brazeau was collecting a housing allowance while living in the National Capital Region, a breach of Senate rules. Two days later, the Senate appointed a bipartisan subcommittee of the Internal Economy Board to examine Brazeau's housing expenses. Senate reform was in the air and the members of the Red Chamber did not want to give their critics more ammunition to support either radical change or outright abolition of the institution. If Senator Brazeau were indeed claiming a home in Maniwaki as his primary residence, then the Senate itself could and would put it right.

Other problems had occurred with the man Stephen Harper had made a senator at the tender age of thirty-four. Brazeau's attendance record had not been stellar. He missed 25 percent of seventy-two sittings of the Senate and 65 percent of the Aboriginal Peoples Senate committee meetings between June 2011 and April 2012. Sensitive to any behaviour that could put the Red

Chamber in a bad light, Marjory LeBreton, government house leader in the Senate, announced that the chair of the Internal Economy Committee was reviewing Senate attendance rules.

Truancy was one thing; trashing people on Twitter, quite another. Brazeau had used the social media to strike back at his critics, sometimes in language that was less than senatorial. After Jennifer Ditchburn of Canadian Press wrote about his sketchy Senate attendance in a June 2012 article, Brazeau advised her in a tweet to change the "D" in her last name to a "B." It did not win the young senator many friends and he later called the reporter to say he was sorry. While Brazeau was offering apologies, MP Justin Trudeau offered some advice to the flamboyant senator with a knack for getting himself in trouble: "Pat, I say this against my own self-interest, but for god's sake stop tweeting. PMO goons hit harder than I do."

Trudeau was referring to the charity boxing match in which he defeated the powerfully built Brazeau on the night of March 31, 2012. It shocked the gathering of Conservative heavies who watched the spectacle from tables around the ring in the Hampton Inn Convention Centre. The event was televised live on the Sun News Network, an agency sarcastically dubbed Stephen Harper's unofficial second communications office. The network was run by the PM's former director of communications Kory Teneyke, who was not overly critical of the Harper government on Canada's anemic imitation of Fox News.

Stephen Harper was reportedly watching as Brazeau, not Trudeau, ended up the loser with a bloody nose and a welt under his eye. The crowd booed when the fight was stopped midway through the third round because Brazeau was taking too many head shots and was unable to defend himself. As a result of the "stunning upset," Trudeau got to cut Brazeau's flowing mane of raven hair in the foyer of the House of Commons, in front of the cameras. Brazeau also had to wear a Liberal "Team Trudeau" sweater for a week on Parliament Hill. The public relations coup the Conservatives hoped to make of the boxing match—a triumphant Conservative senator standing over the prostrate body of the Great Liberal Hope—had turned into a disaster.

Trudeau had pulled off a Rocky. But it had been a close thing, as the victor subsequently told me: "The guy hit me so hard he wobbled my knees. It was a feeling I had never experienced before. But my dad taught me to keep throwing punches and that's what I did. At first they missed, then they started landing."

One of the reasons the Senate leadership moved so expeditiously on the allegations against Brazeau was that it had other expense problems brewing. Rumours swirled on the Hill that Senate Finance members had uncovered "a few bad apples" with respect to expense claims. An internal review of Senator Pamela Wallin's travel expenses had begun quietly in August 2012. The review was prompted by a letter sent by Wallin's former executive assistant to Senator Carolyn Stewart Olsen, a member of the Senate Internal Economy Committee. The letter alleged improprieties in Wallin's travel expenses. The Senate Finance branch looked into the allegations and produced a report in October 2012. It was troubling, and the Senate leadership pondered its next move.

Behind the scenes, another name was added to the "bad apple" list: Liberal senator Mac Harb. In Harb's case, Senate authorities were focusing on his primary residence and related expense claims. News of the internal examinations leaked out and CTV's Robert Fife ran a story about Harb. It was not flattering. Three months after he had been named to the Senate in 2003, Harb bought a house in Cobden, Ontario. Although it was virtually uninhabitable for three years, he designated it as his principal dwelling and began claiming a housing allowance. After a little shoe-leather journalism, Fife discovered from Harb's neighbours that he didn't live there.

Fife's story on Mac Harb spelled trouble for Patrick Brazeau. One of the people who watched the Harb report on television was Brazeau's ex-wife. If what she was saying were true, Brazeau was not entitled to his annual $22,000 housing allowance either. That was because he did not live in Maniwaki outside the National Capital Region, but in a rented house in Gatineau with his girlfriend. The rules said that if a senator's principal dwelling is at least 100 kilometres outside Ottawa, then he was entitled to the annual housing allowance. If not, he wasn't. According to another CTV investigation, the only Brazeau living in the house in Maniwaki was the senator's father.

The media stories kept coming. On December 3, 2012, Mike Duffy found himself in the sights of one of the best investigative journalists in the country, Glen McGregor. McGregor and his partner Stephen Maher had swept every major news prize for breaking the robocalls scandal in a series of compelling investigative pieces. Now the *Ottawa Citizen* was raising questions about Senator Mike Duffy's living allowance for his house in Kanata, while claiming as his principal dwelling a cottage in Cavendish, Prince Edward Island.

Everyone in Ottawa, including Prime Minister Harper, knew that Duffy had lived in Ottawa for thirty years before his appointment to the Senate in 2008. (A well-placed source told me that Duffy wanted the prime minister to name him from Ontario, but that Harper insisted on PEI, telling Duffy his critics "would get over it.") McGregor wondered how Duffy's housing situation was different from Harb's and Brazeau's. Senator David Tkachuk, chair of the Internal Economy Committee, told McGregor that Duffy's expenses were entirely within the rules, "When you travel to Ottawa, you get expensed for living in Ottawa. In his case he has a home here, so he would charge off whatever the daily rate was."

The senator from PEI (or Ontario) was not amused. Duffy claimed that the story was a "smear"—vindictive payback for his lawsuit against *Frank Magazine*, where McGregor had worked before coming to Ottawa in 1998. After the magazine ran a story calling him "a fat-faced liar," Duffy launched a libel action seeking $600,000. The case was reputedly settled out of court for $30,000.

Duffy went on private radio in Ottawa and talked about what he considered to be a personal attack from an old adversary. McGregor responded that his story was about Senate expenses, an issue of public interest, not a smear. He had worked in the "Hot Room," the parliamentary press gallery in Centre Block, and he and Duffy had enjoyed conversations many times. There was even a rumour that after his lawsuit, Duffy became a source for the gossip magazine.

Senator Duffy was sufficiently bothered by McGregor's story that he contacted the prime minister's chief of staff to debunk it. On December 4, 2012, Nigel Wright responded via his private email to Duffy's explanation: "I am told that you have complied with all the applicable rules and that there would be several senators with similar arrangements. I think that the Standing Committee might review those rules. This sure seems to be a smear. I don't know whether this is actionable, my guess is that it is not. This reporter is usually careful that way."

It was noteworthy that Wright used his private email to respond to Duffy. As Greg Weston, national affairs specialist at CBC, pointed out in a September 2, 2013, article, "the promised new era of accountability, is really the golden age of secrecy."[1] Less information, not more, is being released under the Harper government. MPs and senators are exempt from access to information laws, and political staff often conduct sensitive business verbally without notes, or through private email addresses. As for ministerial business, a lot of that is done on the patio of the Metropolitan, a trendy bistro a stone's throw from Parliament Hill.

The PMO was getting nervous about the tremors of scandal coming out of the Senate, and so was the Senate leadership. On December 6, 2012, the Senate Internal Economy Committee announced a plan. It would eventually audit all senators to deter- · mine if their declarations of primary and secondary residences were supported by the required documents.

The new year began with a deepening of the Senate expenses scandal. On January 3, 2013, the Senate moved beyond its internal review and hired outside auditor Deloitte to examine Senator Pamela Wallin's travel expenses from April 2011 to September 2012. By early February, the Senate's own investigation of residency claims was expanded to include all senators, who were asked to provide their health cards, driver's licences, voting registration, and tax records as proof of where they lived.

Nigel Wright was now watching developments closely as the first whiff of smoke from the Senate scandal wafted through the PMO. On February 5, 2013, Wright found out through national media reports that Senator Duffy had tried in December 2012 to apply for a fast-tracked health card in PEI. Coming as it did on the heels of the Senate's decision to require proof of residency, it looked bad. The next day, Wright called Senator David Tkachuk for an assessment of the situation.

Tkachuk reported that Duffy had spent only sixty-two days in the last year in PEI, so there was a common-sense problem at the very least with claiming that his primary residence was the family cottage in Cavendish. The Duffys had purchased the property in 1998 and were considered non-resident owners, a categorization that meant paying 50 percent more property tax than residents. To qualify as residents, property owners were required to reside in the province for 183 consecutive days.

Locals claimed they rarely saw the senator, except at official municipal events or funding announcements. The man who could read a balance sheet could also see what was on the political horizon. Wright informed PMO staff in an email that he wasn't optimistic about the outcome, even though Duffy had winterized his cottage after his appointment to the Senate: ". . . let this small group be under no illusion. I think this is going to end badly."

As Wright had intuited, the sky continued to fall, but in an unexpected way. On February 7, 2013, Senator Brazeau, who was already under investigation for improper housing expenses, was arrested on domestic assault charges at 9:10 a.m. in response to a 911 call. In the hours before his arrest he ignored Justin Trudeau's advice, issuing more than sixty tweets, many of them attacking CTV for a story the network had broadcast that night about his alleged expense improprieties.

As for the assault charges, court documents alleged Brazeau pushed the female victim violently enough to break the handrail of a staircase she was clutching, and touched her in a sexually aggressive way. Brazeau and his accuser had been arguing over Aboriginal issues the night of February 6, 2013, and the dispute continued the next morning. The physical confrontation allegedly occurred after Brazeau ordered her to leave his house.

It was a major blow to the prime minister's judgment. He had appointed Brazeau to the Senate despite allegations of sexual harassment against him dating from his days as vice-chief and chief of the Congress of Aboriginal Peoples (CAP). There were also stories about missed child support payments, accounts Brazeau dismissed as vicious rumours circulated by his enemies in the Aboriginal leadership.

Brazeau's credentials for his Senate appointment were strictly political—he had helped Stephen Harper to power. One of the architects of Harper's victory in the watershed election of 2006,

Tom Flanagan, thought that the Aboriginal reserve system was "anomalous and dysfunctional." If government cut off federal cash to reserves, the reserve population would stop growing. So the better course for the federal government was to focus on Aboriginals who chose to live off-reserve. Flanagan's ideas appeared in a book called *First Nations? Second Thoughts*, which was described as "racist, ethnocentric, and ill-thought out" by a reviewer in *Quill & Quire*.

But Stephen Harper was listening. Just seventy-two hours after the Kelowna Accord was agreed to by all stakeholders, the Martin government fell. With an election on, CAP wrote to each federal party and asked where they stood on the issue of federal support for off-reserve natives. Following Flanagan's advice, Harper gave a detailed reply to CAP on how a government led by him would improve support to off-reserve Aboriginals.

It was music to the ears of CAP, as the congress represented eight hundred thousand off-reserve natives. Despite having signed on to Kelowna, CAP's national chief, Dwight Dorey, and vice-chief, Patrick Brazeau, issued a letter supporting the Conservatives. Chief Dorey was in the Calgary ballroom when Stephen Harper celebrated his minority victory in the 2006 election. A few weeks later, Brazeau became the national chief of an organization that now had a stronger voice in Ottawa than the Assembly of First Nations.

Brazeau cemented his relationship with Harper in November 2006 when he spoke to a parliamentary committee that was discussing the Kelowna Accord. Paul Martin had put forward a private member's bill asking the Harper government to honour the government's financial obligations under Kelowna. Harper needed a credible Native leader to criticize the deal. Brazeau fit the bill. "Kelowna provided false hope for grassroots people— real people in real need—while enriching organizations and the aboriginal elite," Brazeau told the committee.

The Harper government added $1.3 million to Brazeau's budget at CAP and could now promise new approaches to Aboriginal issues with the full backing of his organization, avoiding the appearance of neglecting Native issues. No matter what he said in the election, Stephen Harper had no intention of honouring the letter, spirit, or cash component of the Kelowna Accord. Two years later, in December 2008, Patrick Brazeau became the fifteenth Aboriginal senator, a platform he used to continue his campaign against various First Nations leaders for what he claimed were their unaccountable fiscal ways.

The same Patrick Brazeau had now spent a night in jail after being charged with assault and sexual assault. Stephen Harper could only hope that his part in elevating Brazeau would not become part of the story. Though not yet convicted of anything, Brazeau was immediately removed from the Conservative caucus. A senior government official said that Harper had reacted strongly to the allegations of domestic abuse: "The prime minister was appalled and saddened when he heard the allegations and took immediate action."

THE WEEK BEFORE Valentine's Day was not a time of hearts and flowers for Conservative senators. On the same day that Brazeau was charged, Senator Mike Duffy was informed that there was going to be an independent audit of his expenses by Deloitte, prompting him to call his lawyer. The Conservative Party's star fundraiser was upset. He resented the fact that he was now going to be lumped in with Senators Harb and Brazeau. Duffy believed he had followed the rules and wanted to publicly defend himself on political talk shows. He emailed Senators Tkachuk and Stewart Olsen asking for a meeting. They forwarded his message to Nigel Wright in the PMO. "I have no interest in claiming expenses to which I am not entitled," Duffy wrote. "Can we discuss this matter before you issue any media release naming me, as I believe we can resolve this expense issue without the need of an audit."

It can't have been a happy day for Wright. In addition to investigations into Brazeau and Duffy, and Brazeau's criminal charges, there were now questions being asked about Senator Wallin's residency status.

Mike Duffy didn't get his meeting. The next day, the Senate publicly announced that outside auditors from Deloitte would assess the residency claims and expenses of three senators: Brazeau, Harb, and Duffy. Deloitte asked for a meeting with Duffy and requested documents. On a separate front, the Senate was also seeking legal advice about Duffy's residency status. That was a crucial turn of events. If it were to be found that Duffy was not a resident of Prince Edward Island, his Senate seat could be in jeopardy.

On February 11, 2013, the same day that Kathleen Wynne was sworn in as Ontario's first female premier, a nervous, unhappy, and argumentative Mike Duffy had a fifty-minute mid-day meeting with Nigel Wright in room 204 of the Langevin Block. His visit was initially redacted from the visitors' log. Duffy expressed his biggest fear to the prime minister's chief of staff. If he didn't claim a primary residence in PEI, he would not qualify to be a senator from that province. Wright assured him that his appointment was not in play. But he told Duffy that if he lived primarily in Ottawa, it would be morally wrong for him to claim a housing allowance. Unpalatable as Duffy found it, the bottom line from Wright was that the senator should pay back the money. Wright wrote in an email, "I met with Duff today. He will repay, with a couple of conditions. . . ." At the time of their meeting, the amount Duffy was believed to owe was $32,000.

Duffy's version of the meeting with Wright was that it was the first time that the "fake scheme" to repay his housing expenses was broached. In return for meeting certain conditions, Duffy would repay the expenses and stop talking to the media. A meeting was scheduled with the prime minister after the next caucus, "just the three of them," according to Duffy.

As Nigel Wright set out to resolve the Duffy matter, party leaders in the Senate were making his task harder. They released a joint statement saying that any senator found to have broken Senate spending rules should repay every cent, with interest. When Patrick Rogers, manager of parliamentary affairs in the PMO, emailed Wright about the new development, Wright replied, "Can the leadership PLEASE coordinate every move with us before taking ANY steps?" He knew how unhappy Duffy would be about the statement.

That same evening at 5:05 p.m., Duffy emailed Wright on the chief of staff's personal account: "What does Marjory's letter mean for our talks?" he asked. Eighteen minutes later, Wright replied via his PMO email account. He tried to reassure Duffy that their arrangement would not be affected: "I had no foreknowledge of it. When I learned of it I asked for all unilateral action from that office to cease before being cleared with me. I was not pleased. On its face, it does not make our task more complicated I think, although 'with interest' is new to me." Among other things, Nigel Wright was making clear that the affairs of the Senate should be in the hands of the PMO, not the Senate leadership.

In two emails sent to others in the PMO, Wright showed flashes of the anger he was beginning to feel toward the Senate leadership: "Please convey my thanks to Sen. LeBreton's office for making this more difficult. . . ." and "To repeat Patrick [Rogers], no further action from that office at all without pre-clearance from us."

On February 11, 2013, Wright's plan to dispose of the Duffy expenses problem appeared to be going backwards. Duffy had consulted his lawyer, employment expert Janice Payne, and provided Wright with several talking points outlining why Duffy felt legally entitled to his National Capital Region housing allowance. But Duffy also outlined possible terms under which he might repay his expenses. He wanted to be extricated from the Deloitte audit, reimbursed for his legal fees, and given mutually acceptable media lines that would be followed by his colleagues in the Senate.

The next day, Senator Tkachuk visited the Langevin Block and huddled with Wright for a twenty-minute meeting. Tkachuk wanted to explain the audit process the Senate had put in motion. Both men agreed that Duffy had to repay the money, even though technicalities in Senate rules may have allowed his claim. To Nigel Wright it was not a matter of technical compliance but of morality. He became more convinced than ever that a way had to be found to repay Duffy's expenses in a fashion that would bring the unhappy senator on board.

After Tkachuk left, Senator Irving Gerstein arrived for a two-hour meeting. The visitors' log didn't say who he was there to see or who was with him. Two names are redacted.[2] As head of the Conservative Party Fund, Gerstein had asked Wright if there was any way he could help. If the Fund picked up Duffy's $32,000 in disputed expenses, there would be no need for Duffy to be subjected to the Deloitte audit. But a question hung over that possibility. If Duffy's housing expenses were cleared up, why was it important for him to avoid the audit?

The Senate, meanwhile, was bailing desperately as the water continued to come in over the gunwales. On February 12, the Red Chamber suspended Patrick Brazeau. The Conservative motion to put him on a paid leave of absence "in order to protect the dignity and reputation of the Senate" passed unanimously, save for Brazeau's lone shout of "no" that echoed through the Senate. He had been freed on $1,000 bail after spending one night in jail.

If Mike Duffy was hoping for an early Valentine's present from Stephen Harper, he was disappointed. The meeting with the prime minister that Duffy and Wright had agreed to after Wednesday morning's caucus took place on February 13, 2013. According to Duffy, as he would explain in a sensational speech to the Senate eight months later, the PM said, "It's not about what you did. It's about the perception of what you did that has been created in the media. The rules are inexplicable to our base."

Duffy attempted to defend his housing claims to the PM. Nigel Wright took the opposite position. As he would later remember it, the PM listened to both men and then told Duffy to pay the money back because the public "would not expect or accept such claims" since he actually lived in Ottawa rather than Prince Edward Island. Duffy pressed his argument that he was just following the rules like all the others, but the PM bluntly ordered him to "pay the money back."

Senator Duffy had been around politics long enough to know that what a prime minister wants, he gets. But he was also well aware of how perilous his situation could become if he agreed to pay back money he did not believe he owed. It would be an admission of guilt, a blow to his reputation, and most important of all, it might put his Senate seat in jeopardy since it would be tantamount to the admission that he wasn't a resident of Prince Edward Island.

The political opposition smelled blood in the water. On the same day that Harper, Duffy, and Wright met, the leader of the Official Opposition kicked off Question Period with the Senate scandal. Thomas Mulcair asked about Senator Wallin's claim for over $300,000 in travel expenses and made the accusation that she was actually running up big bills while doing partisan work for the Conservative Party: "Less than 10 percent of these expenses were for travel in Saskatchewan, the province she is supposed to represent. Senator Wallin is using taxpayers' money to travel around the country and to star in the Conservative party's fundraising activities."

Despite the ongoing audit, the PM made the blunder of defending Wallin's expenses in the House, saying he had personally reviewed them: "I have looked at the numbers. Her travel costs are comparable to any parliamentarian travelling from that particular area of the country over that period of time." Less than two weeks later, with Wallin's problems worsening, the PM's communications director, Andrew MacDougall, told reporters in an email that the PM never intended to suggest he had personally reviewed and approved Wallin's expenses. It would be one of many times in the Senate scandal that the PM would "clarify" what he had said.

The Opposition also raised questions about whether another Conservative senator, Dennis Patterson, actually lived in Nunavut, the territory he had represented since 2009. In fact, he owned a home in Vancouver, and was rarely seen in Nunavut except at official functions, although he too collected the annual $22,000 housing allowance. Although he was the legal leaseholder of a property in Iqaluit, it had allegedly been rented to someone else. Was it Mike Duffy, Patrick Brazeau, and Mac Harb all over again? How many other senators were sponging off the public? The Senate's Internal Economy Committee interviewed Patterson and deemed his claims to be in order. But these days, no one was taking the Senate's judgment of its own activities as the final word.

The perception of Conservative foul play was reinforced on February 15, 2013, when Aboriginal affairs minister John Duncan had to resign after it became public that he had written to a tax court judge on behalf of a constituent. The latest contretemps forced the prime minister to have a mini–cabinet shuffle. The PMO was getting twitchy.

Watching events in Ottawa from PEI, Mike Duffy had several conversations with Wright, who was also working hard on the Comprehensive Economic and Trade Agreement (CETA) negotiations at the time and no doubt begrudging the time he had to invest in the Senate mess. Duffy was not pleased that some Senate colleagues had called him in PEI, urging him to repay his expenses. According to Duffy, one of them left several nasty messages on his answering machine, including one that implied he should stop acting selfishly: "Do it for the PM and the good of the party."

As for his greatest fear—losing his Senate seat—Duffy was told that the PM would publicly confirm that he was entitled to sit as the senator from PEI, provided he went along with the plan to repay his expenses. Several lawyers representing the PMO, the Conservative Party, and Duffy were now involved in behind-the-scenes negotiations. Duffy was insisting that any proposed deal be put in writing, a sign that perhaps an earlier verbal deal had not worked out to his satisfaction. It seemed that he wasn't about to make the same mistake again—trusting his political masters to keep their word.

While Duffy was being reassured that the PMO would protect his Senate seat, Nigel Wright was worried. The PMO had been discussing a proposed definition of residency. In a February 15, 2013, email to Benjamin Perrin, special advisor and legal counsel to the prime minister, Wright wrote, "I am gravely concerned that Duffy would be considered a resident of Ontario under this ITB. Possibly Sen. Patterson in BC too. If this were adopted as the Senate's view about whether the constitutional qualification were met, the consequences are obvious."

The PMO was clearly worried that the Conservatives were facing the real prospect of losing senators. In Wright's view, getting something agreed to by the Senate on residency was all that stood in the way of Duffy paying back the $32,000 and ending the matter. Nigel Wright cast himself as puppet master, pulling the Senate's strings from the PMO because the government's own leadership in the Red Chamber had so far failed to deliver. In a memo to Patrick Rogers, manager of parliamentary affairs in the PMO, Wright wrote:

> We are going to need to manage the briefing of the Conservative Senators. . . . We cannot rely on the Senate Leader's office to get this right. . . . have to do this in a way that does not lead to the Chinese water torture of new facts in the public domain, that the PM does not want. . . . I think we should lay out the scenario in a brief memo to the PM. . . . It is clear to me that Ben [Perrin] and I should brief Senator LeBreton directly. Chris [Montgomery] simply does not believe in our goal of circling the wagons. Because of his lack of buy-in, it was impossible to discuss meaningfully the parliamentary strategy. . . . will work with Ben to get something for the Prime Minister tonight. . . . I will look to you Patrick, involving Ben, me and Joanne as much as necessary. . . . because getting confirmation of qualification residency is all that is needed to close out the Duffy situation . . . and to stop our public agony.

Wright's stunning memo made a lot of things clear, from the political price the Conservatives were paying for the Senate scandal, to the fact that Prime Minister Harper was being briefed on the Duffy situation. Harper received a memo that his office was working with Senate leadership "to seek to bring an end to concerns regarding the constitutional residency of some of your Senators." This separate and dangerous issue had become entangled in the expenses debacle surrounding Duffy and Wallin.

By February 19, 2013, the PMO was discussing proposed media lines, and Senator LeBreton's office, having felt the full force of Nigel Wright's displeasure, was working closely with the PMO. LeBreton conveyed her zeal to cooperate in an email to Wright: ". . . My office will work very closely with PMO and Carolyn [Stewart Olsen] as we go forward. We are making progress."

Just when things seemed to be looking up, Senator Duffy threw Nigel Wright a curveball. In a call from PEI, the senator informed Wright that he didn't have the money to repay the expenses. Duffy asked Wright for the name of a government lawyer his own lawyer could contact. Wright told him to have Janice Payne contact Benjamin Perrin, special advisor and legal counsel to the prime minister. It was the final straw for Wright as far as the personal touch was concerned. Unhappy with the new level of complexity Duffy had injected into his best efforts to make the problem go away, Wright informed Duffy that from now on the matter would be dealt with lawyer-to-lawyer.

But that was before help appeared and Wright renewed his direct discussions with Senator Duffy. On February 20, 2013, Senator Tkachuk called Wright with a solution to everyone's problems that he and Senator Carolyn Stewart Olsen had devised. Duffy would write to Deloitte requesting the amount of his inappropriate expenses, admit to an honest mistake, and pay back the money. The Senate Steering Committee would then stop the Deloitte audit. Wright later told Duffy that the PMO would assist with the communications approach. More importantly, Wright would also look into potential financial sources to provide the cash.

Despite Wright's assurances, Duffy kept the pressure on in his own way. On the day that Tkachuk communicated his proposal for a solution to the PMO, Senator Duffy told Nigel Wright that he would be forwarding redacted copies of his diaries for the past four years, along with other information that would back up his claim that he was a resident of PEI. Wright in turn emailed the director of issues management in the PMO, Chris Woodcock; the PM's legal counsel, Benjamin Perrin; and others in the PMO, alerting them that documents from Duffy were on the way.

Was there more to the Old Duff's decision to send his diaries to the PMO than met the eye? The diaries covered four years, and contained detailed notes of the senator's travel, meetings, teleconferences, social events, holidays, important current events, speeches, and political interactions. Opposition leader Thomas Mulcair had already accused Senator Pamela Wallin of running up huge travel bills, raising money for the Conservative Party on the taxpayers' dime. Would Duffy's diaries confirm that she wasn't the only one? And just as important, had the senator from PEI done it with instructions from on high?

Wright was cautious about using the diaries. In an email to his PMO staff, he wrote, "Our team will have to look at that to see if there is anything in it that we would not want his lawyer to send to the Senate steering committee. Maybe it will persuade us to let him take his chances with Deloitte's findings. If not, then I have told him I will be back on his case about repayment. I have told him that we have comms and issues management materials in preparation."

After reviewing the Duffy diaries, the PMO decided to meet the senator's terms, but they also demanded that he meet theirs. Wright called Duffy and told him that the PMO had been working on lines and a scenario for Duffy to use in the media and that all of his other concerns, including cash for payment, would be met. For his part, Duffy would have to repay his debts with interest and stop talking about the issue in the media. But according to Duffy, Wright applied a little pressure of his own to persuade him to accept the deal. The senator remembered being told that the Steering Committee of the Internal Economy Board was preparing to issue its own report on the question of his residency and they were not looking favourably on him.

At a news conference held October 21, 2013, the day before Duffy's passionate speech in the Senate, his criminal lawyer, Donald Bayne, read from a memo Duffy had written to his lawyer on February 20, 2013, after talking to Nigel Wright. Duffy wrote,

Somewhere in the midst of this, he [Nigel] said that the steering committee of the Internal Economy was preparing to issue their own report on the issue of residency. . . . they would trump Deloitte by saying that their analysis of my file is going to say that I was in violation of the rules and wasn't eligible to sit as a senator from PEI. I asked where does this committee get the power to pronounce on these things? Sounds to me like they are way out of their depth. No one gave them authority to make these findings on their own. He said David Tkachuk and Carolyn Stewart Olsen were the majority on the steering committee, and they wanted this.

The way Duffy told it, it was either take the deal being proposed by the PMO or lose his Senate seat.

Whatever the machinations, Duffy agreed to what he later called a "dirty scheme." Under the deal with the PMO, Duffy would repay his housing allowances, admit he made a mistake, and stop defending his entitlements in the media. And he was not to tell anyone about the special arrangement with the PMO. In return he would be reimbursed for the repayment, the Steering Committee would not attack him in the media, and he would be withdrawn from the Deloitte audit.

There was one last practical detail to establish: who would actually pay Duffy's improper expenses? According to Nigel Wright, Senator Irving Gerstein had previously approached the PM's chief of staff to ask if he could assist in any way. On February 22, Wright called the chair of the Conservative Party Fund and took him up on his offer. Gerstein agreed to pay $32,000, plus interest, in the matter of Duffy's wrongful housing allowance expenses. The justification for the Fund's involvement would be that Duffy had made the claims in error. Wright passed on the good news to PMO staff that the deal was all but done—a welcome turn of events for a group that had been grappling with the Senate expenses scandal for months without much success.

After perusing Duffy's diaries, and conferring many times with the embattled senator, Wright also agreed that "a senior government source" would confirm in a statement that Duffy was qualified to sit as a senator from PEI. "The PM will also give this answer is [*sic*] asked, as will other authorized spokespeople for the government," Wright noted.

Wright even agreed to Payne's request that Duffy be reimbursed for his legal fees in addition to his expenses, as long as he kept his part of the bargain. The party "would not inform anyone" of the payment, and Wright expected Duffy to keep their secret arrangement secret. But he wasn't taking any chances. He asked Benjamin Perrin to go back to Duffy's lawyer and confirm that everything was understood. "I would like it to be explicit. . . . I do not want to speak to the PM before everything is considered final."

Less than an hour later, Wright did a follow-up email: "We are good to go from the PM once Ben has his confirmation from Payne." An email from Perrin said that Duffy's lawyer, Janice Payne, wanted the agreement in writing. Wright was indignant and refused. Perrin emailed Wright, "I explained that was not happening. We aren't selling a car or settling a lawsuit here. She seemed to get it eventually."

Wright directed that the "government lines" be sent to Senators Tkachuk and LeBreton, noting that Duffy still had to send his letter to the Steering Committee, "mimicking his public lines." The PMO prepared talking points for both before and after the Senate Standing Committee met. The last line of Wright's orchestrated response turned out to be wishful thinking: "The Committee considers all issues relating to Senator Duffy now resolved."

As for the calamitous star at the centre of the controversy, he followed through on the agreement. On February 22, 2013,

Duffy wrote Senator Tkachuk to say he had filled out the expense forms in good faith but "may have been mistaken." Even though he found the forms confusing, Duffy expressed his intention to repay the housing allowance, and asked for the amount. Duffy's letter to Tkachuk had actually been drafted by Chris Woodcock in the PMO. Duffy's legal bill landed on Wright's desk in the PMO—28.7 hours at $475 per hour for a total of $13,632.50.

The experienced media star kept marching to Nigel Wright's drum. Duffy went on CTV Atlantic from Charlottetown to say he would be repaying his housing allowance, blaming unclear Senate rules for the whole mess, and saying he "may have been mistaken" when he filled out the forms. "Canadians know Mike Duffy," he said. "They've known me for years and they know that I would never do anything that was inappropriate and I would never, ever take advantage of my position."

But at the moment of his triumph, the strings broke in the hands of the puppet master. Nigel Wright was told by the government house leader in the Senate that meals and per diems included, the total bailout bill for Mike Duffy was not $32,000 but approximately $80,000. Wright was apoplectic. "I am beyond furious," he wrote. "This will all be repaid." Wright fumed over the fact that Duffy was apparently getting paid for meals he ate in his own home in Ottawa.

More bad news was on the way. On February 27, 2013, Senator David Tkachuk informed the PMO that the full amount owed by Duffy since his appointment in 2008 was $90,172.24. It was a dicey situation. Tkachuk asked auditors from Deloitte at one of their briefings if they would stop their audit if Duffy made restitution for the improper expenses. It was a crucial question for the Conservatives. If the extent of the Senate expenses scandal became public, there would be hell to pay. The auditors just looked at Tkachuk and didn't reply. They were, after all, independent professionals and this was a forensic investigation.

On the same day, Janice Payne also informed the PMO of the revised amount of her client's expenses. In a note to Benjamin Perrin, Payne said that her client still required assurances from the Internal Economy Committee that repayment would result in his being withdrawn from the audit. In a second email sent the same day, Payne said, "Essentially, we need confirmation expenses are in order, withdrawal from Deloitte, and the $ arrangements."

Perrin passed Payne's request on to Nigel Wright, who was still fuming and was now even angrier: "Ben, I do find this frustrating. There is a letter from the Subcommittee stating precisely what expenses are owed relating to the primary residence claim. Once those are paid, the subcommittee can scarcely say that it got the amount wrong and needs more. Does Janice truly understand that if Mike has improperly charged for travel on Senate business when no Senate business actually took place that we cannot now say to him that those expenses are in order? . . . Withdrawal of Deloitte is as we noted earlier—I agree that the Subcommittee has to do its work on that."

Another serious problem loomed up. With the new, much higher figure for Duffy's expenses, which included possibly dubious per diem and meal claims, the Conservative Party Fund backed out of its agreement to ante up the cash.[3] Nigel Wright now had to find a new source of funds to pay off Duffy's expenses. It was an unwanted task, since he was also a man caught between two audits—the internal audit in the Senate and the external forensic investigation by Deloitte. In order to close the deal on Duffy, Wright had to meet the senator's demands, a task that required influencing or even controlling the conclusions of both investigations. It was necessary to portray Duffy in the right light. With a Conservative majority in the Senate, Wright had reason to believe that things would go smoothly there. They didn't. Senators resented Duffy's outbursts in caucus and felt that his questionable expense claims made them all look bad.

Wright's go-to person in the Senate was Carolyn Stewart Olsen. On February 28, 2013, news broke that a Senate investigation found that there were no other questionable housing expenses beyond those of Senators Harb, Brazeau, and Duffy. Stewart Olsen emailed Wright saying she was "always ready to do exactly what is asked" of her by the PMO, but needed "to know in advance what the strategy was." Wright told her to stay close to Chris Woodcock, the director of issues management and Patrick Rogers, manager of parliamentary affairs in the PMO. "As for strategy," he continued, "I am extremely frustrated that we seem to be unable to get either the subcommittee or Deloitte to the point where it is agreed that the Deloitte examination of Duffy's secondary residence claim is completed by the combination of (i) Deloitte determining the amount of expenses incurred by reason of the claim of secondary residence, and (ii) Mike agreeing to repay that amount. Once we know that repayment will permit the subcommittee and Deloitte to state that that matter is resolved, then the repayment will follow forthwith."

Wright also registered his displeasure at the lacklustre support he was getting from the Senate leadership on the matter of controlling the Deloitte audit. He believed there had been a deal with Senators Stewart Olsen, David Tkachuk, and Marjory LeBreton and they weren't keeping it. "No one on the Senate side is delivering," he wrote to Stewart Olsen. In her reply, Stewart Olsen offered Nigel a nugget of inside information: "Confidentially both Marj [LeBreton] and David [Tkachuk] are telling each other the audit will not be pulled. . . . I think the only way to do this is to tell Deloitte that we are satisfied with the repayment and end the audit. The non-partisan nature of the committee is a problem, as is the Clerk, who seems to have his own agenda."

As for Wright, he had definite ideas of what the Deloitte audit should report about Senator Duffy, responding to Stewart Olsen, "I agree that the auditor (it's not really an audit) should report. But the report can be—if Kanata were a primary residence, here is how much would be owed. It shouldn't conclude that 'Kanata is the primary residence,' and it doesn't need to conclude that because Mike has committed to repay the money as if that were the case. I could use your help getting them to understand that and making it happen."

Pressure was building. On March 1, Janice Payne requested an update from Benjamin Perrin on ending the audit for her client. Wright needed to know if Deloitte were amenable to dropping Duffy from the audit after repayment of his troubled expenses. He forwarded his email exchange with Senator Stewart Olsen to Woodcock and Rogers in the PMO and then wrote to Benjamin Perrin about a highly questionable new strategy:

> Today I asked Sen. Gerstein to actually work through senior contacts at Deloitte and with Sen. LeBreton. . . . the outcome we are pushing for is for Deloitte to report publicly that IF Kanata were the primary residence then the amount owing would be the $90 thousand figure and that since Sen. Duffy has committed to repay this amount then Deloitte's work in determining primary residence is no longer needed. . . . The nub of what I said to Mike is that his expenses would have to be repaid, so his choice was between having that plus a finding that they were inappropriate or that without such a finding. That is what we are working towards.

Despite pre-clearing his plan with the senators on the sub-committee, Nigel Wright told Perrin, "I am no longer 100% sure we can deliver, but if we can't then we and Mike have a bigger problem."

On March 1, 2013, Senator Irving Gerstein, Conservative Party lawyer Arthur Hamilton, and the executive director of the Conservative Party, Dan Hilton, received an email from Nigel Wright advising them that he had a solution to the Duffy problem. In the course of a telephone call with Senator Gerstein, Wright revealed that he had decided to pay Duffy's expenses personally. Gerstein was surprised, but agreed that the Conservative Party Fund would pick up Duffy's legal bill, through party lawyer Arthur Hamilton.

Wright's plan was finally beginning to roll. On March 4, 2013, Janice Payne invoiced Conservative Party lawyer Arthur Hamilton at Cassels Brock & Blackwell LLP for $13,560. A few days later, on March 8, Wright got good news from the PMO's manager of parliamentary affairs. Senator Irving Gerstein had spoken to his contact at Deloitte, senior partner Michael Runia, and asked about getting Duffy removed from the forensic investigation if he paid back his improper expenses. In an email to Wright, Patrick Rogers reported, "Senator Gerstein has just called. He agrees with our understanding of the situation and his Deloitte contact agrees. The stage we're at now is waiting for the Senator's contact to get the actual Deloitte auditor on the file to agree. The Senator will call back once we have Deloitte locked in."

The PMO was now apparently in the business of interfering in an independent forensic investigation ordered by a parliamentary body. With so many negotiations going on, word was bound to leak out that something big was happening in the Langevin Block. On March 8, 2013, the PMO received a media inquiry asking if the Conservative Party was paying off Duffy's expenses. Chris Woodcock alerted Nigel Wright, who replied in part, ". . . For you only: I am personally covering Duffy's $90,000. . . ." The executive director of the Conservative Party, the Conservative Party lawyer, and the chair of the Conservative Party Fund all knew about Wright's momentous, and highly unusual, deal to pay off Duffy's expenses. Now the word had spread to a senior staffer in the PMO.

As the month of March guttered down, Janice Payne was still pushing Benjamin Perrin and Arthur Hamilton about ending the audit of her client upon repayment of his expenses. She also emailed Senator David Tkachuk seeking confirmation that with payment by her client, the audit would stop. Tkachuk contacted the PMO for a suggested response. PMO staffer Chris Woodcock passed along the senator's question and Nigel Wright offered a sharp answer: "Very dangerous tactic by her. Also, I wonder if she is paying attention, because Ben [Perrin] will have explained to her several times that it is not 'the audit being called off,' but rather Deloitte not having to come to a conclusion on primary vs secondary residence. . . ."

On March 21, 2013, the day then federal finance minister Jim Flaherty was slipping into new shoes and delivering the 2013 federal budget, Senator Gerstein contacted Patrick Rogers in the PMO with the final word from Deloitte and his insider contact. Deloitte would not be stopping the audit because it was part of their mandate to determine residency. But Rogers had some very good news for Nigel Wright: ". . . However, they [Deloitte] can't reach a conclusion on residency because Duffy's lawyer has not provided them anything."

It was a remarkable note. The PMO appeared to know what Deloitte would say even though their report would not be issued for weeks. The question is how? Was it through Michael Runia, who had made inquiries at Deloitte for Senator Gerstein, who was in turn acting on behalf of Nigel Wright? Or was it through the Senate? Deloitte auditors had provided verbal briefings to two Senate committees in late February, including the one that was examining Senator Duffy's expenses. That committee had three members: Senators Furey, Tkachuk, and Stewart Olsen.

Wherever the tip came from, the PMO was not slow to seize the advantage and see the way forward. The manager of parliamentary affairs in the PMO, Patrick Rogers, wrote, "I would propose that the Senator continue not to engage with Deloitte. I

believe that we should make arrangements for repayment knowing that Deloitte will not say one way or another on his residency."
Benjamin Perrin, added his thoughts: "At a minimum, I think in
good faith they [Senator Duffy and his lawyer] need to know the
info you found out. We would then need to convince them why
they should do nothing. The Senator's instinct may be to go in and
fight this out again with Deloitte. . . ."

Nigel Wright agreed with his PMO colleagues. "I do agree with
Patrick's suggestion. . . . I would suggest that they send a similar
response . . . that since Sen. Duffy has taken off the table the one
issue DT [Deloitte] was asked to review, they do not see a purpose
for that review. They will want to add 'or any reason to provide the
information requested.' We can never suggest they say this latter
bit, because we cannot trust them never to say that the PMO told
them not to respond to DT's requests for information. . . ."

On March 22, 2013, Wright and Benjamin Perrin called Janice
Payne to persuade her that the best course for the senator was to
pay his expenses and stay away from Deloitte. The next day, Payne
sent over a draft of her letter to Deloitte, adopting the PMO line
that their review was now moot, given Duffy's decision to repay
his expenses. She asked for comments from Wright and Perrin.
In an email to Perrin, a triumphant Nigel Wright gave his bless-
ing to what were virtually the PMO's own words: "I think this is
perfectly fine (and I resist making minor suggestions since I would
prefer to be able to answer, if necessary, that the PMO did not
write it)."

It was now time to get the cash to Duffy. Wright emailed his
executive assistant David van Hemmen with his final instructions
on the matter: "My cheque is in the correspondence folder. I don't
have enough funds in my chequing account, so I have emailed
Murray Culligan to ask him to transfer them in from another
account." The trust requirement was that Duffy repay the expenses

before he received the money from Wright on March 26, 2013. On that day, PMO lawyer Benjamin Perrin received an email from Janice Payne's office informing him that "we have just sent the cheque to Senator Tkachuk by courier." It was the final, revealing step of the deal, confirming as it did that the PMO knew about the plan to make it appear that Duffy was repaying his expenses himself through his personal RBC account. The man Nigel Wright said didn't have the money, or the means of raising it, had managed to secure a $90,000 bank loan to complete the deception.

On the same day that Payne informed the PMO of Duffy's repayment, she also apprised Deloitte, telling the auditor that their review was now unnecessary—just as the PMO advised. As long as everyone involved kept their mouths shut, the public would never know what had actually happened.

Cash from the deal continued to flow. On April 4, 2013, Conservative lawyer Arthur Hamilton sent a cheque for $13,560 "Re: Agency Matter," to Janice Payne, drawn on his firm's trust account with the Bank of Nova Scotia. The money that went to pay Duffy's lawyer, who had negotiated the deal between her client and the PMO, came from Conservative Party donations subsidized by taxpayers.

On April 16, 2013, three Deloitte auditors gave a verbal presentation of facts to the subcommittee, including more expense trouble for Duffy. It appeared that he had made improper per diem claims while he was actually vacationing in Florida. That evening, weeks before Deloitte issued their report, Tkachuk tipped Duffy to what he had learned from the auditors. "Mike, you have a problem," Tkachuk said, advising him to straighten things out. Two days later, Duffy sent a confidential letter to Tkachuk, blaming a temporary worker in his office for the Florida per diem mistake. He offered to immediately reimburse the Senate and appear before the auditors or subcommittee. No one wanted Duffy anywhere near a microphone in a public place, and the Senate decided his appearance would only prolong a process that needed to end.

Senator Tkachuk also talked to another embattled senator, Pamela Wallin, before the auditors had finished their work, allegedly telling her to omit information from her calendar that was not relevant to the claims under scrutiny, before she turned the calendars over to Deloitte. As things got worse in the Wallin case, the prime minister asked the PMO to begin developing "scenarios" for responding to her gathering expenses scandal.

Reporter Duffy had spent most of his working life with his ear to the ground in Ottawa. Senator Duffy still excelled at picking up information and what he was hearing was sufficiently troubling that he paid a visit to the government house leader in the Senate, Marjory LeBreton. Duffy sought assurances from LeBreton that his deal with the PMO was being honoured. LeBreton told him not to talk to the media, and to wait for the results of the audit. She assured him they were working on a plan to manage things once they had received the audits and prepared the Senate reports. "I told him once again that he must trust us on this and not complicate the issue by talking to the media."

More than three weeks after the senator received Nigel Wright's hand-delivered bank draft at Janice Payne's office, Mike Duffy finally issued a public statement that he had repaid the $90,000—though he didn't mention when. He had crossed the Rubicon—or been dragged across it by all the prime minister's men. Following media lines from the PMO, the Senate confirmed the payment but, like the senator, didn't say when the transaction took place.

Nigel Wright still worried about whether the Senate would keep Duffy's residency issue out of their upcoming reports. Duffy's lawyer continued to press the PMO for further assurances that her client would not be booted from the Senate or investigated further by Deloitte or any other party. Since he already knew what Deloitte would be saying, Wright understood that everything now depended on the Senate report. Wright had to be sure that senators LeBreton and Tkachuk were onside—a delicate task, as Wright explained to Benjamin Perrin and Patrick Rogers: "It has to be handled very delicately. We are not asking the Senators to absolve him of anything—they would refuse that, quite properly. We are asking them to treat the repayment as the final chapter of the expenses issue relating to his designation of the PEI cottage as his primary residence to this point in time." According to Wright, both Tkachuk and LeBreton had already agreed. It was now merely a matter of coming through for the PMO, something in Wright's opinion they had not done a very good job of doing, as he would shortly report in a secret memo to the prime minister.

LeBreton responded to an email from Wright on April 28, assuring Wright that she was doing her best to keep a lid on the residency issue: ". . . Just to assure you, I will double my efforts to ensure that there is no reference to the legitimacy of Senate seats in the report to be tabled as a result of the audits. It has never been the Internal Economy's mandate to adjudicate on such issues. . . ."

The next day, Wright personally attended a meeting with Senators LeBreton, Tkachuk, Stewart Olsen, and others to discuss the Deloitte reports they had received. For the first time, he was officially informed that Deloitte could not determine residency in Duffy's case—information Wright already received from Patrick Rogers through Senator Irving Gerstein on March 21.

The heavy hand of the PMO in an exclusively Senate matter did not go over well with Christopher Montgomery, issues manager for the government in the Senate. Senator Stewart Olsen passed on to the PMO what Montgomery had been telling senators. In an email to Patrick Rogers, she wrote, "Montgomery says we as Senators should not compromise ourselves." Rogers forwarded the email to Wright, and curtly responded to Stewart Olsen: "This is the direction. You are not compromising yourself. You are fulfilling commitments that were made."

Caught between the expectations of the PMO and the better judgment of the PCO, the Senate committee went to work on a draft report that would be issued in the Senate's name. Liberals in the Senate were clamouring for the information to be sent to the RCMP. On May 7, 2013, the PMO was provided with a copy of the draft Senate report. Wright claimed that he never saw the report, but other PMO staffers did and briefed him. They weren't happy with the wording, "as they felt it did not reflect the Deloitte findings." Senior PMO staffers Chris Woodcock and Patrick Rogers worked on changes. Emailing Rogers and Woodcock, Wright offered a glum appraisal of what the senators were trying to do and what they were actually achieving: "They think they are hurting Duffy, but they will end up hurting the Prime Minister."

The Steering Committee met again on May 8, 2013, at 2 p.m. Before that meeting, Patrick Rogers presented Senator Stewart Olsen with the PMO's changes and reported back to the PMO: "I gave her our changes. She agreed with them 100%. I reinforced with her that implementing all of the changes to the report was the fulfillment of her commitment to Nigel and our building. She indicated she understood this." Wright offered a wry reply, revealing his appraisal of how Senator Stewart Olsen operated: ". . . I am sure she blamed someone else for the inflammatory language." Rogers replied, "You are correct. It was all Tkachuk's fault."

The most damaging findings touching Duffy in the draft report were that his travel patterns were not consistent with maintaining a primary residence in PEI, and that the Senate's residency rules were "very clear" and "unambiguous"—contrary to the Senator's public statements that he found the forms confusing.

On May 8, 2013, Senator David Tkachuk paid a visit to the clerk
of the Senate, Gary O'Brien. He explained to the clerk that he
and Senator Stewart Olsen wanted to make changes to the Senate
report dealing with Duffy. Since Tkachuk needed the report for a
meeting of the fifteen-member Internal Economy Committee to
take place that afternoon, he simply made the changes that had
been asked for by the PMO without convening the committee.

On May 9, 2013, the Deloitte report and the final Senate report
were made public. Senator LeBreton emailed Wright to ask if there
was any way to get Duffy to stay away, "and most importantly avoid
any media." Woodcock followed up; "I spoke to Duffy. He won't do
any media and will stay away from the Chamber today."

The revised Senate report mimicked the scripted lines out of
the PMO and the conclusion of the Deloitte report regarding
Duffy's primary residence. But though the two reports conformed
to the outline of the Wright/Duffy deal, the price had been an
immense internal contradiction in the Senate report. Where Duffy
was exonerated because of the complexity of the Senate's rules
governing residency, Senators Brazeau and Harb were castigated
for breaking rules that were allegedly crystal clear. The Senate
report went on to say that since Duffy had repaid the expenses,
the Deloitte review was no longer necessary. Senator Tkachuk told
reporters the news Nigel Wright had been longing to hear for
months: the case was now closed.

Not every Conservative senator was satisfied that the culprits
had been properly dealt with. On May 9, 2013, Senator Linda
Frum emailed Ray Novak, deputy chief of staff in the PMO: "Feel
compelled to speak out. . . . By protecting our own we are making
Marjory and the PM look terrible. . . . I feel safe in telling you
that our caucus would support forced resignations. These are my
friends so this is painful to even write. But the PM's reputation—
and that of the Senate caucus—is going down in flames."

Less than a week later, Robert Fife lifted the lid off the Pandora's box of Duffygate. Prime Minister Stephen Harper made a statement that was even more bizarre than Wright's $90,000 gift to Duffy. He didn't know a thing about the deal, and except for Nigel Wright, no one else in the PMO did either.

fourteen

WRECKING BALL

On May 14, 2013, a sunny spring day in the capital, the government of Stephen Harper was hit by a wrecking ball from the near space of network television. It was in every way a remarkable turn of events.

For seven long years, the Conservatives had successfully hobbled the national press by restricting the flow of information. Bureaucrats, government scientists, and cabinet ministers had all been silenced, except for the speaking points provided to them by the PMO. Even the location of cabinet meetings was secret. Journalists were banned from the second floor of the Langevin Block, where the prime minister has his office. Government workers were forced to sign "silence for life" loyalty agreements if they wanted to keep their jobs. As for the prime minister himself, he rarely held press conferences and always restricted the number of questions.

So it was particularly fitting that the story that changed everything came from Parliament Hill veteran Robert Fife, who didn't think journalists should have relationships with politicians, and wasn't much interested in photo ops. He conducted himself in the best traditions of print journalism, where his career had begun. He lived with a phone in his ear and dug into things. The walls of Fife's fourteenth-storey office in downtown Ottawa are festooned with awards: two citations of merit from the National Newspaper Awards, the Edward Dunlop Award, and a 2012 Canadian Association of Journalists Award for television. Fife had broken a string of big stories, including the then defence minister, Peter MacKay's, publicly provided helicopter ride from a private salmon camp on the Gander River in Newfoundland.[1] But none of them compared to the story he had put together in twenty-four hours and was about to break that spring night. It was, simply put, the biggest story of his life.

The backstory had already been in the news for some time. Arising out of reviews by the Senate Internal Economy Committee, irregularities had been found in the expenses of a handful of senators, including Mac Harb, Patrick Brazeau, Pamela Wallin, and Mike Duffy. In Duffy's case, he had paid back $90,000 in "inappropriate" expenses in March, claiming that his mistake had been an innocent one based on confusing Senate rules governing housing allowances.

Citing the results of an independent Deloitte forensic investigation (although Duffy did not cooperate with Deloitte), both the prime minister and the government house leader in the Senate, Marjory LeBreton, agreed with Duffy. On May 10, Government House Leader Peter Van Loan even praised Duffy in the House of Commons for his "leadership" in the expenses scandal, pointing out that he had repaid the money himself in March before Deloitte had even finished its audit.

The Senate had called in Deloitte to conduct an independent forensic investigation of the senators' expenses, after its own attempts to quell demand for action in what the public saw as a sleazy entitlement scandal had failed. As one senator described it to me, "It was better to take care of a few bad apples in our chamber than have every senator investigated by the auditor-general." When Deloitte reported to the Senate in April, it appeared to support Duffy's explanation. The auditors said that the Senate's residency regulations and guidelines do not include criteria for determining "primary residence," so they had not been able to determine which of Duffy's properties—the one in Ottawa or the cottage in Cavendish, Prince Edward Island—was his primary one.

Hill watchers had expected the story to develop, but not in the sensational way it did. According to CTV News, Mike Duffy had not paid back taxpayers at all. The bombshell was who had in fact made the payment—none other than Prime Minister Harper's superstar chief of staff, Nigel Wright. For Fife, this was big-game hunting at its most perilous. Tory bloggers and trolls had sharp claws. The party was rumoured to have a lot of young operatives working in shifts, paid to watch news reports and respond. And Nigel Wright was not just the darling of Conservative circles, he was the PM's right-hand man. When jolted, Stephen Harper was a political player who took down numbers. As Fife told me, he was "scared shitless" about putting the story on air.

The second irony of the story was that it involved Mike Duffy. Duffy had been a fixture on Parliament Hill for decades. Legendary CBC News boss Trina McQueen had once told Duffy that she was going to make him the first successful "fat man" on television. Neither of them could have known how successful that enterprise would be. Duffy entered the TV-news stratosphere. For a time, he was the third musketeer along with Peter Mansbridge and Brian Stewart in the glory days of the CBC's *The National*. Before his Senate appointment in late 2008, Mike Duffy had his own public affairs show on CTV and was easily the most

recognizable journalist in Canada. There was no one in the business who could match him in live broadcasting, and when he gave
that intimate little wink to the camera when signing off, individual
viewers really did think that the "Old Duff" was winking at them.

Like all stars in the often ego-driven business of television
news, Duffy had his detractors—too schmoozy for some, too pro-
Conservative for others. But he was also something of an elder
statesman in the press gallery, with a cultural memory and résumé
few on the Hill could match. He often took rookie reporters under
his wing, sharing contacts and offering advice. One of the ben-
eficiaries of his largesse was Robert Fife. Sitting on Fife's office
bookcase was a picture of him with two legends of the business:
Craig Oliver and Mike Duffy.

When Stockwell Day, as the leader of the Canadian Alliance,
tried to forbid scrums because he thought they lacked decorum, it
had been Duffy who took him aside and told him, "Stock, you're
not in Alberta anymore." It was the kindest way of telling Day that
he was playing in the big leagues now, that journalists in Ottawa
wouldn't put up with tacky restrictions on their right to seek information from public officials. No one had yet met a future leader
named Stephen Harper.

Fife had the two essential assets required to publish a story
of this magnitude: impeccable sources and a media lawyer, Peter
Jacobson, more interested in finding a way to get the news out
than avoiding all possible lawsuits. Before airing his blockbuster
story on the late-night news, Fife placed the duty calls to the
PMO, Conservative Party headquarters, and Senator Duffy for
a response.

It was actually the second time in two days that Fife had called
party headquarters, where the story of Wright's payment to Duffy
had been officially denied. Then another source, who was "out-
raged about the negotiations with Duffy and the payout," came

forward with more details. This time when Fife made his duty calls, he got near-identical statements from the PMO and Senator Duffy. Their answers came with more topspin than Rafael Nadal's forehand. According to the PMO, "Mr. Duffy had paid back the expenses in question, and no taxpayer resources were used." The senator from PEI replied to CTV with an email that was exquisitely misleading but true: "The Royal Bank helped me. . . . I dealt with my bank personally. Nigel played no role."

The next day, the sunny skies in Ottawa gave way to clouds; by noon a thunderstorm was roiling across the city. But nothing in the skies compared to the thunderheads gathering over the government. On May 15, 2013, the most shocking element of Fife's story was belatedly confirmed by the PMO in plain language: Nigel Wright had indeed given Senator Duffy $90,000 to pay his expenses. And there was an added wrinkle—the money was not a loan, but a gift.

It was a *volte-face* from the original story that Duffy himself had repaid his improper expenses. Fred DeLorey continued to insist there was "no party money involved in any way." The morning after Fife broke the story, deep in the shadows of the PMO, staffer Chris Woodcock sent an email to Senator Duffy: "Can you confirm whether you advised the Senate ethics office of any loan/gifts involved in the March 25th payment?. . . Trying to cover off all the angles." The PMO was in pandemonium. A story that no one in the office ever thought would become public was out there for Canadians to see—or at least they could see the tantalizing tip of a much larger iceberg. The PMO's objective was to come up with a "narrative" that would keep what lay beneath the surface hidden. Job one was protecting the prime minister.

Stephen Harper was so anxious to distance himself from the affair that he told the public an implausible, possibly panic-stricken story. He insisted that he, like everyone else, first learned of the Wright payment to Duffy on May 15, 2013. But how could that be, since Fife had aired a news story the night before, May 14, and made confirming calls to the PMO before the broadcast? The prime minister was asking Canadians to believe that a professional staff expressly recruited to advise, inform, and protect him didn't tell him about the dramatic news report of the night before, making explosive allegations about his own chief of staff and one of his highest-profile Senate appointments. It would not be the last of the fact-challenged stories from the prime minister about the Wright/Duffy affair.

On May 16, the prime minister was in New York pitching the controversial Keystone XL pipeline to the Council on Foreign Relations, a non-partisan US think-tank that also publishes the prestigious journal *Foreign Affairs*. (Nigel Wright was also in New York, celebrating a personal milestone with friends: his fiftieth birthday. It can't have been much of a party.) Harper told his American audience that the pipeline would create forty thousand jobs in the United States. He stressed that Keystone XL also offered oil from allied Canada rather than from an ideologically unfriendly Venezuela. Thanks to advertising in US publications placed in advance of the PM's appearance, pro-environment protesters were also alerted to demonstrate outside the event.

While the prime minister wooed his elite audience in the Big Apple, Senator Mike Duffy was being designated as the Rotten Apple back in Canada. The man who had co-hosted the Conservative Party Convention after the 2011 general election received a telephone call from Ray Novak, senior PMO staffer and trusted ally of Stephen Harper. According to Duffy, the government house leader in the Senate, Marjory LeBreton, was also on the line. Duffy claimed that he was told that if he didn't resign from the Conservative caucus immediately, his case would be sent to the Senate ethics officer and he would risk being thrown out of the Red Chamber. LeBreton insisted, "You've got to do this, Mike. Do what I'm telling you. Quit the caucus within the next ninety minutes. It's the only way to save your paycheque."

The Conservative brain trust was moving quickly to put as much distance between the party and its former star-fundraiser as possible. Duffy complied with the PMO request, explaining that he was resigning from caucus because the public controversy over his debt settlement had become "a significant distraction to my caucus colleagues and to the government."

More to the point, there were potentially dangerous rumours swirling around Ottawa that Duffy may have charged the Senate for expenses he incurred while campaigning for colleagues in the House of Commons during the 2011 election. Though ostensibly disgraced, Duffy said that he looked forward to all the relevant facts of his expenses being made public in due course, adding that once the public knew what had happened, they would see that he had done nothing wrong. After that, the path to rejoining the Conservative caucus would be clear.

That was a tall order. The Harper government's damage-control strategy was taking shape, with Senator Duffy as the main culprit. But the other participant in the $90,000 payoff was a different matter. Nigel Wright was a blue-chip political asset to the prime minister, with a long history of involvement in Conservative Party policy and finance going back thirty years.[2] If there was any doubt that the PMO would try to come up with a narrative to save him from the scandal, it was quickly removed by the prime minister's director of communications. Andrew MacDougall told the media that Nigel Wright had "the full confidence of the prime minister" and "he will not resign."

MacDougall attempted to rag the puck by declaring that the PMO was cooperating with a probe by Parliamentary Ethics Commissioner Mary Dawson. If the Conservatives could give the impression that something was being done about the extraordinary deal between the prime minister's chief of staff and his celebrity senator, the brewing scandal might slip behind the fog banks of yesterday's news.

It was not Mary Dawson's first dealing with Nigel Wright. When Wright had taken the top job in the PMO, Dawson had helped devise the "ethical wall" designed to protect him from conflicts between his role in the PMO and his past life as a Bay Street whiz kid at Onex Corporation. The ethical wall would be administered by the deputy chief of staff to the prime minister. Then in 2012, Dawson got a chance to assess the height and thickness of Wright's ethical wall. It became public that Barrick Gold, founded by Peter Munk, had lobbied Wright three times in May about international relations and international trade.[3] Wright was personal friends with both Munk and his son Anthony, who had worked with Wright at Onex. The ties were close. Wright was godfather to Anthony's son.

The calls were of interest because Barrick was the world's largest gold mining company. It had an $8.5 billion investment at the troubled Pascua Lama mine in the Andes, straddling the border of Chile and Argentina. The project came to a grinding halt in Chile in April 2013 when Chile's environmental regulator stopped construction of the mine on its side of the border, citing serious environmental violations affecting the water supply of the indigenous Diaguita Indian community living below the site.

For as long as anyone could remember, the Indians had taken their water directly from their glacier-fed river. Now toxic chemicals, including arsenic and sulfates, were flowing into the headwaters, causing health problems. Barrick was fined $16.4 million, after authorities confirmed that the company had not told the full truth when reporting environmental failures in their operation. Diaguita protesters held up signs that didn't enhance Canada's image on the evening news: "Canada: What's HARPERing here?" and "Harper go home."

Foreign affairs minister John Baird vigorously defended Wright over conflict allegations arising out of the calls from Barrick Gold. The calls were made in May 2012, shortly after Harper blocked a resolution on Argentina's claim to the Falkland Islands at the Summit of the Americas in Colombia. Canadian mining companies were concerned this move would make it harder for them to obtain permits from the Argentinian government, and Barrick planned to continue construction on the Argentinian side of Pascua Lama. According to Baird, Wright listened to Barrick's concerns, said nothing, and directed the matter to the proper officials. Since Barrick called Wright on May 14, 25, and 29, one wonders if the "proper officials" were on a long lunch.[4]

Dawson discontinued her examination of a possible conflict of interest for Wright over Barrick's contacts with him. As she often does, she did this without issuing a notice, ruling, or report. When CP reporter Joan Bryden pressed Dawson on the disposition of the file, the commissioner told her that she was satisfied there had been no violation on Wright's part of the Conflict of Interest Act. It was transparency and accountability Harper-style. The PMO claimed vindication. Andrew MacDougall issued a statement: "As we have said all along, Mr. Wright conducted himself properly and in accordance with the rules."[5]

NDP ethics critic Charlie Angus wasn't buying it. "It's who you know in the PMO and this is what the prime minister said he was going to change, this is the culture that he said was going to get cleaned up." There were good reasons for the political opposition and the public to worry about the shadowy interface between big business and big government. Access to the highest legislative levels is a huge priority for companies like Barrick, and their executives were not shy about bringing in the politicians when they had a problem.

That's exactly how Barrick recovered most of its losses from investing in asset-backed commercial paper (ABCP) that was being sold by Canada's chartered banks by the late 1980s. Barrick was advised by CIBC World Markets that their $66-million investment was safe in a third-party ABCP trust called Ironstone. But when it turned out that the investment was freighted with a lot of toxic subprime mortgage debt, the big banks could not protect all investors and Barrick lost its money. Barrick sued the CIBC, and after years of legal wrangling got some satisfaction in May 2008. But it didn't happen before a call went out from finance minister Jim Flaherty to the bank. As Bruce Livesey wrote in his book *Thieves of Bay Street*, "Federal finance minister Jim Flaherty had stepped in and telephoned senior executives at the bank, pressing them to return Barrick's cash. CIBC reluctantly handed over $49 million to settle the matter."[6]

Access to government by corporations was a priceless commodity, as evidenced by the king's ransom paid by Barrick Gold to acquire the services of John Thornton. The veteran international banker, a former president of Goldman Sachs Group, received a "golden hello" of $11.9 million in cash when he joined Barrick as co-chair on June 5, 2012. As reported by Bloomberg News, "Barrick Chairman Peter Munk told investors . . . that he needed the former banker, 'a highly desirable, well known commodity' to secure access to governments and protect against possible losses of mineral rights."[7]

Just as the government had circled the wagons around the PM's chief of staff in the matter of Barrick Gold, the Conservatives came to his rescue in the immediate fallout from the Wright/Duffy affair. Former Harper communications director Dimitri Soudas emailed CBC in response to their May 16 story about the Wright payment to Duffy. Even though he was out of government as a member of the Canadian Olympic Committee, Soudas weighed in with what would be the government's first "narrative" to find a way out of the scandal; Wright's payment was the act of a Good Samaritan.

In December 2013, Dimitri Soudas was brought back from the Olympic Committee, just before the Winter Games in Sochi, to become the new executive director of the Conservative Party of Canada. Someone had obviously been pleased enough with his remarks about Nigel to make Soudas the party's principal election organizer. Four months later, Soudas was out the door again after he was accused of meddling in the nomination process of his fiancée, MP Eve Adams.

Soudas's strategic encomium notwithstanding, the Opposition had always been troubled by the appointment to the PMO of a person with such deep corporate connections as Nigel Wright. The sheer size of Onex Corporation as the largest private investment capital firm in Canada meant to Wright's critics that there was scarcely a file that would cross his desk that wouldn't present a conflict of interest. The company had assets of $44 billion, revenues of $34 billion, managed $16 billion, and had 229,000 employees worldwide.

On November 2, 2010, Nigel Wright had appeared before Parliament's Standing Committee on Access to Information, Privacy, and Ethics as the prime minister's chief of staff designate. Liberal MP Wayne Easter pointed out forty Onex holdings that were connected to federal government departments. An ethical wall might protect Wright when it came to the aerospace industry—his area of expertise at Onex, where he sat on the board of two affiliated companies, Hawker Beechcraft and Spirit AeroSystems. But would an addition to Wright's ethical wall be necessary to cover off special taxation, taxation on the private equity sector, and issues of tax deductibility?

Easter produced a chart showing an Onex connection to Cineplex and Indigo in cultural industries, Allison Transmission in heavy equipment and fluids, Hawker Beechcraft in aviation, and ResCare in health. Bloc Québécois MP Carole Freeman pointed out that Wright was moving from the largest private corporation in Canada to the most influential position in the country next to the prime minister. Since the activities of Onex were so pervasive, how could he advise Stephen Harper without putting himself in perpetual conflict? Wright replied that he had sent a memo through the Privy Council Office that no matters touching Onex were to be sent to him.

NDP MP Pat Martin flatly rejected Wright's "ethical wall" defence against his many built-in conflict-of-interest issues. He jokingly observed that the PMO couldn't even send out for pizza because Onex had an interest in CiCi's Pizza. On a more serious note, Martin raised the issue of the timing of Wright's appointment. He said that journalists were initially told that the prime minister had offered Wright the chief of staff position just weeks before his appointment was announced in September 2010. Under questioning from Martin, Wright confirmed that he had actually accepted the position six months earlier, in March. That meant that when he accepted the offer to run the PMO, Wright was on the board of Hawker Beechcraft, a company with tie-ins to the F-35 project. This in turn led to the question that was uppermost on Martin's mind: had Wright played any role in promoting the F-35 between March, when he was still at Onex, and October, when he took up his post in the PMO?

It was the elephant in the room, since Ottawa was embroiled in controversy over buying the hugely expensive high-tech aircraft to replace Canada's fleet of CF-18s. Wright replied with icy precision. "Mr. Chair, I can say I have not had any conversations regarding the F-35 or Lockheed Martin with any public official, and I have not promoted—" Martin, who was listening as carefully as Wright was speaking, cut him off. "No, not with a government official, but marketing it internationally?" Again, Wright was measured in his response. "I have not promoted in any way to anybody the sale of that airplane, or the purchase of that airplane for that matter."

Their final exchange cut to the quick. Martin opined that the idea of an "ethical wall" was fatuous. "Walls in and of themselves don't have ethics. The ethics have to reside within individuals, and it seems like this is a construct of convenience to defend the indefensible, which is your position as chief of staff." Unflappable, Wright smoothly replied that the ethics of the person administering the ethical wall were vital. He talked about the "common-sense" protection of his own reputation and the reputation of the prime minister being "critical," and promised to get the working relationship right. He also said that the prime minister's values and his values were aligned in every way. And then this: ". . . not only my first loyalty but also the first loyalty of the deputy chief of staff, of every staff member in the PMO, and the Prime Minister himself is to the law of the land."

If the Opposition seemed obsessed about Nigel Wright's possible conflicts, Stephen Harper was partly responsible. The Harper government had actually tightened the connection between the federal government and big business in a way that made necessary the close scrutiny of appointments like Nigel Wright's. Getting this magnitude of a star out of the private sector and into public service was seen in business circles as a big accomplishment for Stephen Harper. Commenting on the Wright takeover of the PMO from outgoing chief of staff Guy Giorno, Duncan Dee, then chief operating officer of Air Canada, said, "This is as close to a coup as it comes. . . . Nigel is one of the brightest Canadians I know, and he's incredibly focused on doing the right thing. He'll bring a tremendous sense of the economy and of politics. . . . There aren't many people who can synthesize both the economy and politics."

Wright earned about $2 million a year at Onex, and had millions of dollars in stock options. When he was asked to become the prime minister's chief of staff, Wright said it was "a once in a lifetime privilege, impossible to do anything with other than say yes." He had always been interested in public policy, and the skills he used to negotiate multi-billion-dollar business deals were no doubt useful in negotiating foreign-trade deals. It was understood that he would return to Onex after his time in the PMO.

The ease with which Wright planned to move between these two worlds shows how little space there is between business and government in Canada today. The Canadian Pension Plan Investment Board (CPPIB) is a case in point. In 2007, the passage of Bill C-36 transferred all CPP assets to the control of the "arm's length" CPPIB. The CPPIB was created in 1997 by the then finance minister, Paul Martin, to manage the investments of the CPP. Under the Harper government, the formerly conservative management approach has shifted toward a willingness to take on riskier investments for better returns. Offices were opened in London and in Hong Kong in 2007, and in New York and Sao Paulo, Brazil, in 2014. CPPIB participates directly in mergers and acquisitions to boost returns. In October 2013, the organization led the $6.3 billion buyout of Neiman Marcus group, which owns Bergdorf Goodman. The fund has also invested in Formula One racing, and $700 million worth of Manhattan office towers.

As of December 31, 2013, the CPPIB had assets of $201.5 billion, making it one of the ten largest pension funds in the world. CCPIB chief executive officer Mark Wiseman said the board continues to diversify its portfolio, as evidenced by its real estate investments in South Korea, Brazil, and China in the third quarter of 2013.[8]

Wiseman joined CPPIB in 2005 as senior vice-president of private investments, and became CEO in July 2012. Nigel

Wright's former and future boss at Onex Corporation, Gerry Schwartz, told *Canadian Business* magazine that you can feel the weight of the CPPIB in the marketplace, and Wiseman's influence. "He's done a marvellous job," Schwartz said. The pension board is not just an investor, "it's actively engaged with the assets it acquires and firms it works with."

The CPPIB is now partnering with companies such as Onex Corporation. In July 2010 CPPIB and Onex partnered to purchase Tomkins PLC for $4.5 billion. Takeover talks had begun in March, the same month Wright had agreed to join the PMO. It was the largest global private equity transaction in 2010. The then British-based company provided hydraulics to the oil, gas, and mining industries.

According to Bloomberg, the bid was 41 percent higher than Tomkins's closing price the day before the takeover bid. The manufacturer had reported losses in the previous two years, and CPPIB and Onex were the only suitors in a leveraged buyout. Tomkins's chief executive officer, James Nicol, would remain. Nicol had spent his early years in management at Magna International Inc., where he became president and chief operating officer. CPPIB investments also include Magna Corporation.

In November 2012, CPPIB partnered with Onex again to purchase Tomkins Air Distribution for $1.1 billion. One of the spinoffs from the parent company is Titus, which provides data security to the military in Canada, the United States, Australia, Belgium, and Denmark. Titus also provides services for governments, the aerospace industry, police forces, and the financial industries.

Onex, Magna, and the CPPIB—a cozy, interconnected world of high finance that Nigel Wright had once navigated with extraordinary success. (Onex and CPPIB put Tomkins PLC up for sale in November 2013 and sold it in early April 2014 for $5.4 billion.) CPPIB has also invested $80 million in Syncrude,

$553 million in Exxon, $62 million in Nexen, $218 million in the TransCanada Corporation (Keystone XL), and $201 million in Enbridge (Northern Gateway). RBC is the pension plan's largest domestic holding, with $707 million invested in the bank according to a series of articles in the *Huffington Post* by Amy MacPherson.[9]

Nigel Wright may have been able to negotiate multi-billion-dollar deals with ease, but his negotiations with Mike Duffy were turning into an ethical meltdown and a political disaster. On May 16, 2013, the same day Duffy resigned from the Senate, RCMP superintendent Biage Carrese sent a letter to Clerk of the Senate Gary O'Brien, informing him that the Force was "conducting a review of the examinations conducted by Deloitte. . . ." The RCMP requested Senate policy documents for the last ten years. By this time, Duffy was holed up in his Cavendish cottage looking at a clutch of journalists who were gathered on his property, though they would soon be ordered to leave by police.

The next day, May 17, 2013, PMO damage control kicked into high gear. Senator Pamela Wallin, co-host with Senator Duffy at the Conservatives' 2011 Convention, announced that she too was leaving the Tory caucus over disputed expenses arising out of the Deloitte audit. Like Duffy, Wallin denied any intentional wrongdoing and was effectively ordered to leave caucus. She had already stepped down as chair of the Senate's National Security and Defence Committee, the Foreign Affairs Committee, and the Subcommittee on Veterans' Affairs in April 2013. At the time, she cited personal reasons, though few doubted it also had to do with multiple reviews of her expenses.

If the PMO thought that defenestrating another high-profile Conservative senator would blunt the momentum of the scandal and possibly save the public service career of Nigel Wright, they were dead wrong. Legalities to one side, there was an appearance of a double standard in the PMO's game plan. If it was a hanging offence for Mike Duffy to have taken a $90,000 gift to pay back improper expenses, it was surely a hanging offence to have given him the money to do it.

Nigel Wright was just days away from the end of his exempt staff career. Retaining him, now that the payment to Duffy was public knowledge, would be an unmistakable sign to Canadians that the prime minister approved of Wright's "gift" to Duffy. And there was one more thing. On the day that Senator Wallin left the Tory caucus, CTV's Robert Fife filed another devastating story about the Wright/Duffy affair. He reported that the Senate's Internal Economy Committee had sanitized the original Senate report of Mike Duffy's expenses, a document that concluded that he in fact had broken residency rules. The rot appeared to run deeper than a single transaction between Wright and Duffy.

The prime minister decided it was time to cut bait. Early on Sunday, May 19, 2013, the PMO released two statements. In one of them, Wright reported that the PM had accepted his resignation. Already constructing his and the prime minister's defence, Wright said that what he did was in the public interest, and that he accepted sole responsibility. His words were as carefully chosen as the ones he used in front of the Parliamentary Ethics Committee. "I did not advise the Prime Minister of the means by which Senator Duffy's expenses were repaid, either before or after the fact."

In his first personal comment since Fife broke the story, Prime Minister Harper confirmed that he had accepted Wright's resignation. "It is with great regret that I have accepted the resignation of Nigel Wright as my Chief of Staff. I accept that Nigel believed he was acting in the public interest, but I understand the decision he has taken to resign. I want to thank Nigel for his tremendous contribution to our government over the past two and a half years."

The piece on Stephen Harper's political chessboard that he most wanted to keep had been sacrificed. It was an unusually humiliating moment for Harper, smacking of connivance rather than conviction. Just a few days before, he had said through his director of communications that Wright enjoyed his full confidence and wouldn't be resigning. Now he had reversed himself without explaining what had changed. And if the goal had been as strategic as it looked—to stop the political bleeding—it was also a bad chess move.

The day after the prime minister accepted Nigel Wright's resignation, Fife reported that Harper's former special counsel and legal advisor Benjamin Perrin had worked on the legal deal between Wright and Duffy's lawyer. According to Fife's report, Perrin helped draft a memorandum of understanding: money would be provided for the payment of expenses and the Senate investigation would go easy on Duffy. According to Fife, the PMO declined to release the agreement, claiming that it was in the hands of Ethics Commissioner Dawson, who was investigating the payment.

Perrin, who left the PMO in April 2013, denied involvement. In a carefully worded statement released after the CTV story linking him to the payment, Perrin said, "Last night's CTV story in relation to me, which is based on unattributed sources, is false. I was not consulted on, and did not participate in, Nigel Wright's decision to write a personal cheque to reimburse Senator Duffy's expenses. I have never communicated with the prime minister on this matter. In all my work, I have been committed to making our country a better place and I hope my record of service speaks for itself." Perrin had left the PMO the month before to return to a teaching position at the University of British Columbia.[10]

The Senate scandal was turning into an exploding pumpkin for the government. The body count was growing—Duffy, Wallin, and Wright—and the prime minister's credibility was now in play.

He was either clueless or conniving in relation to what was now being called Duffygate. With Fife's latest story, there was a strong suggestion that there was much more to come. It was time for the prime minister to get out of Dodge.

Two days after the initial CTV story broke, the PMO had announced a trip to South America for the prime minister. He would visit Peru and Colombia, meeting with leaders and representatives of the private mining sector.[11] With the flames of scandal licking at his office door, Harper was off to something called the Pacific Alliance Leaders Summit in Cali, Colombia, an alliance formed by Chile, Colombia, Mexico, and Peru in 2011. This was the first time the prime minister participated in the forum—a trading bloc that even some Tories had not been sure Canada should join. Pro–free trade Conservative MP Ed Holder pointed out to a House of Commons hearing in March 2013 that there was no real reason to join the Alliance since Canada already had free-trade agreements with all four members of the group.

Two hours before boarding the Challenger that would take him to South America, Stephen Harper conducted an unusual Tuesday caucus to address his MPs. It was normal Harper rules—a photo op without questions from reporters. Without mentioning any of the players involved in the story the whole country was talking about, Harper called the scandal a "distraction" from the government's work and said that he was angry about it. "When distractions arise, as they inevitably will, we will deal with them firmly." The PM ignored reporters who shouted out questions. The journalists were quickly drowned out by the applause of caucus members and then asked to leave. Liberal MP Ralph Goodale called Harper's speech "totally vacuous" and "tone deaf."

Relations between CTV and the PMO soured. The network had previously had an arrangement with the government to be apprised of big announcements the evening before they were made.

The news item would be previewed on CTV's huge platform of over a million viewers, and the next day, the network would give full coverage when the initiative was officially announced. After the Wright/Duffy story was broadcast, that arrangement came to an end.

CTV's Robert Fife gave me his own assessment of how the Harper government had reacted to his story of cash payments, shady deals, and possibly illegal acts rolling out of the Prime Minister's Office: "Basically, it's been one lie after another."

fifteen

THE PINOCCHIO FACTOR

I f Stephen Harper thought that shuffling off to South America would rid him of unwelcome questions about the Senate scandal back home, he must have been disappointed. The first question asked at his news conference in Peru, 6,000 kilometres from Ottawa, was posed by CBC journalist Terry Milewski. Predictably, the tenacious Milewski asked about the Wright/Duffy affair.

Harper insisted he knew nothing about it except what he had seen on television news, that he hadn't been consulted in advance, and that if he had been, he would not have signed off on the arrangement. "I think we've been very clear that I did not know, but let me be very specific about this, I learned of this after stories appeared in the media last week speculating on the source of Mr. Duffy's repayments. . . . Obviously I am very sorry that this has occurred. I am not only sorry, I've been through the range of emotions. I'm sorry, I'm frustrated, I'm extremely angry about it."

The prime minister's bland denials usually worked. But not this time. There were too many things that didn't make sense. Why had he flip-flopped on Nigel Wright's resignation? First, Wright was remaining as chief of staff; then, a few days later he was leaving. What had changed? Was it plausible that Nigel Wright—a lawyer and the PM's chief of staff—would make a $90,000 cash payment to a sitting Conservative senator and not inform the prime minister?

In his own resignation press release, Wright himself said only that neither before nor after the Duffy transaction did he inform the prime minister of the "means" of the payment. But that was a long way from saying the PM didn't know about the Duffy expense problem and what, if anything, he wanted done about it. A series of nagging questions trumped Harper's standard dismissiveness. How was the deal negotiated and who was involved? Could Wright freelance such a deal, even had he wanted to, without involving others? Most unbelievable of all, how could a leader with a well-earned reputation as a micromanager know nothing about a most unusual action, undertaken by his second-in-command, that had the potential to topple the government?

While Harper clung to his talking points in Peru, the political pot was on the boil back in Canada. Government MPs were getting blowback over the Senate scandal as the Conservative base registered its anger and disapproval over Duffygate. For many Tory supporters, the skullduggery in the PMO and the abuse of expenses in the Senate were what they expected from Liberals—not from the self-declared party of law and order, transparency, and accountability. The Conservatives began to slide in the polls. Like the $16 glass of orange juice at the Savoy Hotel in London that cost Bev Oda her cabinet post, this was one of those "water-cooler scandals" that got ordinary people talking.

Frustrated for years by Harper's smothering information control, the political opposition sensed a genuine opening. Opposition leader Thomas Mulcair urged the government to disclose all documents about the transaction: "Be clear, be forthright, stop hiding out in the Andes, get back up here, tell people what actually happened."

With Harper out of the country, Foreign Affairs Minister John Baird was left to answer questions. He officially launched the government into the cover-up phase of the Wright/Duffy scandal. Baird repeated that the prime minister knew nothing about the deal until after it was reported on television. However, he made an important addition to the narrative, claiming that there was no paper trail connected to the story. "Our understanding is there is no document," he said, without elaborating on what that understanding was based on.

Baird said that the matter of Wright's payment had been referred to a pair of "independent authorities," but refused to state who they were. In fact, he was referring to federal ethics commissioner Mary Dawson, and the Senate's own Internal Economy Committee, the very committee that had whitewashed the original Senate report on Mike Duffy's expenses. The Harper government's self-proclaimed tough new accountability rules for public office holders were looking pretty flimsy. A finding by the ethics commissioner carried no sanction, and the Senate was too hopelessly enmeshed in the scandal to judge any other participants. Liberal Senate leader James Cowan explained why the payment needed to be thoroughly investigated: "If money was paid that would influence a decision of a Senate committee, then that is contempt of Parliament." Stephen Harper was the only prime minister in the Commonwealth for whom that was familiar territory.

Just as the prime minister's comments about Nigel Wright began to change, the Conservative Party's characterization of Mike Duffy also evolved. Five days after Duffy was praised for his "leadership" in the Senate expenses scandal by government house leader Peter Van Loan, the PMO issued a statement saying that taxpayers should not be on the hook for improper housing expenses. It was as if they sensed that more bad news was on the way. They were right. On May 21, 2013, veteran investigative reporter Tim Naumetz reported in the *Hill Times* that Senator Duffy was part of a series of 2011 campaign stops by high-profile party members to boost the electability of local candidates. The tour was organized by the Conservative Party's national campaign headquarters. One of the reporter's sources was a Nova Scotia MP who had shared the bill with others for Duffy's expenses.

The next day the *Toronto Star* advanced the story. The newspaper reported that not only was Duffy billing Conservative campaigns in Nova Scotia during the 2011 election, he was also receiving his Senate allowance as if he were in Ottawa. All told, Senator Duffy helped out in seven ridings during the trip, including Scott Armstrong's in Truro and David Morse's in Kentville, Nova Scotia. The senator had a policy advisor travelling with him on the campaign trip organized by Conservative national party headquarters.

Nigel Wright's worst fear—that the failure to contain the Duffy expense scandal would lead to "the Chinese water torture of new facts in the public domain that the PM does not want"— was coming to pass. It turned out that Senator Duffy had also campaigned for Sandy Lee in Yellowknife. Unspecified hotel costs in the GTA with Stephen Harper, and flights from Ottawa to Toronto to Yellowknife and back to Ottawa, were charged directly to the Conservative Party. Taxis in Toronto were listed on April 5 and April 7, 2011, as expenses. The Deloitte audit indicated Duffy was outside Ottawa on Senate business on those days.

According to Elections Canada, Duffy billed the campaigns of Joe Oliver, Wladyslaw Lizon, Gin Siow, and John Carmichael for $169.45 each for flights between Ottawa and Toronto, taxis, and a night at the Yorkdale Holiday Inn for an April 27–28 tour. The Deloitte review, meanwhile, said he was outside Ottawa on

Senate business. Duffy's invoice stipulated that the total cost of $1,355 would be split between eight ridings he visited. Only four candidates named Duffy as a supplier in their Elections Canada returns. All told, Duffy campaigned with seventeen Conservative candidates during the writ period, claiming Senate per diems for some days he was actually campaigning.

Once again, media stories prompted the Senate to take another look at Senator Duffy's expense claims. The agony continued for the government house leader in the Senate. Marjory LeBreton was caught between an unhappy PMO and the media in hot pursuit. On May 22, 2013, LeBreton gave a lengthy speech during a debate in the Senate on proposed rule changes as part of the government's response to the audits. She was aggrieved that the Senate was facing this "crisis" because it had voluntarily flung open the door that revealed what was going on inside. Instead of getting credit for being candid, the Senate was being pilloried in "hyped-up media stories." Having blamed the media, LeBreton resorted to the tried-and-true line of a politician at bay. "We are not perfect," she insisted, "but we have conducted ourselves in an appropriate and honourable way."

Knowing that the Senate's Internal Economy Committee was reviewing his expenses again, Senator Duffy broke his silence on the payment he had received from Nigel Wright. Stressing that he had done nothing wrong, he expressed confidence that his fellow senators would conclude, as Deloitte already had, that his actions did not merit criticism. He welcomed a "full and open inquiry," and said, "I think Canadians have a right to know all the facts and I'm quite prepared, in the right place and time, to give them the whole story."

Despite the bravado, the walls were beginning to close in on Mike Duffy. On May 28, 2013, the Senate's full Board of Internal Economy held an extraordinary meeting under the glare of TV lights. The senators announced that they had completed a re-examination of Senator Duffy's per-diem expenses and had come to a grave decision. The fact that the Conservatives held a majority in the Senate made what was about to happen next even more spectacular. In light of what Senator Duffy's peers saw as a pattern of false expense claims, his case was being referred to the RCMP. It was another reversal for LeBreton. Early in the controversy, she had said that the Duffy affair was not a police matter. In a little more than a month, LeBreton would resign as government house leader in the Senate, amid little doubt that the PMO had given her a hearty push.

The RCMP had already been looking into the circumstances of the Deloitte audit. Their additional involvement in the matter of Duffy's expenses did not go unnoticed in the PMO. Although Stephen Harper had kept the information to himself since the story broke, the PMO announced on May 31, 2013, that the prime minister had in fact discussed expenses with the embattled senator after the February 13, 2013, Conservative caucus.

Code-named Project Amble, the examination of Senator Duffy's financial affairs began with the RCMP picking up records from Elections Canada without a warrant on June 5 and 13 for twelve Conservatives Duffy had helped during the 2011 election. The list included Gerald Keddy, Greg Kerr, and Joe Oliver, but did not appear to include Julian Fantino. During the same period, the RCMP made a second request for documents from the Senate. The Mounties were trying to determine if Duffy had in fact claimed Senate per diems while campaigning for the Conservative Party in Atlantic Canada, the GTA, and the Northwest Territories, as various newspapers had reported.

That Mike Duffy was a key Conservative fundraiser was beyond question. Citing a series of emails, journalist Leslie MacKinnon posted a CBC piece on May 31, 2013, that showed Duffy had been discussing an expanded role in the party within months of being appointed to the Senate. He was the star speaker at fundraisers and Conservative riding associations across the country. People loved his folksy, funny style, described as "Hilarious, engaging and delightfully risqué." "Did you hear the one about Michael Ignatieff doing the work of three people—Curly, Larry and Moe," offered a gleeful Duffy.

Partisan crowds in towns such as Lacombe, Alberta, loved him, and small-town newspapers that relied on government ads eagerly quoted his speeches. Everyone wanted to put his star power to work, and that included Stephen Harper. In June 2009, Duffy had hosted a $100,000 campaign-style town-hall event featuring the prime minister and his Economic Action Plan in Cambridge, Ontario. The CBC obtained a July 2009 email exchange between Duffy and an unnamed party insider. Just six months after his appointment, Duffy was looking for ways for the party to pay his expenses and fees for what he called his "expanded role in the party."

According to a July 27, 2009, email from Duffy, the newly minted senator planned to speak with Irving Gerstein at the Senate golf tournament banquet that evening. Apparently Duffy had already suggested to the party bagman that he be named a minister without portfolio so he could get staff, a car, and more resources to assist in his travelling fundraising show. In the email, Duffy reported, "He [Gerstein] laughed and said he didn't think THAT was within the realm of the Cons fund. So my question is: what do I demand?" Duffy answers his own question "(That the Cons fund hire my private company, and I use that cash to hire additional staff to assist with these gigs?)." He asks should he have a meeting with Marjory, or "Should I request a one-on-one with Stephen?" A few hours later, Duffy's obviously well-connected correspondent replies,

I would keep the discussion with Irving. Expanding it at this time would attract too much attention. Any money, staff, resources paid for by the fund should be done by the fund. Keep it out of your company and office budget or it will hurt you down the road. If he can set up a travel budget for you at the fund and support a staffer, fantastic. What you really need now is travel paid by them so you don't get in trouble or run out of points. Have a billing acct, [name deletion] knows to book certain trips to them and not you etc. Don't take a credit card, just expense them.

Asked to comment on the story, party spokesperson Fred DeLorey replied, "Any events Mr. Duffy participated in on behalf of the party would have been paid for by the party. The party does not pay Mr. Duffy compensation." After hearing the story, MP Michelle Rempel told Evan Solomon, the host of CBC TV's *Power & Politics*, "The prime minister himself has expressed deep regret for appointing Mike Duffy."

After the Wright/Duffy affair blew up, Harper may have regretted the Duffy appointment, but he was certainly happy with it when the former television personality was on hand to help win coveted Toronto seats. On November 16, 2010, Duffy hosted a successful town hall for the Vaughan by-election that sent Julian Fantino to Ottawa. The call went out to 40,000 homes and 15,000 people stayed on the line. The event, organized by Andrew Harris of Picea Partners, was closed to the media. Harris had been the manager of direct voter contact for the Conservative Party of Canada from May 2006 to November 2008.

But there was mystery attached to the event. Although a media release said Duffy was on hand in Mr. Fantino's office to facilitate the meeting, Duffy denied it: "I wasn't in Vaughan, I can't remember where I was but I was at the end of a phone, as was

Mr. Fantino. I wasn't paid, nor did I incur expenses. I know nothing about the Elections Canada Act and reporting."

If he wasn't paid for the Vaughan town hall and if he incurred no expenses, he certainly did so in other ridings. In September 2009, Duffy emailed the executive director of the Conservative Party, Dan Hilton, and asked about billing procedures: "Dan: Shud [*sic*] I send you a one-page note re fees and expenses?" Duffy requested a staffer be assigned to him to help answer emails from supporters sent in response to a party email appeal, "before people get pissed off that we haven't responded." The emails were from Conservative VIPs and others who expected to hear from the party directly. "The Old Duff" sent out personalized video messages from the Conservative Party. He called the recipients by their first names and invited them to fill out a survey.

Duffy had asked people to write to him about suggestions for the party, and he was concerned that he was the mere front man for an enterprise controlled by others. In an email to Dan Hilton on September 28, 2009, he laid out his fears: "If my name is out front, then I want to be part of the decision making process. If it goes bad, I'm the one our members will blame." Hilton replied, "I have arranged to set funds aside where it makes sense and I have discussed this with Jenni Byrne. She should be the primary person on our end to square up the appropriateness of visits etc and she can review the schedule from your assistant to see if their ridings are of influence in the area."

Duffy was addressing university clubs, riding associations, and fundraisers since, as a minority government, the party was in permanent campaign mode. The question was whether this was Senate business or party business or funny business. Duffy's friends would later be quoted telling the *National Post* that "political appearances on the Senate tab were not only tolerated, they were expected by the Prime Minister."

While the PMO, Duffy's lawyers, and the Senate leadership had been cobbling together a deal to repay Duffy's "improper" housing allowance and expenses, the RCMP had been quietly looking into the Deloitte audit since March 2013. One of the things that caught their eye was a series of payments made by Senator Duffy to a company called Maple Ridge Media Inc. Maple Ridge was paid out of Senator Duffy's office budget at the rate of $200 per hour. The payments began in March 2009, and by 2013 amounted to a total of $64,916.50.

The billing seemed straightforward enough from the paperwork. For example, Duffy submitted an invoice to the Senate for $10,500 for "Consulting/editorial Services—research, writing & revisions for Heritage Project." In November 2010, Duffy submitted a contract for Maple Ridge that he requested be backdated to April. After being informed that backdating was not permitted by the Senate human resources officer, Senator Duffy resubmitted the $12,000 contract, plus tax, in December. There was only one problem: the man behind Maple Ridge, Gerald Donohue, had no experience as a media consultant. Donohue had spent most of his working life as a television technician, and ended his career in human resources. He had first met the TV star in 1989 while Duffy was hosting a public affairs show, *Sunday Edition*, broadcast out of CJOH in Ottawa. The RCMP decided to interview the man on the senator's payroll to find out exactly what Maple Ridge had done to earn its money.

They were in for a surprise. Although Donohue refused to give a sworn statement, he told the RCMP that he did not personally receive any money from the senator and that "he never funneled any of the money back to Duffy." Donohue's wife and son were officers of Maple Ridge, but he told police that they "had nothing to do with the work done for Senator Duffy." (Both declined to be interviewed by the RCMP.) It was a conundrum. If Donohue's family was not involved in working for the senator, and Donohue never received any money or remitted any to Duffy, where did the nearly $65,000 go? The Donohues decided to consult a lawyer, and the RCMP went away from the interview believing that little or no work had been done by Maple Ridge, a conclusion they noted in their report. Their next stop was to scoop the bank records to follow the money trail.

Unaware of this element in the Duffy case, the Senate had been reduced to desperate measures. The expenses scandal was not only not going away, it was getting worse. The NDP were calling for the abolition of the unelected Upper Chamber, and from the prime minister's point of view, it seemed like a good time to start that debate—anything to change the channel from corruption in his own office. Attacking the Senate had never been better politics.

In full panic that the institution itself was in danger, the Senate acted. On June 6, 2013, the leadership agreed to have federal auditor general Michael Ferguson do a "comprehensive audit" of Senate spending—including that of individual senators. It was one way to restore public faith in the probity of the Senate. Although Sheila Fraser had prised open the books of the Senate in 2011, shortly before she retired, her audit had not included senators' expense accounts. The Senate had decided to conduct its own random audits instead, and inadvertently got the expense scandal rolling, to the chagrin of the PMO.

Michael Ferguson's audit was the real deal, right down to powers of subpoena. The audit could include physical inspections of primary and secondary residences, and even interviews with neighbours to see if senators really lived in their designated residences. Numbered letters were sent to each senator. Consent letters had to be mailed back to the AG's office. Secrecy would be maintained by forbidding reproduction and distribution of the documents.

The formal motion to bring in Michael Ferguson was moved by Senator Marjory LeBreton: "That the Senate invite the auditor general of Canada to conduct a comprehensive audit of Senate expenses, including senators' expenses." It was an ironic turn of events. The Senate had initially wanted to deal with "a few bad apples" in its midst to avoid the very thing they were now proposing: a universal audit of all members. Under LeBreton's doomed leadership, the Senate was no longer master in its own house.

The Senate, the PMO, and the Conservative Party of Canada were now firmly tangled in the net of Duffygate. On June 7, 2013, the Conservative Party responded to a story by the CBC's Greg Weston. Weston's report said that there was a secret Conservative fund in the PMO controlled by one person, Nigel Wright. Weston quoted unnamed sources who told him that at times the fund had contained up to a million dollars. The political air in Ottawa was electric with the possibility that the secret fund—beyond the reach of Elections Canada and the auditor general—was in some way connected to Wright's $90,000 gift to Senator Duffy. "No Conservative Party funds were used to repay Mike Duffy's inappropriate expenses," party spokesperson Fred DeLorey claimed. "No taxpayer funds were used. Nigel Wright was not reimbursed by anyone."

After PMO spokesperson Andrew MacDougall, Fred DeLorey, and a variety of anonymous sources had all but confirmed the existence of the PMO fund, the Conservative Party tried to backtrack. It now called Weston's story about a "secret fund" false. But its contradictory attempts to deny the existence of the fund, in effect, confirmed the story. Finally, Chris Alexander, the parliamentary secretary to the minister of national defence, told CBC Radio's *The House* on June 8, 2013, that "No one [was] denying" the existence of the fund. Although parties must reveal all donations to Elections Canada, political parties are under no obligation to account for how they spend their party funds between elections.

The pressure was beginning to take its toll. On June 11, 2013, Senator David Tkachuk stepped down as chair of the powerful Internal Economy Committee. He announced that he was being treated for bladder cancer: "It's really important I have no stress and I give it all the opportunity to succeed, because if I don't succeed, the consequences aren't that good." In passing, the outgoing chair acknowledged that he found it personally difficult to read the emails he was receiving from ordinary Canadians angered by the Senate scandal.

Tkachuk's empty seat on the committee was still warm when Canadians learned that it was not merely a scandal they were watching unfold in some of the highest offices in the land, but quite possibly a crime.

sixteen

MOUNTIES AT THE DOOR

O n June 13, 2013, the RCMP announced that it had launched a criminal investigation into Nigel Wright's secret $90,000 gift to Senator Mike Duffy. According to their press release, the police were trying to "determine whether a criminal act has taken place. It [the investigation] must be meticulous and carefully examine all information." Stephen Harper's director of communications of the day, Andrew MacDougall, made clear that the PMO wasn't volunteering anything but "would provide any possible assistance if asked." It was a novel reaction from a law-and-order government: passive cooperation.

Since the RCMP was now involved, Ethics Commissioner Mary Dawson suspended her investigation into the propriety of Wright's payment to Duffy. News of the criminal investigation broke just before Question Period in the House of Commons. The prime minister was in Europe attending the G8 and high-level trade talks, leaving heritage minister James Moore to take the heat from the opposition, and, if possible, change the channel.

The incoming from the enemy lines started early. NDP MP Megan Leslie launched the first rocket, telling the government to "stop hiding," to produce Wright's cheque, and to tell the House who else in the PMO was involved in the secret deal. The affable Moore parried with sarcasm, asking rhetorically why NDP leader Thomas Mulcair wasn't in the House. "We know he is on the Hill," Moore quipped, drawing laughter from the government benches. It had made the news earlier that day that Mulcair had driven his car through a security checkpoint on the Hill without stopping, a small act of petulance creating a minor dust devil that disappeared in the act of forming.

The big story just kept getting bigger. Given the new development, Nigel Wright may have wished he had gone into the priesthood after all. The announcement of a criminal investigation changed everything for both men at the centre of the affair. They were no longer dealing with a political scandal but with a serious and personal legal problem. One Canadian senator, Raymond Lavigne, was already collecting his pension in jail after being convicted of fraud and breach of trust. Senator Duffy hired respected Ottawa criminal lawyer Donald Bayne, whose advice to the senator was to keep his powder dry. Wright's legal team took a very different approach.

On the very day the Mounties announced their criminal probe, one of Wright's lawyers called the RCMP to say that they would be sending information to investigators. The next day police received a letter in which Wright claimed he had been unaware of any fraudulent expense claims by the senator at the time he had given Duffy the $90,000. It was an answer to a question no one had yet asked him face to face. Had someone tipped off the prime minister's former chief of staff about what the Mounties were looking into? Had they found incriminating documents?

From the outset of the crisis, the Harper government claimed that there was no paper trail in the case. The outcome of twenty-three access-to-information requests by the media seemed to bear that out. The Privy Council Office, the prime minister's department, responded in every case that not a single piece of paper, letter, or email dealing with the Wright/Duffy affair existed. Nearly six months would pass before a red-faced PCO was forced to change its story, raising serious questions about how high the cover-up of the secret payment went.

Unlike the PMO and his department, Wright was the model of proactive cooperation, telling investigators he was willing to meet with them and provide whatever information they required. On June 19, 2013, Wright's lawyers, Patrick McCann and Peter Mantas, huddled with RCMP supterintendent Biage Carrese and Staff Sergeant Jean Francois Arbour to talk over a future interview with their client. The lawyers told the Mounties that Wright's role in the PMO was to manage the Conservative caucus members and handle any matters that could cause embarrassment to the prime minister or the party.

Then came the bombshell. Wright's lawyers said that the Conservative Party Fund, controlled by Senator Irving Gerstein, was initially going to repay Duffy's improper expenses. But that changed when the amount owing soared from $32,000 to $90,000. The Fund quickly closed its coffers to Senator Duffy. Then, and only then, did the prime minister's chief of staff decide to retire Duffy's expenses with a $90,000 personal "gift."

It was an odd piece of information. If the Conservative Party Fund was willing to pay back $32,000, why not $90,000? It certainly didn't seem to be a matter of principle. Was it the sheer increase in the amount of money owing that changed Senator Gerstein's mind, or the nature of the other $58,000 in claimed expenses? And there was another question. Why hadn't other Conservative senators with expense problems been bailed out? There were no "gifts" for Pamela Wallin or Patrick Brazeau—just invoices.

Wright's lawyers explained that their client had personally covered the costs of the Duffy settlement because he thought that taxpayers should not be out the money, making it "the proper ethical decision." It was a noble explanation even if it left another issue unexplained. Nigel Wright made it sound as if he were the only person who could make the public whole again. In fact, there was another person who could ensure that the taxpayers would get their money back and from whom a cheque made much more sense: Mike Duffy. Why hadn't the senator who claimed the improper expenses paid them back, instead of depending on the kindness of Nigel Wright? He did, after all, raise the total amount at the bank. Or was there something more to the arrangement than remarkable generosity?

The lawyers told police that Wright had imposed two conditions on Senator Duffy in return for his very big plum: that the improper expenses be paid back immediately, and that the former TV star stop talking to the media about his expense problems. Through his lawyers, Wright denied that anyone had directed him to make the payment to Duffy, and insisted that the prime minister was not aware of the "means" of the secret arrangement.

But Wright provided a declaration, via his lawyers, that flatly contradicted Stephen Harper's statement, on May 23, 2013, that the gift to Duffy "was a matter he [Wright] kept to himself until Wednesday, May 15." According to Wright's lawyers, several other unnamed people in the PMO knew about the deal with Duffy. The last thing McCann and Mantas told investigators in their meeting was that they "were not aware of any involvement this deal may have had regarding the altered Senate report draft." It was an important point. CTV's Robert Fife had reported the same two conditions that the lawyers told police Wright had attached to the $90,000 gift to Duffy. But Fife had reported a third—that if the senator acknowledged his improper expenses and repaid them, then the Senate committee looking into senators' expenses would go easy on Duffy.

Two days after meeting with the RCMP, one of Wright's lawyers, Peter Mantas, provided investigators with a letter in which his client gave the names of the four people, three of them in the PMO, who were told about the $90,000 deal: David van Hemmen, Nigel Wright's executive assistant; Benjamin Perrin, the prime minister's legal counsel; Chris Woodcock, the director of issues management; and Senator Irving Gerstein. There was also an interesting enclosure. Attached to the letter was a copy of the CIBC bank draft that NDP MP Megan Leslie had wanted to see. It was made out to Senator's Duffy's employment lawyer, Janice Payne, in the amount of $90,172.24 and dated March 25, 2013.

The investigation was now at the prime minister's door and the police had possible fraud and breach of trust on their minds. In making requests for additional documents, investigators made public the names of the three PMO staffers and the senator who knew about the deal. The public was reminded once again of the lack of truth in what the prime minister had repeatedly said, and indeed said again on June 5, 2013: "It was Mr. Wright who made the decision to take his personal funds and give those to Mr. Duffy. Those were his decisions. They were not communicated to me or to members of my staff."

Meanwhile, the Wright/Duffy scandal ended another career in the Senate leadership. On July 4, her seventy-third birthday, Marjory LeBreton announced she was stepping down from her post as government house leader in the Senate. Coincidentally, it was the same day the first batch of RCMP court documents regarding Mike Duffy were unsealed and became public. Just a few months earlier, LeBreton had insisted that Senator Duffy's expenses did not rise to the level of a police matter and that the whole scandal was the result of over-hyped stories from the national media. It was an open secret in Ottawa that the PMO was disenchanted with the performance of top Tories in the Senate, including LeBreton. That became blatantly obvious when the prime minister announced in the wake of LeBreton's "retirement" that the government house leader in the Senate would no longer have a seat in the Harper cabinet.

Harper's anger toward the Senate was hypocritical. The Conservative majority in the Upper Chamber may have created an embarrassing situation, but it took operatives from the PMO to turn it into a police matter. Harper was now paying the price in the media, even with his base. As the PMO lurched from one version of the facts to another, even the pro-Conservative *Globe and Mail* ridiculed the amateurish cover-up by people with a reputation for tight political control. "It's getting awkward to watch," wrote columnist Tabatha Southey. "It's like the whole exquisitely polite country is trapped at karaoke night with the guy who thinks his version of 'Total Eclipse of the Heart' is rocking your world." The Conservative Party had been willing to pay $32,000, but decided to be "tough on crime over $90,000."

The prime minister was beginning to look shifty. The sensational details laid out in the sworn RCMP affidavit blew out his story that no one but Nigel Wright knew about the secret deal with Duffy. Just hours before the Conservative leader was to attend a major fundraiser for his Calgary Southwest constituency association, Harper had to change his story, telling reporters, "When I answered questions about this in the House of Commons, I answered to the best of my knowledge."

The real question was, had the prime minister made his best effort to find out? The answer was clearly "no" as far as the political opposition was concerned. Harper's constant revisionism looked more like wilful blindness than the truth. "It's really depressing to see the prime minister of Canada acting like the piano player in the bordello, saying he didn't know what was going on upstairs," NDP PM Nathan Cullen said.

Judging by an Ipsos Reid poll published in July 2013, NDP MP Charlie Angus wasn't the only one who thought Harper was lying. Only 13 percent believed that the prime minister didn't know about Wright's payment to Duffy. A whopping 70 percent of respondents also disapproved of the prime minister's handling of the scandal—a head-in-the-sand combination of evasion, half-truths, and confabulations.

And now there was a new accusation against the PMO. On July 17, 2013, CTV's Ottawa bureau chief, Robert Fife, reported that the February 20 email sent by Senator Duffy to unspecified recipients—the document that broke the Wright/Duffy affair wide open—was being withheld from the police by the PMO. In another example of passive cooperation, the PMO responded by saying that investigators had not yet asked for the document.

The RCMP had not decided where Nigel Wright fit within their investigation. Was he a witness or a suspect? On July 18, 2013, Wright was interviewed under caution by Superintendent Carrese and Corporal Greg Horton. While Wright was answering questions, the Canadian Taxpayers Federation (CTF) was making a statement of its own. The scandal had angered the CTF's 84,000 supporters, and 65 percent of them now wanted the Senate abolished. Senator Duffy became the symbol of their wrath and the affair moved into its circus phase. The CTF hoisted a giant hot-air balloon of Mike Duffy two-and-a-half stories high into the summer sky off Victoria Island.[1] The senator was carrying a briefcase bulging with twenty-dollar bills—taxpayers' money. When the wind blew in the right direction, the effigy of Duffy twisted eerily toward Parliament Hill.

By July 24, 2013, RCMP investigators officially asked for information from the PMO. Press secretary Julie Vaux confirmed that the Mounties had indeed made a formal request for information. Harper's official story was modified again. He no longer said that no one else in the PMO knew of Wright's secret payment to Duffy, only that the lone villain of the piece was Nigel Wright. "This file was handled by Nigel Wright and he has taken sole responsibility," Vaux said.

If anyone were looking for a sign of Stephen Harper's anger at the Senate, his new minister for democratic reform provided them one on July 31, 2013. Pierre Poilievre unveiled the federal government's position for the Supreme Court reference on Senate reform. In keeping with Harper's unilateral approach in constitutional affairs, Ottawa asserted the right to make changes to the Senate without consulting the provinces.

But the claim that sent a shiver down the spine of sitting senators was Ottawa's position that it needed the support of only seven provinces representing 50 percent of the population to abolish the Upper Chamber of sober second thought. Within a month, Alberta, Saskatchewan, and British Columbia sided with the federal government.[2]

On August 26, Liberal senator Mac Harb briefly diverted the spotlight from the Wright/Duffy affair with his surprise resignation from the Senate. It was a dramatic about-face for a man who had insisted that his disputed housing allowance was in order and who had commenced a legal action against the Senate. He not only dropped the litigation but also repaid $231,649.07 in ineligible expenses. Harb predicted that the ongoing review by the auditor general would confirm that many other senators shared his understanding of the rule and had made similar expense claims. One of the "bad apples" was no longer in the barrel. The question now was whether Harb's resignation and repayment would end his troubles. They would not.

By late summer, the RCMP had still not interviewed Senator Mike Duffy, but documents filed into court showed that investigators had been busily looking into the affairs of the senator from Prince Edward Island. (In fact, though no one knew it, the police had begun investigating Duffy back in early March.) The documents were published in the *National Post* on August 9, 2013, and alleged that Duffy had charged the Senate for travel and daily expenses while he had in fact been campaigning for the Conservatives in far-flung parts of the country. Corporal Greg Horton, who was now in charge of the investigation, wrote, "I believe that Senator Duffy has demonstrated a pattern of filing fraudulent expense claims."

All told, the police alleged that Duffy charged the Senate for expenses while campaigning for three defeated candidates and eight elected MPs between April 12 and April 21, 2011. The senator also allegedly double-dipped by sending bills to each campaign—bills that were then submitted to Elections Canada as election expenses. A report from FINTRAC (Canada's independent financial intelligence unit reporting to the minister of finance) also revealed to investigators that Duffy changed the address on his personal bank account to his address in PEI on December 10, 2012—mere days after the Senate announced it was conducting an audit of housing claims.

Instead of fading away, the Senate expenses scandal settled in like a low-pressure zone over the Harper government. The headlines just kept coming. On September 14, Senator Pamela Wallin repaid the Senate nearly $114,000 for rejected expense claims, stressing that she had done nothing wrong. How strange it must have seemed for the woman who had introduced Stephen Harper when he made the keynote address at the party convention in 2011 to be fighting to keep her place in the Senate.

Two days after Senator Wallin wrote the cheque to repay expenses she still believed were legitimate, the RCMP sat down with one of the most powerful men in the Senate, Irving Gerstein, chair of the Conservative Party Fund. Under Senator Gerstein, the Conservative Party of Canada had built the most successful fund-raising operation of any political party in the country. Every weeknight, the party's phone banks call people who have shown an interest in contributing, or who have given money to the Conservative Party in the past. The operation isn't just to raise money. It's also about keeping a visceral connection to the base—about seeking political intelligence, the mood of Conservative Party supporters, and the issues they care about.

The Conservative Party phone bank tracks it all, and the prime minister receives regular reports from Jenni Byrne, the former director of political operations for the party, now in the PMO. It goes to the heart of the Conservative formula for winning: holding the base at 30 percent and adding 7 to 8 percent more at election time equals a majority government—or at least for as long as the progressive vote is divided.

Money and politics is sometimes a shady combination. Gerstein and three other senior Conservatives—Michael Donison, Susan Kehoe, and the late Doug Finley—were all charged by Elections Canada with devising an illegal scheme that allowed them to spend a million dollars above the limit on advertising during the 2006 federal election.[3] It also allowed local candidates to claim rebates for expenses they never incurred. The so-called in-and-out scandal was settled when the party pleaded guilty to a lesser charge in return for the charges against the individuals being dropped. In the end, the party paid a $52,000 fine and returned $230,000 to the government.

Just as Nigel Wright had already told investigators, Gerstein confirmed that he had spoken on a conference call with Wright in

February 2013. The Mounties discovered that Conservative Party lawyer Arthur Hamilton was also on the line. Wright had told police that Gerstein had initially offered to help with the Duffy matter. Gerstein told investigators a slightly different story—that Wright had asked him to pay Duffy's expenses and legal bill, and Gerstein had said "it was something he would consider."

One of the concerns the party bagman had was that Duffy might not keep the arrangement confidential. If Conservative Party donors were to find out that their money had been used to bail out an expenses cheater, there would be outrage. And there were also tax implications, since donors get a generous tax rebate for political donations. Taxpayers as well as Conservative Party contributors would not be happy if they learned they were picking up the tab for Mike Duffy or any other senator, beyond what the rules allowed.

Gerstein explained that Wright had initially told him that the senator owed $32,000 but afterwards confirmed that the amount was $90,000. The chair of the Conservative Party Fund emphatically refused to write the cheque. Nigel Wright was apparently left holding the bag. When next Gerstein spoke to the PM's chief of staff, on March 1, 2013, Wright surprised the senator by telling him that he had decided to personally repay Duffy's expenses. According to what Gerstein told the RCMP, word was certainly getting around. The president of the Conservative Party of Canada, Dan Hilton, also knew about the secret payment.

Two weeks later, the Senate scandal widened to include someone very close to Stephen Harper. Carolyn Stewart Olsen had been the prime minister's long-time press secretary and strategic communications advisor before Harper appointed her to the Senate in 2009. He can't have been happy to see *The Huffington Post* reporting that Stewart Olsen had claimed per diems and other expenses when the Senate was not in session for a three-month period ending February 28, 2011. Stewart Olsen vigorously denied the allegation, but the new chair of the Internal Economy Committee, Senator Gerald Commeau, asked Senate finance officials to review Stewart Olsen's expenses. Stewart Olsen chose this moment to step down from her spot on the committee, joining Marjory LeBreton and David Tkachuk as high-ranking Conservative casualties of what was now being described as the bloodbath in the Senate.

The narrative was about to turn pure Hollywood. Police and paramedics were called to Senator Patrick Brazeau's house twice during the night of October 2, 2013. The calamitous senator who had been arrested eight months earlier and charged with violent assault and sexual assault was taken to hospital, possibly suffering from depression or other health issues. No further details emerged.

Just two weeks later, Senator Mike Duffy issued a press release about his health. With a long history of heart problems behind him, including open-heart surgery, he said that his doctor wanted him to take immediate medical leave because of his deteriorating condition.[4] The press release came one week after court documents revealed that the RCMP was now investigating the senator for potentially new breach-of-trust and fraud charges related to contracts paid out of his Senate office budget to an old friend from his CTV days with no known experience as a consultant.

Duffy's press release came just hours before the Harper government's new leader in the Senate dropped a bomb of his own. Claude Carignan announced that he would be tabling a motion to suspend Senators Duffy, Brazeau, and Wallin without pay on the grounds of "gross negligence." The warfare was now open and brutal, and no one was taking any prisoners.

On October 21, Senator Duffy's criminal lawyer, Donald Bayne, held a packed press conference at which all the skills that made him a crack criminal lawyer were on display. As though he were playing to a skeptical jury, Bayne stated his client's case energetically and eloquently. He read from the now-famous February 20, 2013, email giving details about the Wright/Duffy deal and emphasized that all roads in the scandal led back to the PMO. It was the PMO, he declared, that worked out the "lines" and "scenarios" to meet Duffy's concerns, "including cash for payment." The virtuoso performance also featured a tease. Protesting that he wasn't about to try Senator Duffy's case in the media, Bayne said that his client had information about what the prime minister knew about the deal that the press would find most interesting.

Bayne's press conference was mere prologue. Over the next two days, the three senators showed up in the Red Chamber to personally challenge the motions to suspend them without pay. Though he was just weeks away from more open-heart surgery, Duffy made a remarkable speech. Forty years of communicating for a living—on radio, television, and countless stages across the country—were on display. Duffy was critical and contrite, painting a picture of ruthless schemers in the PMO who had forced him to do something that was against his will: "I allowed myself to be intimidated into doing what I knew in my heart was wrong out of fear of losing my job and out of a misguided sense of loyalty." With his fellow senators, journalists, and a large part of the country listening to the famous voice, Mike Duffy lowered the boom: "I wish I'd had the courage to say no back in February when this monstrous political scheme was first ordered."

The next day it was Pamela Wallin—another star Harper Senate appointee who had had her expenses forwarded to the RCMP—who took the stand. As falls from grace go, it was almost Shakespearean. A celebrated television personality and former diplomat, she had received the Order of Canada, once chaired the powerful defence committee, and served on the Foreign Affairs Committee. Then there were the corporate connections. As a senator, Wallin had been on the boards of several companies, including Bell Globemedia, Oilsands Quest Inc., Porter Airlines, and wealth management firm Gluskin Sheff & Associates. Since becoming a senator, Wallin had earned $1 million in fees and stock options from these connections, beyond her Senate salary of $132,300. Oilsands Quest was the most lucrative, earning Wallin almost $648,000 in cash and offered options between June 2007 and December 2011.

Although all this extra income was allowed under Senate rules, the connection with Oilsands Quest was not without controversy. The company filed for bankruptcy in an Alberta court in November 2011, and under Chapter 15 protection in the United States. Its assets in northern Saskatchewan were sold to energy giant Cenovus. In August 2013, a US court approved a multi-million-dollar settlement in a securities fraud case against Oilsands Quest and its directors. In a lawsuit filed in New York in 2011, investors alleged that the company overstated its assets by $136 million and fraudulently pumped up the stock price. The judge who signed off on the $10.2 million settlement had also presided over the case involving infamous ponzi schemer Bernie Madoff. Luckily for Wallin and the other directors, the insurer of the bankrupt energy exploration company paid the fine.

Wallin's speech to the Senate was a passionate defence. She accused fellow Conservative senators Marjory LeBreton and Carolyn Stewart Olsen of having a personal vendetta against her. As for the audit that found her guilty of running up improper expenses, the former CTV television personality called it a "fundamentally flawed and unfair process." Five days later, the RCMP laid out fraud and breach-of-trust allegations against Wallin in court documents. Investigators were seeking more documents from the Senate related to changes the senator had made in her daily calendars. They cited "inconsistencies and discrepancies" in the calendars that warranted further investigation. The RCMP also believed that Toronto, rather than Wadena, Saskatchewan, was Wallin's primary residence.

With the Conservative leadership in the Senate flexing its muscles, the prime minister decided to personally join the effort to sink Duffy, Wallin, and Brazeau. On October 26, Harper took to the airwaves in Toronto on John Tory's CFRB drive-home show in a carefully controlled event with a government-friendly host. The PM claimed that he had ordered Senator Duffy to repay his expenses because it was "beyond a shadow of a doubt" that Senate rules were broken over a long period of time. Harper also repeated a story that fewer and fewer Canadians believed—that he knew nothing about the $90,000 gift from Nigel Wright to Mike Duffy: "Look, John, obviously I didn't know, and obviously had I known about this, I would have told Mr. Wright not to undertake these actions." A new element was creeping into the PM's account—a faint note of feeling aggrieved that would fully declare itself two days later, with serious implications for his former chief of staff. "I should have been told, I think I should have been consulted. I was not."

The fact that the PM was doing radio interviews was a tell-tale sign that, far from losing momentum, the scandal was gaining traction by the day. The damage to both the party and the prime minister was showing up in the polls. Since it had taken four days for the prime minister to accept Nigel Wright's resignation, it looked as though he was condoning what had happened. His false claims that no one else in the PMO knew about Wright's secret payment were now almost laughable. The real issue seemed to be that Stephen Harper was the only one who didn't know—despite being the most controlling prime minister Canada has ever had.

So on October 28, 2013, Harper changed his story again, casting himself as a decisive leader who wouldn't put up with lies and deception. He told Jordi Morgan—a former Canadian Alliance candidate and host of News 95.7's *Maritime Morning* show—that Nigel Wright "was dismissed." This was a jarring departure from Harper's previous statements: first, that Wright enjoyed his full confidence and would not be leaving his post, and then his reluctant acceptance of Wright's resignation four days later. Now the PM was claiming for the first time that Nigel Wright had been fired.[5]

Wright had a cadre of longstanding supporters who were taken aback at the news, some of them openly doubting the credibility of the prime minister's latest version of events touching the scandal. Praising Wright as one of the most able and ethical people he had ever met in politics and business, Preston Manning suggested he would be vindicated, noting, "I think it's his [Wright's] account, at the end of the day, that will be the most credible account of what actually happened." Manning also suggested darker motives that might be behind Harper's new claim. "I think the first story was the correct one," he told Mark Kennedy of the *National Post*. "The deeper these things get, the more people are backed into corners." It had been Manning's experience that "Stephen doesn't think words mean much."[6]

Even Conservative cabinet ministers seemed uncomfortable with Harper's latest version of events. Both Jason Kenney and Peter MacKay lauded Wright's hard work for the party and vouched for his integrity. Charles McMillan, who had worked with Wright in Brian Mulroney's PMO, delivered the sharpest rebuke of Stephen Harper's scapegoating of his former chief of staff: ". . . to put the blame of this whole saga on Nigel is nuts. . . . I think there is a larger story here with a whole series of players. . . . It's like an iceberg. There's a larger story under the water."

It was at that moment that the man nicknamed "the Killer Whale" by government insiders breached the surface again and rocked the government's boat. Coming straight from Ottawa's Heart Institute, Mike Duffy's passionate voice rang out in the

Senate chamber a second time. It was another headline event, occurring as it did just three days before the Conservatives held their national convention in Calgary on Halloween.

Not only had Nigel Wright paid $90,000 of Duffy's disputed expenses, but Canadians learned that he had arranged a second cheque from the Conservative Party Fund for the senator's legal fees—$13,560. The cheque had been sent by Arthur Hamilton to Duffy's lawyer, Janice Payne. Duffy gave another masterful speech proving again that he was skilled in the art of the political knife fight. And just so there was no doubt the party had paid his legal bills, he tabled both the cheque and the transmittal letter in the Senate. Duffy knew that, in just a week, the Senate would be voting on Claude Carignan's motion to suspend him from the Senate without pay, and he may have been trying to make clear that there would be consequences for the party if that happened.

Senator Wallin, also facing expulsion without pay and an RCMP investigation, paid back a total of $152,908.77 in improper expenses hoping that it would be enough to persuade her colleagues not to vote in favour of the motion. She insisted once more that she had been mistreated by the Senate and the auditors at Deloitte.

Senator Duffy's revelation of a second cheque turned Question Period into an inquisition directed at the prime minister. Day after day, Opposition leader Thomas Mulcair skewered him. It was the NDP leader's strongest performance, with Mulcair outshining the more reserved Justin Trudeau and showing brilliant flashes of a person who could be prime minister. When Harper tried to pass off the payment of Duffy's legal bill as "normal," Mulcair shot back, "The prime minister, therefore, sees nothing wrong with using the money of the Conservative Party to reimburse the legal expenses of someone he says has broken the law. That is the ethics of the prime minister. Duly noted." Liberal leader Justin Trudeau had an observation of his own that was on a lot of people's minds: "I think donors are beginning to wonder how this party administers their donations."

On October 29, 2013, the opposition continued to grill Harper over Duffygate, and a hapless Stephen Harper stuck to his already discredited story that it was all Nigel Wright's fault: "On our side, there is one person responsible for this deception and that person is Mr. Wright, by his own admission. For that reason, Mr. Wright no longer works for us. Mr. Duffy should not either." Liberal MP Scott Andrews pounced on the PM's hypocrisy. Why should Duffy be dumped from the public payroll? Conservative MP Dean Del Mastro was actually charged with violating election expenses laws and the taxpayers were still paying his salary. When Harper was asked if party lawyer Arthur Hamilton should be fired, the prime minister replied, "This individual is not accused of anything."

The prime minister's confabulations and contradictory stories were beginning to catch up with him. It was not true that no one in the PMO other than Wright knew about the secret payment to Duffy. Harper's longstanding claim that no taxpayer money had been used to pay Duffy was not true. (Taxpayers remit a generous tax credit to donors to political parties, so they in fact paid a portion of the senator's legal bill.) And if it were true that it was "normal" to pay the legal bills of caucus members, as the PM stated in the House of Commons, why hadn't Pamela Wallin or Patrick Brazeau been treated normally?

Up until November 2, 2013, the only people Senator Irving Gerstein had spoken to about the Wright/Duffy affair were members of the RCMP. The senator was a very busy man and not only with Senate business. Gerstein collected $290,000 in director's fees and attended dozens of corporate board meetings in 2012. He is chair of the board of Boston-based Atlantic Power Corporation, which has power generation projects in the United States and Canada. He is also on the board of Medical Facilities

Corporation, whose specialty is private surgical hospitals in the US offering "five-star hotel" surroundings and service.

After it became public that the Conservative Party had paid Duffy's legal bill, a fact Gerstein himself had never revealed, there was no way even a senator as busy as Gerstein could avoid the question about paying Duffy's expenses. He gave his answer at the Conservative convention, where, with the exception of guard dogs and bouncers, the party did everything it could to keep the media away from the action.

In his explanation to delegates, Gerstein followed the prime minister's line and laid it all on Harper's former chief of staff. It was Wright who asked the party to pay for Duffy's lawyer, he claimed, and Wright who asked the party to pay off his $90,000 in expenses. "I made it absolutely clear to Nigel Wright that the Conservative Fund of Canada would not pay for Senator Mike Duffy's disputed expenses and never did." It sounded like a principled position. But if the party wouldn't pay as a matter of principle, why had Gerstein told the RCMP the Fund considered paying Duffy's bills when the amount was $32,000? And why hadn't he made it absolutely clear that the Fund wouldn't pay Duffy's legal bill if using party donations was truly a matter of principle?

The PMO would soon come up with an answer through Stephen Harper's latest press spokesperson, Jason MacDonald. MacDonald wrote in an email, "The party was assured the invoice was for valid legal fees related to the audit process, and the party paid them on the basis of those assurances." The mischaracterizations were getting silly. Not only did MacDonald's story contradict the PM's explanation that the party had paid because it was "normal" to do so. If that were true, why hadn't senators Wallin and Brazeau had their bills paid? The PMO knew perfectly well that Janice Payne was an employment lawyer primarily looking after Senator Duffy's negotiations with the PMO to secretly pay off his expenses. And then there was the most inconvenient fact of them all: how could the bill have been related to the audit? Senator Duffy never participated in it. And the PMO knew that because it was the PMO that advised him to stay away from it. Nigel Wright's lawyer responded to the latest piece of PMO fiction with a few icy words that suggested the truth would come out later. "No comment at this time to the latest characterization of events."

On November 5, 2013, the four hundred and eighth anniversary of the Gunpowder Plot to blow up the British House of Lords, two political explosions shook the foundations of Canada's political establishment. Guy Fawkes would have been impressed with the panic they set off in the political establishment.

The mayor of Canada's biggest city, Rob Ford, admitted after months of public denials that he smoked crack cocaine. The man who was the prime minister's fishing buddy and the Tories' key to suburban federal seats around Toronto assured his supporters he was not an addict or a liar; he merely used drugs and only responded truthfully to the "right" question. As for that pesky video in which he appeared to be smoking crack cocaine with fellows who were not Boy Scouts, he had simply been too drunk to remember it. It was not the most shining moment for the party of law and order and family values.[7]

Three hundred and fifty-three kilometres northeast of Toronto, the Senate of Canada carried out the prime minister's wishes and voted to suspend Senators Duffy, Wallin, and Brazeau without pay. Although the rules said that such an action could be taken "to protect the dignity and reputation of the Senate and public trust and confidence in Parliament," the motion to suspend had faced vocal opposition from some senior senators in the Conservative caucus.

Senators Hugh Segal and Don Plett (a former president of the Conservative Party) declared that the motion was in effect sentencing the three senators before they had been charged, let alone convicted, of anything. In Segal's view, kicking the senators out and taking away their pay turned "the Senate Chamber into the Star Chamber." Despite his eloquence, the Conservative majority in the Harper-stacked Senate did the deed in a lopsided vote: Wallin, fifty-two to twenty-seven; Duffy, fifty-two to twenty-eight; and Brazeau, fifty to twenty-nine—all results in favour of suspension for two years without pay. Thirty-six senators abstained from the vote.

Among those sitting in the Senate Chamber looking down at the historic vote (only once before had a senator been suspended) was the journalist who had broken the story, Robert Fife. It was a wrenching moment. "I'd known two of these people for thirty years," Fife told me. "Mike Duffy helped me a lot when I was a young reporter in Ottawa, a lot. People think doing these stories is easy. It isn't. I felt sick to my stomach that night."

Senator Patrick Brazeau sat stone still in his place as the results were announced. Earlier, he had pleaded with his colleagues not to believe all the things they had heard about him. "It is very important that you know that I am not a thief, a scammer, a drunken Indian, a drug addict, a failed experiment or a human tragedy." The last items in his list were a direct dig at Senator LeBreton, who had used those terms to describe his appointment to the Senate.

There was a lot on Brazeau's mind as he sat there dazed by what had just happened—the criminal charges he was facing, the $49,000 in expenses he had to repay, the loss of his Senate paycheque, and his banishment from the Senate. But there was also gratitude. He walked over to Liberal senator James Munson, a friend and supporter, and shook his hand. In just over three months' time, Patrick Brazeau would be managing a strip club in the Byward Market. In April 2014, he was charged in another domestic assault, and with cocaine possession. Reporters arrived at the home to find his personal belongings thrown out in the snow—clothing, a violin, family photographs, his Indian Status card, a legal envelope from the Senate. Brazeau was sent to a rehabilitation facility in Saint-André-d'Argenteuil as a condition of his bail.[8]

As for the now-suspended Senator Pamela Wallin, she took a moment to talk to the retinue of reporters looking for a comment as she exited the Chamber for what was likely the last time. "I think it's an extremely sad day for democracy. If we can't expect the rule of law in Canada, then where on earth can we expect it?" There was no appealing the judgment that her Senate colleagues had brought down on her. She was now a senator in name only, without a paycheque or an office, though all three suspendees retained their health benefits. Wallin walked out into the dark November night and slipped into the back seat of a waiting car. Turning to the throng of reporters, she managed to pull up one last smile. Even through the window, it could not disguise her dismay at her stunning fall from grace. F. Scott Fitzgerald's brilliant coinage came to mind: the rock of the world is built on a fairy's wing.

As desperately as Stephen Harper wanted the Senate scandal to just go away, the suspension of the three senators under conditions that even some Tory MPs found unfair dominated Question Period the following day. The leader of the Opposition bluntly asked the prime minister if Jenni Byrne, the domineering and abrasive director of the Conservative Party at the time of the Wright/Duffy deal, knew about the plan to repay Duffy's expenses using party funds. The question got under Harper's skin. "Without proof, the NDP is making allegations against people. Clearly Mr. Wright acted alone and accepted responsibility for that."[9]

Partisan help for the non-answering prime minister came from the Speaker's chair. Andrew Scheer repeatedly warned Mulcair to stick to government business, not party business. Mulcair schooled the youthful Speaker on his mistaken premise, and he did it by playing on the most overused meaningless word in the prime minister's vocabulary: "Just to be clear, perfectly clear, this is about a cover-up in the Prime Minister's Office. This is government business. This is the public's business."

Just as Stephen Harper thought he was making progress on the Senate scandal with the removal of Duffy, Wallin, and Brazeau, Corporal Greg Horton filed his blockbuster Information to Obtain (ITO) to Justice Hugh Fraser on November 15, 2013. An ITO is an affidavit sworn by an investigator stating the grounds for seeking additional documents from their custodians. The contents of Horton's eighty-one-page ITO provided a spectacular rebuttal to the prime minister's assertion that the Wright/Duffy affair was not known to others in the PMO. According to the ITO, several senior staffers not only knew about it but were deeply involved in negotiations to settle the matter in a way that might prove illegal. The prime minister had either been misled or he himself had misled the House of Commons.

Often, ITOs remain sealed, but Horton's was made public five days after he swore out his affidavit. As hard as the prime minister had tried to restrict the Senate scandal to a few bad apples in the Upper Chamber and one deceitful member of his staff (all hand-picked appointees of Harper), this limited version of the story was obviously untrue. But the issue of Wright's $90,000 secret gift to Senator Duffy was eclipsed by even more serious allegations. Corporal Horton alleged new evidence that the PMO interfered in an independent audit commissioned by the Senate, and conspired through multiple PMO staffers to have an official report of the Senate altered to accommodate the demands of Senator Duffy.

Outed by Corporal Horton's ITO, the Harper government responded with monosyllabic answers or the Cone of Silence. The most important new fact that had been added to the public discussion was that the chair of the Conservative Party Fund, Senator Irving Gerstein, had been asked by the PMO to approach internal sources at Deloitte to find out if the Duffy audit could be shut down if Senator Duffy repaid his expenses. Gerstein, it was revealed, went to Michael Runia, who was a senior partner at Deloitte, which also audited the Conservative Party Fund. Was Runia the hidden source who supplied PMO staff with an answer to their question and a preview of what Deloitte would conclude about Duffy's residency issue?

Although the members of the Red Chamber had the urgent duty to get to the bottom of a possibly illegal breach of an independent audit the Senate itself had commissioned, they opted instead to participate in a cover-up. The Conservative majority on the Internal Economy Committee refused to call either Senator Gerstein or Michael Runia. This was not the decision of a body interested in discovering the facts. It was the ignoble ploy of people who wanted to hide them.

Senate Speaker Noel Kinsella also ruled against a Liberal request to look into how the findings of the Deloitte audit got into the hands of the PMO weeks before they were presented to the Senate committee. Even Senator Gerstein got into the act. As chair of the Senate Finance Committee, he ruled out of order a motion calling for him to step aside while the RCMP was investigating a case in which he was involved. Since the Senate wouldn't go after the facts, Liberal justice critic Sean Casey asked the RCMP to investigate Gerstein's role in a scandal that had a very well-known centre but no known circumference.[10]

On November 28, 2013, the three Deloitte auditors who had reviewed Duffy's expenses made a seventy-minute appearance in front of a Senate committee. It was as close as the public would get to knowing more about Gerstein and Runia's dealings on the Duffy audit. Auditor Gary Timm confirmed that Ontario managing partner Michael Runia had indeed called him to ask about the audit, and Timm suggested in his testimony that the call was not appropriate. He told the senators, "It was a short call and it ended there," with the auditor directing Runia to public information.

Asked about the fact that PMO staffer Patrick Rogers knew in mid-March that Deloitte would not reach a definite conclusion on Duffy's primary residence, auditor Alan Stewart called the information "troubling" and testified, "I don't know where that information came from, but it did not come from the investigative team."

Peter Dent, the national leader of Deloitte's forensic advisory practice insisted that independence was maintained throughout the audit. "At no time was confidential information shared outside of the forensic team," he stated, "and Deloitte stands by the content, the quality and the objectivity of the information we provided." Dent insisted that the call from Michael Runia prompted by Senator Gerstein's intervention on behalf of the PMO had no effect on their conclusions. When *Hill Times* reporter Tim Naumetz asked Dent how Senator Gerstein could have known that Deloitte was unlikely to make a conclusive finding about the legitimacy of Senator Duffy's residency claims, Dent replied, "We have no idea."

Deloitte, which has received over $135 million in major contracts since the Conservatives came to power, was mindful of its international reputation. On June 18, 2013, New York governor Andrew Cuomo had announced that his administration had reached an agreement with Deloitte that would see the auditing firm make a $10-million payment to the state of New York and agree to a one-year voluntary suspension from consulting work at financial institutions regulated by the state.[11] The firm would also agree to implement reforms designed to address conflicts of interest. In the US, Deloitte LLP consultants had hidden from regulators money-laundering details about Standard Chartered Bank's transactions with Iranian clients. The New York State superintendent of financial services said, "At times, the consulting industry has been infected by an 'I'll scratch your back if you scratch mine' culture and a stunning lack of independence. Today, we are taking an important step in helping ensure that consultants are independent voices—rather than beholden to the large institutions that pay their fees."

In April 2014, Deloitte was ordered by the court to pay $84.8 million in damages to Livent creditors. Justice Arthur Gans of the Ontario Superior Court ruled that as auditors of Livent, Deloitte failed to detect fraud at the company, even though there were plenty of warning signs that something wrong was going on by the end of August 1997: "The red flags were certainly aflutter by that time." Had Deloitte detected the fraud, the firm could have refused to sign Livent's improper financial statements, which were in turn used to solicit funds from investors.[12]

Just when it seemed that the Harper government's credibility couldn't sink any lower, the PMO was caught in another false assertion. Since May, the office had insisted to the RCMP that the emails of the prime minister's legal advisor, Benjamin Perrin, had been erased. Those emails were crucial to understanding how deeply others were involved in the Wright/Duffy affair. CTV ran an anonymously sourced story that Perrin was involved in the negotiations between the PMO and Senator Duffy's lawyer that eventually led to the secret payment. Perrin called the story false and subsequently hired a lawyer. The RCMP wanted access to Perrin's emails to confirm or deny the report that the PM's lawyer may even have drafted a memorandum of understanding between the PMO and Duffy. In May 2013, the PMO explained to lead RCMP investigator Corporal Greg Horton that it was policy to delete emails of staff who left the office. Since Perrin had left the office in April, his emails no longer existed.

Fortunately the RCMP kept asking for them. The PMO, as it turned out, was wrong on both counts. It was not policy to delete all the emails of departing staff members, only the "casual communications" or transitional ones. Perrin's emails were available.[13] Privy Council Office rules require that information with "business value" that accounts for the activities of government be kept. The PCO took responsibility for misinforming the prime minister about Perrin's emails, which had been retained because of an unrelated pending court case. (It was possibly the privacy breach of 583,000 students when an external hard drive went missing at Employment and Social Development Canada.)

Liberal deputy leader Ralph Goodale wasn't buying the explanation and asked a question no one on the other side could answer. "Who ordered the retention of Perrin's files? Who had custody of them? Has that person been unconscious for the last six months?" The prime minister burned what was left of his credibility—it was not a bonfire.

According to documents released in June 2014 to Tim Naumetz of the *Hill Times* under the Access to Information Act, Perrin actually left his job in the PMO on March 27, 2013, the day after Wright's payment to Duffy. Perrin had a crucial role in the negotiations. After the PCO found the emails on November 29, 2013, RCMP commissioner Robert Paulson was informed within two hours. Harper's national security advisor Stephen Rigby was emailed first about the newly found Perrin documents. Other than the emails in Corporal Greg Horton's November 2013 court affidavit, Perrin's emails have not been made public. A source close to the investigation told me that Mike Duffy has a cache of over eight hundred emails involving Perrin.

During the federal by-elections, on November 25, 2013, Stephen Harper was in Winnipeg at the opening of an expressway, and was asked by a reporter if either he or the PMO approved Irving Gerstein contacting Deloitte about the ongoing Duffy audit. "No," he said, despite the fact that the whole country now knew that Nigel Wright had done exactly that. His director of communications later scrambled to once again "clarify" what the PM had said: "He had no knowledge of Gerstein's efforts to contact Deloitte or that he had been asked to do it." The leader who knew nothing continued to know nothing—evidence or no evidence.

For decades, the unelected Senate had been master in its own house, a rich pasture for party loyalists and more than a few Canadians of note. Now the anachronistic institution that costs Canadians $95 million a year was under the microscope of independent auditors, the RCMP, and the auditor general's office. The results to date were disturbing. With all the revelations of corruption, and the fatal decision not to call principal witnesses to get to the bottom of the rot, the senators themselves guaranteed one thing: change was coming.

It exploded onto the political landscape on January 29, 2014. In a dramatic move that thrilled, angered, and befuddled, Liberal leader Justin Trudeau cut loose all Liberal senators from the parliamentary caucus. Henceforth, all senators who had been appointed as Liberals would sit as independents. Critics immediately speculated that Trudeau was trying to get in front of possibly damaging findings from the investigation of federal auditor general Michael Ferguson. According to the polls, most Canadians liked the idea, including voices from the West who saw Trudeau's decision as a practical way to change the reformproof and unelected institution without starting a constitutional war.

Six days after Trudeau's bombshell, the serpentine chain of events in the Senate expenses scandal snaked its way to a destination that had been inevitable from the moment investigators put a searchlight on an institution unaccustomed to outside scrutiny.

On Tuesday, February 4, at just after 11 a.m., RCMP assistant commissioner Gilles Michaud announced that Senator Patrick Brazeau and retired senator Mac Harb were each being charged with one count of breach of trust and one count of fraud under sections 122 and 380 of the Criminal Code.

In May 2013, Stephen Harper had called the Wright/Duffy affair a "distraction" involving two men. Nine months later, the Conservative Party hierarchy, the PMO, and the Conservative leadership in the Senate had been decimated. The executive director of the party, Dan Hilton, gone. The prime minister's chief of staff, Nigel Wright, gone and under criminal investigation. Four senior PMO staffers, including the prime minister's legal counsel, his director of issues management and his manager of public affairs—all gone.

On the Senate side, the government house leader in the Senate, Marjory LeBreton—gone. Gone too was LeBreton's policy advisor, Chris Montgomery, one of the few people who wouldn't go along with the PMO's intervention in the Senate audit or reports about Duffy's expenses. Gone was the chair of the Internal Economy Committee, Senator David Tkachuk, as was fellow committee member Senator Carolyn Stewart Olsen. Senators Duffy and Wallin—gone. Senator Brazeau—gone and facing multiple charges. Three other Conservative senators, including Hugh Segal, resigned from the Senate. The only two people who retained their positions who played intimate roles in the Wright/Duffy affair were Senator Irving Gerstein, chair of the Conservative Party Fund, and Arthur Hamilton, lawyer for the Conservative Party of Canada. In April 2014, the RCMP ended its investigation of Nigel Wright, saying the evidence "does not support" criminal charges against him. No explanation was given. The federal opposition sent a letter to RCMP commissioner Bob Paulson on April 24, 2014, asking several important questions, including who made the decision not to charge Wright. NDP MP Charlie Angus wondered how the act of writing a secret personal payment to a sitting senator didn't contravene the law: "If Mr. Wright's actions did not cross this line, the average Canadian is justifiably left wondering where exactly the legal and ethical line is in Ottawa today." In June 2014, Onex CEO Gerald Schwartz told Bloomberg News that Nigel Wright would be returning to Onex, posted to their London office.

The decision not to charge Wright was announced almost five months after the Perrin emails mysteriously appeared. In his November 2013 affidavit, Corporal Horton had attested that he believed Wright did, "without the consent in writing of the head of the branch of that government," pay a reward or confer an advantage to Mr. Duffy. If the Perrin emails, or other documents that surface, contain written proof that the prime minister had consented to the deal, according to the law Nigel Wright has not committed an offence under the Criminal Code.

Mike Duffy was charged with thirty-one counts relating to fraud and breach of trust on July 17, 2014, and a press conference was called by the RCMP to lay out the charges. No questions were allowed from the media, "out of respect for the court process." This was Stephen Harper's Ottawa. Included in the charges was that Duffy "did for his benefit and without the consent in writing of the head of the branch of government of which he is an official, accept an advantage from Nigel Wright."

Duffy's lawyer, Donald Bayne, issued a statement that began with how difficult the last sixteen months had been for Mike and Heather Duffy, financially, emotionally, and for the senator himself, healthwise.[14] Bayne was confident that when the full story was told, supported by many forms of evidence, "it will be clear that Senator Duffy is innocent of any criminal wrong-doing." In his prepared statement, Bayne also said, "I am sure that I am not the only Canadian who will now wonder openly, how what was not a crime or bribe when Nigel Wright paid it on his own initiative, became however mysteriously, a crime or bribe when received by Senator Duffy."

The prime minister might yet find himself in a place where you get to tell your story only once and under oath—should Senator Mike Duffy make good on his promise to call Stephen Harper as a witness for the defence. Harper's office was already ahead of the curve on that possibility. His director of communications, Jason MacDonald, said the prime minister does not intend to testify because he has no useful information to offer. MacDonald also said, "We have assisted the RCMP throughout their investigation, and congratulate them on the progress they have made. . . . Those who break the rules must suffer the consequences. The conduct described in the numerous charges against Mr. Duffy is disgraceful. As this is now a criminal matter before the courts we have nothing further to add."[15]

Duffy is scheduled to appear in court on September 16, 2014, the day after MPs return to the House from the summer recess. And that means parliamentary privilege for the prime minister— just in case someone dares to issue a subpoena.

seventeen

PARLIAMENT
ON THE BRINK

S heila Fraser has a quality of dependability about her, of
solidity—she seems like a person who would always show
up with the heart medication on time, take care of the phone bill,
remember to let the cat in.

It could be her roots. The eldest of six children, five girls and a
boy, Fraser grew up on a farm in Dundee, Quebec. Life on a dairy
farm includes a lot of chores, few of them optional. In those circumstances, it might be thought that getting an education would
have been difficult for the future auditor general of Canada. In fact,
just the opposite was true. The Frasers, who had worked the land
for generations, valued education. Fraser's parents, Ken and Lily,
both had high school diplomas. Her father had always wanted to
be a lawyer, and he satisfied his unrealized professional desires by
entering politics, serving as a member of the Quebec legislature
from 1966 to 1976. Meanwhile, the five Fraser daughters benefitted from the duties of their lone male sibling, Ken. It was the men

in the family who were expected to stay on the land, freeing the Fraser women to pursue higher education.

One of Fraser's aunts, Doris Fraser, earned a doctorate from McGill University, setting the example for Sheila and her siblings. All six, including her farming brother, became professionals—three accountants, two doctors, and a lawyer. Fraser's path to McGill began in a three-room rural schoolhouse, Dundee Consolidated, and passed through Huntington High. She decided to take mathematics in university, but it ended badly. Fraser contracted mononucleosis as a sophomore and failed her second year. She was "devastated." On the advice of her family physician, Dr. Kenneth Cameron, she decided to try accounting. "The normal path then for a woman was a teacher or a nurse. Being an accountant and a woman was a very rare thing," she told me. "While other kids were demonstrating against the war in Vietnam, I was learning to be an accountant."

Today people talk about the glass ceiling restraining female executives. When Fraser was looking for a job after McGill, the problem was the front door. Women were simply not hired for what was considered to be a man's profession. Fraser made a strategic adjustment. When applying for interviews, she began leaving out her first name and gender. "So when I walked into the room, you could see the shocked expressions." The one firm that wasn't averse to taking on female accountants was Clarkson Gordon, later Ernst & Young. When Fraser sat down at her desk in the firm's Montreal offices, she wasn't quite sure what she was getting herself into: the 150-person operation was overwhelmingly staffed by males. She became the first woman on the company's audit team.

Things worked out well for both parties. Fraser joined the firm in 1972, and was promoted to manager four years later. Five years after that, she became a partner, only the second woman in the country to hold that position in a major accounting firm. Another first awaited her in 1983. Fraser was the first female partner in the accounting business in Canada, the United States, and the United Kingdom to have a child. The professionals who were accustomed to toting up beans now had to take babies into account. The worldwide maternity policy for the accounting industry was kick-started by the woman whose work would later run the Liberals out of office in the notorious Quebec sponsorship scandal.

Fraser stayed with Ernst & Young at the Quebec City office until the then auditor general of Canada, Denis Desautels, called with an invitation for her to come to Ottawa. After listening to his pitch, she made the jump from the private sector to government. Two years later, Fraser was approached by other staff in the auditor general's office to let her name stand for the top job. Although the position of auditor general (AG) was rarely filled by anyone currently serving in the office, Fraser applied. She was quizzed by the then president of the Treasury Board, Madame Lucienne Robillard. The interview, which began in French, was supposed to last an hour. It ended after a mere thirty-five minutes. Sheila didn't know if she had impressed her formidable interviewer or bombed. It would be two months before she was informed by the Privy Council Office that she had landed the biggest auditing gig in the country.

In her career as AG, Sheila Fraser worked with three prime ministers. The first was, Jean Chrétien, whom she never met in person—though she told me that their relationship was "professional." Given the deep shadow cast by the sponsorship scandal over Chrétien's last government, that is something in the order of a small miracle. Although Canadians would come to admire and trust "Sheila"[1] for her exposure of the Liberals' stunning abuse of public funds, few understood just how difficult it was for an auditor general to hold any government to account. The decision to take such a risky step depends as much on the mettle of the office holder as on the statutory powers of the office itself.

For one thing, politicians constantly try to use the auditor general's office as a weapon in their partisan wars. That's why Fraser did not generally accept the frequent requests from individual politicians for audits. She wanted to maintain the independence of her office, which ideally meant that the AG decides which audits to undertake. But when it came to requests from cabinet ministers or parliamentary committees, it was Fraser's practice to look into the matters they raised. Conducting full-blown audits was tough enough; with all the power and ego of politics thrown in for good measure, it made an already thorny task even trickier. With a strategic adjustment of her famous bifocals, Sheila Fraser had a way of winning most of the staring contests. "Every audit begins with two lies," Fraser explained to me. "They say 'Glad to see you'; we reply 'we're here to help.'"

When it came to the ad sponsorship program, it was Liberal Don Boudria in his capacity as minister of public works who requested the audit. Persistent questions had been raised in the House of Commons about two contracts with a Montreal firm called Groupaction, each worth $500,000. Fraser thought that the minister's request was transparent: "I have always believed that the political motivation was to take the subject off the radar." But if Boudria thought that the sponsorship scandal would disappear into a bureaucracy that moved at geologic speed, he was in for an unpleasant surprise. Fraser got his request for the audit in March 2002. She called her audit team together and set it an ambitious agenda; she wanted the investigation completed in the current parliamentary session.

Just over two months later, the AG must have thought she was reading a thriller by her favourite author, Louise Penny, rather than a government report. Her team confirmed two very dodgy contracts, and came up with a third one the opposition hadn't known about. It was the stuff of fiction: the sponsorship scandal had tendrils everywhere. Sheila immediately ordered a government-wide audit. In her report to the Chrétien government, she notified Minister Boudria that she had also referred the matter to the RCMP.

What made the situation "extremely offensive" to Fraser was that internal audits had already revealed problems with ad sponsorship contracts, yet nothing had been done. And that was despite the fact that the person in charge of the program was the prime minister himself. An estimated $100 million had been funnelled to government-friendly ad agencies in Quebec, for which the public got little or nothing in return. "I was really shocked that all this was happening in an era of cutbacks," Fraser told me. "Money was being spent, millions of dollars, for nothing. Even the RCMP was in on it."[2]

TV Cinq in France picked up the story, and it was quickly shared with French-speaking countries in Africa. At an international conference of supreme auditors in Budapest, African auditors general approached Auditor General Fraser with questions and deprecating comments about the sponsorship scandal. There was considerable embarrassment, she recalled, because "we were supposed to be a world model of good governance."

The sponsorship scandal marked the bitter end for the little guy from Shawinigan, and a rocky start for his successor. Sheila Fraser may never have met Jean Chrétien, but she and Prime Minister Paul Martin kept running into each other by "happenstance." At one such chance meeting in Europe, Martin quipped, "Sheila, we've got to stop meeting like this." Although she noted that Martin and his people could be "quite nasty" (Martin's president of the Treasury Board, the late Reg Alcock, had tried to cut the AG's budget), Sheila described her relationship with the new prime minister as "polite and correct." That rapport was remarkable, given that the AG's final report on the sponsorship scandal landed on Martin's desk just two weeks after he assumed office. "It caused an enormous flurry," Fraser recalled.

Indeed. The report left the newly minted prime minister faced with one of the deadliest dilemmas in Canadian political history: whether to hold a public inquiry into an episode so sleazy that it threatened the foundational credibility of the Liberal Party, or to brazen it out. If Martin went ahead with an inquiry, it also stood to overshadow his laudable stewardship of the economy as minister of finance, which had included taming Canada's deficit, paying down the debt, and recording seven straight budget surpluses.

Martin did the right rather than the political thing. He went with an inquiry and left it to Mr. Justice John Gomery of the Quebec Superior Court to lift all the rocks in the sponsorship affair—a decision that blighted his prime ministership and mortally wounded his party. But it also gave the country a degree of closure on one of the low points in Canada's national life—and garnered respect for Martin on the long hours of the historical clock.

Rather than shooting the messenger—in this case, Sheila Fraser—Martin's approach was to deal with issues outside of the scandal fairly, and as they arose. Fraser wanted to see, for example, what the Liberals had done with huge surpluses Martin had built up after reducing dangerously high deficits from the Mulroney era. Ten billion dollars had been moved into special "foundations" such as the Innovation, Millennium, and Scholarship funds. The oddity about these transfers was that the government did not control the money. Instead, it was administered by a board of directors. If the fund failed, the remaining money in it did not go back to the government but rather to those who had been receiving it. The auditor general wanted that changed. Following her recommendation, the prime minister agreed to put the finances of these cash-rich foundations back into the financial statement of the Government of Canada. Although Fraser concluded after investigating that the board of directors had actually done a "pretty good job" of managing the money, the funds were now more accountable and transparent.

Despite the devastating impact of Fraser's work on his government, Prime Minister Martin actually increased the powers of the auditor general. After the scandal, the AG was given access to all Crown corporations, including Canada Post, whose boss, André Ouellet, had famously refused to cooperate with her office. The only exception under Martin's reforms was the Bank of Canada. "There is some preoccupation with the independence of central banks," Fraser told me with a wan smile.

Shortly after the 2006 election, Sheila Fraser had a personal meeting with the third prime minister of her public service career, Stephen Harper. It took place in his office in the Langevin Block. For the most part, the relationship was "fine." One difference the AG noticed was that while she still worked closely with senior bureaucrats, Harper ministers were less accessible. From the very beginning of their dealings, Harper also tried to persuade Fraser to modify the powers of the auditor general. As stated in the Conservative election platform, the PM planned to grant the AG power to audit all loans and grants over a million dollars. On the surface, it looked like a responsible means of keeping a sharper eye on taxpayers' money. But was it also a clever way of usurping the AG's options, and more important, her independence? Would it turn an auditor into an exalted management consultant?

Fraser demurred. For one thing, accepting the PM's reforms would mean that her office would be inundated with an avalanche of small audits—something she didn't think was an appropriate task for the auditor general. It was up to agencies such as the Economic Development Corporation and the Federal Business Development Bank to devise their own financial administration systems, which would then be audited by the AG. The prime minister was "very courteous" in climbing down from his suggested reforms—though, as a lot of people would learn about him, he had a way of circling back until he got what he wanted. But the auditor general is a powerful player. "They didn't want to mess with me," Fraser recalled.

Inevitably, Harper did take her on. Fraser doggedly stood her ground. The collision took place over the interpretation of the order-in-council that laid out the rights of the auditor general to information—a confrontation she attributed as much to over-zealous justice department lawyers as to politics. In those early days, Fraser perhaps underestimated the degree to which information control would become the central obsession of the Harper government. The Conservatives wanted virtually everything to be a cabinet confidence, a demand that would have placed the government's actions beyond the scrutiny of the auditor general. (As it is, the Ministries of Information Technology and National Security enjoy that status.) Even though the Treasury Board Secretariat had a role in Information Technology programs (the auditor general's meetings with the Treasury Board and the Secretariat were important because both briefed cabinet), even that body wanted to refuse all documents to the AG, including emails between bureaucrats.[3]

Sheila Fraser eventually got the Harper government to adopt a new order-in-council clarifying the access rules from the 1980s in her favour. Perhaps there was a soft spot for the AG's office in certain quarters of the Conservative administration. John Baird's stepmother had once worked in the office and the future Treasury Board president had "read AG reports as a kid." But soft spot or not, Fraser didn't get everything she wanted from Stephen Harper. Although the AG had the right to see cabinet directives, for example, she was shown only the final decision, not the drafts. The distinction is significant. Only the drafts of those decisions contain the reports and the rationale upon which cabinet has acted.

Holding those drafts secret, Stephen Harper's decision-making process was still opaque. The struggle over access to information taught Fraser that the AG's office had "always" to be vigilant on matters of interpretation with the Harper government.

Vigilance was also the order of the day when it came to how the Harper government tried to piggyback on Sheila Fraser's universal reputation for probity. When the Conservatives hosted the G8 and G20 Summits in Ontario in the summer of 2010—spending $1.1 million on posters and even using taxpayers' money to construct a fake lake—they faced a firestorm of opposition criticism. The event was notorious in its own right, with mass arrests and the kettling of innocent bystanders by overly aggressive police, who were later found to have abused their authority. In an odd way, the over-the-top Liberal ad showing troops in Canadian cities that appeared on the party's website during the 2006 election found its haunting echo over that weekend in Toronto—some ten thousand uniformed police and another thousand private security guards were deployed.

But the self-styled prudent managers of the Harper government had also burned through nearly a billion dollars of taxpayers' money in hosting the planet's potentates. It was ten times the amount anyone else had ever spent on these events—and ten times the deplorable financial waste resulting from the sponsorship program. The Harper government's largesse included $50 million for widespread and unauthorized rural renewal of cabinet minister Tony Clement's Muskoka riding (site of the G8 Summit)—monies lifted from the Canada Border Services budget and never separately approved by Parliament. Sheila Fraser was not impressed. "Look at the fuss over $900 for an honour guard the RCMP had to repay and it makes the point," Fraser told me. "Yet $50 million blown in Tony Clement's riding didn't get a hearing. It was completely unacceptable from a financial administration point of view."

Given her feeling about "Gazebo Tony" and public washrooms built 20 kilometres from summit venue sites, "unacceptable" was about to become "outrageous." At the height of opposition attacks, the Harper government reported to Parliament that the auditor general herself had praised its summit spending. "I never said that," she recalled thinking when she read the false report. "What the hell are they talking about?" In fact, the quote used by the Conservatives had been uttered by Fraser—but in praise of a former Liberal government initiative from years earlier. Outgoing Harper cabinet minister Stockwell Day later apologized to the AG, who graciously accepted the government's claim that the misleading quote had not been issued intentionally. "Still," Fraser told me, "you would think someone might have checked before making that kind of public blunder."

Other attempts were made to exert control over Fraser's office. The Harper government tried to force the auditor general to seek approval from the minister of finance for any expenditure over $5,000, a gauche attempt to remind Fraser's office who was really in charge. Fraser took the battle straight to the clerk of the Privy Council, Wayne Wouters. "There was no way we were going to have an expenditure of the office okayed by politicians or ministers." The "offensive section was removed"—with one exception. Harper refused to permit the auditor general to run recruitment ads for her office bearing Canada's coat of arms—a practice adopted by Fraser expressly to assert independence from the government. As an item of "communications policy," Harper insisted that any advertising from the AG's office had to be accompanied by the Canada logo.[4] On the issue of branding, this was a Conservative priority carried to outlandish and, some have argued, improper lengths. Harper never budged, the AG never blinked, and the ad never saw the light of day.

But after winning his majority, Harper did succeed in making a major change to the role of the auditor general that diminished the office and reinforced the government's chokehold on public information. In the previous Conservative minority governments, the auditor general had been actively engaged with parliamentary committees—in particular, the Public Accounts Committee. After the 2011 election, Fraser made written offers to continue the practice but was greeted with a terse "No thanks." As the committee system and the bureaucracy became steadily more politicized, Fraser thought that her independent input was needed more than ever. Invited or not, she decided to do something about it, especially when politicized bureaucrats began stretching the truth. "There were a number of committee meetings where deputy ministers were called in but not the auditor general," Fraser told me. "I would have to put up my hand as an observer to 'clarify' what the deputy ministers were claiming as fact."

If Sheila Fraser was becoming skeptical of the Harper government's commitment to openness and transparency, the list of reasons was long and growing. She had watched as colleagues such as the information commissioner tussled with the Treasury Board over budget requests. Fraser herself was turned down when she wanted to do a major audit across the entire government. "No one in government wants a 'systemic audit across government,' which would reveal how the broader system is working and what best practices might be," she commented. "You can't pick them up with a transactional audit. But the government refused funding."

As her experience with the Harper government accumulated, Fraser became increasingly aware of a much graver development—the breakdown in parliamentary traditions and safeguards. It was evident in things both large and small. At the Public Accounts Committee, the practice had always been for the Opposition to ask the first question. That privilege was usurped by the government. The Harper government also worked assiduously to shut down debate as quickly as possible. It moved committee proceedings behind closed doors, where members could not talk about the content of the in-camera sessions. The intention was information control, and the first casualty was public debate. And another big blanket was used to suffocate the free flow of information: the shadow of the PM's department, the Privy Council Office, fell across every decision. In Stephen Harper's Ottawa, all roads led back to the prime minister. Those who worked most closely in the system, including Sheila Fraser, were appalled. "This government has the worst record on time allocation issues[5] of any government I have seen. It is becoming a charade," Fraser told me. Time allocation, limiting debate to a specific period of time, reduces the role of the opposition in debate and puts more power in the hands of senior management in the PMO. The executive gains more control at the expense of parliamentary debate. Even government members are silenced if they have questions about a particular measure.

The Harper PCO also vets all government decisions, even ones that were once made by individual government departments. Fraser said, "There are very few things where a decision gets made without vetting by the Privy Council Office. There was a time when individual departments could decide certain matters on their own. The Harper government has replaced that with a system where everything must now be vetted by the PCO."

Nor had Sheila Fraser ever seen an administration so willing to use the crushing power of incumbency against individual civil servants who traditionally operated at arm's length from government. Distinguished public servants, from former Statistics Canada chief Munir Sheikh, to former parliamentary budget officer Kevin Page, had felt the lash of the government's public displeasure after speaking out to oppose certain measures. And other victims had been on the receiving end of the government's political wrath. Fraser knew the backstory of what really happened to the former chair of the Nuclear Safety Commission, and was alarmed at how

Linda Keen, an exceptionally able public servant, had been driven out of office in January 2008. "What happened to Linda Keen put a chill through the federal system. This was not about Chalk River. This was about a government flexing its muscles at the 'independent' head of an agency," she said.

Beyond individual cases of abuse, Fraser was concerned about the clear and present danger that the Harper government's legislative approach represented to Canada's democracy. A striking assault was being mounted on the traditions of Parliament, which was actually paralyzing the institutions by which Canadians were governed. Though Fraser had seen many improvements in the AG's situation over her career—including increased powers, better audit personnel, and personal immunity from lawsuits—the authoritarian reflex of the Harper government was as unmistakable as the deliberate suppression of public information. "Parliament has become so undermined it is almost unable to do the job that people expect of it," Fraser asserted. "A glaring example is the budget bill, where there was no thoughtful debate or scrutiny of the legislation. And the legislation was massive, much of it with little to do with the budget."

The government had pushed through omnibus budget bills containing non-budgetary measures such as overhauls to employment insurance, old age security, food safety, immigration, fisheries, and environmental assessment laws with little or no scrutiny or debate. Many people saw this as dismantling the progressive state and social safety net that had been built over the last forty years. Bill C-38, introduced in March 2012, amended sixty different laws, repealed six, and added three more, including a rewritten Environmental Assessment Act. It drew protests even in Calgary.

The government used the bill to cut the budget to Environment Canada and gutted the regulations. The Navigable Waters Protection Act (NWPA) of 1882, considered Canada's first environmental law, was changed to the Navigation Protection Act (NPA). The focus now is to protect navigation rather than navigable waters. Under NWPA, roughly thirty-two thousand lakes were protected. Under the new NPA, just ninety-seven lakes are protected, most of them in Conservative ridings. (Sixty-two rivers and three oceans are also protected under the NPA.) The rest of the waterways, an estimated 98 percent of the rivers and lakes in Canada, no longer have federal protection.[6] Under the new act, construction of dams, bridges, and other projects would be permitted on unprotected waterways without prior environmental approval. The National Energy Board is now responsible for the oversight of navigable waters and fish related to pipeline and international power line crossings. Grassroots Conservatives at the riding association level wrote letters of concern to their members. The list of protected species was shortened, and the Kyoto Protocol Implementation Act was abolished. Parliament in effect rubberstamped the Harper government agenda by passing the 425-page bill after a marathon session on June 13, 2012. Bill C-45, introduced in the fall, was more of the same.

The former farm girl from Dundee was not the only parliamentary insider who was beginning to worry about the direction Canada's democracy was taking.

AS IDYLLIC RETREATS go, Peter Milliken's cottage on Hurds Lake is something special. The lake itself is deep, spring-fed, and crystal clear. The cottages that dot the heavily wooded shoreline are well spaced and private, but the one belonging to the longest-serving Speaker in the House of Commons history is splendidly aloof. A fifteen-minute boat ride gets you from the mainland to Milliken's Island, where the owner is the lone human inhabitant. All along the route, Milliken relatives wave from their docks, tanned and relaxed as characters from an F. Scott Fitzgerald novel.

The vintage cottage in the heart of Greater Madawaska near Renfrew is a transplant. Set back from its wooden wharf, encircled by trees, it was "pulled over the ice" from its original location 2.5 kilometres down the lake after Milliken bought it in 1971. Milliken asks me to carry a box of wine to the cottage. A quick peek at the labels makes me choose my steps very carefully—any one of the bottles could have caused excitement at Sotheby's. Inside the building is an enamel and stainless steel woodstove that vents through the roof. The musk of family history is as strong as the old-wood smell of the cottage itself.

The walls are festooned with Milliken's grandmother's oil paintings, many of them depicting Peter frozen in the childhood of long-gone summer days. While my host gets me a beer, I stop for a moment in front of one painting where he is again the subject—a cosseted boy of seven or eight lounging in bright blue pajamas. Resting in the rafters is a gleaming red canoe—symbol of Milliken's lifelong passion for extended paddling expeditions in Canada's Far North. Outside, down a path through the woods, is the privy—on its door, a hand-carved sign that always wins a smile from visitors: "The Leaker of the House."

Like Sheila Fraser, Peter Milliken came from a large family—the eldest of seven siblings. His father was a doctor in Kingston, and the family had roots going back to the United Empire Loyalists. From the beginning, politics intrigued him. At sixteen, he was already a subscriber to the official record of the House of Commons, Hansard. His route to public life followed a rigorous path of higher education, with stops at Queen's, Oxford, and Dalhousie Universities. While at Queen's, there were intimations of his future: he served as Speaker of the Student Government's Assembly. In 1973, he was called to the bar and eventually became a partner in the well-known Kingston law firm Cunningham Swan Carty Little & Bonham.

The Liberal Party could not have found a better candidate to run against Progressive Conservative legend Flora MacDonald in the 1988 "free trade" election. Milliken's community credentials were blue-chip—respected lawyer, trustee in his church, a governor at Kingston General Hospital, and member on the board of the Kingston Symphony. Although the Mulroney Conservatives won a majority that year against John Turner's Liberals, Milliken bested MacDonald by nearly three thousand votes and became his party's critic for electoral reform.

Soon afterwards, Milliken was named to the parliamentary committee that dealt with elections, privileges, procedures, and private member's business. He came into public life with an extensive knowledge about parliamentary procedure dating back to his boyhood fascination with Parliament; after just a few years as an MP, he became a formidable expert. In January 2001, after five gruelling ballots, Milliken was elected Speaker of the House by a vote of all MPs. It was the beginning of a remarkable four terms in the Speaker's chair. On October 12, 2009, he officially set the record for the longest-serving Speaker of the House of Commons in Canadian history.

From their first meeting, Milliken found Stephen Harper to be distant and taciturn, traits the Reform MP shared to a degree with Pierre Trudeau but without the Liberal icon's engaging intellect. "Harper wasn't a big personality and didn't make much of an impression," Milliken told me. "The truth is I can't remember him very well. He was not a friendly guy, he was standoffish and aloof. He was not one of those guys who wanted to be friends." Even after Harper became prime minister, Milliken observed that he was almost never seen outside the House of Commons: "You rarely see him at parties. He doesn't drink and that may be part of it." In Milliken's experience, about the only place you might "run into Harper" was at state functions—Rideau Hall, military awards, or foreign receptions. When Milliken was sworn in as a privy councillor, the prime minister and the deputy clerk of the PCO showed up. It was something of a Quaker meeting. No personal conversation took place and no congratulations were offered. "I had good office-to-office relations with him," Milliken recalled, "but no personal relationship. Zero."

There was another oddity. As Speaker of the House of Commons, Milliken had become concerned over the bitter atmosphere in Parliament. In an effort to temper the often crude political jousting, Milliken thought it would be a good idea to provide a forum where the contact between MPs could occasionally be social rather than political and adversarial. So every Tuesday evening in the Speaker's dining room, Room 216, Peter Milliken hosted get-togethers. "I held Speaker's dinners for all MPs and leaders," Milliken told me. "The idea was to get people to know each other, to not be so partisan. . . . The tenor in the House of Commons today is more caustic than it has ever been in my experience. . . . Harper never accepted one of those invitations."

The prime minister was no better at extending invitations than he was at accepting them. The Speaker of the House of Commons is the fifth-highest officer in Canada's parliamentary pecking order, yet when Prime Minister Harper entertained at home, Peter Milliken was never among his guests. "As Speaker, I was never invited once to a reception at 24 Sussex. In fact, there are not many parties at this PM's house. That's a real departure from Chrétien and Mulroney. Once or twice a year, they did major entertaining at the PM's residence."

One of the things that Speaker Milliken had become famous for was hosting lunches at Foreign Affairs whenever a departing ambassador was in need of an official farewell. His speeches were erudite, his toasts witty, and the man who could also sing like an angel from years in two choirs in Kingston was much sought after in the diplomatic community—at least until Stephen Harper moved into 24 Sussex. Milliken found it "amazing" that the prime minister showed no interest in diplomatic matters, an aversion he expressed by sending junior officials to host those lunches on the upper floor of the Pearson Building. Milliken observed that Harper's comfort levels were highest with people who often had the least experience and the least to offer: "I find it shocking these people have been at times so inexperienced and incompetent, but seem to enjoy telling seasoned public servants with decades of experience what to do."

In a career full of drama and history-making events, including casting more tie-breaking votes in Parliament than any other Speaker (five of the ten such votes since Confederation were his), Peter Milliken will go down in history for a series of rulings he made that went to the heart of the powers of Parliament and so to the heart of Canadian democracy. Yet remarkably it was met with public indifference. In the first one, rendered on April 27, 2010, he addressed a point of privilege, having to rule whether Parliament had the right to send for persons, papers, and uncensored records, and whether government had the obligation to provide them. The Opposition had demanded documents on the transfer of Afghan detainees into the hands of local authorities who may have tortured them; the government had stonewalled. Milliken decided that parliamentary privileges had been breached.

But in typical Milliken fashion, the grave process unfolded with a light touch and an appeal to compromise. In making his ruling that the government indeed had an obligation to produce documents to Parliament, the Speaker deftly handed the issue back to the politicians, asking that all House leaders, ministers, and MPs work out a collective solution to hand over the required documents, but without compromising national security. Although the MPs took longer to work out a compromise than Milliken's ruling had stipulated, a solution of sorts was produced. An all-party committee would examine the documents to determine which could be made public without violating security or confidentiality requirements. If the committee disagreed, a special panel of three judges, including two former justices of the Supreme Court, would consider the matter. The NDP did not participate in the committee because they did not have confidence in the document vetting process. The party accused the government of trying to suppress the truth by keeping the vast majority of the forty thousand documents about prisoner transfers from Canadians. Instead, the NDP demanded a full public inquiry.

Less than a year later, Peter Milliken made a historic ruling, finding Stephen Harper's government in contempt of Parliament—the first time in the British Commonwealth that a sitting government had been so judged. Milliken's finding was sent to the Procedure Committee, which agreed with the Speaker's ruling. On March 25, 2011, the full House of Commons voted non-confidence in the Harper government, triggering an election. Milliken remains convinced that the government had earned the ultimate rebuke in the Canadian system of government: "Harper deserved to be found in contempt of Parliament. Committees of Parliament have the right to demand the production of documents; the government didn't oblige. The PM seems to have forgotten that the government is the servant of the House. And that is all governments."

If it was a historic procedural defeat for a government whose first instinct was to flout the rules, it didn't resonate with the Canadian people. In the ensuing election, Harper won his previously elusive majority government. One of the first things he did in June 2011 was to kill the all-party panel looking into the Afghan detainee issue.[7] The NDP had been right about one thing: Canadians would never learn the facts about the detainee issue under the flawed process that had been set up. The end came in the form of a declaration by Harper cabinet minister John Baird that the work of the all-party panel was over. Baird made two claims in his announcement: that the accusations of wrongdoing by Canadian forces had been "unfounded" and that the process had cost $12 million.

Neither statement was true. In the end, the government had released only four thousand of the forty thousand requested documents, and even those were censored—hardly the warrant to dismiss the serious allegations of Canada's number-two diplomat in Afghanistan, Richard Colvin. And Baird's $12-million figure was not just for the work of the all-party Afghan panel. It also included the costs of finding and redacting documents for two proceedings of the Military Police Complaints Commission, which the government had also stonewalled.

Andrew MacDougall, the then PMO director of communications, provided another slant to shift blame from the government over the fact that the panel was being disbanded long before its work was completed. MacDougall told reporters that the opposition parties had actually been responsible for killing the process, by supporting a non-confidence motion to defeat the Harper government. Like so many other things coming out of the PMO, this was simply not true. "I've never heard what happened on the [all-party Afghanistan] panel," Peter Milliken told me. "I've asked Stéphane [Dion] but he's been sworn to secrecy. As far as I know, the documents have never been produced. I guess some might think that the whole process was dissolved when Parliament was dissolved for the last election. That's not so. The panel was not created as a committee of Parliament. It was set up by Order of the House. It still exists."

Outside the cottage, we take a path to the point of land where Milliken's small guest cabin sits. He talks about institutional developments that endanger Parliament as it has never been threatened before. At the top of his list is the steady, disturbing, and pernicious growth of the power of party leaders in Canada, most especially the prime minister. Milliken notes that other prime ministers, such as Pierre Trudeau, certainly expanded the powers of the PMO and diminished the role of MPs. But Stephen Harper has become the "leader" of this democracy-killing centralization. This centralization is leading to a "qualitative" change in Canada's governance model, Milliken told me. For every increase in the power of leaders and the prime minister, a corresponding reduction occurs in the status of MPs. "They are far less important today than they once were," said Milliken. "I don't think that's the way it's supposed to be. MPs are supposed to represent their constituents. They're supposed to be free to speak on their behalf. They're supposed to have diverse views within the party. Harper does not encourage that conversation. It used to be speaking in the Parliament and answering questions was an MP's prerogative. . . . There are actually Conservative backbenchers who literally haven't spoken for years in the House."

In fact, until Milliken's successor, Speaker Andrew Scheer, ruled differently on the matter, the Harper PMO decided who would speak in debate in Parliament, drawing up lists of Conservative MPs who were authorized to speak.[8] It was also the leader who unilaterally threw members out of caucus, and retained the dubious ability to trump the decisions of riding associations on candidates. "Another extraordinary thing that Harper did was to throw Helena Guergis out of caucus," Milliken recalled. "She was kicked out by a party leader. I feel strongly that this should be a caucus decision. I also strongly believe that no leader should have the power to veto a candidate who is chosen by their riding association. Leaders should never be allowed to choose candidates."

Milliken, like Sheila Fraser, was appalled by the government's extensive use of omnibus legislation. Loading huge amounts of unrelated legislation into one indigestible bill not only made it impossible for opposition MPs to discharge their fundamental task—the scrutiny of the government's legislation program—it also turned the budget process into a farce. Scores of bills that had nothing to do with the budget were being tacked on with one purpose in mind: to introduce radical change without debate, scrutiny, or financial information. From Peter Milliken's perspective, the practice could collapse Parliament unless reforms are brought in to regulate how omnibus legislation is used. His misgivings were nicely expressed in an intriguing question: "What are we going to do when a private member brings in a bill that amends fifteen or twenty pieces of legislation?"

When Milliken retired after serving ten years as Speaker of the House of Commons, he received accolades from both sides of the House. One of the highest came from the then government house leader, John Baird. Stephen Harper's right-hand man recounted how the Speaker of the British House of Commons had told him that he and Speakers from around the Commonwealth saw Milliken, six times elected MP and favourite son of Kingston, as their leader and model. That day on Hurds Lake, the consummate parliamentarian and passionate Canadian offered an appraisal of his own about the government in which Baird plays so central a role: "Parliament can hardly be weakened any more than it already is. Harper can't go much further without making the institution dysfunctional. He is trying to control every aspect of House business. In fact, it will have to be returned to its former state by someone if we are to have a democracy."

DUNN'S FAMOUS DELI at 220 Elgin Street was a good place to meet the man who just can't seem to retire—Robert Marleau. Dunn's is just a hop and skip across the street from his latest office: he is now the integrity ombudsman at Ottawa City Hall. During his thirty-one years in the federal public service, Marleau has faced plenty of problems, but a lack of job offers has not been one of them.

In fact, he may hold the record in Ottawa for paths not taken. Consider the posts that were offered and declined: clerk of the Ontario legislature, 1986; privacy commissioner, 2003; ethics commissioner, 2004; access to information commissioner, 2005; and the Senate seat of retiring franco-Ontarian Senator Robert Gauthier. Marleau did accept an offer of Senate ethics commissioner from the then government leader in the upper chamber, Jack Austin, but doubt crept in. "A few days later, just before the motion for appointment went on the notice paper, I withdrew. Sober second thought . . . narrow escape in hindsight," Marleau told me.

But all the refusals did not stop Marleau from becoming one of the legendary figures of the federal public service. He is a kind of commissioner of important nouns, having served in the country's top job in Privacy and also Information at the federal level—after initially turning the posts down. Marleau was also clerk of the House of Commons for thirteen years, making him one of the keenest experts on parliamentary practice in the country. (A manual he published is now a reference book on house procedure in many parts of the Commonwealth.) Ironically, he never applied for the post that came his way in 1987. "I was called in one day and told I was now the Clerk [of the House of Commons]."

Marleau had certainly come up in the world since his student days when he worked at the Central Experimental Farm, Animal Division. His main task was forking manure, a chore he quipped was "good prep" for his future career. As healthy as the work sounded, it was not without its perils. "When we would pass out from methane exposure in the manure pens, Barn Boss would send us up the mow to haul hay bales. I was deadly allergic to hay dust, but I needed the $1.65 an hour." A strong work ethic was ingrained in the Cornwall native by the francophone family he grew up in. His father, Roland was a dental technician, and his mother worked as a checkout cashier and sometime waitress. Robert attended Cornwall Classical College, where he got what he described as "Jesuit" training from people who "knew how to educate and build strong character."

He also showed a strong athletic side. Marleau was a hard-tackling corner linebacker in college football and was the Most Valuable Player on his team in 1965. He finished off his university days at the University of Ottawa in 1969. After graduating, he joined the House of Commons in 1970, planning to stay for two years. His calculation was slightly off; he left in 2001.

Marleau escapes from the stresses of his high-pressure jobs into his tightly knit family. He met his wife in 1964 on a swimming raft in the St. Lawrence. The girl in the bright orange one-piece made quite an impression. They started "going steady" in 1965. Two sons, four grandchildren, and forty-three years later, they are "still going strong." For deeper escape, Marleau built himself a wilderness cabin. To this day, it is off the grid and has no running water. Like his former colleague, Peter Milliken, Marleau likes an early-morning canoe paddle.

Information commissioner of Canada from January 2007 to June 2009, Marleau has seen a lot changes, many of them for the worse, over his three decades in public life. He is a firm believer that the quality of a democracy can be measured by the depth of information its citizens hold about their government's actions. Long-time public servants like Marleau remember a healthier time in Canadian governance: a time when releasing public information was actually done by getting answers to questions on the Order Paper in the House of Commons. A time, before changes brought in by Pierre Trudeau, when the old Committee of Supply went through the budget estimates, or the Blue Book, line by line—no matter how long it took. Now the "guillotine" date of

June 30 must be met and, in Marleau's words, "The House has abandoned its constitutional obligation with respect to reviewing the estimates. . . . There is a very tight hold on information."

The man who has had a front-row seat to the sea change in Parliament's traditional morphology thinks the public was better served by the former methods of getting information out. Getting direct answers to direct questions was much better than resorting to the codified provisions of today's Access to Information Act, freighted as it is with tools for manipulation, delay, and inconvenience. "The federal government used to be the best at sharing information," Marleau recalls. "Now we are last in our own confederation. Mexico has a better record than Canada."

Marleau first met Stephen Harper when Harper worked for Calgary MP Jim Hawkes and Marleau was clerk-assistant in the House of Commons. Marleau's main job was to call votes, so the two men were often thrown together. At the time, Hawkes was the chief party whip for the Conservatives. The "whip" could substitute people on committees by signing a form and giving it to the clerk. Harper's duties with Hawkes included keeping Conservative MPs who sat on parliamentary committees in line. In those days, Marleau didn't particularly see Harper as a control freak; working for the whip, control was merely his job. "The idea was to populate committees with friendlies, move in your goons, and get things done," Marleau told me.

On a personal level, Marleau's first impression of Harper was that "he did not fill a room with charisma." But he had a professional demeanor, and was a solid political staffer loyal to Hawkes. He even had an eye for better office space for his boss, or so Marleau suspects. As clerk-assistant, Marleau had a prime, ground-floor office on the west side of Centre Block. After having some dealings with Harper, he coincidentally received notice that he was to move to new quarters—a cubbyhole on the north side of the building. The new occupant of his old office was none other than Jim Hawkes—along with his faithful employee, Stephen Harper.

Suspicions of strategic evictions aside, the working respect between the two men continued after Stephen Harper was elected as a Reform MP. Marleau noted that Harper's demeanour did not change from his days as a staffer with Jim Hawkes. Marleau regarded Harper as a professional politician reminiscent of Joe Clark—a person whose early experience outside politics was narrow and unremarkable. As for Harper, he must have been impressed with Marleau. Just before the election that made him prime minister, Harper confided in the then-retired Marleau, "I'm having a hard time getting people to fill senior positions." Marleau advised Harper to "give it some time," pointing out that while he was still leader of the Opposition, any truly non-partisan candidates for public service positions would be hesitant to commit to him. But all that would change if he became prime minister. Harper made no offer to Marleau, but did probe for his intentions. The man who had retired in January 2001 told Harper he was "content in retirement."

After becoming prime minister, Stephen Harper continued to court Robert Marleau. The approaches were deft, discreet, and persistent. The first came in the summer of 2006, when senior personnel from the PCO informally asked Marleau if he would participate in an open competition for the job of information commissioner. Marleau respectfully declined. A few weeks later, Marleau received a phone call from Margaret Bloodworth in the cabinet office. She extended a breakfast invitation. Bloodworth explained that she was calling at the prime minister's request. The offer was straightforward. Harper wanted Marleau to become interim information commissioner for a six-month term under the statute. Administrative "renewal" in the office was needed, along the lines of what Marleau had already brought about as privacy commissioner

It was a tricky matter. Marleau knew better than most that reform was needed in the government's Access to Information office: he had faced similar issues as privacy commissioner. But he also knew that six months was not enough time, as he put it, "to change anything." Once other public servants learned of the term of his proposed posting, they would simply wait him out. Marleau was also concerned about Stephen Harper and his relationship with the institutions of government. He remembered how Harper had made clear that he believed the system was against him: a Liberal Senate that would limit his actions as PM, an interventionist Supreme Court that would challenge his policies, and a Liberal-appointed public service that would only reluctantly implement his plans.

In the end, Marleau signed on for a seven-year term with a mandate to deliver a legislative renewal package for Canada's Access to Information office. To clean house and come up with something better was no mean task, not with more than five thousand information requests in arrears to work through the system. But the experienced public servant set clear conditions on the deal, some of which were not public at the time. His appointment was to have the unanimous support of the House of Commons and the Senate. It was also agreed in advance that he would not complete a full seven-year term—a detail known to both the prime minister and the PCO. Instead, after putting a legislative proposal to Parliament and arranging a succession plan for a new commissioner that the government "could not easily manipulate," Marleau would be free to leave whenever he wished: "I always leave posts at the time of my own choosing. . . . Saw too many egos go bust on the steps of the Centre Block."[9]

Robert Marleau had many reasons for serving only two years of a seven-year appointment—the principal one being that a partial term had been the plan from the beginning. But other considerations contributed to hastening his departure. Because of the resistance he felt from the Harper government to the kind of change he thought was needed, Marleau came to the conclusion that the remaining years of his seven-year appointment would be "given over to advocacy at a disputatious level, rather than doing the main job." So what might be in dispute? Playing well with others. Marleau thought "relationships" were needed to improve information flow, including the kind of partnerships he proposed before committee, which I asked him about. "When you mention my committee hearing comments on the need for government to have relationships with Parliament, the public and the media, I have to say there is no relationship under this government. All of those relationships have regressed. House committees are prevented from travelling the country; witness selection for committee appearances is done behind closed doors in in-camera meetings."

The feeling in the air was that Stephen Harper did not much care for Parliament. As Marleau put it, "When his government was found in contempt, Harper treated it like a minor, partisan irritation. Parliament is now a minor process obstacle." For a lot of Ottawa's most experienced deputy ministers, a malaise had set in; it was so intense that many of the most senior public servants opted for early retirement. This was not because of the government's policies, which they were prepared to implement as professional public servants. It was because of the way the prime minister related to parliamentary institutions. A circling of the wagons had occurred in Harper's Ottawa that left the impression you had to be onside to be on the inside. Paranoia, not the promised perestroika, ruled.

Remarkably, the very man Stephen Harper courted to become his information commissioner arrived at the conclusion that the prime minister had "done nothing to improve transparency and information flow." Not that the Liberals had done much better when they were in office, but the Conservatives' Accountability

Act promised better days for access, starting with the duty it created for deputy ministers to "assist" information seekers in their access to information applications. The new rule was supposed to have been "when in doubt, give the requester the benefit and disclose the information." With few exceptions (the Department of Justice under Deputy Minister John Simms had a five-star access rating), it just didn't happen.

This was partly because deputy ministers were "very unhappy" with their statutory duty to assist. They feared that if things went south on a request, that part of the legislation would expose them to blame. But the greater reason was that the public service had seen that the Harper government not only lacked a commitment to greater access to information, it was in fact the most secretive information regime the country had ever known. Silence was not just golden; it was Stephen Harper's platinum standard. Harper said all the right words, but that was where his commitment to making information available came to an end. "It is no longer a trickle of information coming down from the top; it's shut off," Marleau noted. "In 2006, it was at first a fog over information in Ottawa, a fog over communications. Now, in 2013, there is a fear over information release and a black hole over communication. A foggy night in Newfoundland has turned into a dark night in Nunavut."

What troubles Marleau most about the suppression of information under Stephen Harper comes down to four simple words: "Government spending goes unverified"—a stiletto through the heart of Canada's parliamentary democracy. The Harper government creates new programs but suppresses their costs. It makes substantial cuts at the departmental level, but the details of what services are affected are kept secret. It proclaims policy without white papers or a word of debate. The late finance minister Jim Flaherty would bring in a budget but wouldn't table the Planning and Priorities report to show how the funds would be allocated. Not even Canada's parliamentary budget officer can penetrate the darkness. "The Harper government botched the Parliamentary Budget Office by putting it in the [Parliamentary] Library and then not giving it the resources to do its job. In particular, the role of the PBO in the estimates process should have been spelled out clearly in the legislation," Marleau told me.

It was a subject he had thought about. Marleau had drafted an ingenious system to improve the way agents of Parliament and the Treasury Board worked together. Under the old system, budget estimates went to the Treasury Board and it was "something like going into a black hole." The estimates came out again as decisions, but the decisions were offered without explanation. Marleau worked out a "preview system" so that the Treasury Board's agents and officers of the House of Commons could better discuss relevant issues. If the parties couldn't agree in direct discussions, there was an all-party panel that acted as a kind of dispute-resolution body. Since neither party wanted to end up in front of the panel, the system worked "exceptionally well"—as long as the budgetary demands fit the government's fiscal framework. Stephen Harper ended the practice. Marleau made a last-ditch attempt to brief the then Treasury Board president, Vic Toews, about the advantages of a better relationship between officers of Parliament and the Treasury Board, but "it went right over his head."

In conjunction with another development under the Harper government—the clear politicization of the clerk of the Privy Council and the PCO—this lack of cooperation between officers of Parliament and the Treasury Board made for a deadly combination. Canada's chief public servant, Wayne Wouters, told an officer of Parliament operating under his statute that he couldn't have budgetary details required to support the work of parliamentarians. Now it was not secretive politicians saying no to a legitimate request for public information; it was the top civil servant in the land. "When the clerk of the Privy Council says to a parliamentary officer, 'You can't have public information you need to do your job' that is a political action," Marleau told me.

Like his colleagues, Sheila Fraser and Peter Milliken, Robert Marleau sees a quiet and destructive revolution taking place under the nose of a country seemingly in a trance. "I see a government that is dismantling, piece by piece, a Canadian mosaic that in a small way a lot of us here helped to build. It is happening behind people's consciousness of it, without the knowledge that it is happening. Canadians are sleepwalking through dramatic, social, economic, and political changes surreptitiously being implemented by a government abusing omnibus bills and stifling public and parliamentary debate. . . . We operate under Westminster rules—an honourable understanding that you will play within the rules and by the rules. Mr. Harper has not played within the rules. Having attained absolute power, he has absolutely abused that power to the maximum."

eighteen

DELAY, DENY, AND DIE

On May 10, 2012, with the expansive lawns of Parliament Hill turning green under a warm spring sun behind him, renowned war artist Allan Harding MacKay tore up four original pieces of his art.[1] A few days earlier, he had destroyed another piece of artwork on CBC TV's *Power & Politics*. The artist, who has more than seventy works hanging in Canada's war museum and other public collections, called it a "lone wolf" protest against the treatment of veterans by the Harper government. "I absolutely feel vets have been abused," he told me. "They are given a one-time paycheque to deal with a lifetime of injury."

It didn't seem possible that the Conservative government could ever be criticized for its treatment of the military. During the Afghanistan War, it had promoted the highly successful "Support Our Troops" campaigns, and many Canadians began wearing red on Fridays. Stephen Harper admired, and did not hesitate to deploy, Canada's soldiers, sailors, and pilots. When he was a member of the Official Opposition, Harper had wanted Canada to go to war in Iraq, and had abjectly apologized to Americans after Prime Minister Jean Chrétien refused to join in the invasion. As prime minister, Harper committed Canadian forces to topple Libyan leader Muammar Gaddafi in March 2011, and was proud of the fact that a Canadian led the NATO mission. The Harper government had spent $850,000 on a November 2011 flyover to mark the end of the Canadian mission in Libya, where the only casualties were Libyan. Retired general Lewis MacKenzie told me, "The trouble with that victory fly-past in Ottawa, which reminded me of Bush and the 'Mission Accomplished' speech, is we don't really know who we ended up supporting in the end. Now the warring has started again between the Libyan factions."

Stephen Harper had always been quick to turn to the military option with a less than perfect understanding of the issues. In the middle of peace negotiations by the major powers aimed at persuading Iran not to develop a nuclear weapon, Harper all but gave his approval for a military strike against Tehran—even withdrawing Canada's ambassador. Most recently, while other countries struggled to find a diplomatic solution to the bloodletting in Ukraine, Stephen Harper dispatched six Canadian CF-18 fighter jets to bolster Western forces in the event of a shooting war with the Russians. He also sent a series of belligerent messages to Russia's czar-like leader Vladimir Putin. Harper would rather join a NATO mission than a peace mission. Like the men and women of the military, he too was a man of action. At a Toronto fundraiser in late May 2014 for Tribute to Liberty, a monument to the "hundred million souls" who were victims of Communism, Harper criticized Putin's expansionism and militarism that threatened global security. He repeated his support for Ukraine: "We feel this pain so acutely because nearly one quarter of all Canadians were either held captive by communism's chains or are the sons and daughters of those who were."[2]

The prime minister's interest in all things military, especially the pomp and circumstance, is in part inherited. After he won the leadership of the Conservative Party, Harper was asked by CBC's Peter Mansbridge who had been the most influential person in his life. He answered without hesitation, "my dad." His dad was in turn influenced by his father, Harris Harper. Harris was only twelve when the First World War began. But while attending normal school,[3] he served in the militia as a sergeant in the Seventh Battalion Canadian Machine Gun Corps in Fredericton, New Brunswick. When he became principal at Prince Edward School in Moncton, he established a cadet corps and moulded the members into prizewinning marksmen. They practised their shooting in the basement of the school—on the girls' side.

June LeBlanc, then June Thurber, was in Harris Harper's grade-seven class. She told me he was a strict disciplinarian who once gave her the strap for talking in class: "Mr. Harper ran the school like the army. We marched into the building in pairs to the beating of drums. Twice a week, he drilled us around the schoolyard. If you got out of step, he'd tap you on the ankle with his baton. On the coldest winter days, he had the grade six and seven kids run the grade ones around the schoolyard." But Harris Harper was not all marching and manliness. June remembered him teaching the girls Irish dancing and square dancing. And on bitterly cold days, he personally drove home all the youngest students from grades one to four. "I don't know how he did it, he must have gotten home at 7 p.m.," she told me. And she remembered one other thing about her teacher: "He was not a bad looking man. Looked like Diefenbaker."

During the Second World War, Harris was commissioned as a lieutenant in the Fifth Reserve Armoured Regiment of the Princess Louise's Hussars, drilling militia recruits in the summer. His son Joseph, the prime minister's father, was only eleven when the Second World War broke out, but he became an army cadet during high school. He loved Canadian military history, and had a keen interest in military insignia, which he collected. He wrote two books about regimental flags and badges. Joseph Harper, who died in 2003, became a consultant to the Department of National Defence (DND).

Stephen Harper's office houses a military uniform encased in glass. The prime minister followed the family tradition of an interest in military insignia and badges, which he indulged with a real army. But that didn't stop Harper from violating military protocol when he was shown wearing a Canadian Forces flight jacket complete with pilot wings while flying in a military plane to survey flood damage in Alberta. Troops do not approve of civilians wearing military gear, even if that civilian is the prime minister.[4] The footage of Harper reminded some people of George W. Bush flying over New Orleans in the wake of Hurricane Katrina.

On July 19, 2012, the Canadian Forces were given pins to wear commemorating the War of 1812. The pin has a red maple leaf with two crossed swords on a blue background. Harper authorized members of the Canadian Forces to wear the pin on their uniforms for three years. Military units will also fly a similar commemorative banner. The then defence minister, Peter MacKay, made the sales pitch: "This tribute will be a daily reminder of a key chapter in Canada's history, and of the courageous efforts made by the regular and militia soldiers, provincial marine[5] and the aboriginal allies who helped define who we are today."

Despite a concerted effort to popularize a two-hundred-year-old war, which involved Harper's personal participation in some of the promotional events, Canadians did not respond as expected to the government's campaign. The public relations campaign—which included a new national monument, historical re-enactments, museum exhibits, a special silver dollar that sold for $60, and even a mobile-phone app—did not elicit much public support. Instead, a lot of people were upset that the government was spending $28 million on the War of 1812 while slashing spending on Library and Archives Canada by $9.6 million. But the deepest reason for public apathy toward the attempt by the government to whip up nostalgia for an antique war was that veterans returning from Afghanistan felt they had been betrayed by the Harper government.

The war in Afghanistan drew Canada's biggest military deployment since the Korean War. Forty thousand Canadians served during the twelve-year mission, mostly in the deadliest combat zone around Kandahar. From the arrival of Canadian special forces in December 2001 to the final withdrawal of troops in early 2014, 162 Canadians and 40 Americans under Canadian command were killed in Afghanistan. Thousands of others suffered debilitating, life-changing wounds, both physical and psychological. Of the 2,179 wounded Canadian soldiers, an estimated 637 are suffering from non-battle injuries; the remaining 1,542 were wounded in action.

Unlike previous wars the nation's military has been involved in, Canadians were deeply divided by the moral dilemma presented by the Afghanistan mission. On the one hand, no one was against the goal of building schools, educating girls, and assisting Afghans to break the fundamentalist grip of the Taliban. But on the other hand, not much proof existed that these actions were actually taking place. The news was full of far less noble accomplishments: midnight raids on ordinary people's homes, lawless detentions, and the killing of innocent people by bombs not quite as smart as their inventors believed. Indeed, persistent stories conveyed that the national honour was being besmirched by the alleged practice of handing over Afghan detainees to national authorities, who in turn tortured or abused them. According to the Geneva Convention, that is a war crime. Many of those stories came from a Canadian diplomat, Richard Colvin.

Colvin had been with Foreign Affairs since 1994, with postings to Sri Lanka, Russia, and the Palestinian territories. He travelled on a bloody ticket to Afghanistan. Colvin was the replacement for diplomat Glyn Berry, the brave civilian on Canada's Provincial Reconstruction Team who was killed by a car bomb on January 15, 2006, at the height of the insurgency around Kandahar. What Colvin, a native of the UK, liked most about his adopted country was Canada's deeply held value of tolerance. He admired the Canadian virtues of acceptance, fairness, and social protection for the unfortunate. As he put it to me, "Canada believed in human rights and stood for something, unlike the UK, which suffered from its Imperial past. Canada's instinct in those days was to be a helpful fixer, a peace-keeper.[6] Canada was a middle power committed to bilateralism and playing a useful role."

Colvin said that when he took up his new post, the International Red Cross immediately wanted to know what was happening to Afghans taken prisoner by Canadian Forces. The diplomat was surprised to learn that Canadian commanders were not notifying the humanitarian agency in time to allow for visits to check on the health and identity of detainees. At first, Colvin thought the Red Cross was exaggerating, because Canada had always been known as a humanitarian country that took its obligation to uphold international law seriously. Although he received a litany of complaints in the weeks after his arrival, Colvin held off on reporting back to Ottawa because he simply didn't think that what the Red Cross was saying could be true.[7]

Instead, he met three times with the Red Cross and with senior military personnel who had a policy of not talking to the humanitarian agency. He learned that NATO was also complaining about Canadian Forces not advising the organization of detainee transfers. "They were really focused. We, by comparison, did not seem to care," he told me. Colvin eventually forwarded prisoner

abuse reports to the Canadian government through C-5, a classified communications system, hoping to raise an alarm in official
Ottawa. "I needed to get it right. There was no one else." Despite
Afghanistan being the foreign policy priority of the Harper government, only two Canadian diplomats were on the ground—just
Colvin and one other person. Colvin had to look to CSIS for
intelligence on the situation in theatre because the military viewed
civilian authorities like him as the enemy.

To his surprise, instead of earning the government's appreciation for alerting it about the detainee situation, Colvin was reprimanded. He was informed that his report had created "anxiety"
in the department of justice and among the generals. Colvin told
me, "I don't consider myself a whistle-blower. I suppose I became
one." The Harper government simply didn't want to talk about it.
It fought public hearings tooth and nail, arguing that they could
damage the reputation of senior officers involved and risk revealing
military secrets. But Colvin finally gave his testimony in front of
a special parliamentary committee looking into the detainee issue,
and was forcefully and publicly attacked by defence minister Peter
MacKay. Looking back on it, Colvin told me, "It was dirty to slag
me personally. MacKay did that aggressively. I knew there would be
a big fight and they would try to destroy me. They were obliged to
do something. The fighting started the day after I testified."

The Harper government's secrecy about everything to do with
the Afghanistan mission was staggering. It was perhaps the most
damaging single issue the government faced. Emotions were running so high that the Tories prorogued Parliament for two months
in early 2010, and faced a contempt ruling. To this day, the records
dealing with Afghanistan remain heavily censored, and cabinet
papers and legal opinions are excluded from those documents that
are released. But according to Colvin, because of him, "The message had finally gotten out."

The Harper government vehemently denied Colvin's testimony, insisting that Canada did not approve of torture and had not participated in it. It was a defence that rang hollow after a secret order given by defence minister MacKay became public. On April 13, 2014, Jim Bronskill of the Canadian Press reported that the Harper government had secretly ordered the Canadian military to share information with allies even when there was a "substantial risk" it could lead to torture. CP obtained a copy of the November 2011 memo under the Access to Information Act. A basic tenet of Canada's identity—upholding international law that forbade such transfers—was changed without ordinary citizens being the wiser. The newly released memo was expressly prepared for MacKay by DND officials, the fifth federal agency to apply the Harper government's instruction to exchange information with a foreign agency, even if there was a "substantial risk" of torture. (The other agencies were CSIS, the RCMP, the Canadian Border Services and Communications Security Establishment Canada.)[8]

Meanwhile, the government tried to say that Canadian forces and companies were succeeding in modernizing Afghanistan by building infrastructure projects such as schools and roads and by defeating the Taliban. It was third-rate propaganda, and many of the schools Canada had built were crumbling. When the clerk of the Privy Council showed up for a visit to Afghanistan in 2006, Richard Colvin found him uninterested in the true progress of the war but insistent on one thing: "All he wanted was to set up a televised connection between children in rural Afghanistan and Canadian kids." A good-news public-relations event couldn't have been further from the facts on the ground.

The $50-million reconstruction of the Dahla Dam on the Arghandab River 34 kilometres northeast of Kandahar has been a massive failure mired in corruption. It was to have been Canada's signature project. The reservoir was to feed 40 kilometres of irrigation ditches to bring water to farmland. Despite the project, won by the scandal-ridden firm SNC-Lavalin, Kandahar still has its water crisis. Further, violence marred voting in April 2014, and not much has improved for ordinary people.[9] The current government is widely viewed as corrupt. According to US intelligence estimates, when US troops are drawn down and leave the country, Afghanistan will return to chaos by as soon as 2017. It has left the bitterest of memories of the war for Richard Colvin: "People died for nothing, to prop up drug dealers and killers."

The government has been evasive about the true progress of the war, about possible violations of international law by Canadian personnel, and even about how much the mission cost. The most conservative estimate is $12 billion, including $8.4 billion on the combat mission alone. As of 2008, the Parliamentary Budget Office put the actual cost at $18 billion. The "all-in costs" up to 2014, when the Canadian troops came home, have been estimated at $28 billion, a number that can't be verified because of the lack of transparency at the DND. These estimates do not include costs for the future care of returning soldiers who were left with physical or mental injuries.

Until the troops started coming home from Afghanistan, the relationship between the military and the Harper government had been good. Three things changed that. First, the government was determined to balance the budget through deep spending cuts, $13.6 billion by 2017. In a unanimous vote in the House of Commons, the government benches refused to exempt the Department of Veterans Affairs from the new austerity.

Second, the New Veterans Charter (NVC) was fatally flawed. It was adopted without amendment or debate, as a result of a unanimous motion in the House of Commons to prevent the bill from dying on the order paper in the final days of the Paul Martin government. The aim of NVC was well intentioned: to focus on wellness and productivity rather than illness and dependence. It was originally intended to be a long-term, cost-neutral way of caring for veterans, but it was anything but that. Under the charter's terms, wounded soldiers who had once been eligible for lifelong pensions were now given a one-time lump-sum payment. Adopted in 2006, the NVC has proven very unpopular—being met by court challenges, two reviews in 2009 and 2011, and a current parliamentary review.

Third, health services provided by the military to men and women wounded in body and mind have been woefully inadequate. The troops had been handed an impossible mission and now they were paying the price. As retired major-general Lewis MacKenzie told me, "The impossibility in Afghanistan was partly the unrealistic expectation . . . to peace-keep, do humanitarian work, and make war—all at once." The mutually exclusive missions took a terrible toll. More than two thousand members of the Canadian Armed Forces came back wounded from Afghanistan. Many suffered alone because of the continuing stigma attached to admitting to any form of mental distress. The most common operational stress injuries are post-traumatic stress disorder (PTSD) and depression. PTSD's symptoms include unrelieved edginess, insomnia, anxiety, and irritability. The symptoms can take months to emerge and may never disappear. There is no drug for treating PTSD. Without proper and timely care, the emotional demons begin to take their toll, just as the IEDs, bullets, and unspeakable sights did to the soldiers during their active duty in Afghanistan. Victims of PTSD often try to anaesthetize themselves with alcohol or drugs. Many isolate themselves from those around them. An alarming number commit suicide. Homelessness is a growing problem for those who suffer mental health issues attributed to their time in the military. Adjusting to civilian life is hard. "Being able to shoot someone at 600 metres is not necessarily in high demand by civilian companies," says Captain Victoria Ryan. A former corporal who served under her was found frozen to death on an Ottawa street in February 2013. It broke her heart, and Ryan has launched a volunteer organization to find help for homeless veterans.[10]

Roméo Dallaire, a former general, has been a strong advocate for soldiers with PTSD. In May 2014, he announced his retirement from the Senate to spend more time crusading for veterans' rights and on PTSD research.[11] Dallaire's answer to this massive problem is to allow Canada's two thousand wounded or injured soldiers to continue to serve in the military, despite a diagnosis of PTSD. (There are about sixty-eight thousand full-time soldiers in the Canadian Armed Forces.) As reported by CP, Dallaire gave an explosive interview shortly before testifying on April 3, 2014, before the House of Commons Veterans Committee, which is reviewing the New Veterans Charter. Despite the Conservative messaging that it supports veterans, Dallaire described a number of recent encounters with "politicians who are second-guessing the cost of veterans. . . . This has been sniffing its way around the Conservative hallways and it's pissing me off." Dallaire called for a legislated social covenant with soldiers to ensure that the wounded are properly looked after.

The Harper government has a different answer: the Joint Personnel Support Unit (JPSU). The JPSU is the umbrella unit for a network of support for injured veterans. It takes them through a complex treatment regimen known as the "three Rs": recovery, rehabilitation, and reintegration. The three Rs are in turn anchored to the "universality of service" rule, which dictates that after treatment is over, soldiers have to be physically fit, employable without significant limitations, and deployable for operational duties. Those who don't meet this standard are mustered out of the military and channelled back to a civilian life for which many of them are unprepared. And if they happen not to have ten years of service when that happens, they fail to qualify for an indexed pension.

That is what happened to Corporal David Hawkins, a reserve combat engineer released from the military before qualifying for an indexed pension at the ten-year mark. His PTSD diagnosis means that he is unable to be deployed overseas. Hawkins spent a tour in Afghanistan from September 2008 to April 2009 as a member of the "quick reaction" force, soldiers who were called out to deal with suicide attacks and roadside bombs. For his own safety, Hawkins slept in a light-armoured truck while deployed in Afghanistan. When he came home, the only place he could sleep was in his own truck. He was prescribed thirteen medications for his PTSD. Jennifer Wild, a clinical psychologist at Oxford University who treats British soldiers suffering from PTSD, said that was the wrong way to go: "Medication is not recommended—there is no good medication for PTSD. A pill does nothing for their PTSD symptoms." Instead, Wild uses cognitive behavioural therapy in her practice, which is the most beneficial treatment for PTSD. She observed, "Soldiers may feel ashamed or excessively guilty about an action they took or didn't take, and may be judging themselves on superhuman standards."

After Hawkins's time limit for recovery was up, he was given an ultimatum: either go back to work or "we can drop your funding right now." Knowing that he was not ready for an operational redeployment, he declined the option to return to work. He was then released from the military with nine years of service, and didn't qualify for his indexed pension. Lost in the no man's land of PTSD, he has filed a grievance against the military, which can take four years, sometimes even longer, to review.

Like Hawkins, Corporal Glen Kirkland did not meet the universality of service rule. Kirkland was injured in a Taliban bombing attack that killed three of his comrades in 2008, and was subsequently diagnosed with PTSD. Leaving the army before the ten-year mark would have meant no pension for Kirkland. Defence minister Peter MacKay told him that he could stay in the army until he qualified, despite his diagnosis of PTSD. Kirkland refused to accept the offer unless it also applied to other veterans. As Kirkland told the *Toronto Star*, "I joined as a member of a team, as a family. So, when I was offered an opportunity when no one else was, it just goes against everything I joined for."

Even after the vote in Parliament, in which the entire Conservative caucus voted against an exemption for Veterans Affairs from government-wide cuts, soldiers had a hard time believing what was happening to them. It got harder when they learned that Ottawa had pledged $557 million to Afghanistan, including $330 million for the Afghan Army between 2014 and 2017. At home, the Harper government was cutting the budget of Veterans Affairs and reducing veterans' benefits. It was hard to understand. One person who was not surprised about the cuts was former interim Liberal leader Bob Rae. He noticed that as support for the war in Afghanistan waned in Canada, so, too, did the prime minister's commitment to the troops. "He is very cold-blooded about these things," Rae told me. "Harper's objectives and methods tend to be pragmatic. . . . I find him one of the most deeply partisan and divisive people in Canadian history. I've never seen a politician act with less compassion, or so intent on never going beyond partisanship."

The Department of Veterans Affairs had been forecast to spend $163.2 million more on disability awards and allowances, and $10 million more in earnings loss benefits than originally expected. But there was a big problem. Senior bureaucrats in the department were reluctant to ask the Treasury Board for more money, knowing the Harper government was hell-bent on balancing the budget in time for the 2015 election. In the final analysis, Stephen Harper made no distinction between ending postal delivery, closing scientific facilities, and cutting veterans' benefits.

They were all simply steps on the road to his party's re-election. Bureaucrats were so afraid of him that even money that had been allocated to departments routinely went unspent.

So instead of fighting for more funding for medical care for the troops, senior managers in Veterans Affairs earned $700,000 in bonuses in 2011 for coming up with cuts.[12] Bureaucrats reported that the department would be spending more on memorials and monuments, and less on activities with veterans' groups. That raised the ire of the Royal Canadian Legion, which implored the Harper government to exempt Veterans Affairs from the proposed spending cuts, just as President Obama had once promised in the United States. Veterans affairs minister Steven Blaney then said he would make reductions by cutting red tape. That way, soldiers would not feel the impact. It was pure rhetoric, but for a while it looked like it might be true. Rear Admiral Andrew Smith, chief of military personnel, told CTV News the government was only considering cuts for now: "It's more an advisement there may be changes. It's not a hard determination of changes. It remains under reviews, and we're going to continue to study it going forward."

Admiral Smith and the Forces' top commander, General Walter Natynczyk, insisted that everything was being done to protect front-line health services. Opposition MPs and unions representing government employees called on defence minister MacKay to intervene and stop the proposed cuts. MacKay claimed the Forces had 378 full-time mental health professionals and that the department was working diligently to hire more. But the cuts would not be rolled back. The Harper government's true intentions became clear after it lost the only committee vote since forming a majority government in 2011.

Liberals on the Veterans Affairs committee managed to win a motion demanding a study of planned cuts of more than $226 million to veterans' services in November 2011. The department's plans and priorities report, which outlined spending to 2014, showed that financial support for ex-soldiers would see the biggest reduction. The number of Second World War and Korean vets was declining. Veteran Affairs Canada (VAC) pays out about $3.1 billion in transfer payments to veterans and their families, out of a total budget of $3.5 billion. The $226 million in cuts over two years is from the operations budget of about $380 million. At $113 million a year, that is almost a 30 percent reduction in operational funding.

The Liberal committee win was made possible by Conservative Eve Adams, the then parliamentary secretary to the minister of veterans affairs. It was Adams's job to monitor the committee, but she herself had been late for the vote, causing her party's loss. The Liberal victory was short-lived, however. The Tories quickly put an end to the study of the budget cuts at Veterans Affairs at the very next committee meeting. No amount of rhetoric could dissuade angry soldiers that the government no longer had their back but had stabbed it.

The opposition agreed. NDP MP Sylvain Chicoine opened debate in the House, saying that as many as twenty thousand veterans would be affected by the announced closure of Veterans Affairs Canada offices, and said such a move showed a lack of respect for the people who had fought for the country. NDP veterans affairs critic Peter Stoffer stated that if the NDP won the next election they would reopen the offices. Liberal leader Justin Trudeau made the same promise. The opposition argued that veterans needed one-on-one support that only experienced VAC case managers can provide, not a 1-800 number.

The Harper government's answer was that veterans could have their needs met through Service Canada Centres—general referral offices for anyone seeking a government service. It showed a lack of understanding of the problems that veterans were facing. At the Service Canada Centres, men and women suffering from

PTSD would be lumped in with people inquiring about employment insurance and parents applying for maternity benefits. The sessions with veterans often ended with breakdowns, hard enough to bear in any venue, but next to impossible in such a public one. The veterans needed the privacy and professional attention provided by the VAC offices, and they set up a meeting with Veterans Affairs minister Julian Fantino on January 28, 2014, to say so.

The minister turned up seventy minutes late for the scheduled meeting in Ottawa. The veterans wanted him to reverse the scheduled closure of nine VAC centres across the country. Some of the veterans at the Fantino meeting were in their eighties, and had been travelling non-stop for twelve hours to get to Ottawa. They were hungry, weary, and upset that the minister had stood them up. Upbraided by the angry veterans when he finally did show up, Fantino stormed out as if he were the injured party. Compounding the political damage caused by the minister's arrogant exit, Fantino then accused the vets of being duped by unions fighting to keep their VAC centres open. Eight centres were closed three days later, on January 31, 2014; one in Prince George, British Columbia, had already been closed. According to the Public Service Alliance of Canada (PSAC), approximately seventy union jobs were lost. Included in that number were twenty-five case managers who worked on the most complex cases, often doing home visits to deliver their highly specialized help. The wait times, already long for home visits, had just become much longer.

Stephen Harper tried to downplay the VAC closures. He said that these "duplicate" veterans offices had "very small caseloads." But figures presented to Parliament in 2012 showed caseloads of between 2,065 and 4,113 for each of the closed offices. The remaining Veterans Affairs offices would now be saddled with huge new caseloads due to the closures. The Halifax office had just inherited over 4,000 new client files from the shuttered Sydney office, a third more than its present caseload. Already down five client agents since cuts in 2012, the Halifax VAC was only given three more case managers to deal with the influx of thousands of new clients.

The Harper government argued that the same service would be offered by Service Canada Centres, staffed by experienced VAC officers and backed up by online help. Employing Orwellian logic, Julian Fantino claimed that the cuts would actually improve services. He dismissed the public outcry against the cuts as union manufactured. "One group in particular has questioned our loyalty to veterans," Fantino said. "I'm speaking of the Public Service Alliance of Canada. They've tried to paint themselves as the champions of veterans. Let me be absolutely clear, they are anything but." After trying to demonize the union, a spokesperson from Fantino's office was forced to acknowledge reality. Case managers who had thirty-one clients before the closures would now have forty. That number was certain to rise with the 2014 end of the Afghanistan mission. No one knew how many more troubled vets would be coming forward in years to come seeking service that had just become a lot harder to get.

The day after the disastrous meeting with veterans, Fantino issued an apology: "Due to a cabinet meeting that ran long, I was very late in meeting a group of veterans that had come to Ottawa to discuss their concerns. I sincerely apologize for how this was handled. Today, I am reaching out to those veterans to reiterate that apology personally." Ron Clarke, for one, wasn't impressed. The veteran from North Sydney, Nova Scotia, was disgusted at Fantino's late arrival, and rejected the minister's apology. He told CBC News, "I thought he would be a lot more professional than what he was. As a matter of fact, I found him very disgusting. . . . I want to see him resign, that's what I want to see. Either he resigns or I'd like to see his boss fire him. He's not a very compassionate man. He was ignorant, forceful, and actually disgraceful." Alphie

Burt seconded that assessment. Speaking from the lobby of his shuttered VAC centre in Cape Breton, the veteran of the Royal Canadian Armoured Corps was blunt: "What the frig is wrong with that guy?"

Bruce Moncur, a veteran who was wounded in Afghanistan in 2006 by American "friendly fire," was also at the Fantino meeting and blogged that it was easier fighting the Taliban than being a wounded veteran fighting for benefits back home. On September 4, 2006, Moncur was having breakfast with his platoon in Panjwaii when at about 5 a.m., a US A-10 Thunderbolt fighter jet mistook them for the Taliban and opened fire. A private was instantly killed and two dozen soldiers injured. Moncur took shrapnel to the head and lower back. He was told by fellow soldiers they could see part of his brain. Blood ran from the wound, and yellow liquid trickled from his ear. He lost control of an arm temporarily, and had to have two brain surgeries.

For the shrapnel wound to the head, Moncur received $22,000, payment for what the military calculated was the loss of 5 percent of his brain. He was also diagnosed with PTSD, a condition he believes was aggravated by the failures within the Department of Veterans Affairs since he returned home. He wrote, "I am not the only soldier who feels they have not been taken care of when coming home." After weeks in hospital, Moncur needed help to learn to read and write properly again, as well as to walk and talk. When he returned to Windsor, the VAC office referred him to physiotherapists, occupational therapists, doctors, and specialists.

The greatest help came from his VAC case manager. She had read a story about his struggle in the local newspaper and asked to meet him. The office became a "lifeline" as Moncur recuperated physically and mentally. His VAC centre in Windsor was one of the offices that closed. Help was now two hours away in London, Ontario. Before the cuts, the London office had a caseload of

6,400; with the clients from Windsor, the load ballooned overnight to 9,000.

It was a story that was repeated across the country. For veterans from Thunder Bay, Ontario, the closest office was now in Winnipeg, Manitoba, eight hours by car in the best of weather. Since travel costs to visit case managers are not covered under the New Veterans Charter, veterans could easily spend over a thousand dollars getting the help they needed. As Moncur told reporter Donovan Vincent of the *Toronto Star*, "It's like we've become an inconvenience. If veterans aren't safe from budget cuts, I guarantee you, no one else is. Every Canadian needs to take notice of this."

Moncur had always voted Conservative and believed the Harper government were the only ones "who had our backs." But that was when declaring such support was convenient for the government. "It's a betrayal is what it is," he said. Referring to the Conservative boast of actually improving service with nearly six hundred "points of service access" at Service Canada Centres, Moncur practised some black humour. He suggested that the Harper government should just put the forms behind the counter of every McDonalds and have *thousands* of points of contact. He was convinced that the closures were a deliberate strategy to reduce use of services: "If you are told 'no' enough times, you'll go away." According to Moncur, it was all a part of the Harper government's triple-D credo: "delay, deny, and die."

Moncur suggested that instead of commemorating D-Day and the start of the First World War, the money would be better spent on veterans who needed help now. Funding for programs to honour veterans has increased by more than 20 percent to over $50 million for 2014–2015. In contrast, the government spends $38.6 million annually on mental health for the Canadian Forces. In 2012, Peter MacKay promised to make mental health a priority, announcing extra funding of $11.4 million to hire more expert staff to treat mentally injured Afghanistan veterans.[13] It was a promise he didn't keep.

Bruce Moncur made his case for fair compensation and proper treatment, "only to be repeatedly denied, called a liar, told there was not enough proof, and to be given a fraction of what I should rightfully have." He has been denied a Permanent Impairment Allowance and has spent the last eight years appealing his pension. He felt reduced to an unwanted claim in an insurance company.

Just at the moment that minister Fantino was taking heat for his insensitive treatment of needy veterans, he announced $50,000 to fund a monument to honour veterans who fought in Italy in the Second World War. Meanwhile, flesh-and-blood veterans were losing their VAC centres—and money. Under the cuts, funding for disability and death compensation, health care, and re-establishment services for veterans decreased by 4 percent. Even though the mental health treatment system was in crisis, the DND actually planned to reduce the number of medical professionals involved in suicide prevention and the treatment of minds that had been wounded in Afghanistan. It was a risky move.

Psychiatrist Neil Greenberg at King's Centre for Military Health Research in London headed a study that found a correlation between PTSD and suicide. Greenberg said, "We found high rates of PTSD and risk of suicide in those who are on deployments longer than six months. We also found reservist combat troops are also at a higher risk." Veterans' advocate Michael Blais reported that Canadian Forces men and women can wait five months to get to see a psychiatrist, a dangerously long waiting period: "This could end in catastrophe if we don't provide treatment in an expedient and effective manner." Liberal defence critic John McKay told reporters, "[Peter] MacKay loves to wrap himself in the military, and as long as these guys are healthy and look like they can take on the world, he's happy to stand beside them.

When they return and they have to transition to civilian life and they're no longer deployable because of mental health issues, then he's nowhere to be found."

The military surgeon-general, Brigadier-General Jean-Robert Bernier, testified before the all-party House of Commons defence committee on April 8, 2014, that depression, especially among male members of the Forces, was "a major concern." It was double the rate of the civilian population. Depression is also one of the symptoms in the diagnosis of PTSD. Soldiers were exposed to many triggers for that condition in Afghanistan. They saw their comrades and Afghan children blown to bits, and witnessed Afghan troops sexually abusing small boys without consequences. Drug use in Afghanistan's national army was routine and rampant. Those same Afghan "partners" also killed their NATO allies at the rate of about one per week. A Canadian soldier never knew who most to fear—the Taliban or the Canadian military's supposed allies. And the ubiquitous and depressing spectacle of abject poverty was also acutely affecting. When all of these things were mixed with survivor guilt, it often led to Canadian soldiers becoming addicted to the only thing that kept the horrors in check—Oxycontin and Percocet as well as street drugs and alcohol. None of this is surprising, as it is common for PTSD sufferers to engage in high-risk behaviours.

The impact of the cuts to Veterans Affairs on the prime minister's credibility was like a direct hit from a mortar. Retired sergeant-major Barry Westholm, the director of Armed Forces Engagement for Canadian Veterans Advocacy, quit the Conservative Party. He said that the government showed a shocking lack of respect toward veterans. Westholm told Chris Cobb of the *Ottawa Citizen*, "There are so many red flags flapping across the country, but the government doesn't appear to see them." He informed his MP, Conservative Cheryl Gallant, that he was severing all ties with the

Conservatives with "great regret—regret not for my actions, but regret in that the CPC has strayed so far from the path of reason and respect regarding our veterans. . . ." Westholm was particularly upset that MP Gallant had said soldiers with mental injuries weren't getting help because they chose not to, rather than because help wasn't available. He wrote to Gallant, "When you spoke before Parliament recently to chide our veterans and promote a dysfunctional organization, the Joint Personnel Support Unit, I was left in shock, disillusioned and most certainly dismayed." While Westholm was still working at the JPSU, he had written to MP Gallant, "Many soldiers have committed suicide since my first email to you, and I can only ponder those that could have been better supported, assisted or saved if action was taken—but no action was taken."

Westholm, who had served in Cambodia, Syria, and Haiti, said he had received messages of support from other veterans, also brimming with anger about the Fantino meeting and statements by Conservative cabinet ministers and MPs in the House of Commons. Westholm couldn't understand why the government blamed the union, or made the Orwellian claim that closing VACs to save $3.78 million would improve service. When the narrative that closing VACs would actually improve service didn't work, the Conservatives had gone on the attack, accusing the veterans of being duped by the Public Service Alliance of Canada. Veterans Affairs spent an additional $4 million on advertising in 2014, including expensive spots during the NHL hockey playoffs, to tell Canadians what a great job the department was doing helping vets make the transition to civilian life—more than they saved by closing the centres. PSAC was trying desperately to save eight hundred jobs on the chopping block at Veterans Affairs. The government's belligerence came across as thuggish arrogance—just like Julian Fantino's performance in front of the vets and the TV cameras in Ottawa. But this group had been under attack before and wasn't about to buckle.

AS REPORTED BY Scott Taylor in the Halifax *Chronicle Herald*, Corporal Stuart Langridge took his own life on March 15, 2008. He had served in Bosnia and then in August 2004 was deployed to Afghanistan. Langridge had been involved in reconnaissance missions for seven months, and was described as "a member of a crew that put a lot of Taliban in the dirt." When he returned to Canada, he began a metamorphosis from an easygoing, sports-loving young man to a depressed recluse. He spoke very little about his time on patrol in the mountains, but his mother told reporters, "The incredible poverty bothered him." Langridge also battled addictions to both drugs and alcohol. He began having night terrors. His suicide note explained why he was ending his life: "Sorry, I cannot take it any more. Please know I need to stop the pain." The military withheld his note from his family for fourteen months. It also contained his wish for a small funeral, "just family." Instead, he was buried with a full military ceremony. Paperwork to change payment of his benefits from his former girlfriend to his mother was lost behind a filing cabinet.

On January 20, 2014, the Canadian Press reported that the eighth member of the Canadian Armed Forces had taken his life in a period of just over two months. Lieutenant-Colonel Stéphane Beauchemin, who served in Haiti and Bosnia, died on January 16 in an apparent suicide. The helicopter pilot had been a client of the Joint Personnel Support Unit in Ottawa. Another former soldier, Corporal Leona MacEachern, committed suicide on Christmas Day in a car crash that was an "intentional final desperate act," according to her husband. MacEachern had been receiving monthly disability payments. The military's letter of condolence to the family included a request for a repayment of $581.67.

Veterans Affairs explained, "Earnings Loss benefits paid under the Canadian Forces Members and Veterans Re-establishment and Compensation Act are payable up to the day of Mrs. MacEachern's death." After the letter was made public, veterans affairs minister Julian Fantino told CTV News on January 28, 2014, that the decision to collect the money had been reversed. He also expressed his "deepest condolences to the MacEachern family during this difficult time." Her husband accepted the apology at face value, but said in an email to CTV News, "Of course it's a very small amount of money considering a life was lost that should have been saved." Leona MacEachern had suffered from PTSD. Her family felt she had "slipped through the cracks of a system that barely exists."

Another apology was in order after a soldier's mother received a one-cent cheque from the government two and a half years after her son, Corporal Justin Stark, committed suicide in October 2011. He had returned from a seven-month tour of Afghanistan earlier in the year. He was twenty-two years old. Several tribunals were held to try to determine whether his suicide, at the John Weir Foote VC Armouries in Hamilton, was related to his tour. The results were unclear. Canada's defence minister, Rob Nicholson, said an "insensitive bureaucratic screw-up" was the cause of the one-cent cheque. The cheque, dated February 28, 2014, was sent marked "Canadian Forces release pay."

Despite the "Support Our Troops" message from the Harper government, the Canadian Armed Forces published numbers documenting that twenty-one Canadian soldiers killed themselves in 2011, an increase from twelve the previous year. There were ten suicides in 2012. Ascertaining the true number of suicides is difficult because the Canadian Forces do not include army reservists, retired soldiers, or female soldiers in that sad statistic. What is known is that suicide rates in the Canadian military are higher than those in Britain's armed forces. Thirteen Canadian soldiers killed themselves in 2013, compared to five in the British regular forces. The British military is three times the size of Canada's armed forces. Nor is the trend slowing down. As of January 30, 2014, at least eight soldiers had taken their lives in the previous two months. And by mid-April, five suicides had already been recorded in the Canadian Forces for 2014.

It is important to note that the statistics for suicides only include those who kill themselves while deployed. Canadian soldiers are fighting a less defined enemy than their grandfathers were. No one knows what the long-term psychological impact of serving in Afghanistan will be, although Statistics Canada is scheduled to release a comprehensive study on mental health in the military in November 2014. Although nothing can be said with certainty until that study is published, many experts in the mental health field believe the death rates are much higher than reported. Mental health facilities for Canadian Forces are chronically short-staffed, although the Harper government has been promising an increase in staffing levels since 2012. So far, the promised fifty-one additional psychiatrists, psychologists, nurses, and addictions counsellors haven't been hired.

According to December 2013 staffing figures, the Forces' medical facilities had only 388 mental health professional and support staff to deal with troubled soldiers and veterans. The military's former chief medical officer, retired surgeon general Hans Jung,[14] blames the staff shortages on the Harper government's hiring freeze—one of the grimmer realities of balancing the budget through cutting services. Meanwhile, an estimated seventy-five boards of inquiry into possible military suicides remain outstanding. Despite the Harper government's boast about the excellent care afforded to wounded Canadian soldiers, many veterans face long waits for help as stress injuries multiply, and the suicide rate keeps going up.

People who know what war can do have demanded action. In a discussion about military suicides and the psychological after-effects of war, retired general Rick Hillier told CBC Radio, "I don't think we had any idea of the scale and scope of what the impact might be." Hillier had commanded troops in Afghanistan, and became chief of the defence staff. The general from Newfoundland affectionately known as the "Big Cod" asked for a public inquiry to find out why vets with mental health problems were being let down. The public was angry that cuts to the budget were more important than the well-being of former soldiers. Hillier said, "This is beyond a medical issue. I think that many of our young men and women have lost confidence in our country to support them."

Corporal Alain Lacasse committed suicide just as the last troops returned home from Afghanistan in March 2014. He was found dead in his home. He had served six tours of duty, including two in Bosnia. Master Corporal Tyson Washburn was found dead of apparent suicide over the same weekend. Both men had done tours in Afghanistan. Lacasse had been stationed in Kandahar from July 2007 to February 2008, and had several brushes with death. A suicide bomber had jumped in front of his vehicle just days before the end of his mission.

THE LAST TROOPS to leave Afghanistan were greeted by the prime minister in March 2014. As Harper welcomed them home, they could not know that his government had just instructed federal lawyers to argue in court that no legally binding covenant existed that obliged Ottawa to look after the troops.

In October 2012, six veterans of the Afghanistan war had filed a suit in the BC Supreme Court. They called their group the Equitas Society. The veterans launched the suit to challenge the New Veterans Charter, which came into effect in 2006. Under the old system, disabled veterans received a tax-free benefit of about $31,000 per year for life. The new legislation replaced that with a lump-sum payment up to a maximum of $301,000. As of September 2013, only 148 people had received the maximum award since 2006. The average award is $45,000, $2,000 less than the Harper government paid for a photo op of the then defence minister, Peter MacKay, climbing in and out of a plywood mock-up of the F-35.

The Equitas Society veterans argued that the government had a "social contract" with the soldiers who put their lives on the line for their country. Since the sixteenth century, under the reign of Elizabeth I, British legislation required each parish to care for sick and wounded soldiers and mariners. But the litigants also cited the words of a former Canadian prime minister to bolster their case. In the spring of 1917, Sir Robert Borden, the Canadian prime minister during the First World War, attended the first imperial war cabinet and conference in Britain. He made regular visits to Canadian soldiers in military hospitals. On the eve of the Battle of Vimy Ridge, which took place on April 9, 1917, Borden made a pledge to Canadian soldiers, many of them wounded:

> You can go into this action feeling assured of this, and as head of the government I give you this assurance: That you need not fear that the government and the country will fail to show just appreciation of your service to the country and Empire in what you are about to do and what you have already done. The government and the country will consider it their first duty to see that a proper appreciation of your effort and of your courage is brought to the notice of people at home, that no man, whether he goes back or whether he remains in Flanders, will have just cause to reproach the government for having broken faith with the men who won and the men who died.

The soldiers expected the government to honour this promise made by a previous Conservative prime minister.

The Harper government wanted the case thrown out without a hearing of the facts, a tactic it had used against former Conservative cabinet minister Helena Guergis and the Council of Canadians when each of these parties sued the government. But a BC Supreme Court Justice, Gordon Weatherill, rejected Ottawa's request in the fall of 2013 and allowed the Equitas case to proceed. Lawyers for the vets argued that the government had a sacred obligation to care for soldiers injured overseas.[15] The justice department denied this in a written submission and is appealing the Supreme Court's decision to allow the matter to go forward. This was odd. Stephen Harper's own veterans ombudsman, a position his government created, had reported that the New Veterans Charter needed to be changed. Colonel Pat Stogran found that senior officers benefitted most under the new charter, while the most severely injured soldiers were the biggest losers. Stogran had commanded the Princess Patricia's Canadian Light Infantry in Afghanistan in 2002 and pushed hard for improvements to benefits for wounded soldiers.

Court papers filed by federal lawyers in a statement of defence against the class action suit on January 31, 2014, were not made public until March 18, 2014—the same day Stephen Harper greeted the last Canadian soldiers returning from Afghanistan. In the statement, the government argued it did not have a special obligation to soldiers who fought for Canada: "The defendant further pleads that at no time in Canada's history has any alleged 'social contract' or 'social covenant' having the attributes pleaded by the plaintiffs been given effect in any statute, regulation, or as a constitutional principle, written or unwritten." It was therefore unfair to bind the government to a statement made by another prime minister almost one hundred years ago: "The defendant pleads that Parliament, within the bounds of constitutional limits, has the unfettered discretion to change or reverse any policy set by a previous government."

The Harper government's lawyers argued that what Prime Minister Borden had said to the troops just before ten thousand of them would be killed or injured in the Battle of Vimy Ridge amounted to just words—nothing more than a speech by a politician. Ottawa's thirty-seven-page filing maintained that the speech merely reflected the policy positions of the government of the day, and was never intended to create a contract, or to bind future governments.

Ironically, at the launch of the New Veterans Charter on April 6, 2006, Stephen Harper had offered a few words of his own that sounded a lot like Prime Minister Borden's: "In future, when our servicemen and women leave our military family, they can rest assured the Government will help them and their families' transition to civilian life. Our troops' commitment and service to Canada entitles them to the very best treatment possible. This Charter is but the first step towards according Canadian veterans the respect and support they deserve." The prime minister's rhetoric notwithstanding, Canada's veterans had to do a surprising amount of fending for themselves in court actions against the government that promised them the "best" of care.

In March 2007, a class action suit was filed on behalf of Dennis Manuge and over 4,500 other disabled veterans. Their long-term disability benefits were reduced by the amount of their Veterans Affairs disability pension—the payment they received for pain and suffering. Once the legal battle got under way, a review of files increased the number of vets eligible for back payments to 7,500. After a five-year battle, the Federal Court of Canada finally ruled on May 1, 2012. The court agreed with the veterans. Judge Robert Barnes ruled that monthly Veterans Affairs pensions for pain and suffering were not "income benefits," and that the clawback would create "a particularly harsh effect on the most seriously disabled Canadian Forces members who have been released from active service." The judge rejected this outcome "unreservedly." Manuge, who had battled hard for his fellow soldiers before the federal veterans ombudsman, Parliament, and the Senate for years, was pleased but not jubilant: "The money will never fix any of us, but it will provide that little bit of dignity."

The then defence minister, Peter MacKay, waited nearly a month before announcing that the federal government would not appeal the ruling. MacKay appointed a negotiator to make a deal with disabled veterans. The agreement was reached in January 2013 and rubber-stamped by the court. Ottawa would repay thousands of disabled veterans whose benefits they had clawed back, to the tune of $887 million, including $424.3 million in payments retroactive to 1976. The rest of the money was interest, $35 million in legal fees, and an estimate of what the veterans would be owed in the future. Julian Fantino's office noted that unlike the DND, Veterans Affairs was not compelled by the courts to halt the clawback. Still, he saw the legal handwriting on the wall. According to his spokesperson, "Our government voluntarily decided to cease the deductions as an additional action to recognize the sacrifices of Canada's veterans."[16]

Although Dennis Manuge won his case, it raised another troubling issue about Ottawa's treatment of veterans—and critics. Manuge discovered that his personal file had been accessed almost a thousand times. Most of the access was legitimate, but several cases of access by political staff in the office of a senior assistant deputy minister were a clear violation of Manuge's privacy. The Harper government did not seem to take breaches of privacy of ex-soldiers or their advocates seriously. Private information—a diagnosis of PTSD—was also used to smear veterans champion

Sean Bruyea, a retired Air Force intelligence officer and an ardent critic of the government's New Veterans Charter.

The government ignored almost every recommendation from veterans groups for changes to the new charter. By November 2010, veterans across the country were protesting against the Harper government—the first such protest in almost ninety years. Sean Bruyea was the first person to publicly oppose the New Veterans Charter, even before it was implemented in 2006. His private information (including psychiatric reports) was provided to a cabinet minister and other members of Parliament. It was also the basis of a briefing to staff in the PMO. Over eight hundred Veterans Affairs employees saw his personal file, where it was also noted he was an advocate for veterans.

In October 2010, Privacy Commissioner Jennifer Stoddart reprimanded the government for the illegal distribution of Bruyea's "sensitive medical and personal information." She called the widely distributed breaches "alarming" as well as "entirely inappropriate." Retired colonel Michel Drapeau described this as the worst privacy breach he had seen: "It's despicable. It's dishonourable. It's unethical. And also illegal." Backed into a corner, the Harper government surrendered. With the government facing widespread condemnation by Canadians as well as veterans, a lawsuit launched by Bruyea was mediated. In October 2010, Bruyea became only the second individual to receive an apology from the Harper government. (The first was Maher Arar, who had been imprisoned and tortured in Syria based on information from Canadian intelligence sources.) Former veterans affairs minister Jean-Pierre Blackburn issued the apology in a news release and on the floor of the House of Commons. He later called Bruyea personally.

Bruyea became a military activist, standing up for other injured soldiers such as Corporal Steve Stoesz. Stoesz was worn down by the red tape that veterans had to wade through to get counselling, physiotherapy, and other medical care. He waited three years to get surgery for some of his injuries, and believed his depression and anxiety were caused by years of fighting to get help from the Forces, not by his tour of duty. Stoesz concluded that loyalty was a one-way street with the Harper government: "They expect it from us but they don't give it in return." Eventually, Stoesz spoke out about the lack of health services in the military, despite being ordered by a superior not to talk to the media or face punishment. Stoesz said his fight to get help for injured soldiers was worse than the battle he endured in Afghanistan. He returned from Afghanistan having survived three bomb attacks, but suffering speech and balance problems. He told CBC News, "They broke me in the fight after, in the dealing with my own country. The country that I fought for now has broken me."

Other advocates, such as Harold Leduc, who sat on the Veterans Review and Appeal Board, got the same treatment as Manuge, Bruyea, and Stoesz. The board gives vets a chance to appeal benefit claims rejected by Veterans Affairs. Leduc was known to give veterans the benefit of the doubt. The RCMP conducted an investigation after Leduc claimed that fellow board members leaked private information about his PTSD diagnosis in order to discredit his decisions at the board. The Human Rights Commission ordered the veterans board to pay Leduc $4,000, including legal costs, for harassment he suffered from other board members.

As it has done with several civilian critics, the Harper government tried to muzzle its detractors in the military. Wounded soldiers were required to sign a form giving their agreement not to criticize senior officers on social media. The form was leaked by members of the military who saw it as a way of preventing them from making the case that the New Veterans Charter was not working. On April 1, 2014, the man in charge of the Joint Personnel Support Unit, Colonel Gerry Blais, gave MPs the government's line that the form was intended to benefit the wounded, not to stifle criticism: "The form is there more for the protection of the individuals because unfortunately there are occasions where people, especially when they are suffering from mental health issues, will make comments or become involved in discussions that, later on in the full light of day, they would probably prefer that they had not been involved." So the victims were to blame.

Not everyone embraced Colonel Blais and his notion of compassionate muzzling. Veterans advocate Sean Bruyea described the JPSU form as "right out of something you would see during the Soviet era." The form, introduced in March 2013, stipulates that those in the JPSU are not to disclose their "views on any military subject," which, as everyone knew, included complaints about health care. Ironically, it had been through leaking to the media that the new policy ending danger pay during the Afghanistan War was rescinded.[17] Military personnel in the JPSU would be held responsible for their comments on social media, as well as for the comments of their friends. Some people getting treatment under the JPSU refused to sign because it took away their freedom of speech. Colonel Blais said the form is "not restrictive, per se." Rather, "It is guidance."

The Afghanistan mission officially ended on March 12, 2014. The Harper government declared May 9, 2014, a National Day of Honour "to commemorate our service and our sacrifices in order to achieve the security and stability we brought to Afghanistan." Not everyone thought this was a good use of taxpayers' money. Priscilla Blake, who lost her husband, Petty Officer Craig Blake, in a deadly explosion in Kabul, said that the money used for the commemoration should be spent helping returning veterans who suffered mental and physical injuries.

After Canada's Afghanistan mission ended, the father of Corporal Jordan Anderson, who was killed on July 4, 2007, by a roadside bomb outside of Kandahar, gave an appraisal free of the empty rhetoric of politicians. Rejecting the PM's claims of success in Afghanistan on the day the mission ended, James Anderson of Yellowknife told CBC, "I think it was a waste in all respects. The personal cost, the emotional cost, the financial cost, and Canada's place in the world, quite frankly." [18]

The National Day of Honour went ahead as planned. Family members of fallen soldiers received letters inviting them to the memorial event in Ottawa. But the letter included a stunning piece of information: it advised that attendance "would be at your own expense." The letter was obtained by CTV News and the story broadcast April 2, 2014. The father of Captain Nichola Goddard, the first female Canadian soldier killed in Afghanistan, said from his home in Charlottetown what a lot of Canadians were thinking after seeing the letter on television: "It was kind of like, 'we're having this big special event and you can come if you want, but you have to buy your own ticket.'"

When the story became public, the Harper government resorted to the usual tactic—blame the bureaucrats. Defence minister Nicholson said the letter telling family members they had to pay their own way to the tribute "had absolutely nothing to do with [his] office." When the blowback increased, his parliamentary secretary, MP James Bezan, said in the House of Commons that the letter was "premature, incorrect and contained false information." Outed and embarrassed, the government had decided to pay after all. Then corporate sponsors stepped forward to provide funding for transportation and accommodation for the families. The prime minister caused a protocol flap when he decided to receive the last Canadian flag flown in Afganistan from a relay team of injured vets, rather than our real commander-in-chief, Governor General David Johnston. It was a Harper event: A twenty-one-gun salute, parades, helicopters landing, planes overhead, tanks in the street, and, having closed the file on Afghanistan, photo ops for 2015.

The problem was, returning veterans with mental and physical wounds inhabit a harsh and ongoing reality: how to push your kid on a swing minus an arm or a leg, or how to fill a war-weary heart with good human emotions again. The party that had courted, lionized, and used the military now turned its back on them when priorities changed.

nineteen

A WALK WITH FARLEY

L ike that magical line where a fog bank meets the incandes-
cent brilliance of a summer day, the Strait of Canso divides
elementally different worlds: mainland Nova Scotia and the rugged island of Cape Breton. In days gone by, as you approached
Cape Porcupine—half its enormous rock face blasted away for
the 10 million tonnes of granite that built the causeway—there
was a toll booth and a modest wait before crossing to the other
side. But the link to Cape Breton has long since been paid for
and the toll booths have disappeared. Now you drive unim-
peded across the green swing bridge on the island side, with the
words "Welcome to Cape Breton" painted in yellow on one of
the crossbeams. The only delay might be an amber flashing light,
signalling that the bridge is about to swing open so that a sail-
boat, its mast rising surrealistically above the girders, can glide
silently through.

It is said that the Canso Causeway is the deepest and among
the longest in the world. But like all great feats of engineering,
it has had unintended consequences. The tourists came, but the

herring and lobster left, cut off from their traditional migration routes by the causeway. No one had thought to ask the fishermen their opinion of a structure that would forever seal off a large part of the strait from the open ocean. The lobster traps are no longer on the ocean floor in the old places, but fastened to the roof racks of cars from Ontario and Quebec—tourists headed home with a memento of their visit.

The last time I passed over that bridge was in the late summer of 2009. I was on my way to St. Anthony Daniel Church in Sydney to attend the funeral of a remarkable person, Donald Marshall Jr. I had written my first book, *Justice Denied*, about his wrongful imprisonment of eleven years for a murder he had not committed. The case of the young Mi'kmaq Indian became a national *cause célèbre*, a black mark against the courts and police, and a reminder that Canada had its own version of racism to worry about. It was also my personal schooling in the fact that everything that can go wrong in the justice system sometimes does go wrong. Marshall had been so confused at his one-day murder trial, he later told me he couldn't tell the difference between his own lawyers and the prosecutors. Since then I have never discounted a story, however improbable, without looking into it.

A few years after the publication of the Marshall book, a young waiter, Shane Earle, told me about the decades-old cover-up of sexual and physical abuse of boys at Newfoundland's Mount Cashel Orphanage. He had read an editorial I had written in *The Sunday Express*[1] entitled "Justice for All" and asked why there had been none for the boys of Mount Cashel. The scandal was not that no one had known about it; it was that many powerful people officially covered up the story because it involved a lay order of the Roman Catholic Church. Earle's story, told barely above a whisper, became my next book, *Unholy Orders*. When I found myself explaining the tragedy of Mount Cashel on *Oprah* with Shane beside me, I was thinking of the lesson Donald Marshall Jr., had taught me: listen to everyone, lift every rock, because you never know where the truth might be hiding.

And I learned one other thing. Ordinary people can do extraordinary things, no matter what personal torments or travesties they have endured. Years after his release from prison, remarkably unbroken by his ordeal, Marshall was charged with catching and selling 220 kilograms of eels out of season and without a licence. On Maliseet and Mi'kmaq reserves, where unemployment stands at 85 percent, making an extra $787.10 from illegal fishing, as Marshall did, is an attractive proposition. Donald Marshall Jr., the shy and unlikely icon of indomitable survival, was headed back to court, but this time with a very different result. In 1999, the Supreme Court of Canada brought down a landmark decision that held that Marshall had the right to fish under a 1761 treaty the British had signed with the Mi'kmaq. The boy who had been sent to prison at seventeen for something he hadn't done, and came out as a graduate of Dorchester Penitentiary at twenty-nine, had successfully extended native fishing and treaty rights for an entire people.

But this day I was not headed to Marshall's home reserve, Membertou, a journey I had made so many times while working on his story. My destination was not Sydney, but a place where I had never been, River Bourgeois, to interview a man I had never met, though he was very famous: Farley Mowat. Yes, I wanted to interview Farley Mowat for a book about Canadian politics, Mowat the ninety-two-year-old author. Over the years, I have observed that official sources, party spokespeople, and now computer-assisted journalism, have left a hole in the telling of our national story. Where were all the other people in the newspaper articles and on television: the non-experts, the non-insiders, the thinkers, the painters, the eccentrics?

Writing a book about the Harper government carried its imperatives to be sure—talking to a great many people in politics and public service, and gathering as many documents, secret or otherwise, as one could. But to me, it also meant listening to different voices with a unique point of view: an eighty-year-old former student of Stephen Harper's grandfather; a Stockwell Day delegate who claimed the Harper team had cheated at the convention that chose Harper to be leader of the Canadian Alliance party; a girl who went to university with Harper and has never forgotten that cold, blue stare.

And then there was "Dennis." He did not make his living writing about politics. But he was still an expert on the prime minister in a totally original way, for Dennis was Stephen Harper's hairstylist. His recollections ran from the banal to the hilarious. Starting with the banal, it takes half an hour to cut the prime minister's hair, which Dennis does every three to four weeks. Sometimes this special customer only wants it thinned. Although Opposition leader Harper used to come to Rinaldo's, the elegant salon on George Street in Ottawa's Byward Market, Dennis now travels to 24 Sussex Drive and cuts the PM's hair in an alcove under the stairs on the ground floor.

One day, Dennis forgot his barber's cape. The prime minister whipped the cloth off the breakfast table, threw it around his shoulders, and Dennis was back in business. "I was shocked at how shabby the table was when he took the table cloth off. It was shocking to see cracks in the baseboards that didn't seem to get fixed," he told me. Only once in their working relationship did Harper ever make a special request—a haircut on a Saturday. The rest of the time, it was early mornings, right after the PM had breakfast with the children. When Harper was in Opposition, Dennis had told him that one day he would be prime minister. "Harper liked that," Dennis remembered. "A lot of people hate

Stephen Harper, but I think he's a smart guy." Dennis also noted another important thing about his famous client: Stephen Harper was apparently a good tipper.

Dennis also cuts Laureen Harper's hair. According to the stylist who has a cleaning business on the side, the prime minister's wife never asks for a particular style, is most comfortable in blue jeans and a T-shirt (like her husband), and is unpretentious. When he asked her where she was going for her vacation when Parliament rose, she replied, "Into the woods."[2]

Finally, the improbable and hilarious. As Dennis explained to me in the salon, cutting the hair of powerful people has its unexpected benefits. Margaret Trudeau arranged for Dennis to meet President Jimmy Carter—and even Fidel Castro on his secret trip to Canada to attend Pierre Trudeau's funeral. "Fidel Castro's security detail really impressed me—female, Russian, and the meanest-looking people I ever saw."

The only person guarding Farley Mowat this August day was his handyman, Mark, the maintenance chief at the local fish-plant. Mark explained how to get to Farley's place, but contrived to show up a little later to make sure that the local legend was not being pestered by unwanted camp followers from the mainland. The Mowat homestead sits on 80 hectares of unspoiled wilderness overlooking the ocean, a fitting location for the writer of forty-four books and Mother Nature's first, big-time, Canadian bodyguard. He calls the property the Mowat Research Institute. Hyperbole is his first instinct, winning a laugh from you, his highest pleasure. I had been told to arrive at a certain hour and not to interfere with his needed rest. Don't come too early and don't stay too late. In the end, I was invited to stay overnight, an invitation I foolishly declined.

I drove down the long lane to the farmhouse, which he later claimed "was rotting from the top down"—Farley's explanation of how the ants got in. The famous writer was standing there with his hands on his hips, wearing Bermuda shorts and looking like a boy dressed up as an old man for Halloween. The expression on his face was a mixture of delight and canny curiosity. I could see the skinny kid who so worried his librarian-mother when, at age ten, the "Shrimp" barely looked six. I could also see the shrewd assessor.

I passed his sniff test and was offered a tour of the Mowat Research Institute. He showed me how he had rigged up a water system from two ponds—which he called the White and the Blue Nile. The ponds were not spring-fed, but depended entirely on rainfall. I noticed that there were frogs in Farley's drinking water. He laughed: "They have a language with just one word in it—harrrumph. That one-word language can keep you awake all night."

Back down the lane was the guest house, which Farley had once used to shelter a "fugitive from injustice," his friend Paul Watson. The anti-whaling, direct-action environmentalist has faced two "red alerts"—international arrest warrants issued by Interpol—over allegedly obstructing Japanese whaling vessels. Farley claimed that Watson's only crimes were stopping the Japanese from whaling in designated sanctuaries. "No one in Canada knows this, but I entertained Paul recently when the authorities didn't officially know where he was. Those same authorities used to listen to my phone calls. I was one of the Friends of Cuba and a known "left-wing rebel." I just laughed about it and said 'good morning chaps' to the listeners when I used my phone."

From the crest of the hill where the white frame house sits, no other domicile or building is visible—just the unspoiled land, a crescent beach below, and the ocean stretching all the way to the horizon. As we passed a well-chewed tennis ball, Farley stopped and said, "My old dog, Chester, died last year. The night before we were about to head back to Port Hope, he crawled in his bed and went to sleep. He didn't want to go back to Ontario."

The boyish old man talked for a moment about his latest crusade—keeping oil rigs out of the Gulf of St. Lawrence. He saw the gulf as the last, vital internal body of salt water on the East Coast that could support the restoration of endangered species. And if that happened, it could also support traditional human activities. But he was well aware of the potential cost to him. "I am doing this against my will in a way, getting involved at this time in life, when I might get the Big Call tomorrow. But the bastards who have set this thing in motion are taking a perverse pleasure in doing it and must be opposed . . . to exploit what's left of the gulf will be the dagger driven into the corpse."

If a *Deepwater Horizon*–type of event were to take place in the Gulf of St. Lawrence, the results could be catastrophic.[3] The channels and straits that make up the gulf move in a counter-clockwise direction, which means that the vast area is only flushed into the wider ocean once a year. Spilled oil would ride the mostly landlocked gulf currents for a long time. Worse, the site of the proposed development is the Laurentian Channel, the deep main artery in and out of the gulf for 2,200 marine species.

Listening to Farley talk, I am surprised at the discouragement in that clear, quick voice, stating and restating his thoughts until the words were just right. His heart told him that drilling for oil in the Gulf of St. Lawrence was wrong; his head said it would almost certainly happen. His convictions told him that environmentalists were doing Gaia's work, but his head understood that the forces lined up against them were all but invincible. Farley was profoundly worried. "We don't elect pacifists. We admire the killer instinct in leaders. It's genetic. It is inevitable that people in high positions like Harper reach out for a bloody stick or sword. The people who run the world today are psychopaths. Everybody can see it, so why are we so obedient? All they care about is the economy because that means money. A virus is sweeping through the human race. At the top, all over the world, we are rotting away as a species from the top down. The leaders have gone beyond greed to the sheer amassing of power. There is no effective morality, just power."

Farley leads me to his swimming hole, a secluded second pond surrounded by gorse and thicket so dense it can't be seen from the laneway. There is a wooden plank extending out into the water, though so small that only a child—or a child-sized man, could use it. It was a good place to skinny-dip, he assured me. I ask him his thoughts on the country. "Canada is a fermentation process that has gone wrong," he replies. "Instead of wine, we got vinegar. 'We create the reality,' those in power say. Every dictator the world has ever seen operates like that." He stops to nibble the green shoot of something plucked from the side of the pond.

Farley explains that governments worldwide, including Canada's, are doing their best to diminish nature because of the fundamental collision between the environment and resource development. It is, of course, his great subject. "Under the current system," he says, "the environment and resource development cannot be reconciled. The ones in power just don't think the right way. It's as if we are being governed by an alien species. It's as if something in the miasma of the Ottawa River rises and affects them all. They become zombies. People don't understand that a biosphere either lives or dies. They're finding it out in the Gulf of Mexico."

Writers go in and out of favour like the width of lapels and the height of hemlines. Pierre Trudeau was a big fan of Farley Mowat, a natural enough affinity since both loved the wilderness with a passion. When Farley and his wife, Claire, were living on the Magdalen Islands, the prime minister showed up with Margaret for a visit with one of his favourite Canadian writers. "Trudeau was travelling quietly when he came to visit us. He arrived on an icebreaker and helicoptered into our place with a pregnant wife and one security officer. Margaret was pregnant with Justin. It turned out they were in the market for a dog. So our dog, a black Lab and water dog mixture, was pregnant and we offered them a puppy. That's how Farley Trudeau got to join the Trudeau household. But he got banished to British Columbia shortly after his arrival for pissing on Trudeau's Tibetan prayer rug."

These days there are not many invitations to go to Rideau Hall and none to 24 Sussex Drive. I ask him about Margaret Atwood's comment that Stephen Harper's modus operandi was "Stalinist." "Stalin had small balls compared to this guy. Stephen Harper is probably the most dangerous human being ever elevated to power in Canada. How the population has acquiesced in following this son of a bitch, and to let him take over their lives, I'll never know. You have to create warrior nations, they are not born. They have to be made. It is the preliminary step of a tyrant. And this son of a bitch incited Canada into becoming a warrior nation."

Unlike Stephen Harper, Farley Mowat has been a real warrior, and written about it in one of his books. There is a part of him that tries to make a joke of everything—even the Second World War: "I don't feel guilty about anything from the war. I was such a bad shot that whenever I aimed at a German, I missed." But the levity is mostly for show. His face darkens as he remembers calling in the heavy artillery on a German counter-attack around Casino, in Italy. The carnage was stupefying. "Three days later, I had the chance to go back up the road they were on when the bombardment started," he says. "I didn't go because I didn't want to be haunted by what I might see."

Back in the house, Farley's wife, Claire, author of six of her own books, grants permission for a glass of otherwise forbidden Chardonnay. Farley has lined up his medications on the table like toy soldiers and explains that wine wars with his army of pre-scriptions. There are pink peonies on the table from the bee-filled gardens and a quiche set off with greens from the Mowats' fenced vegetable patch. I ask Farley which of his books he liked best. "If you mean the one that was the most important, it would be *Sea of Slaughter*. If you mean my favourite, it would be *And No Birds Sang*." The war book.

Over dinner, Farley returns to politics. He remarks that the parliamentary system is no longer working in Canada and what we have now is the imitation of Parliament. "We took Parliament for granted, but, like the environment, it turns out that it is an incredibly delicate and fragile structure. Harper has smothered MPs and is destroying Parliament. Elizabeth May is our one ray of hope, the only light in that vast, dark institution, our flickering little candle." It is not for nothing that Farley Mowat is godfa-ther of the Green Party leader's daughter, Victoria Cate. Summer and Christmas holidays, the Mowats and the Mays come together like family.

With a five-hour drive ahead of me, I start to say my goodbyes half an hour before I know I will be allowed to leave. With Farley, there is always one more story, all of them filling in some part of his extraordinary life. With a chill in the Cape Breton air, and the sun sinking, I rise to go.

"You should stay you know. Come in here a minute."

It is Farley's writing room, and there on the desk sits his old Underwood. The typewriter is so big it looks as though Farley could ride it. I stop in front of a work hanging on the wall; it is a picture of Farley that his publisher Jack McClelland had done up as/a Wanted poster. "Jack thought it would be a good idea because I had been stopped trying to enter the US on a book tour. I wrote about my discovery of America. I wrote it in three weeks—fastest book I ever did."

I thanked Farley for letting a fellow writer into his inner sanctum and started to leave. "Care for some reading material?" he asked, leading me to a closet door in his study. Inside were all his books, carefully laid out on shelves. I chose *And No Birds Sang*, his memoir of the Second World War, with a stylized crow taking up most of the cover. Its beak was open and black except the blood-red, protruding tongue. Even to its author, the subject matter was next to unbearable: ". . . a bloody awful thing it was," he wrote of the war. "So awful that through three decades I kept the deeper agonies of it wrapped in the cottonwool of protective forgetfulness. . . ." Farley took the book from my hands and inscribed it. We walked to the door and then down to my pickup. His face clouded over and he lowered his voice. "About the country and our future. It is like an aura that seems to have gone wrong. I have the sound of old cannon fired in 1812 in my ears. It is the sound of war again. War is coming back. There is an inevitable sense about it. I'm pretty pessimistic."

I was told to come back and spend a weekend in the guest house in September, which I promised to do. But I was a prisoner of words that summer and did not make it back. My new promise, made in a letter, was to come next summer when the book was done. "Sure, you could camp in the sacred precincts of the Mowat Environmental Inst. Overnight," he wrote back. "No cockroaches! See you at Brock Point next summer. I bloody well hope. IF the Seapuss let's [*sic*] us come back. The Seapuss gets us all in the end!"

The ocean came in and went out again, the Seapuss intervened, and Farley was gone before that next summer. Drilling in the Gulf of St. Lawrence has since been approved, but the bullfrogs still harrumph in the Blue Nile, and the battle goes on for the soul of the nation, as Farley had surely known it would, no matter how powerful the enemy, or how depleted the ranks of those who love the land.

WAR IS PEACE

I t took just over a year for Farley Mowat's premonition that Canada was going back to war to come true.

On October 7, 2014, the Harper government voted to send six fighter jets, support planes, and six hundred Canadian personnel to a coalition combat mission in Iraq against Islamic State militants (ISIS). The prime minister was redeploying Canadian forces in a combat zone just seven months after ending the country's twelve-year mission in Afghanistan.

With oil prices plummeting and the economy stalling, the mission against ISIS was a political godsend for the government—just as the Falklands War had brought Margaret Thatcher back from the political dead in 1982. Before ISIS burst onto the scene, Stephen Harper had been polling badly. An EKOS poll done in August 2014 had the Liberals leading the Conservatives 38.7 to 25.6 percent, with the NDP threatening opposition status at 23.4 percent. Even the Green Party was surging with 7.1 percent support. Harper had a job approval rating of only 29 percent, 20 points behind Justin Trudeau's. Thomas Mulcair scored the highest approval at 54 percent. Almost 57 percent of Canadians thought the country was moving in the wrong direction.

The first job in any war is selling it, a tough task at the best of times, but even harder in a war-weary nation that had seen 40,000 Canadians serve in Afghanistan and 162 of them die there. The first step is demonizing the enemy, which in the case of ISIS was easy to do. With its penchant for making videos of the beheadings of its foreign captives and enemies, the latest Islamic terrorist organization from the Middle East was easy to depict as heartless barbarians.

Unlike al Qaeda, which operates worldwide, ISIS believes it is carrying out a prophesy by re-establishing a Muslim caliphate in the Middle East. Followers of ISIS think they will defeat the "crusaders" on a plain near the village of Dabiq, northeast of Aleppo, Syria, about ten kilometres from the Turkish border. After the Antichrist appears, it is believed there will be a final battle at the gates of Rum (believed to be Istanbul), where Issa ibn-Maryam (known as Jesus to Christians) will descend from heaven to kill the Antichrist with a spear, marking the end of the world—a kind of Muslim Armageddon. The first duty of jihad is to make a pilgrimage to the Islamic State. So far ISIS has captured nearly a third of Iraq and Syria, proving to be a formidable fighting force despite having no air power.

Both main opposition parties voted against the mission, but the Harper majority approved the motion by a vote of 157 to 134. Thomas Mulcair accused the government of "plunging Canada into a prolonged war" without a credible plan to help the victims of ISIS. He wanted to increase humanitarian aid and supply arms to local fighters. Liberal leader Justin Trudeau said his caucus voted against the mission because the government had not clearly explained its objectives to Canadians: "They have no exit strategy beyond an illusory end date set for next March."

Marketing the war against ISIS got a huge boost from two tragic events that rocked the domestic political landscape in Canada. On October 20, 2014, Warrant Officer Patrice Vincent died after twenty-five-year-old Martin Couture-Rouleau ran down two soldiers in a hit-and-run attack. Rouleau had converted to Islam in 2013. According to a friend, the troubled man was angry that Canada supported the bombing of ISIS in Iraq and Syria, and dreamed of martyrdom in the cause. His vehicle idling, he waited patiently for two hours until two soldiers, one of them in uniform, emerged from a Service Canada building. Rouleau ran them down in cold blood.

After the hit-and-run, Rouleau was pursued by police from Saint-Jean-Sur-Richelieu. He was shot dead after crawling out the window of his car, which had overturned in a ditch after a four-kilometre chase. According to news reports, he initially put his hands up, but then allegedly charged police officers with a hunting knife that was found at the scene.

It was a strange case. Rouleau, like many converts, had unresolved difficulties in his life. He had had a minor run-in with the law, overdid the party scene, and gambled. He tried to start a pressure-washing business without success. There was also a custody battle with a former girlfriend over his young son. Even Rouleau's Facebook profile seemed to be a dark harbinger of what was to come. It showed two doors: one leading to heaven, the other to hell.

Rouleau had reportedly told his father that he wanted to join ISIS. He tried to leave the country for Pakistan in February 2014. When he started using "the language of jihad" in April and May 2014, his concerned father called the police. Rouleau was placed on an RCMP watch list in June 2014 as a possible Islamist extremist.

In the wake of the tragedy, a *Globe and Mail* editorial on October 21, 2014, asked the question that no one in authority was particularly anxious to answer: "Why were no charges laid when [Couture-Rouleau] tried to leave the country, apparently with violent intent?"

It was a good question, since laws were obviously in place to apprehend Mohammad Hasan Hersi for the same thing. In July 2014, the month Rouleau was arrested for his second attempt to join ISIS, Hersi was sentenced to ten years in prison for trying to fly from Pearson Airport to join the terrorist group al-Shabab in Somalia. Why was Rouleau different?

In addition to enlisting the help of police, Rouleau's father had also taken him to the hospital for psychiatric help. His son was released the next day. After police were tipped by his father that Rouleau was on his way to Turkey in July 2014, he was arrested and his passport was revoked. Rouleau was one of ninety-three suspected extremists the force was closely monitoring.

In a statement released shortly after the hit-and-run killing, a spokesperson for Stephen Harper said, "The individual who struck the two [Canadian Armed Forces] members with his car is known to federal authorities, including the Integrated National Security Enforcement Team." So why wasn't he detained? Existing laws on the detention of such individuals using security certificates were already in place.

RCMP outreach officers had talked to Rouleau as recently as October 9, two days after the Harper government made the decision to go to war in Iraq. Police got the impression they were making progress and that Rouleau was changing his ways. Alerted by the RCMP, the imam from Rouleau's mosque had also talked to the young man, trying to "de-radicalize" him. RCMP Superintendent Martine Fontaine said, "The meeting ended on a very positive note, so we had no reason to believe after he would commit a criminal act in Canada." On October 21, the day after the hit-and-run, six CF-18 fighter jets left Cold Lake, Alberta, for Kuwait to join in the coalition air strikes against ISIS.

As unimaginable as it seemed, lightning was about to strike again. The next day, on October 22, 2014, another troubled Muslim convert, Michael Zehaf-Bibeau, shot dead Corporal Nathan Cirillo, a young, unarmed Canadian reservist who was guarding the National War Memorial in Ottawa. Normally the ceremonial sentry duty was held for tourists during only the summer months. But in 2014, the sentry duty had for the first time been extended to Remembrance Day because Stephen Harper wanted to commemorate the start of World War I.

Bibeau should have been on the radar of the authorities. He had a history of drug use and run-ins with the law. At one point, he was so desperate to break his cocaine habit that he tried to get himself sent to jail. In 2012, Bibeau turned himself in to Vancouver police, confessing to an armed robbery he said he had committed in Quebec. Finding no record of the incident, the police released him. That same night, he sharpened a stick and tried to rob a McDonald's restaurant. He waited outside for the police to arrive and arrest him.

Once in court, he begged the judge for a long sentence so that he could get the counselling he needed to break his drug habit. It was details like this that led Andrea Polko, the girlfriend of murdered soldier Nathan Cirillo, to ask for a national "wake-up" call on how society treats people who struggle with mental illness. Stephen Harper's terrorist was Polko's "deeply disturbed man." She posted on Facebook that Canadians should focus on "how we can prevent another event like this through more accessible and effective mental health treatment programs that target the real sources of this tragedy."

Bibeau had tried to get a Canadian passport in Vancouver in August 2014, but was informed the application was subject to review. So he made his way to Ottawa, hitchhiking and riding a Greyhound bus. He told fellow passengers he was on his way to Ottawa to get a passport. A dual citizen of Canada and Libya,

Bibeau went to the Libyan Embassy on October 2, 2014, to renew his expired passport. Authorities told him the process would take three to four weeks because of discrepancies in his documents. Two days later, he took a guided tour of Centre Block in the Parliament Buildings. Days later it was announced that Canada would be sending six F-18s to bomb ISIS in Iraq.

The mayhem Bibeau wreaked on the morning of October 22 was all but incredible. The killer had been able to park on busy Wellington Street in downtown Ottawa, shoot the soldier at the War Memorial brandishing a rifle only partly hidden by an umbrella, run up the drive to Centre Block, get past the RCMP security patrol, commandeer a cabinet minister's car, drive to the entrance, and get inside Centre Block after shooting an unarmed security guard in the leg.

While his caucus members fashioned crude weapons and barred the door when they heard gunshots, Prime Minister Stephen Harper hid in a closet for "protocol" reasons. Bibeau quickly went down in a hail of bullets just outside the entrance to the Parliamentary Library.

Later at a Mount Allison University convocation honouring him, former House of Commons Sergeant-at-Arms Kevin Vickers recalled that he found himself on one side of a pillar facing the gunman on the other side, so close he could almost "reach out and grab the gun." The gunman fired and Vickers fired back. The day was a blur, but when Vickers woke up at 5:30 the next morning after a night spent in anguish for taking a life, he was crying. Now Canada's ambassador to Ireland, Vickers recalled, "It was the loneliest moment of my life."

Three days later, during a long overnight drive back to his family in Miramichi, Vickers decided he should pray for the gunman. He arranged for his priest to say a private mass at the family home. His mother prayed for the mothers of both Corporal Cirillo and Bibeau. With his grandchildren in his arms, Vickers said a prayer for "Michael." He recalled, "It kind of occurred to me that [Jesus], after he was crucified, the first person he let into the Kingdom of Heaven was the man crucified next to him—a convicted criminal."

The Harper government quickly announced the RCMP would now be given overall authority for security on Parliament Hill in the wake of the attack. It was an odd decision. The RCMP hadn't stopped the gunman from gaining entrance to Parliament; it had been House of Commons security staff in the person of Sergeant-at-Arms Kevin Vickers who took down the shooter. The RCMP reports to Cabinet, which raises the question of Parliament's independence from the government of the day. As with many other Harper initiatives, the changing of security responsibilities on Parliament Hill may lead to a constitutional challenge.

Later it was discovered that moments before his attack at the War Memorial, Bibeau had left a video on his cellphone explaining the murder in his own words. He said he intended to commit a terrorist act against the military because of Canada's role in Afghanistan and the decision by the Harper government to send troops to Iraq. "So we are retaliating," he said, "the mujahedin of this world. Canada's officially become one of our enemies by fighting and bombing us and creating a lot of terror in our countries and killing us and killing our innocents. So just aiming to hit some soldiers just to show that you're not even safe in your own land, and you gotta be careful."

The night of the Cirillo shooting, the prime minister took to television and made an explicit connection between what had happened in Ottawa and Canada's bombing against ISIS in Iraq. He said that Canada would "fight against the terrorist organizations who brutalize those in other countries with the hope of bringing their savagery to our shores."

The government repeatedly tied the murder of both soldiers to ISIS, which in Bibeau's case was patently false. The photo of Bibeau taken during the shooting at the War Memorial did not originate from an ISIS website, although initial press reports quickly alleged a link. It was in fact tweeted from a US site. Nor was Bibeau originally planning to go to Syria if he got a passport, as the RCMP claimed, but rather Saudi Arabia—a crucially important difference. Even after Bibeau's mother corrected the RCMP about her son's actual destination, she had to go to the press to finally get a public correction from the police.

In a move straight out of tactics described in Naomi Klein's book *The Shock Doctrine*, the PM used the public disorientation and grief caused by the death of two soldiers to beat the drums of war. Hoping to paint the opposition as soft on terrorism, he and his ministers hammered away at the grave danger ISIS presented to the world and to Canada. Defence Minister Jason Kenney depicted ISIS as the most evil force on earth. He even tweeted photos of Muslim girls in burkas and chains as an example of ISIS depravity, turning young girls into slaves. Unhappily for Kenney, the photos turned out to be scenes from a ceremonial religious enactment, like a passion play, that made the rounds of the internet before ISIS had even appeared on the world stage. Caught out in clumsy propaganda, the minister refused to apologize.

The Harper government's rhetoric may have been overblown, but it achieved the desired result with a frightened citizenry. Conservative polling showed that Canadians supported the mission because they believed ISIS was a threat to Canada. Stephen Harper had Canadians just where he wanted them—shaking in their boots.

Oddly enough, neither Justin Bourque nor Glen Gieshen were charged with terrorist acts, though their crimes amounted to an assault on the government. Gieschen was convicted of plotting to blow up a Veterans Affairs Centre in Calgary's Bantrel Tower. Decked out in camouflage, Bourque shot five Mounties in Moncton, New Brunswick, killing three of them. He had spoken openly about a revolution against the Canadian government. Bourque and Gieshen shared three similarities. Both were captured alive, both entered guilty pleas to criminal charges, and neither was Muslim.

ALTHOUGH THE PRIME MINISTER stressed that our troops would not be involved in ground combat in Iraq, it turned out that Canadian Special Forces in fact accompanied coalition forces and returned enemy fire on several occasions. Neither the Americans nor the British had permitted their special forces to engage with ISIS.

Despite clear evidence of mission creep that contradicted the prime minister's pledge in Parliament, then Defence Minister Rob Nicholson insisted that all activities were consistent with the mandate to "advise and assist." In the process, General Tom Lawson, the chief of the Defence Staff, was humiliated by the Harper government. He had to publicly insist that returning fire with militants at the front lines in Iraq was not "combat."

Lawson also said that the US and Canada were the only countries deploying advanced precision-guided weapons—a fact that would later be used to justify Canada's expansion of the bombing mission into Syria, since Canada was the only other member of the coalition with smart bombs. Again, General Lawson and Minister Kenney were wrong. Other members of the US coalition involved in air strikes in Syria also had smart bombs, including Saudi Arabia and the United Arab Emirates.

It looked like the old Tory tactic of misleading Parliament yet again. The NDP's defence critic, Jack Harris, requested that Kenney be investigated for breach of privilege, since he had repeated false and misleading information in Parliament several times. The NDP alleged that Kenney breached his privilege by using that false information to justify Canada's involvement in the expanded mission.

On April 29, 2015, Speaker Andrew Scheer ruled that Kenney did not breach privilege when he told the House that Canada was the only country besides the US with precision-guided munitions—even though he was factually wrong. Kenney refused to apologize and turned instead to the now standard behaviour of a Harper cabinet minister caught with his foot in his mouth. He blamed his military briefings for the mistake, forcing General Tom Lawson's office to express regret for the inaccurate information.

The motion to extend Canada's mission passed 142 to 129 on March 30, 2015. Both the NDP and the Liberals voted against the expanded mission, just as they had opposed the original deployment, although Liberal MP Irwin Cotler abstained on principle.

As with the Senate scandal and the cost of new fighter jets, Stephen Harper had difficulty keeping his story straight about the war plan in Iraq and Syria. Initially, he had said that Canada would not bomb Syria without the permission of the Assad government. Then on March 24, 2015, Harper said, "The government has now decided we will not seek the express consent of the Syrian government." No reasons were given for the flip-flop.

Harper had also told Parliament that he would keep the Canadian Forces on the ground in a non-combat role. The death of Special Forces soldier Sergeant Andrew Joseph Dorion by friendly fire near the fluid front line of the war showed how empty that pledge was. After a series of investigations, in May 2015, the death of Canada's first soldier to die in the Iraq mission was ruled "a tragic case of mistaken identity."

The first six months of the mission had cost $166 million. On March 26, 2015, Jean-Denis Grechette, the parliamentary budget watchdog, released a report saying that the Harper government's defence spending was "unsustainable." The government currently spends $21.5 billion on defence. This is 1.1 percent of GDP, but according to Grechette they need to spend 1.6 percent of GDP, an increase of at least $3 billion annually, in order to sustain the current level of troops, bases, and equipment. The government will have to spend more on defence or scale back its missions.

The war in Iraq and Syria is expected to cost Canada over $528.5 million by 2016, according to Defence Minister Jason Kenney. The numbers were not revealed in Parliament, though, but during an interview with Kenney and the ethnic media. In fact, MPs had been expressly denied the costing of the expansion of the mission into Syria while it was being debated in Parliament.

The prime minister made a surprise visit to Iraq on May 2, 2015, no doubt for photos for the next federal election showing him as the strong leader protecting Canada from ISIS. It was a more marketable image than the caricatures of the prime minister cowering in a closet that filled the country's newspapers after the attack on Centre Block. He had a red-carpet meeting with Iraqi Prime Minister Haider al-Abadi, which took place in Saddam Hussein's old palace. Harper said, "Canada will not stand by idly while ISIS threatens Canadians and commits barbaric acts of violence and injustice in Iraq against innocent civilians." In what has become the norm, he did not take questions from the press.

The prime minister had good reason to fear them. What would he say about the fact that the West had been standing idly by for four years while President Assad's regime had slaughtered more than 200,000 of his own people in a gruesome civil war? How would he justify being allied with Iran in the fight against ISIS, when his then Foreign Affairs Minister John Baird said Iran was "the most significant threat to global peace and security in the world today"?

There were other contradictions and embarrassments over Canada's new military bedfellows. The Iraqi government's ground forces that fought to retake Tikrit included Iranian troops led by Major-General Quassim Suleimani, considered by the United States to be a terrorist. Canada withdrew its ambassador to Iran in

September 2012 because the Harper government said the country was a sponsor of terror. One of the reasons cited for that conclusion was Iran's support for Syrian President Bashar al-Assad's regime. Israel's prime minister praised the move as a courageous act of leadership on Canada's part. So an inquiring mind could fairly ask, Mr. Prime Minister, how did Canada come to be an ally of two of the original members of President Bush's Axis of Evil?

And where did the prime minister think ISIS came from? US President Barack Obama said in an interview with VICE news on March 17, 2015, that ISIS was the product of George Bush's invasion of Iraq, the other war Stephen Harper wanted in on: "ISIS is a direct outgrowth of al-Qaeda in Iraq that grew out of our invasion." Obama went on to say that this was an example of the law of unintended consequences. "Which is why we should generally aim before we shoot," the president added. Even Republican presidential candidates such as Jeb Bush now believe the Iraq invasion in 2003 was a mistake. His brother George W. Bush had launched the war.

The other big evildoer in Harper's world—Russia—also supports Assad, so Canada has some strange partners in the Middle East. Immigration Minister Chris Alexander has said that Putin is actually the biggest threat to global security. Defence Minister Kenney misreported that a Canadian ship, the HMCS *Fredericton*, had been buzzed by Russian fighter jets and confronted by Russian ships in the Black Sea. On April 14, 2015, Canada announced that Canadian troops were on their way to Ukraine to train local forces in their fight against Russian-backed rebels claiming parts of the eastern region of the country. The troops will be stationed at a NATO base close to the Polish border. A former diplomat, James Bissett, said Canada could end up training neo-Nazi militia members who have integrated with the regular army. Canada has also imposed sanctions against Russia.

Stephen Harper also used the deaths of the two Canadian soldiers at home, which he personally tied to ISIS, to bring in an omnibus anti-terrorist bill that added a new front to the battle for public opinion over the war. Bill C-51 raised a storm of protest. Many, including *The Globe and Mail* editorial board, four former prime ministers, five former Supreme Court judges, and the Canadian Bar Association, expressed deep concerns about the draconian legislation. Thousands of people across the country gathered to protest the bill. More than a hundred Canadian law professors signed an open letter to members of Parliament asking the government to either amend the bill or kill it, expressing fear that Bill C-51 was "a dangerous piece of legislation in terms of its potential impact on the rule of law, on constitutionally and internationally protected rights, and on the health of Canada's democracy."

Green Party leader Elizabeth May was in the vanguard of the opposition to a piece of legislation that had not been requested by any law enforcement agency. In fact, since 9/11, Canada had passed eight new pieces of anti-terror legislation and spent $12 billion on security measures. May believed those measures were adequate and that Bill C-51 simply went dangerously over the top toward a police state: "This bill gives CSIS vague and wide-ranging powers. The limits on those powers are themselves chilling. Part 4 specifically says CSIS cannot directly kill or harm people or 'violate the sexual integrity of an individual.'" In the eyes of its many detractors, Bill C-51 was sixty-two pages of potential McCarthyism.

As public opposition to Bill C-51 began to mount, the video left by Corporal. Nathan Cirillo's killer was made public. Although RCMP Commissioner Bob Paulson had initially said the police wanted to release the video, he had quickly changed his mind, declaring that the video would likely never be released. Then on

March 6, 2015, the video was suddenly available—carefully edited by the RCMP, although the deletions were later made public.

A couple of days before the initial release, the prime minister told a news conference he had not seen the video but had been briefed on its contents. He linked the government's new anti-terror legislation to Bibeau's actions: "I think Canadians are well aware, not just because of the October 22 attacks but what they see around the world, that unfortunately the threat of terrorism and violent jihadism is very real."

Bill C-51 passed first reading without any of the 112 proposed amendments from the opposition, although four Conservative amendments would eventually be included when the legislation passed in the House of Commons on May 6, 2015, with the support of the Liberals. Had the Mounties been ordered to release the edited Bibeau video just at the moment when the resistance to Bill C-51 was at its zenith? Commissioner Paulson assured the Commons Public Safety Committee the release was in no way motivated or influenced by Parliament's debate on Bill C-51. Although the RCMP believes Bibeau was a terrorist under Section 83.01 (1) (b) of the Criminal Code, there was no public evidence of a connection between the shooter and ISIS. It also remains unknown at this time if Bibeau had an accomplice or an enabler, or was a so-called lone wolf.

A report by the Ontario Provincial Police (OPP) on Bibeau's shooting concluded that security forces were justified in using lethal force against the gunman. Kevin Vickers fired fifteen rounds at Bibeau, who had also been shot by another guard. Vickers was less than a metre away, close enough to hear him breathing. In total, Bibeau was shot thirty-one times, including a fatal bullet to the back of the head.

By February 2015, polls showed that the majority of Canadians supported the Iraq mission. But the bounce in the polls the PM got from playing the fear card proved to be temporary. On April 1, 2015, *The Globe and Mail* published a survey done by Nik Nanos which found that 90 percent of respondents said that the party with the best plan for the economy will be more important than the party with the best plan to fight terrorists. Only 4 percent of respondents said fighting terrorists was more important than the economy.

The air was slowly leaking out of Stephen Harper's war balloon. By April 7, 2015, Forum Research published a poll that found that 55 percent of Canadians of voting age opposed the expansion of the war to include Syrian air strikes, and a majority opposed lengthening the Iraq mission. The field survey was done only a week after the Conservative majority voted to expand the mission on March 24.

The Forum poll showed Canadians also favoured infrastructure spending over tax cuts to give the economy a boost, even though the Conservatives decided to go the tax cut route that would cost the treasury $5 billion a year. (Like his Republican brethren, Harper would boost spending on defence and security, and slash social spending.) Harper delayed the budget as the economy worsened. Bank of Canada Governor Stephen Poloz warned that Canada would record an "atrocious" growth figure for the first quarter of 2015 due mainly to low oil prices.

When the budget was finally delivered on April 21, 2015, it was the Conservative's first balanced budget in nine years, but it was more parlor trick than parsimony. Finance Minister Joe Oliver had pulled it off by selling the government's last General Motors shares to US investment banker Goldman Sachs at a loss to taxpayers, reducing the government's Contingency Fund by two-thirds to $1 billion heading into what the minister himself said were troubled economic times, and by helping himself to $3.4 billion from the Employment Insurance fund operating surplus—something the late Jim Flaherty said he would never do as finance minister to balance the books. In Harperland, appearance continued to trump reality.

More troubling than that, Harper spent $13.5 million of tax-payers' money to stage a media blitz to sell the budget to Canadians.

THE HARPER CONSERVATIVES weren't just fighting battles in the court of public opinion or on distant battlefields. Many of the deepest scandals touching the government were moving through the criminal courts—at glacial speed. One of the biggest unsolved crimes in Canadian political history, the robocalls scandal, still had a final act to be played featuring a judge and the only man convicted in the wide-ranging voter suppression conspiracy during the 2011 election—Michael Sona.

Submissions on sentencing were heard on October 17, 2014, with the reasons for the sentence released by Justice G.F. Hearn on November 19, 2014. The previous August, the court had found that Sona was an active participant "with one or more other persons" in an ill-conceived plan to send out a false message that directed voters to the wrong polling station in Guelph to prevent them from voting in the 2011 federal election. Although the court did not necessarily believe Sona activated the calls, it had no doubt he was involved.

Despite graduating with a degree from the University of Guelph, Sona now works as a machinist's apprentice at a company owned by a member of his church. He is described as a "fantastic employee" and a "great friend," as well as someone of "high integrity and character." Since his conviction, Sona has gone through periods of great stress and has had emergency treatment for an ulcer.

On the advice of his counsel, Norman Boxall, Sona chose not to make a statement in court about his conviction. Defence asked for a non-custodial sentence or "a short sharp sentence" of fourteen to thirty days, followed by probation with community service. The

Crown argued that Sona's lack of remorse and contrition in view
of the serious nature of the charge merited a period of custody—a
sentence of eighteen to twenty months.

Sona, who worked for the Conservative candidate in Guelph,
Marty Burke, was the first person to be convicted of interfering
in the electoral process under the Canada Elections Act, so there
were no sentencing precedents. Judge Hearn stated, "This is a difficult and troublesome sentencing." He considered the absence of
a guilty plea, "an absence of a mitigating factor." The judge rea-
soned, "The lack of remorse is simply an indicator to the court
that the prospect for rehabilitation may be lessened." He felt a
period of deterrence and denunciation in a traditional prison setting was appropriate to show that the courts treated the matter
seriously, and he sentenced Sona to nine months in jail followed
by twelve months of probation. Judge Hearn declined the Crown's
suggestion that a term of Sona's probation include a written apology to the public. There was no value in a forced apology if Sona
remained unrepentant.

Sona's lawyer had advised him that if he truly had nothing to
do with the fake robocalls it would be wrong to pretend remorse.
No matter what the sentence was, he said, "You still have to sleep
at night." Knowing that the judge would be more lenient if he
apologized, Sona maintained his innocence. As he told the author
on August 23, 2014, "I have to do a pre-sentence interview in the
coming weeks. Apparently, if I say I'm sorry for what I've done, the
judge will be lenient. But if I maintain my innocence, the judge
will bring the hammer down on me because I have no remorse.
How can you be remorseful of something you haven't done? By
their logic, no innocent person has ever gone to prison. But it is
why I know the judge will be very hard on me."

As the judge pronounced sentence, Sona's family members
wept. He put his head down and sent a text to his employer to

inform him of what had happened. There were numerous texts to Sona from people who thought the verdict was unjust. "No one—lawyers, media, friends, and observers—saw the verdict coming," Sona later told me. He believes they should have won the case "on the rules of evidence, plain and simple." In retrospect, they could have attacked the witnesses harder, but they decided not to do that since the defence was focused on reasonable doubt.

The convicted man was led out of the courtroom by police and taken to Maplehurst Correctional Complex. A social worker who had input in parole decisions told him, "All you have to do is say you did it, and we'll let you out of here in four to six weeks." Sona told her that would not be happening. He was not about to start lying to make things easier on himself.

Sona was granted bail on December 1, 2014, pending an appeal of the sentence. His appeal lawyer, Howard Krongold, argued that his client had already been punished enough. "Quite frankly, he's been front-page news: his life has been completely devastated and turned upside down."

The Crown didn't see it that way. On December 15, prosecutors filed a notice of appeal asking for a tougher sentence. Sona did not testify at his trial and has given no public interviews since the trial. He has maintained his innocence. In a statement released by a friend, Sona continued to insist, just as he had in his first statement to the media, "I had no involvement in the fraudulent phone calls." Sona, like his lawyer, asked for a full public inquiry into robocalls if the government was interested in finding out what had happened.

Told that there would be an update for the paperback edition of *Party of One*, I asked if there was anything he would like me to add. Sona replied, "If there is one thing I'd do different, it would be to not be involved in the Conservative Party. I know too many people that have had similar experiences to mine for it to simply be a coincidence. As one of those acquaintances told me, 'There's enough of us that have been thrown under the bus that we're turning into a voting block.'"

AND THEN THERE IS the strange case of a Canadian businessman, Nathan Jacobson, who has been closely connected to cabinet ministers in the Harper government and to the Conservative Party of Canada. In September 2014, six years after confessing to money laundering in a US court and after failing to appear for sentencing in 2012, a US District Court judge in San Diego granted Jacobson's motion to withdraw his guilty plea. Jacobson argued that his lawyer had given him bad advice.

In a very unusual move, the US government agreed to withdraw the charge, although they did keep Jacobson's "administrative forfeiture" of $4.5 million. When I contacted lawyer Steven Skurka about the status of the lawsuit between him and his former client, Skurka told me, "Jacobson is currently suing me and Marie Henein, who also worked on the file. My counterclaim against Jacobson is proceeding. Jacobson's claim is unfounded and even abusive. We will take steps to have it dismissed as soon as possible. Jacobson mistakes my decency and professionalism for weakness."

THE BIGGEST TRIAL of them all, that of suspended Senator Mike Duffy who is facing thirty-one criminal charges arising out of the Senate expenses scandal, started with a bang. On April 7, 2015, Duffy's lawyer, Donald Bayne, quoted from a previously undisclosed RCMP interview with the prime minister's former chief of staff, Nigel Wright. Wright allegedly described a conversation he had had with Stephen Harper on February 22, 2013: "I was aware of the fact that I was pushing very hard to have a caucus member repay a significant amount of money to which he may have been legally entitled. I needed the PM to know this just in case it ever came up with someone else who couldn't repay, then you have to get kicked out of caucus, whatever, that we're basically forcing someone to repay money they probably didn't owe, and I wanted the prime minister to know that and be comfortable with that." He was. They were famously "good to go."

On the morning of February 22, 2013, the PMO received a copy of Duffy's detailed diaries, showing how hard he had worked across the country helping seventy fellow Conservatives, including the PM, with fundraisers and campaigns, and how he received accolades for his speeches from MPs during caucus meetings. (It could be argued his real home appeared to be an airbus.) The PM had once praised Duffy as "one of my best, hardest-working appointments, ever." Ironically the PMO had also sought Duffy's help handling the media lines during the early days of the robocalls scandal.

According to Donald Bayne, Nigel Wright also told the RCMP that from the very beginning of the controversy, Duffy did not believe he had done anything wrong when it came to the matter of his primary and secondary residences. In Wright's words, Duffy "actually mentioned to Senator Tkachuk he wanted a judge to look at it." Duffy told friends that at the time of his elevation to the Senate he had asked the PM to make the appointment from Ontario. It was the PM who insisted that Duffy represent Prince Edward Island.

According to evidence introduced in court, Duffy was named a senator on December 22, 2008. The next day the Senate administration schooled Duffy and seventeen other new appointees about residency rules. Based on what he was told, Duffy travelled to PEI on December 29, his first official trip there as a senator. He got his PEI driver's license on January 2, 2009, and provided "property documentation" to the clerk of the Senate, Paul Bélisle, at a meeting on January 5, 2009. Bélisle had been the clerk for fifteen years.

Duffy filled out his residency declaration on January 6, 2009, claiming his cottage in PEI as his primary residence. This allowed him to claim about $20,000 a year in living expenses for his Ottawa residence. Both Duffy and Pamela Wallin were told by Senate Leader Marjory LeBreton's office that "so long as a senator owns property in his or her province of appointment, then they are allowed to sit as a senator from that province," even if they live in Ottawa most of the time.

One of the ironies of the trial is that a woman who was instrumental in following the PMO's orders pertaining to Duffy, Senator Carolyn Stewart Olsen, was herself a long-time resident of Ottawa. She had worked for Stephen Harper as his press secretary and was a close political advisor. Stewart Olsen was appointed to the Senate in 2009 by Harper to represent New Brunswick, where she also had a home. She too collected a housing allowance for her Ottawa home by declaring it as her secondary residence. Since she had worked for Stephen Harper since 2002, the PM could hardly claim he didn't know where she lived.

Picking up on the likelihood that there were other senators in the same boat as Duffy, Bayne asked for a secret internal Senate report overseen by the Internal Economy Committee in 2013 to be tabled at trial. It may show other senators have residency problems. The Senate is claiming parliamentary privilege and refusing to honour a subpoena asking for the report and minutes of a closed-door meeting discussing it. A voir dire will help the judge decide on the issue when the trial resumes on June 1, 2015.

According to an April 2, 2015, article in the *Toronto Star*, the suspended senators will get their salaries back by mid-September or when the election is called. Under the rules of the Senate, the suspension order ends with the session, and they would be entitled to their basic salary of $142,400 a year, unless any of the senators are convicted of an indictable offence by that time. On May 10, 2015, the new Senate speaker, Leo Housakos, told CTV News that the Senate is looking at ways to maintain the suspension without pay of Senators Brazeau, Wallin, and Duffy after the session ends.

Most observers believe there will not be a verdict in the Duffy case before the October 19, 2015, general election. Ethics and accountability just may be the key in that next election campaign.

One of the hotly debated issues surrounding Donald Bayne's epic defence of Duffy is whether the prime minister will be called as a witness. Mr. Harper, in a year-end interview with CBC's *The National*, said it was highly unlikely to happen. "I'm told that a lawyer looked at this for me. He said there's absolutely no reasonable reason you would be called as a witness because I'm not a witness." The Prime Minister's Office did not respond to a question from *The Hill Times* about whether Mr. Harper has in fact been served a subpoena. The prime minister continued with his claim that he didn't know anything of importance about the case, even after the trial began with the startling description of what Nigel Wright allegedly told the PM on February 22, 2013.

After the first half of Senator Duffy's trial, the Crown's case is spinning its wheels, with Donald Bayne persuasively arguing that Duffy's behaviour was "normative" considering the unclear nature of Senate rules. As one journalist, Tasha Kheiriddin, put it in iPolitics.ca, the smoking gun against the beleaguered senator has blown up in the prime minister's face.

AS OF THE WRITING of this Afterword, other cases mentioned in this book are, like Michael Sona's, still before the courts. Although convicted of three separate offences under the Elections Act, including knowingly submitting a falsified expenses document to Elections Canada, Dean Del Mastro has yet to be sentenced for election cheating in 2008. There have been several sentencing delays in the case involving Stephen Harper's former parliamentary secretary, who is now scheduled to be sentenced on June 26, 2015. The Crown is seeking a sentence of nine to twelve months for the former parliamentary secretary. The defence wants a discharge or small fine. In the wake of his criminal conviction, Del Mastro resigned his seat in the House of Commons.

Former top Harper energy advisor Bruce Carson has been committed to stand trial on influence peddling charges, but health issues have delayed his day in court. Arthur Porter, the man Stephen Harper made the watchdog of Canada's spy service, CSIS, remains in Panama fighting extradition to Canada on multiple criminal charges, including receiving a $22.5 million kickback from the building of a new hospital at the Montreal University Health Centre in Quebec. Porter invited Harper to visit him in prison during the PM's recent visit to Panama for the Summit of the Americas (April 10–11, 2015). The PM, who used to do photo ops with Porter, declined to visit his former chair of the Security Intelligence Review Committee. Porter remains a privy councillor, another appointment bestowed on him by the prime minister. If Porter had not been caught, he might still be in charge of the oversight committee monitoring CSIS.

On May 30, 2015, suspended senator Patrick Brazeau was a guest referee at a Great North Wrestling match in Ottawa, starring Hannibal the Death Dealer and Soa (Spirit of Allah) Amin. Brazeau's trial date for Senate fraud and breach of trust is set for March 29, 2016. He also has personal legal problems. A framed photo of Brazeau, the prime minister, and the alleged victim is an exhibit at Brazeau's ongoing sexual assault and assault trial taking place before a judge in Gatineau, Quebec. Brazeau has pleaded not guilty to all charges.

Despite paying back disputed expenses and resigning his seat, ex–Liberal senator Mac Harb is scheduled for trial in 2016. Suspended Conservative senator Pamela Wallin has not been charged in the expenses scandal but continues to be under investigation by the RCMP.

Looming on the parliamentary horizon, Auditor General Michael Ferguson will be reporting the results of his audit of all senators' expenses in June 2015. The audit has cost taxpayers $21 million. Several other senators could soon be in a position similar to those already facing charges for expense abuse. CTV has reported that ten more senators will be referred to the RCMP, and that an additional thirty senators have problems with their expenses and will be required to repay the money.

Of note, the Senate itself has created a process for senators facing questions about their travel or living expenses to quietly take the matter to a special arbiter, former Supreme Court judge Ian Binnie, for binding arbitration. There will be inevitable questions about the double standard that has seen some senators criminally charged and prosecuted, while others could make the problem go away with the stroke of a pen.

AFTER NEARLY TEN YEARS in power, Stephen Harper's mantra remains pure: Republican neo-conservatism, privatization, deregulation, and hobbling of the unions. Foreign policy is about flexing military muscle and making free trade deals. Harper has systematically deconstructed the old Canada like a venture capitalist who buys a corporation to sell off the best parts for profit. He has closed and sold embassies, weakened democratic institutions, and allowed the sale of valuable Canadian assets to countries with questionable human rights records. Apparently the PM sees no contradiction in building a monument to the victims of Communism, while selling off a prized Canadian resource company to a Communist government in China.

Meanwhile, the Harper government has effectively erased the line between big business and big government. Barrick Gold

Corporation confirmed on March 28, 2015, that former Foreign Affairs Minister John Baird, who resigned suddenly in February 2015, would become an international affairs advisor to the firm. Former US Republican lawmaker Newt Gingrich also joined the advisory board at the same time. When Nigel Wright, acting as the PM's chief of staff, had faced conflict-of-interest questions over three calls to him in the PMO in May 2012 from Barrick Gold, Baird insisted that the calls to Wright were above board, a position confirmed by Ethics Commissioner Mary Dawson.

Baird's assurances ring less convincingly today. The firm has interests in fifteen countries, but no one questioned Baird's move from Foreign Affairs to Barrick without a cooling-off period—another sign of just how close politics and business have become in Harperland. Barrick is facing a multi-billion-dollar lawsuit over the Porgera Mine in Papua New Guinea. A group of landowners claimed in a position statement that they had suffered "irreparable losses" as a result of social, economic, and environmental damages caused by the open-pit mine. Barrick has put the mine up for sale to help reduce its debt by $3 billion. Since John Thornton took over as chairman from Barrick founder Peter Munk, the company's shares have dropped 31 percent in trading on the New York Stock Exchange. At its annual meeting in Toronto in April 2015, 75 percent of shareholders voted against the executive compensation model that saw Barrick chairman Thornton paid $12.9 million annually, up from $9.5 million the previous year, particularly when earnings were down. The Canadian Pacific Railway has nominated Baird to serve as a director. With his cabinet seat still warm, Baird has also landed a job as an advisor to Hong Kong billionaire Richard Li, the son of one of the richest men in Asia. The family controls Calgary-based Husky Energy.

As for Nigel Wright, he managed to go straight back to work with Onex Corporation after helping to negotiate CETA, a massive trade deal between Canada and the European Union. The normal laundering period for someone leaving government service did not apply because Wright went to work in the London office of Onex.

THERE ARE SOME who still claim that Stephen Harper has not made radical changes to Canada, but the facts don't bear out that thesis. He is no incrementalist, and he has, and always has had, an agenda, just as former Prime Minister Joe Clark warned back in 2003. As prime minister, Harper has gone down the list of the objectives he set while running the National Citizens Coalition. Almost every one of them has been ticked off: A majority share of the assets of the former Canadian Wheat Board has been sold to Saudi Arabia, a repressive, undemocratic kingdom that now has control over a large part of Canadian food distribution. In January 2015, Canada sold $15 billion worth of military equipment to Saudi Arabia, a country that has recently seen a "macabre spike" in state sanctioned beheadings.

The "jackasses" at Elections Canada (Harper's own description), are definitely under control under the regressive changes ushered in by the Fair Elections Act. EC has no power of subpoena to deal with another robocall affair, and its investigative arm has been transferred to the public prosecutor's office. The point is that EC reports to Parliament, while the public prosecutor does not. If another voter suppression scheme were unleashed in the next election, Canadians would only learn about it if charges are laid. In other words, if voter suppression took place, Canadians would never learn about it during the election. Expect long lineups and confusion at the polls over what constitutes proper voter ID. If you don't have a drivers license or a provincial identity card with a street address, even a passport and voter information card will not be acceptable.

The CBC is dominated by the Conservatives at the board level, and the impact on content and tone is obvious and distressing. It is odd that this once dependable news source is cutting so much slack for a government that intends to bring it to its knees and restructure it into a PBS-style operation paid for by subscribers.

Harper lost in the Supreme Court in 2004 on the issue of allowing unlimited third-party spending during elections, but he continues to try to undermine the power of the top court. He has repeatedly sent bill after unconstitutional bill to the court, the better to make the political argument that the justices have become interventionist busybodies undermining the power of Parliament. Harper is using this carefully picked fight to get at his real objective—undermining the Charter of Rights. As one former Harper cabinet minister told me, Harper hates the charter because it transferred raw power from Parliament to the Supreme Court and because it was the creation of his most-hated foe—the late Pierre Trudeau.

On the issue of election spending, the PM used little-noticed changes brought in with the Fair Elections Act to allow federal parties and their candidates to spend millions of taxpayer-subsidized dollars in three upcoming federal by-elections. The scheme is based on inflating the spending cap by a pro-rated amount whenever a campaign goes beyond the thirty-seven-day minimum.

Accordingly, by-elections were called in early May 2015 for October 19, the expected date of the general federal election. It was pure scheming. That means 169-day campaigns for vacant seats in Ottawa West Nepean, Peterborough, and Sudbury. As a result, a party with deep pockets will be able to spend half a million dollars in a riding like Peterborough—a far cry from the $95,000 each candidate was able to spend in the thirty-seven-day 2011 election campaign. And whatever candidates spend, they are eligible for a 60 percent rebate from Elections Canada. The man who took public financing of political parties off the table has managed to put it back on again to his advantage, with barely a ripple of criticism.

Flush with cash, sporting the best get-out-the-vote apparatus of any federal political party, and facing a divided progressive vote yet again, Stephen Harper, according to polls, is showing that the 2015 election is his to lose. But on May 5, 2015, the universe changed for the Harper Conservatives. Their button-down world of disciplined messaging, avoidance of the media, and precision fundraising was struck by the political equivalent of an asteroid. The NDP, under new leader Rachel Notley, overran the Tory fortress of Alberta and scored a stunning majority victory in the provincial election after thirteen Conservative majority governments. Like Stephen Harper, Premier Jim Prentice stood for Big Oil, the Big Blue Machine, and the tried and true line that an NDP government would be a disaster—a line parroted by meddling federal Conservatives during the campaign that ended forty-four years of Tory dominance in Alberta. Rachel Notley's radiant sincerity in the provincial debate was a deciding moment for many voters.

On May 12, 2015, the Conservatives announced that Stephen Harper would not take part in the traditional Canadian election debate. Run by a consortium of broadcasters for decades, the debate reached over 10 million viewers. Instead, Harper will participate in a debate hosted by *Maclean's* magazine, not known for being overly critical of the prime minister. The debate will reach a much smaller targeted audience, as will the Munk debate on foreign policy and a debate on the economy hosted by Google and *The Globe and Mail* in Calgary.

An EKOS poll done shortly after the Alberta election showed a stunning national NDP surge and that the three main political parties in Canada were in a virtual tie. The winds of change were blowing strongly again, once more from the West. Suddenly, anything was possible in Canadian politics.

NOTES

one · SIGN OF THE TIMES

1 The International Commission of Jurists condemned the prime minister for his public criticism of Canada's top justice, saying it impugned her integrity and was in effect undue interference with the independence of the courts. The ICJ said the PM should withdraw his remarks, and that he and justice minister MacKay should apologize to the chief justice. Harper's communications director responded in an email, "We have noted it. I have nothing further to add." The commission also urged the government to have an open process with prescribed criteria based on merit to choose judges. The ICJ is composed of sixty eminent judges and lawyers who work to protect human rights through the rule of law. See Collin Perkel, "Harper's spat with chief justice Beverley McLachlin was wrong: legal group," CP huffingtonpost.ca, July 25, 2014. Retrieved July 30, 2014, from http://www.huffingtonpost.ca/2014/07/25/harper -beverley-mclachlin-peter-mackay-nadon_n_5621434.html?page _version=legacy&view=print&comm_ref=false.

two · THE GENESIS OF STEVE

1 The NCC was originally set up to undermine support for national medicare, a position similar to present-day Republicans such as the Koch brothers, who oppose Obamacare in the United States. In 2017, federal

funding for medicare will be cut in Canada, leaving the provinces, who have jurisdiction, to pay the shortfall. A lack of national standards will open the door for private delivery of health care.

2 "See the USA in your Chevrolet" was an iconic ad campaign that ran for five years and is still on YouTube. It was remastered for iTunes last year. People were encouraged to drive and burn gas.

3 Although his office is in Irvington, an affluent village in Westchester County, New York, Finkelstein spends a lot of time in Israel. On November 4, 1995, Israeli prime minister Yitzhak Rabin was assassinated at a rally in Tel Aviv, where one hundred thousand Israelis had gathered in support of the Oslo peace process.

Shimon Peres, a dove, cast himself as the natural successor to Rabin the peacemaker. It was a deadly opening for a pro like Finkelstein, who was running the campaign of the underdog—the hawkish Benjamin Netanyahu. Finkelstein smeared Peres as a weak, ineffective leader who would betray Israel to the Arabs. He found the four perfect words in his polling to skewer the peace candidate with voters: "Peres will divide Jerusalem."

With support from powerful US neo-conservatives Richard Perle and Paul Wolfowitz, both of whom opposed the peace process, Finkelstein pulled off an upset. On May 29, 1996, Benjamin Netanyahu became prime minister of Israel by a narrow margin. *The Jerusalem Post* noted, "Finkelstein was largely responsible for the strategy that brought Netanyahu victory. . . ."

Less than a year later, Israel's intelligence agency, Mossad, supplied an assassination squad with forged Canadian passports in the attempt to kill Khaled Mashal, a Hamas official, with nerve gas in Jordan. The life of the Hamas political official was saved when King Hussein demanded that President Bill Clinton intervene.

Prime Minister Netanyahu turned to Arthur Finkelstein for advice on how to handle the international crisis. Netanyahu subsequently acceded to Clinton's demand, apologized, and sent the chief of Mossad, Danny Yatom, to Jordan with the antidote. Since Finkelstein did not have a security clearance in Israel, Israel's attorney general considered opening a criminal investigation against the prime minister for divulging state secrets to a foreign citizen. The urge passed, as it is wont to do in hierarchal organizations where the accuser finds himself looking up.

In the 2013 Israeli election, Finkelstein won a narrow victory for Netanyahu and Avigdor Lieberman by suggesting they form a union of Likud Yisrael Beiteinu.

In 2013, the American Association of Political Consultants (AAPC), the world's biggest organization of political and public affairs specialists, announced that Finkelstein had been inducted into their hall of fame. According to a jns.org post from April 8, 2013, the candidates Finkelstein worked with were not only conservatives "but also strong proponents of the close relationship between the United States and Israel." The consultants, pollsters, and strategists he trained over the years at Arthur J. Finkelstein & Associates are part of his legacy.

4 Norway's sovereign wealth fund has almost doubled since 2010. According to Bloomberg, March 18, 2014, the Norwegian government now predicts the world's largest sovereign fund will grow by 41 percent to $1.2 trillion by 2020. See Saleha Mohsin, "Norway examines $850 billion wealth fund's return measures," Bloomberg, March 18, 2014. Retrieved July 30, 2014, from http://www.bloomberg.com/news/2014 -03-17/norway-examines-return-calculations-for-850-billion-wealth -fund.html.

5 Harper's speech to the CNP was in the same month as the June 1997 election won by the Liberals, but got little coverage at the time, although Harper had been at NCC for about six months by then. When Tom Flanagan became Harper's chief of staff in 2003, he went through Harper's speeches at NCC headquarters; this one was missing. A copy turned up briefly before a debate in the 2006 election, causing a panic because here was Harper cozying up to the Americans. Marjory LeBreton was consulted and it was decided to play the speech down, dismiss it as old stuff, after-dinner humour that didn't represent Harper's views. Conservative pundits such as Tim Powers kept to the speaking points, that the Liberals were dwelling in the past instead of the future. When the speech shows up on the internet, it still gets scrubbed very quickly. Oddly the welfare state comment gets quoted, but not the far more damaging observation that a Canadian prime minister with a majority and an inclination can in effect be a dictator.

6 The $200,000 campaign about pension porkers was managed by Harper. He later talked a lot about the campaigns he did for the NCC with his own campaign workers such as Patrick Muttart.

7 A professor at Simon Fraser University is writing a book about third-party spending in Canada. He says that the Fraser Institute gets $300,000 a year in foreign funding from the Lilly foundation, whose wealth comes from the Eli Lilly family fortune. The American pharmaceutical giant Eli Lilly and Company has filed a $500-million NAFTA suit against Canada over drug patents. The professor also confirmed that it is common knowledge that the Charles Koch Foundation gives a grant of $150,000 a year to the Fraser Institute. Bloomberg recently reported that Koch revenues are now over $100 billion.

three · THE DEMOCRACY BANDITS

1 According to a lawyer very familiar with the CIMS system, the information collected is almost scary. They even know if an individual voted in the last election, as well as a voter's probable voting intentions. The connection between RMG and the Conservative Party apparently goes back to 2003.

2 Byrne was national campaign manager for the Conservative Party during the 2011 election. She became director of political operations for the party in 2009 but returned to the PMO as co–deputy chief of staff in August 2013.

3 Meier said the caller referred to knowing someone in the Conservative Party. Meier claimed that he concluded that someone had given "Pierre" his contact information, and even though he didn't know who that person was, he accepted "Pierre's" business because he was obviously connected.

4 Meier gave Mathews a copy of three PayPal forms called "Transaction Details." The PayPal documents identified "Pierre Jones," of 54 Lajoie Nord, Joliette, Quebec, J6E 3B3, with an email address of pierres1630@gmail.com. The information was confirmed only insofar as there was a prepaid credit or debit card linked to the name, ensuring payment. When "Pierre Jones" contacted PayPal on May 1, 2011, he logged in each time from IP address 64.64.11.139, using the email address pierres1630@gmail.com. This was the same address used to communicate with RackNine.

5 Meier told Mathews that the session logs he recovered identified two IP addresses as having been used by both clients #45 and #93 between April 30 and May 2, 2011. Unlike Prescott, client #93 used only two IP

addresses. The proxy server IP address appears in the session log four times, and was used by client #93, the dubious "Pierre Jones." The IP address 99.225.29.34 appears numerous times in the session logs, and was related to use by client #45, Andrew Prescott. It was the IP address of the Marty Burke campaign.

6 Stephen Maher and Glen McGregor, "Harper advisor delayed robocall witness interview for legal advice, email showed," Postmedia News, November 14, 2013. Retrieved August 8, 2014, from http://o.canada .com/news/harper-adviser-delayed-robocall-witness-interview-for -legal-advice-email-shows. It takes almost three months for investigators to get an opportunity to speak to Prescott on February 24, 2012, and then only after the story breaks in the *National Post*, and briefly by phone with Arthur Hamilton on the line. Even if Byrne needs to consult a lawyer, is this a reasonable amount of time if you are doing everything you can to assist in the investigation? By the time Byrne sends her email to Prescott on November 30, Matt Meier has been in touch with both Prescott and the Party, after his visit from Elections Canada, according to court testimony at the Sona trial.

7 Maher was the engaging cavalier of Ottawa journalism, who sailed, played the guitar, and "caroused" to escape from the rigours of high-impact journalism. He had his professional roots on the East Coast, working first in Gander for Robinson Blackmore, a chain of weeklies owned by Newfoundland businessman Harry Steele. He then moved to Nova Scotia where he was the restaurant critic for the *Chronicle Herald* until he was sent to Ottawa to cover federal politics. His charm was disarming. Behind the ladies' man was a first-class mind that worked imaginatively on the stories he chose to pursue.

8 McGregor's hallmark as a journalist was exceptional research, based in part on wizard-like computer-assisted reporting skills. He had worked at the *Ottawa Citizen* since 1998, but his beginnings in the business were with *Frank Magazine*, the satirical publication that often pulled the tail of the establishment with outrageous stunts, and clever, if unorthodox, approaches. McGregor loved it:

"The most fun were the telephone pranks—calling up public figures with ludicrous premises and asking them to respond. My favourite was the Brian Mulroney Defence Fund, where I called up former PC cabinet ministers and asked them to contribute to his legal costs over Airbus.

Barbara McDougall committed to fifty bucks. Everyone else . . . 'Uh, let me get back to you.'"

When not taking on the government, McGregor has a unique way of easing the pressure of Hot Room journalism on the Hill: "I follow an '80s alternative rock band called Pixies around. It's my mid-life crisis, flying to their shows. Cheaper than sports cars, hair transplants and mistresses," he quipped.

When the government's amiable stenographers in the right-wing media hit back at McGregor for his "Dumpster diving" journalism, it was usually a reference to his days at *Frank Magazine*. They also attacked him for the fact that his mother had once been Ed Broadbent's communications director. What they didn't know was that while the late Mrs. McGregor was doing that job, her son was running messages for Opposition leader Brian Mulroney.

9 Sona told me in a March 9, 2014, interview that Al Mathews told him he didn't know about Sona until he saw his name in the press.

10 Initially in the investigation the information was described as "missing." Blanks in the access logs could possibly mean the identifying data about who made the downloads had been removed by someone. CIMS is closely guarded; authorized people on individual campaigns can access data for their riding with a unique password, but not data for another riding. Only headquarters can do that.

11 Early in 2013, Rougier left the federal party to work for the Ontario Conservatives and Tim Hudak. The provincial Conservatives lost on June 12, 2014. Rougier had also worked for Julian Fantino during his winning 2010 by-election campaign in Vaughan.

12 Although it is not listed on his CV, White was reputed to be involved in the development of C-Vote. The new super-system was intended to replace CIMS for the 2015 election, but had some glitches and was not user friendly. There were so many complaints from the ridings, the acting executive director of the party put out a memo just before the Conservative convention in Calgary reinstituting CIMS: "To be clear, we will never again deploy C-Vote in our ridings." Conservatives had spent over $7 million on C-Vote, which would have taken at least 280,000 donations of $25 to build.

13 White, who holds a master's degree in engineering from the University of Guelph, is the chief technical officer at UnlimitedViz Inc., an

information technology and services company he founded. Over the past ten years he has become an expert in Microsoft SharePoint and business intelligence platforms, and has won numerous awards for his work.

14 The amendment also removes the problem of why the Conservative Party apparently did nothing when one of its campaign workers allegedly tried to get information from headquarters about making poll-moving calls.

four · UNDER THE BUS

1 On March 25, 2011, the Harper government was given the contempt of Parliament citation because it was withholding details of proposed bills and cost estimates from Parliament, including costs for the F-35, the G8 and G20 Summits, the cost to the federal treasury of planned reduction of corporate tax rates, cost of its crime bills, etc. The government eventually fell because of it.

2 By studying workers in Canada, Britain, Australia, and America, Muttart had concluded that working-class voters were "crucially responsible for the rise of centre-right leaders like Harper, Australia's John Howard, and Margaret Thatcher." Like Jenni Byrne and Ray Novak, Muttart had worked for the Reform Party since he was a teenager. He joined the Harper team in 2004 and scripted daily messages. Muttart was chief of staff for Harper from 2006 to 2009, and helped the party cast itself as the champion of Canadians who "work hard, pay their taxes and play by the rules."

Muttart returned to Canada in March 2011, to work on contract during the May 2, 2011, election as a key strategist for Harper. (He travelled back and forth to his home base in Chicago.) But he was suddenly dropped on April 27, 2011, after an apparent attempt at swiftboating Ignatieff backfired.

On April 20, 2011, Sun News ran a story by Brian Lilley: "Ignatieff linked to Iraq war planning." The story said, "He was on the front lines of pre-invasion planning when he worked in the US." Then on April 27, 2011, Sun Media Corp. president Pierre Karl Peladeau published a photo that Sun News and former Harper spokesperson Kory Teneycke said it had received from Muttart. Apparently, according to an editorial by Pierre Peladeau, Muttart had also given the Sun a clip from a Pentagon press briefing in which an American colonel thanked Ignatieff for his work in preparation for the 2003 invasion of Iraq.

According to an *Ottawa Citizen* blog dated April 27, 2011, Peladeau said Muttart had given the *Sun* a fake photo of Ignatieff in combat gear. The photo showed a group of soldiers in front of a military helicopter holding rifles, supposedly in Kuwait prior to the US invasion of Iraq. One of the men was supposedly Ignatieff, but it wasn't.

The Conservatives claimed they had told Sun News they couldn't verify the photo. Muttart's PR firm Mercury issued a press release saying Muttart had provided verbal overviews and material to Sun Media about Ignatieff and the war in Iraq, and Sun Media used the information provided: "At no point did Muttart tell Sun Media that he had positively identified Ignatieff in the photo in question."

The odd thing was that Mercury had been actively involved in the creation and development of Sun TV. Muttart had worked with Sun News to develop the network's original logo, and framed the network's "straight talk" language. Muttart had also introduced potential advertising clients to Sun News. Yet Peladeau now claimed, "It is my belief that this planted information was intended to first and foremost seriously damage Michael Ignatieff's campaign but in the process to damage the integrity and credibility of Sun Media and, more pointedly, that of our new television operation, Sun News."

3 See "Two Republican Dark Money Groups Spent $311 Million Last Year," Bloomberg, November 18, 2013, for reference that AFP focuses on voter turnouts according to president Tim Phillips. See "The GOP War on Voting," *Rolling Stone*, August 30, 2011, for information about the American Legislative Exchange Council (funded in part by Koch brothers) and the information on Weyrich.

4 AFFIDAVIT OF ANNETTE DESGAGNE (sworn April 13, 2012) Federal Court of Canada, Court File No. T- 633-12. This five-page affidavit is a revealing document for voters concerned about the robocalls scandal.

5 See Commissioner of Canada Elections, Summary Investigation Report on Robocalls, April 2014. Retrieved from http://www.elections.ca/content.aspx?section=com&dir=rep/rep2&document=index&lang=e.

The April 24, 2014, Elections Canada report by commissioner Coté found that incorrect poll locations were provided to some electors, and some nuisance calls occurred (see page 4 executive summary). The problem was proving intent to prevent an elector from voting for a particular candidate. The Elections Canada evidence had to be beyond a reasonable doubt. (Under current case law, it is not illegal to impersonate Elections Canada.)

Item 93 page 22 of the Elections Canada report reads: "Investigators found that a number of RMG callers told electors at which poll location they should vote, rather than asking electors to verify the poll location indicated on their VIC as outlined in the script. As well, a number of the RMG calls identifying a specific poll location provided incorrect information." Elections Canada did a sample study of 1,000 calls made by RMG to compare them to 126 complainants calls (see page 23 of report). Wrong poll location information was provided in only 1 percent of the sample cases, but among actual complainants, RMG provided incorrect poll location information 27 percent of the time.

6 Andrew Coyne, "Judge finds smoking gun in robocalls scandal but who pulled the trigger? *National Post*, May 24, 2013. Retrieved July 31, 2014, from http://fullcomment.nationalpost.com/2013/05/24/judge -finds-smoking-gun-in-robocalls-scandal-but-who-pulled-the-trigger/.

7 According to the election commissioner's report on April 24, 2014, Campaign Research "called 89 complainant numbers during the election." The company does not retain recordings of calls, so "investigators were unable to determine the call content." Investigators were told the callers did not provide electors with poll location information.

8 Stephen Maher (with files from Glen McGregor): "Party lawyer's presence in robocall witness interviews may pose problem, lawyers say," canada.com, September 10, 2013.

9 Johnson, who is disabled, was living in Ottawa, where he attended All Nations Church. He graduated in the spring of 2011 with a degree in political studies from the University of Saskatchewan, in Saskatoon. That summer he worked in the PMO, moving in the fall for a few months into the office of Senator Doug Finley. After that, he took a ninety-day job with Human Resources Development Canada in Gatineau in February 2012. While he was there, his parents faxed him with good news: his $43,000 student loan had been forgiven [it is unknown by whom]. Like Michael Sona, Johnson had plans to eventually open his own political consulting business based on the experience he was gaining in Ottawa. Some very senior Conservatives had lent Johnson their support. Guy Giorno, the PM's former chief of staff and national campaign chair for the 2011 election, helped Johnson to apply to the commissioner of

lobbying for an exemption from section 10.11 of the Lobbying Act. That way, he'd have a better chance at getting a job in the private sector, without going through a laundering period before going to work for a firm that did business with government. In the end, Giorno himself hired Johnson as his assistant at the Ottawa office of the law firm Fasken Martineau.

five · THE UNFAIR ELECTIONS ACT

1 After tabling a report in Parliament recommending changes to the law to keep up with new technologies and massive voter databases, Mayrand briefed reporters. On March 28, 2013, he told reporters that in Guelph about 7,000 calls were placed in 15 minutes at a cost of about $160: "It's very cheap to breach the legislation, undermine public confidence and, honestly , to try to deter or prevent people to cast their ballots."

2 Some complainants could not be reached by investigators, some could not provide the incoming calling number nine months after the fact, or provide their telephone service provider at the time. People knew what had happened after the fact, but few had concrete proof. Call data from service providers was unavailable for 80 percent of the 1,726 complainants. Some filed their complaints too late to be included in the investigation, and some individuals and telemarketers simply refused to cooperate. The investigation was doomed from the start.

3 See John Ivison, "Harper reminded he's not omnipotent as court dashes Senate plans and Tories amend election bill," *National Post*, April 25, 2014. Retrieved July 31, 2014, http://fullcomment.nationalpost.com/2014/04/25/john-ivison-harper-reminded-hes-not-omnipotent-as-court-dashes-senate-plans/.

4 Under the old act, if a person showed up at a poll without ID and wasn't on the voters list, a person who knew him and was on the voters list could vouch for who he said he was, and the person could vote. That has been eliminated under the new act. Many poor, older people, Aboriginals, and students do not have the proper photo ID with a street address now required. (An Indian status card, for example, does not include a street address.) Despite wide protests, vouching is still eliminated, affecting hundreds of thousands of people. After an amendment, a person who has proper ID, but without a street address on it, can have someone vouch for the fact they live at a certain address in the riding and they can vote.

5 Michael Sona told me that Prescott swore to him in a church parking lot that he knew nothing about the fake robocalls and Sona believed him.

6 Just before the robocalls story broke, Ken Morgan helped organize the Guelph EDA annual Sir John A. Macdonald dinner on Thursday, February 2, 2012, tweeting on January 24, 2012, "Must confirm by this week everyone!" Michael Sona tweeted back, "Still in Ottawa, unfortunately won't be able to make it. Senator Finley is always a riot! Be sure to ask him about what happened to the guy (MP Paul Szabo) who had House of Commons security drag him out of Committee haha."* Other Guelph Campus Conservatives tweeted their regrets from Ottawa.

Senator Doug Finley was the keynote speaker for the $90-a-plate Sir John A. dinner. Sixty people listened as he started his speech critiquing how the media looks to create the news rather than report it. He also spoke about leadership and the importance of being seen to lead. He compared Stephen Harper to Sir John A. Macdonald for his work ethic.

By this time, Finley, who was the party "fixer," would have known that reporters were working on the robocalls story that would be broken by Maher and McGregor on February 22–23, 2012. Finley could have talked to Morgan about the coming scandal. (Morgan had been the Guelph EDA president since 2006.) In better days, Morgan, Sona, and Andrew Prescott were among the twelve Guelph delegates who had attended the Conservative Policy Convention in Ottawa on June 9–11, 2011, co-hosted by Mike Duffy and Pamela Wallin. By May 2012, a new Guelph EDA board had been elected, Michael Sona had been named as a key suspect in the robocalls scandal by Sun News, and Ken Morgan was about to take a teaching position in Kuwait. Elections Canada cannot prosecute someone out of the jurisdiction. If a person returns to the jurisdiction, EC has one year to prosecute.

*(This was a reference to Finley being escorted from the witness table of a special parliamentary committee hearing into federal Conservative financing of the 2006 election held in August 2008. National Conservative campaign director Finley had shown up two days before his scheduled testimony and insisted on testifying that day. This would have bumped scheduled speakers. His unscheduled appearance was also possibly intended to intimidate some former Conservative candidates who were scheduled to testify that day. This is an example of the "swaggering, bullying style" of the Conservatives observed by Andrew Coyne [NP, February 24, 2012].)

7 Elections Canada did not seek a production order for the CIMS database, relying instead on voluntary cooperation from the Conservative Party. A production order is a court order requiring the custodian of documents to deliver or make available those documents to law enforcement officials within a specified period of time. It is like a search warrant, but instead of the information being seized by investigators, its custodian is ordered to produce it.

8 One of the co-sponsors of the Conservative Political Action Conference is the John Birch Society, which the father of the Koch brothers helped to found.

9 This is an important decision since it will establish new case law, and the judge had to write his decision carefully to prevent the decision being overturned. Elections Canada has never lost a case.

10 On June 19, 2014, the Council of Canadians and the Canadian Federation of Students announced they would challenge the Fair Elections Act in the Superior Court of Ontario, alleging that it violates section 3 of the Charter on the grounds that it infringes on the rights of certain Canadians to vote.

six · THE BIG LIE

1 Real engine trouble occurred for the F-35 on June 23, 2014, at a Florida air base. The Pratt & Whitney engine on an Air Force F-35 A model broke apart and pushed through the top of the plane, catching fire as the pilot was preparing for takeoff. This prevented the jets from appearing at the Farnborough air show in England for a widely publicized event. The incident would also prevent the jets from appearing at the naming of Britain's new aircraft carrier on July 4, 2014. See "F-35 fighter jets to be inspected after major engine fire in US," Reuters, July 2, 2014, and "F-35 fleet cleared to fly after June engine fire prompted grounding," July 15, 2014, by CNN staff.

2 Interview with Kevin Page, June 13, 2012.

3 See, for example, "Drones replace 'The Right Stuff': Fighter pilots make way for remote warfare," washingtontimes.com, April 10, 2013.

4 Edwards is also the controlling shareholder of Imperial Metals Corp., which owns the Mount Polley mine in BC. The mine-waste dam collapsed in August 2014 spilling 10 million cubic metres of tailings into

Polley Lake, Hazelton Creek, and Quesnel Lake. BMO Nesbitt Burns Inc. estimated the cleanup could cost $200 million.

5 See Laura Payton, "MPs battle over F-35 fighter jet costs," CBC News, April 4, 2012.

6 Government did not want lower-level managers called to testify at committee hearings because there had been disagreement about the project within Public Works. In December 2012 Harper tried to escape the growing scandal by suddenly appearing to order the Air Force to re-evaluate options for a new jet. The government announced it would put the procurement process on hold. *The Globe and Mail* said on December 12, 2012: "It was a rare U-turn for an administration that only infrequently acknowledges it was wrong—but one the Tories felt was necessary to repair their fiscal stewardship credentials." The Tories also admitted the planes would cost at least $45 billion, not the $9 billion they had originally estimated. (See Steve Chase, "Ottawa officially scraps F-35 purchase as audit pegs costs at $45-billion," *The Globe and Mail*, December 12, 2012, updated December 13, 2012.)

The so-called independent review panel was a charade. It did not call for open bids. Manufacturers such as Saab, which makes the Gripen NG fighter jet, had so little faith in the review that they did not even bother to participate in the re-evaluation.

seven · THE DEATH OF EVIDENCE

1 See "Science minister's coyness on evolution worries researchers," CBC News, March 17, 2009.

2 Hyer became deputy chief of the Green Party on December 13, 2013.

3 *Yes Minister* was a satirical British situation comedy set in the private office of a cabinet minister.

4 "CEO asks big oil for ELA funds: Says water research important to the sector," *Winnipeg Free Press*, June 20, 2012.

eight · MELTDOWN

1 This is public record material. See "Chalk River shutdown triggers isotope shortage," *Ottawa Citizen* (no byline), December 5, 2007. Retrieved July 31, 2014, from http://www.canada.com/story.html?id=be7892fd-c460-4a8d-aa15-d1f128a3d883.

The news story indicates that the reactor was shut down for regular maintenance on November 18. See also "Lunn knew of reactor issues in September: report," CTV News (Staff), January 9, 2008. Retrieved July 31, 2014, from http://www.ctvnews.ca/lunn-knew-of-reactor-issues -in-september-report-1.270513. This news story is based on a report by auditor general Sheila Fraser about needed safety improvements to the Chalk River reactor. Keen was fired for not starting it up again, because it did not have the required emergency backup power installed.

2 See "Nuclear safety watchdog head fired for 'lack of leadership': minister," CBC News, January 16, 2008.

3 Interview with Keen, August 16, 2012. The NDP voted with the government to reopen the reactor.

4 The pretext was to give them money for the development of the next generation of AECLs CANDUs. See Greg Weston, "Ottawa basically paying SNC to take AECL," CBC News, June 29, 2011. Retrieved July 31, 2014, from http://www.cbc.ca/news/politics/weston -ottawa-basically-paying-snc-to-take-aecl-1.1078128.

5 See "The made-in-Canada isotope shortage facing medical scans," CBC News, May 26, 2014, and "Canada to get out of isotope business, PM says," *The Globe and Mail*, June 10, 2009.

nine · THE EXONERATION BLUES

1 Although Guergis was not Iraqi, the racism during the Gulf War (1990– 1991) was just as strong as in 2003. People assumed someone of her complexion was Iraqi, even though she wasn't—and therefore viewed her as a target to vent their feelings about the war.

2 Rahim Jaffer met Stephen Harper and his wife for the first time at a party at Ezra Levant's house in Calgary. Elected in 1997 when he was only in his twenties, Jaffer told me, "I acted my age on the fun side but worked hard and took the job seriously."

3 The second time Jaffer met Harper was at the Century Grill when a dozen Conservative operatives "came to sniff Harper the potential candidate." Jaffer recalled, "It was interesting hearing his thoughts—a smart guy." But it was the future PM's appearance that got Jaffer's attention: "He was incredibly shabby. His belly was hanging out of his shirt that was unbuttoned. He was wearing a hundred-year-old tweed jacket. I turned to James Rajotte and said that Harper was a candidate

for *Extreme Makeover*. He was not hugely charismatic." Jaffer noted that although Harper definitely listened, "He seemed to always have his mind made up. He had no patience. He did not win 100 percent of the support of the people at the Grill."

4 The loss of Edmonton-Strathcona was attributed to Rahim's work ethic, but this analysis failed to consider the strong progressive elements in the riding that returned candidates such as Liberal Anne McClellan and NDPer Linda Duncan.

5 On March 31, 2010, the Liberals alleged that a letter-writing campaign had been waged on Helena Guergis's behalf after the PEI airport story, by those close to her, including her executive assistant and the assistant's mother, as well as a constituency assistant and former riding president. Rahim Jaffer's arrest on the driving charges had occurred in September 2009.

6 Ironically, the place she had allegedly called a "hellhole," Charlottetown, was her father's birthplace.

7 Interview of Guergis by Peter Mansbridge. See CBC News, May 10, 2010, updated May 11, 2010: "Guergis breaks silence on scandal." Sidebar "Charlottetown tantrum" reports about Mansbridge viewing the tape with Guergis at the Canadian Air Transport Security Authority office in Ottawa. CBC News article includes part of this quote. Cameras were not allowed in to the room, and the tape has never been released to the public. A reporter from *The Enterprise-Bulletin* ("What meltdown?" August 3, 2010) also viewed the tape and reached a similar conclusion to Mansbridge.

8 See report: "Guergis appears on Parliament Hill after P.E.I. incident," CTV News, March 15, 2010.

9 Statement of Arthur L. Hamilton, April 16, 2010. RCMP File #2010-391251. Present: Mr. Arthur L. Hamilton, S/Sgt. Stéphane St-Jacques and Insp. John Keuper.

10 See "Winnipeg O' My Heart," a blog about moving to Winnipeg, June 1, 2011. Many Manitobans are fiercely proud of their unique tradition of wedding socials, fundraisers for a wedding couple known as a "Winnipeg social." You rent a hall and sell tickets to everyone you know. The couple's wedding party organizes the event and hosts it for the bride and groom instead of having showers, stags, and stagettes. It is commonplace in the province. See also "The Social: A Manitoba tradition," *Maclean's*, January 11, 2013, which says, "The wedding fundraisers are almost as ubiquitous as perogies and cold weather."

11 After Jaffer lost his seat, he put in what he believed to be legitimate expense claims. A Conservative MP made an allegation that Jaffer had stolen the money, but the dispute was never resolved. Normally the party would not spread damaging rumours about itself, unless it was trying to target someone, in this case Jaffer.

12 CPIC: Canadian Police Information Centre. This is a computer database that allows law enforcement agencies across the country to access centralized information about aspects such as wanted persons, judicial orders, stolen property, etc. It is maintained by the RCMP.

FINTRAC: Financial Transactions and Reports Analysis Centre of Canada. This is Canada's financial intelligence unit. It reports to the minister of finance, and its mandate is to track money laundering and the financing of terrorist activities.

13 Del Mastro is charged with overspending in the 2008 election under the Elections Act. His case went to trial on June 23, 2014.

Lisa Raitt was investigated by the ethics commissioner over a fundraiser organized in the office of the president of the Port Authority, where she had once been CEO. She was cleared.

14 The RCMP report cleared both Guergis and Jaffer of all the allegations received from the PMO. Guergis is referring to Jaffer's careless driving conviction. She lost her place in caucus because of something her husband did. The groundless sex/drugs scandal diverted everyone's attention from the much more dangerous Afghan detainee scandal. This is much like the PM's Twitter red herring that refocused the media's attention when the Arthur Porter scandal was breaking.

ten · FAREWELL DIPLOMACY

1 My first interview with Paul Heinbecker for this book took place on June 30, 2012. See also "Canada's 'one-sided' position on Mideast conflict could undermine its international influence," *Hill Times*, July 15, 2014.

2 In a diplomatic way, Heinbecker is saying others in the room may not have agreed with his point of view about Iraq, but that his advice carried the day with Chrétien.

3 In November 2007, Harper attended a Commonwealth Heads of Government Meeting in Kampala, Uganda. He stepped off the government airbus, gave an awkward wave to the cameras, accepted a

bouquet, and disappeared. Everyone was tired after a long flight. None of the Canadian journalists saw Harper or his communications staff for two days. Rahim Jaffer was on the trip and recalled witnessing Harper swearing and yelling at his staff. Harper was furious that after a meeting with British prime minister Gordon Brown, he had another meeting his staff had scheduled with the prime minister of India, Manmohan Singh. Jaffer recalled, "He screamed at Ray Novak and kicked over a chair. He would get angry around his staff because no one leaked." Both Tom Flanagan and Bruce Carson have described similar incidents.

4 A fact check showed the State Department cited figures provided by TransCanada, indicating that 50 permanent jobs would be created once the pipeline was completed. Obama said something similar in a *New York Times* interview done in Galesburg, Illinois, on July 24, 2013.

5 See "John Baird vacationed for free at historic Macdonald House in England," CTV News, June 19, 2013. Retrieved August 1, 2014, from http://www.ctvnews.ca/politics/john-baird-vacationed-for-free-at -historic-macdonald-house-in-england-1.1333451.

6 Re: using foreign aid to subsidize mining, see Aaron Wherry, "Is this foreign Aid?" *Maclean's*, January 19, 2012. Retrieved August, 2014, from http://www.macleans.ca/politics/ottawa/is-this-foreign-aid/. See also Daniel Leblanc, "CIDA funds seen to be subsidizing mining firms," *The Globe and Mail*, January 29, 2012. Retrieved August 2, 2014, from http://www.theglobeandmail.com/news/politics/cida-funds-seen-to -be-subsidizing-mining-firms/article1360059/.

7 Stats Canada would rely on the census. In the 2006 census, only 29,435 people self-identified as Tamils in the GTA. This may be due to the 2006 Canadian government designation of the Tamil Tigers as a terrorist organization. See: "The Truth about Tamil Statistics," in the *Star*, April 4, 2009. The 2011 census showed 143,300 people with Tamil as a mother tongue, mostly in the Toronto area. They are an important voting demographic for the government.

8 Morsi was elected, the junta was not.

9 Ezra Levant and others such as Charles Adler at the *Toronto Sun* were very upset. Adler called Clement China's "useful idiot." The *Sun* story called the museum "Canada's shrine of shame." Conservative MP Rob Anders was also very critical. After Harper returned from China in

February 2012, tweets from the base were often not kind. The "Commies" had once been the enemy. See Ezra Levant, "Canada's shrine of shame," *Toronto Sun*, July 14, 2012. Retrieved August 2, 2014, from http://www.torontosun.com/2012/07/13/canadas-shrine-of-shame.

10 Although the US condemned the shelling of a UN school in Gaza by Israel, Canada's prime minister kept his government's hard line saying, "Obviously no one likes to see the suffering and loss of life that has occurred. That said, we hold the terrorist organization Hamas responsible for this. They have initiated and continue this conflict and continue to seek the destruction of the state of Israel." See "Harper sticks to hard line on Hamas; US condemns Israel's deadly shelling of UN School," Reuters and Associated Press, reported in *The Globe and Mail*, July 29, 2014. Retrieved August 2, 2014. from http://www.theglobeandmail.com/news/world/21-palestinians-killed-in-gaza-as-israeli-shelling-continues/article19840971/.

eleven · BAD BOYS

1 Although the PMO quietly put out the story that the photo was taken during Netanyahu's trip to Canada in March 2012, staff did not contact iPolitics demanding a retraction of the 2010 date, as they usually do when they believe errors are made. I kept the date from the Mackenzie Institute site, since all their other dates were accurate.

The Mackenzie Institute (MI) had once shared office space with the NCC at 100 Adelaide St. in Toronto. The NCC had also provided initial funding and continued to use the Mackenzie Institute for research on foreign policy. The right-leaning institute presented itself as an independent organization concerned with issues of political stability, terrorism, warfare, and extremism. It was set up in 1986 as a non-profit group by Middle East intelligence expert Maurice Tugwell.

Tugwell had been an intelligence officer in the British military and participated in the Bloody Sunday massacre in the Bogside district of Derry in Northern Ireland. In the subsequent inquiry into the atrocity, Tugwell had to apologize in 2010 for falsely claiming that the fourteen people shot dead by British forces that day were armed members of the IRA. They were, in fact, unarmed protesters, seven of them teenagers.

It was reported that Stephen Harper was once a board member of the Mackenzie Institute. One of the institute's main preoccupations was political Islam. Members have compared the rise of the Muslim Brotherhood to the rise of Hitler in Nazi Germany. Funding for the MI came from individuals, corporations, and foundations, although none were identified, nor were the member lists published. The institute was also interested in oil security.

According to their old website, the MI is an "independent non-profit organization concerned with issues related to political instability and organized violence." It provided research and commentary, and it claims to promote informed debate. "The Institute is also concerned with the social and political stability of Canada, and works to enhance it when it can." Named after Sir Alexander Mackenzie, the first European to reach the Pacific from Upper Canada in 1793, and the first to trace the Mackenzie River to the Arctic Ocean in 1789, the organization appears to have ready access to Stephen Harper. After the January 2006 election, top-ranking members of the Mackenzie Institute were some of the first people to pose for photo ops with the new PM, posted on their website under the heading "Members in Action."

2　Eran Peer, "PayGea quits Israel activity without warning," *Globes*, April 2, 2012. Retrieved August 2, 2014, from http://www.globes.co.il/en/article-1000738361. Report said "Jacobson was close to leaders in Canada's Conservative party. His aides say that he considered himself as a mediator between Prime Minister Benjamin Netanyahu's office and Canada's Conservative Party." See also Moshe Lichtman, "Nathan Jacobson behind clearers in ICC pornography affair," *Globes*, July 15, 2013. Retrieved August 2, 2014, from http://www.globes.co.il/en/article-1000862242.

3　See Aaron Derfel, "Alleged Quebec hospital fraudster Arthur Porter defies cancer odds inside Panama prison," *National Post*, July 14, 2014. Retrieved August 2, 2014, from http://news.nationalpost.com/2014/07/14/alleged-quebec-hospital-fraudster-arthur-porter-defies-cancer-odds-inside-panama-prison/.

4　On August 8, 2014, Porter was tear-gassed and trampled during a prison riot that erupted during a routine search of cellblock 6 in the La Joya prison outside Panama City. Most of the 506 foreign prisoners in the cellblock had been arrested on drug charges. Porter's family feared for his life.

5 An ITO or Information to Obtain is a document written by police outlining a case. It is shown to a judge to obtain a court order to search someone's home, office, or computer or tap a phone. It is used to obtain more evidence to support charges. A judge decides whether to publicize part or all of an ITO.

twelve · FORKED TONGUE

1 See "Natural Gas: Fuelling British Columbia's growth." Topic paper prepared for the Business Council of British Columbia, May 2010. The natural gas sector in BC grew from $1.1 billion in exploration and development in 1999 to $7.9 billion by 2008, and became one of the "leading drivers of the provincial economy." It is the largest direct source of natural resource revenue for the province of BC. See also James Munson, "The Drilldown: Christy Clark's LNG push hits a snag," ipolitics.ca, August 1, 2014. Retrieved August 2, 2014, from http://www.ipolitics .ca/2014/08/01/the-drilldown-christy-clarks-lng-push-hits-a-snag/.

2 "Oil sands 'allies' and 'adversaries' named in federal documents." CBC News, January 26, 2012.

3 In a ground-breaking decision, on June 26, 2014, the Supreme Court of Canada gave the Tsilhqot'in Nation a big victory. It affirmed their Aboriginal title to over 1,700 square kilometres of frontier land in BC, giving the First Nation the right to protect their waterways and largely intact ecosytem.

4 Each year all bands must sign contribution agreements with Ottawa to receive funding for health care, education, and other services. If the bands don't sign, they don't get the money. In 2013, bands were given very little time to review the document. When they did, they noticed changes in the fine print in appendices that could be interpreted as agreeing to support resource development on their lands. They had not been alerted to the changes. Bands signed under duress. Health Canada also uses contribution agreements.

5 Paul C. Webster, "Canada curbs Aboriginal health leadership," *The Lancet* 379 (9832), June 9, 2012. See also CTV News staff, "Maternal health: Should Harper focus on First nations first?" CTV News, May 27, 2014, updated May 28, 2014; and Kim Mackrael, 'Ottawa commits $3.5 billion to improve maternal health,' *The Globe and Mail*, May 29, 2014.

6 Kinder Morgan Canada operates a number of pipeline systems and terminals in Canada, including the Trans Mountain Pipeline which runs from Alberta to BC. It transports about 20 percent of liquid petroleum products produced in Alberta to markets in Western North America.

7 "Canadian Forces spent virtually all of 2013 watching Idle No More protesters," *National Post*, June 1, 2014; "CSIS spying on citizens at alarming rate, FOIs reveal," *Vancouver Observer*, February 26, 2013; "The Conservative government just doesn't get it when it comes to privacy," *Huffington Post*, July 8, 2014.

8 "Supreme Court sides with Métis in historic Manitoba land claim dispute," *The Canadian Press*, March 8, 2013.

thirteen · A TANGLED WEB

1 Greg Wetson, "Senate Expenses scandal left no paper trail, really?" CBC News, September 2, 2013.

2 "'The prime minister agreed I had not broken the rules': Duffy's account of the PMO's 'fake payback scheme,'" Postmedia News (no byline), October 29, 2013. Article references Gerstein's two-hour visit. The names of who he was there to see and who was with him were redacted from documents released under the Freedom of Information Act.

3 A source close to this matter recently told me that it was the late Senator Doug Finley who advised the Conservative Party not to pay off Duffy's debt. Finley, who is considered the mastermind of the Conservative election triumphs, including the important breakthrough in Ontario, died on May 11, 2013, of colorectal cancer. Finley was in the Senate May 8, 2013, where he debated and moved the third reading on Bill C-383, the Transboundary Waters Protection Act.

fourteen · WRECKING BALL

1 MacKay used one of only three search-and-rescue helicopters in Newfoundland to pick him up from his vacation at Burnt Rattle, a private salmon camp on the Gander River in July 2010. The Cormorant helicopter costs about $32,000 per flying hour to operate, and the trip took half an hour. An informed source told me that the PMO had called, ordering MacKay to be at a meeting at a certain time, making the

helicopter ride necessary to make it on time. Then someone in the PMO allegedly leaked the story.

2 Wright was interested in politics even in high school. He was a member of the Young Conservatives in university, and backed Mulroney in his 1983 leadership campaign. In 1984, Wright interrupted law school at U of T to become a speech writer and policy advisor in the Mulroney PMO. (He worked as executive assistant to senior policy advisor Charles McMillan.) Wright also assisted Mike Harris in Ontario, and helped Kim Campbell to become the first female PM. (Wright went to Onex in 1997, the same year Harper went to the NCC.)

Wright believed Harper was the one who could unite the Conservatives, and he encouraged Harper to go after the Conservative leadership in 2004. He did fundraising, and was a valued policy advisor. Conservative Fund Canada was created with Irving Gerstein, Gordon Reid, and Nigel Wright as the founding directors. Wright sat on the board of the Fund until he joined the Harper PMO in 2010. The Fund paid for the development of CIMS.

3 Joan Bryden of CP broke the story, and Dawson began her investigation only after the story was published. A Council of Canadians site dated May 17, 2013, says Dawson rejected at least eighty complaints made to her office without a public ruling since 2007, and made public rulings in seventeen. The Council asked for a public ruling in the Barrick Gold case.

Joan Bryden, "Nigel Wright Conflict of interest allegations: chief of staff cleared by watchdog," CP in *Huffington Post*, August 1, 2013. Retrieved August 11, 2014. from http://www.huffingtonpost.ca/2013/01/08/nigel-wright-conflict-of-interest-chief-of-staff_n_2435040.html.

"PMO chief lobbied by Barrick Gold despite personal ties," CP on CBC News, August 28, 2012. Retrieved August 11, 2014, from http://www.cbc.ca/news/politics/pmo-chief-lobbied-by-barrick-gold-despite-personal-ties-1.1193101.

Joan Bryden, "Harper's chief of staff faces scrutiny over Barrick Gold links," CP in *The Globe and Mail*, August 28, 2012. Retrieved August 11, 2014, from http://www.theglobeandmail.com/news/politics/harpers-chief-of-staff-faces-scrutiny-over-barrick-gold-links/article4504620/.

Joan Bryden, "Nigel Wright conflict of interest controversy: Harper's chief of staff was lobbied by Barrick Gold 3 times," CP in *Huffington*

Post, August 29, 2012. Retrieved August 3, 2014, from http://www
.huffingtonpost.ca/2012/08/29/nigel-wright-barrick-gold-conflict
-lobbying_n_1841180.html.

4 Cecilia Jamasmie, "Barrick has had enough: Stops construction of
Pascua-Lama, mulls stake sale," Mining.com, October 31, 2013. Retrieved
August 11, 2014, from http://www.mining.com/barrick-has-had-enough
-stops-construction-of-pascua-lama-mulls-stake-sale-89887/.

   Cecilia Jamasmie, "Argentina lobbies to overturn Barrick's Pascua-
Lama freeze in Chile," Mining.com, January 10, 2014. Retrieved
August 11, 2014, from http://www.mining.com/argentina-lobbies-to
-overturn-barricks-pascua-lama-freeze-in-chile-53714/.

   Cecilia Jamasmie, "Chiles's supreme court begins hearing on Barrick
Gold's appeal to $16m fine," Mining.com, July 8, 2014. Retrieved
August 11, 2014 from http://www.mining.com/chiles-supreme-court
-begins-hearings-on-barrick-golds-appeal-to-16m-fine-90958/.

   Fabian Cambero, "Barrick strikes deal with Pascua-Lama mine
opponents," Reuters.com, May 28, 2014. Retrieved August 11, 2014,
from   http://www.reuters.com/article/2014/05/28/barrick-gold-pascua
-idUSL1N0OE0PS20140528.

   This was an agreement to provide project details to the communities
affected by the mine. Construction would not restart until there was a
two-year "dialogue phase" that may include payment of an "indigenous
royalty." The situation has parallels with development projects affecting
Aboriginal communities in Canada.

5 There were reports that Nigel Wright's ethical side occasionally caused
friction in the PMO, particularly with Jenni Byrne, and even the PM.

6 The call by finance minister Flaherty to the CIBC was also reported
in *The Globe and Mail* on May 7, 2008. See Jacquie McNish, "Flaherty
wades into Barrick's CIBC feud," *The Globe and Mail*, May 7, 2008, page
B1, 7. Retrieved August 3, 2014, from http://www.theglobeandmail
.com/report-on-business/flaherty-wades-into-barricks-cibc-feud/
article719623/. See also Doug Alexander, "Flaherty intervened in
Barrick, CIBC dispute, Globe says," Bloomberg, May 7, 2008. Retrieved
August 11, 2014, from http://www.bloomberg.com/apps/news?pid=
newsarchive&sid=aAAVca5V2IwA.

7 The former president of Goldman Sachs Group had spent the last
ten years in China running an elite business school. The $11.9 million

signing bonus did not play well with dissenting investors. The Canada Pension Plan Investment Board was among the six largest pension funds that opposed the payment. Shareholders voted 85 percent against the payment to Thornton, but the vote was not binding. No one was pleased. The CEO of Caisse de Depot told BNN on May 1, 2013, that he would not have supported the compensation plan for a co-chair "even if it were for Jesus Christ."

Leaders of several of the investment groups signed a letter dated April 19, 2013, saying, "This amount for a signing bonus for a Co-Chairman of the board is, to our knowledge, unprecedented in Canada and is in addition to other compensation for the year for a total of $17 million in 2012. This compensation is not consistent with the governance principle of pay-for-performance and is therefore disproportionate. It sets a troubling precedent in Canadian capital markets."

8 In the second quarter of 2013, the investment return was only 1.8 percent, well below the general average return of 3.6 percent on Canadian pension funds during the same quarter.

9 Amy MacPherson, "Where your CPP money really goes," *Huffington Post*, January 22, 2013. In 2009, a year when pension funds around the world took a massive hit, the CPPIB fund had a $24-billion loss, yet CPPIB executives still received millions in bonuses. CPP contributions of $6.6 billion from Canadian workers helped offset the loss. CPPIB holds a $330-million stake in Barrick Gold, and invested $78 million in Lockheed Martin. It also invested $350 million in Progress Energy Resources in 2009. In 2012, a subsidiary of Petronas announced its intention to buy Progress Energy, which had acquired Suncor Energy's northeast British Columbia assets in 2010. Petronas offered $5.5 billion. In October 2012, the Harper government rejected the sale as not likely to be of "net benefit" to Canada. Just two months later, the government changed its mind, approving the deal in December 2012.

10 Mike Duffy's defence team is reported to have a cache of hundreds of emails from Perrin.

11 About seventy-five Canadian mining companies are active in Peru, exploring mainly for gold, silver, and copper. Some in the country see the Canadian government as a representative of the Canadian mining companies in the regions, aimed at maximizing profits at the expense of local people and the environment. See Heather Scoffield, "Harper visit to

Peru targets better use of mining royalties to alleviate poverty," Canadian Press/CTV News, May 22, 2013.

sixteen · MOUNTIES AT THE DOOR

1 Victoria Island is in the Ottawa River at the border between Ontario and Quebec. You can see Parliament Hill from the island. It is important in Aboriginal culture, and Chief Spence staged her hunger strike there.

2 On April 25, 2014, in a unanimous eight-to-zero decision, the Supreme Court ruled that Ottawa could not act alone to reform the Senate, appoint only elected senators, or impose a term limit of nine years. To reform the Senate, it must have the consent of seven provinces with half of the population. Unanimous consent of the provinces and Parliament (including the Senate) was necessary to abolish the Senate. Harper said he was "personally disappointed" in the decision. But in effect the Court had provided a constitutional road map for reforms, signed by the Court as a whole, not by a particular judge. At Confederation, the Senate was originally designed to be a legislative check on government as well as to represent regional interests.

3 The RCMP raided the Conservative Party of Canada headquarters on April 15, 2008. After a five-year investigation, charges were laid under the Canada Elections Act against the Conservative Party and four members, including two senators (Senator Doug Finley [appointed August 2009], Senator Irving Gerstein [appointed December 2008], Michael Donison, and Susan Kehoe), on February 24, 2011. The charges included allegations that elections expense documents submitted to Elections Canada were "false or misleading, and that the party had exceeded spending limits by over a million dollars." On March 6, 2012, a plea deal was reached.

4 Duffy required a second open heart surgery while awaiting charges, and an invasive follow-up procedure. He still has serious heart problems.

5 Saying Wright was "dismissed" prompted others in the party and his friends on Bay Street to defend Wright. Jason Kenney gave a speech at the Albany Club in January 2014 defending Wright, which brought the black-tie Conservative elite to its feet with "thunderous applause" as they hooted and whistled. Gerald Schwartz told *Toronto Life*: "I don't understand it. This isn't an issue of Bay Street defending one of its

own. It's an issue of whether a guy of enormous integrity and capability, donating himself to public service for two and a half years, has been treated shabbily."

According to *Toronto Life*, Harper's treatment of Wright has made many Conservatives question the prime minister's judgment: "To the public, the Senate scandal is a baffling, sometimes comical tale of greed, hyper-partisan politicians and of backroom hacks trying desperately to protect them. But to corporate and political insiders, it's a story of personal betrayal—and a rift that has divided the Conservative party at the highest levels."

See: Kelly Pullen, "With friends like Harper: how Nigel Wright went from golden boy to fall guy," *Toronto Life*, March 25, 2014.

6 Interview with Preston Manning, November 7, 2012.

7 Despite Ford's admitted drug use, most Conservatives have not made negative comments about Rob Ford, who they still believe will help them win ridings in the GTA, particularly in Scarborough. On September 22, 2013, in a surprise Sunday announcement in Toronto, Harper and Flaherty pledged $660 million in federal funding for the $3-billion expansion of the Bloor-Danforth subway line. Harper shook hands with Rob Ford after the announcement. Note the treatment of Helena Guergis when her husband was accused of possession of a small amount of cocaine, a charge that was dropped.

8 According to Brazeau's lawyer, Gerald Larocque, on June 17, 2014, the alleged victims of the assault and threats case want to drop the charges. Brazeau pleaded not guilty to the charges, and the case was put off until September 5, 2014. The trial date for the earlier February 2013 charges is expected to be set in the fall as well.

9 Informed observers have noted rivalry in the PMO; one even suggested to me that the real target of the leak to Fife was Wright, not Duffy.

10 On June 26, 2014, the Senate Ethics Office announced it would not pursue an investigation into allegations that Senator Gerstein tried to intervene in the audit of Mike Duffy's expenses. Gerstein has not commented on the allegations made by the RCMP in court documents. Lyse Ricard did not give a reason for her decision.

11 Joe Mont, "Deloitte Unit agrees to $10 million fine, one year New York consulting ban," *Compliance Week*, June 18, 2013. Retrieved August 8,

2014, from http://www.complianceweek.com/blogs/the-filing-cabinet/deloitte-unit-agrees-to-10-million-fine-one-year-new-york-consulting-ban#.

"Deloitte gets one year New York ban," BBC News business, June 19, 2013. Retrieved August 8, 2014, from http://www.bbc.com/news/business-22958743.

12 Drew Hasselback, "Livent auditor Deloitte ordered to pay $84.5 million for failing to detect fraud," *Financial Post*, April 6, 2014. Retrieved August 8, 2014, from http://business.financialpost.com/2014/04/06/livent-auditor-deloitte-ordered-to-pay-84-8-million-for-failing-detect-fraud/.

According to the *The Globe and Mail*, Deloitte is appealing the April 2014 decision of Justice Gans. See Janet McFarland, "Deloitte ordered to pay another $33 million in Livent negligence case," *The Globe and Mail*, July 15, 2014. Retrieved August 8, 2014, from http://www.theglobeandmail.com/report-on-business/industry-news/the-law-page/deloitte-ordered-to-pay-another-33-million-in-livent-negligence-case/article19613388/.

13 Kady O'Malley, "Ben Perrin failed to protect email from deletion, PMO, PCO say," CBC News, December 5, 2013. Retrieved August 8, 2014, from http://www.cbc.ca/m/touch/politics/story/1.2450711.; Laura Payton, "PMO emails: 3 questions about Ben Perrin's account," CBC News, December 4, 2013. Retrieved August 8, 2014, from http://www.cbc.ca/m/touch/news/story/1.2449591.

14 Although no questions were allowed from reporters after the thirty-one charges against Duffy were announced in spectacular fashion on July 17, 2014, "out of respect for the court process," the RCMP offered more details in a court filing on the charges four days later. The Mounties had already alleged that Duffy had committed fraud by awarding contracts to his friend Gerald Donohue, but on July 21, 2014, they accused the senator of funnelling that money to three other individuals for "illegitimate expenses." The three included Ashley Cain who worked for Duffy in 2010. According to reporter Steven Chase, Cain had been employed in the correspondence unit of the PMO since 2011. PMO director of communications Jason MacDonald said, "Ms. Cain worked for Mr. Duffy in 2010. This is the first we are hearing of any of this. That said, we are not aware of anyone other

than Mr. Duffy who is under investigation or who has been charged in this affair." See Steven Chase, "Duffy billed taxpayers for attending funeral, RCMP allege," *The Globe and Mail*, July 21, 2014. Retrieved August 3, 2014, from http://www.theglobeandmail.com/news/politics/mike-duffy-filed-expenses-for-funerals-ceremonies-court-documents/article19695383/.

After the charges were laid against Duffy, I asked Robert Fife his final thoughts for the book. He told me, "It's a tragedy when you think about what happened to Mike."

15 Mr. MacDonald is Prime Minister Stephen Harper's eighth director of communications.

seventeen · PARLIAMENT ON THE BRINK

1 Joan Bryden, "Fair Elections Act: Sheila Fraser slams Bill C-23 as attack on democracy," *Huffington Post*, March 4, 2014, updated March 6, 2014. Refers to Fraser as becoming a "virtual folk hero" for exposing the sponsorship scandal.

2 Reported by CBC News In Depth, February 17, 2004, re. 125th anniversary of the RCMP. The RCMP received $1.7 million with a commission of $244,350. They bought six horses and two trailers, etc.

3 The Treasury Board Secretariat is the administrative arm of the Treasury Board. The Secretariat has dual mandates: "to support the Treasury Board as a committee of ministers and to fulfill the statutory responsibilities of a central government agency." The Secretariat is headed by a Secretary who reports to the president of the Treasury Board, currently Tony Clement.

4 The Canada logo is a specific font of the word "Canada," with a small Canadian flag above the final letter. The AG still uses coats of arms in reports and job advertising.

5 The Harper government used time allocation to limit debate seventeen times during the nineteen-day marathon Commons sitting at the end of May 2014 before the summer recess. Nineteen bills went through the House of Commons in under four weeks.

6 "Navigation Protection Act: government braces for court battles over waterways," CBC News, July 13, 2014, updated July 14; "Pipeline industry drove changes to Navigable Waters Protection Act, documents show," *Toronto Star*, February 20, 2013.

7 "Government shut down detainee documents panel: judges' letter," CP on CTV News, June 24, 2011. Retrieved August 4, 2014, from http://www.ctvnews.ca/gov-t-shut-down-detainee-documents-panel-judges-letter-1.661814.

8 Steven Chase (with a report from Bill Curry), "Speaker gives backbench MPs freedom from party's whip," *The Globe and Mail*, April 23, 2013. Retrieved August 4, 2014. from http://www.theglobeandmail.com/news/politics/speaker-gives-backbench-mps-freedom-from-partys-whip/article11506636/. A group of ten backbench Harper MPs had complained to the Speaker about Harper's iron grip over what MPs can say in the chamber. They asked Scheer to rule on a point of privilege.

In his first major ruling since being elected to the post nearly two years earlier, Scheer told MPs they are not constrained by caucus lists that dictate who can deliver sixty-second statements or ask questions in Question Period. Scheer's ruling challenged the centralized discipline of the Harper government. In effect, backbenchers had a right to be heard. Party whips could coordinate but not control the backbenchers. Traditionally it is the Speaker's role to decide who speaks. In the UK, members bob up and down for a chance to speak by being recognized by the Speaker. Harper's continuing attempt to control who speaks in the House of Commons is a radical departure from parliamentary practice.

9 An appreciative prime minister called his new information commissioner the day after New Year's in 2007 to say he was "grateful" that Marleau had accepted the appointment. Stephen Harper had obviously ignored what Marleau had previously told him: "Be careful what you wish for." Marleau kept his bargain. After serving for two years, re-engineering the Office of the Information Commissioner (there were many critics), and presenting a legislative review to Parliament, he resigned on June 29, 2009. For his part, Stephen Harper kept his word too—a fact that Marleau appreciated. Although the PM knew of the resignation in advance, Harper allowed Marleau to make it official.

eighteen · DELAY, DENY, AND DIE

1 The art works were described to me by MacKay as video grabs, with heavy use of charcoal, pastel, and wax on them done by hand. Each piece was unique. This is a technique he has used for years, based on taking

hours of video in war zones, then choosing a particular frame to work on as a background, sometimes in sequence. You can also see his work at the Pape TTC station in Toronto.

2 "Stephen Harper attacks Vladimir Putin and 'evil' communism," *Canadian Press*, May 31, 2014.

3 Teachers' college.

4 For comment about Bush comparison, see "Stephen Harper's military jacket is irritating and offensive," *Huffington Post*, July 2, 2013. People I interviewed also mentioned it. Harper is an excellent marketer and very aware of branding. President Bush's first trip after his presidency was to speak to a closed-door Conservative group in Calgary. They loved him.

5 The provincial marine was a coastal protection service that operated in the Great Lakes, and St. Lawrence River, etc. Their schooners were armed and staffed by the Royal Navy during the War of 1812.

6 Colvin is referring to Canada's diplomatic instinct and reputation before he became aware of the treatment of detainees in Afghanistan in 2006— the Pearson legacy as well as his own experiences as a diplomat since the 1990s. He was shocked to see what was happening on the ground to detainees, because of his view of Canada as a humanitarian country. He risked his career and reputation to reveal what he suspected was going on. At the time of my interview, he was first secretary in the Intelligence Section of the Canadian embassy in Washington.

7 According to records recently released under the Access to Information Act, over a thousand prisoners were caught by the Canadian military in Afghanistan. Most were transferred to Afghan authorities, where they faced possible torture at the hands of Afghan jailers. A lawyer who worked for Amnesty International in an attempt to halt the transfers said, "I think Canada really lost its innocence in the detainee controversy." (See "Alleged Afghan prison torture controversy slips quietly into history books," *Canadian Press*, March 10, 2014.)

8 "Tories secretly gave Canadian military OK to share info despite torture risk," by Jim Bronskill, *Canadian Press*, April 13, 2014.

9 In June 2014, the Taliban attacked police outposts and government facilities across several districts in northern Helmand province, as well as neighbouring districts. The deepening crisis in Kabul has put long-term stability in doubt, even before US troops have completed their withdrawal from Afghanistan. Fear and violence are increasing and the

country is facing a humanitarian crisis. Water and food in certain areas are in short supply.

10 There is a looming crisis of homelessness among veterans. The number of homeless people identified as veterans has jumped from 35 in 2009–2010 to 236 in 2013. Like the suicide rate, the actual number is probably much higher. In Toronto, a 2013 study found that 16 percent of people sleeping on the streets identified themselves as veterans. See Annie Bergeron-Oliver, "The number of homeless veterans in Canada is soaring," iPolitics, June 30, 2014; Annie Bergeron-Oliver, "Addictions, mental illness pushing veterans onto the street: expert," iPolitics, July 23, 2014.

11 See "Roméo Dallaire, Senate Liberal, retiring from Parliament," CBC News, May 28, 2014.

12 David Pugliese, "Veterans Affairs paid $700,000 in bonuses," *Ottawa Citizen*, May 26, 2012; Peter Worthington, "Bonus Pay for Veterans Affairs managers has to end," *Toronto Sun*, June 21, 2012.

13 In the 2012 announcement, MacKay said he would target long wait times by recruiting four more psychiatrists, thirteeen more psychologists, ten or more mental health nurses, thirteen more social workers, and eleven more addictions counsellors. Figures updated in December 2013 show that current mental health staffing levels are 388, which is 62 short of the military's own staffing target of 450 back in 2009. If MacKay's promise had been fulfilled, at least 51 more staff would have been recruited.

14 Murray Brewster, "Turf war hindered hiring of mental health staff at National Defence, sources say," Canadian Press, *The Globe and Mail*, January 26, 2014.

15 The lawyers for the vets are doing the case pro bono.

16 Frequently, Ottawa showed that respect and support for Canada's veterans in odd ways. Between 2006 and 2011, it turned down 67 percent of applications made under the Last Post Program. That is the federal program that assisted to the amount of $3,600 in the burial costs of veterans. (After publicity, the amount was raised to $7,376 in 2013.) If a military couple have joint assets of $12,000, they do not qualify for the Last Post benefit.

17 David Pugliese, "It's their fault: MacKay blames military for cut in danger pay for soldiers in Afghanistan," Postmedia News, April 24, 2013. Retrieved August 4, 2014, from http://news.nationalpost.com/

2013/04/24/its-their-fault-mackay-blames-military-for-cutin-danger
-pay-for-soldiers-in-afghanistan/. Soldiers contacted Postmedia News
to complain about cuts to danger pay in Afghanistan. After the public
backlash, the government reversed its position.

18 "Father of slain soldier calls Afghanistan war 'a waste,'" CBC News (no
byline), March 15, 2014. Retrieved August 4, 2014, from http://www
.cbc.ca/news/canada/north/father-of-slain-soldier-calls-afghanistan
-war-a-waste-1.2573058.

nineteen · A WALK WITH FARLEY

1 *The Sunday Express* was a weekly paper started in St. John's,
Newfoundland and Labrador, in 1986 by businessman Harry Steele.
I was the founding publisher and editor-in-chief, and we hired some
great young journalists.

2 Laureen Harper is the third prime minister's wife who has been on
Dennis's list of celebrity clients, though in the case of Mila Mulroney,
only the legendary Rinaldo himself was permitted to cut her hair. It
was acceptable if the blow-dry was performed by a lesser mortal. It was
the same with her husband. "We always knew when the Mulroneys were
coming because you could hear the stairs shaking," Dennis recalled. "He
brought a lot of people."

Dennis had a mind that noted and classified details others might
miss. The "classy" Margaret Trudeau drove a Mercedes; the confident
Mila Mulroney, a Land Rover; and the shy and unassuming Laureen
Harper, a Honda van, and before that, a Ford Escort.

3 *Deepwater Horizon* was the BP oil rig that exploded, causing the largest
marine oil spill in the world. The disaster in the Gulf of Mexico began
April 20, 2010, and it took eighty-seven days to cap the well. An estimated
4.9 million barrels of oil spilled in to the gulf. Dolphins and other marine
species such as tuna continue to die in record numbers there.

afterword · WAR IS PEACE

1 Allan Woods, "How would have new terror legislation affected recent
Canadian cases?" *Toronto Star*, January 30, 2015. Retrieved May 28,

2015, from http://www.thestar.com/news/canada/2015/01/30/how-would-have-new-terror-legislation-affected-recent-canadian-cases.html.

2 René Bruemmer, "From typical teen to jihadist: How Martin Couture-Rouleau became radicalized after converting to Islam," Postmedia News, November 9, 2014; updated January 25, 2015. Retrieved May 28, 2015 from http://news.nationalpost.com/news/canada/from-typical-teen-to-jihadist-how-martin-couture-rouleau-became-radicalized-after-converting-to-islam.

3 "Martin Couture-Rouleau, and the challenge of someone who hasn't broken the law—yet," *The Globe and Mail*, October 21, 2014. Retrieved May 28, 2015, from http://www.theglobeandmail.com/globe-debate/editorials/martin-couture-rouleau-and-the-challenge-of-someone-who-hasnt-broken-the-law-yet/article21216003/.

4 Josh Elliott, "Toronto man handed 10 years on terror charges", CTV News, July 24, 2014. Retrieved May 28, 2015, from http://www.ctvnews.ca/canada/toronto-man-handed-10-years-on-terror-charges-1.1930051.

5 Kieran Corcoran, "Radicalized Canadian Muslim mows down two soldiers 'in the name of Allah,' killing one," Mailonline and Reuters, October 21, 2014; updated October 22, 2014. Retrieved May 28, 2015, from http://www.dailymail.co.uk/news/article-2801102/radicalized-canadian-muslim-convert-runs-two-young-soldiers-car-shot-dead-police.html.

6 Shaamini Yogaretnam, "Ottawa police to guard sentries at National War Memorial," *Ottawa Citizen*, April 8, 2015. Retrieved May 28, 2015 from http://ottawacitizen.com/news/local-news/ottawa-police-to-guard-sentries-at-national-war-memorial. The Ottawa Citizen learned that the Ottawa Police Service will guard the unarmed sentries from 9 a.m. to 5 p.m. at a cost of $450,000 when the program resumes in the summer of 2015. Police had been investigating security at the memorial for a month before the attacks.

7 Scott Taylor, "On Target: Canadian given pass on calling crimes terrorism," *Chronicle Herald*, November 30, 2014. Retrieved May 28, 2015, from http://thechronicleherald.ca/opinion/1254384-on-target-canadian-given-pass-on-calling-crimes-terrorism.

8 Murray Brewster, the Canadian Press, "Ottawa's defence costs 'unsustainable' over next decade, budget watchdog says," *The Globe and Mail*, March 26, 2015. Retrieved May 28, 2015, from

http://www.theglobeandmail.com/news/politics/ottawas-defence-costs-unsustainable-over-next-decade-budget-watchdog-says/article23630687/.

9 Alexander Panetta, the Canadian Press, "Republican reversal on Iraq war, 12 years later: OK, it was a mistake," CTV News, May 19, 2015. Retrieved May 28, 2015, from http://www.ctvnews.ca/politics/republican-reversal-on-the-iraq-war-12-years-later-ok-it-was-a-mistake-1.2380161.

10 Alexander Panetta, the Canadian Press, "Republican reversal on Iraq war, 12 years later: OK, it was a mistake," CTV News, May 19, 2015. Retrieved May 28, 2015, from http://www.ctvnews.ca/politics/republican-reversal-on-the-iraq-war-12-years-later-ok-it-was-a-mistake-1.2380161.

11 David Pugliese, *Ottawa Citizen*, "Canadian training mission warned of neo-Nazi militias," *The StarPhoenix*, April 18, 2015. Retrieved May 28, 2015, from http://www.thestarphoenix.com/life/Canadian+training+mission+warned+Nazi+militias/10983767/story.html.

12 "Open letter to Parliament: Amend C-51 or kill it," signed by more than 100 Canadian professors of law and related disciplines, *National Post*, February 27, 2015. Retrieved May 28, 2015, from http://news.nationalpost.com/full-comment/open-letter-to-parliament-amend-c-51-or-kill-it.

13 While Bill C-51 was passing through Parliament, there were two terrorist trials: the Vancouver pressure cooker bombers and the VIA train bombers, who were convicted. Like the Toronto 18, the accused had been enabled by government agents who had been in on their plots from the beginning. One of the men in the VIA plot was sent for psychiatric assessment after his conviction. The RCMP had reassigned 600 officers to counterterrorism, which had sidelined 321 other criminal investigations. While the bill bans causing bodily harm or rape ("violating an individual's sexual integrity"), it does not include a clause banning torture.

14 Chris Hall, "Parliament Hill shooter Zehaf-Bibeau's cellphone manifesto barely a minute long," CBC News, March 5, 2015. Retrieved May 28, 2015, from http://www.cbc.ca/news/politics/parliament-hill-shooter-zehaf-bibeau-s-cellphone-manifesto-barely-a-minute-long-1.2982104.

15 Tim Naumetz, "Canadian majority opposes Syrian airstrikes:poll," hilltimes.com, April 7, 2015. Retrieved May 28, 2015, from http://www.hilltimes.com/news/news/2015/04/07/canadian-majority-opposes-syrian-airstrikes-poll/41699.

16 Bill Curry, "Economy a higher priority than terrorism for Canadian voters: poll," *The Globe and Mail*, April 1, 2015; updated April 10, 2015. Retrieved May 28, 2015, from http://www.theglobeandmail.com/news/politics/economy-a-higher-priority-than-terrorism-for-canadian-voters-poll/article23728296/?cmpid=rss1.

17 Greg Keenan, "Canadian taxpayers lose \$3.5-billion on 2009 bailout of auto firms," *The Globe and Mail*, April 7, 2015; updated April 8. Retrieved May 28, 2015, from http://www.theglobeandmail.com/report-on-business/canadian-taxpayers-lose-35-billion-on-2009-bailout-of-auto-firms/article23828543/. The auto bailout cost government \$13.7 billion. All in, including the shares sold to Goldman Sachs for \$3.2 billion to balance the budget, the government received \$10.2 billion back, resulting in a net loss to taxpayers of \$3.5 billion.

18 Scott Tracey, "Robocall Mystery figure spotted in Guelph," *Guelph Mercury*, January 27, 2015. Retrieved May 28, 2015, from http://www.insidehalton.com/news-story/5278167-robocalls-mystery-figure-ken-morgan-spotted-in-guelph/Ken. On Sunday January 25, 2015, former Guelph campaign manager Ken Morgan was spotted in Guelph at a south-end restaurant. His friend John White, who had also worked on the campaign with Michael Sona, confirmed that Morgan was in the area but would be returning to Kuwait where he teaches English. According to Crown witness Andrew Prescott at Sona's trial, Morgan had handed him a sheet of paper with the log-in and password for the account used to distribute the misleading robocalls. Morgan left the country and has never been interviewed about his potential role in the affair. According to the commissioner of Elections Canada, the robocall file is officially closed.

19 See Nathan Jacobson's forty-page guilty plea: Case 3:07 CR2016 (18 - IEG) filed in San Diego, California, on May 2, 2008. Retrieved April 29, 2015, from http://media.nacion.com/sites/investigacion/2013/Jacobson/assets/pdf/GUILTY%20PLEA.pdf.

20 "Full text of Peter Mansbridge's interview with Stephen Harper," CBC News, December 17, 2015. Retrieved May 28, 2015, from http://www.cbc.ca/news/politics/full-text-of-peter-mansbridge-s-interview-with-stephen-harper-1.2876934.

21 Tasha Kheiriddin, "The Duffy trial's smoking gun just blew up in Harper's face," ipoli-tics.ca, May 7, 2015. Retrieved May 28, 2015, from

http://www.ipolitics.ca/2015/05/07/the-duffy-trials-smoking-gun-just-blew-up-in-harpers-face/.

22 James Fitz-Morris, "Patrick Brazeau lawyer draws hope from Mike Duffy trial," CBC News, May 1, 2015. Retrieved May 28, 2015, from http://www.cbc.ca/news/politics/patrick-brazeau-lawyer-draws-hope-from-mike-duffy-trial-1.3057271.

23 Cecilia Jamasmie, "Barrick faces multi-billion dollar suit over Porgera mine," Min-ing.com, March 19, 2015. Retrieved May 28, 2015, from http://www.mining.com/barrick-faces-multi-billion-dollar-suit-over-porgera-mine/. See also Liezel Hill, "Barrick Gold Chairman's shakeup keeps investors guessing," bloomberg.com, February 17, 2015. Retrieved May 28, 2015, from http://www.bloomberg.com/news/articles/2015-02-17/barrick-gold-chairman-s-shakeup-keeps-investors-guessing regarding debt of $13.1 billion at Barrick and new management style. On May 26, 2015, Barrick Gold announced it had sold half its stake in the Porgera Mine to China's state-owned Zijin Mining Group Co. for US$298 million. See Peter Koven, "Barrick Gold Corp, Ivanhoe Mines Ltd sell stakes to China's Zijin in Papua New Guinea, Congo Mines," *Financial Post*, May 26, 2015. Retrieved May 28, 2015, from http://business.financialpost.com/news/mining/barrick-gold-corp-sells-50-stake-in-papua-new-guinea-mine-to-china-in-bid-to-forge-closer-ties.

24 Alexandra Posadzki, the Canadian Press, "Barrick Gold revamps approach to executive pay after shareholder vote," CTV News, April 28, 2015. Retrieved May 28, 2015, from http://www.ctvnews.ca/business/barrick-gold-revamps-approach-to-executive-pay-after-shareholder-vote-1.2348229.

25 Heather Saul, "Saudia Arabia beheadings: One chart that reveals the disturbing rise in executions this year," *The Independent*, May 7, 2015. Retrieved May 8, 2015, from http://www.independent.co.uk/news/world/middle-east/saudia-arabia-beheadings-one-chart-that-reveals-the-disturbing-rise-in-executions-this-year-10232782.html.

26 Elections Canada, "Voter Identification." Retrieved May 28, 2015, from http://www.elections.ca/content.aspx?section=vot&dir=ids&document=index&lang=e.

ACKNOWLEDGMENTS

A great may people were involved in the writing of this book, but none more important than Lawrence Martin. It was Martin, the first mainstream journalist to take a critical look at the Harper government in his book *Harperland*, who encouraged me to take on this project. His support and advice were invaluable.

James Baxter, the publisher of iPolitics.ca, gave me generous leeway to complete extensive research and to write *Party of One* on time that would otherwise have been devoted to my job as his national columnist. On both a personal and professional level, his support has been unconditional and constant.

Diane Turbide, my editor and publishing director at Penguin Canada, and Tara Tovell, who copy edited the book, provided insightful and meticulous advice on a project made more difficult by stringent deadlines, driven by events beyond everyone's control. Thank you to production editor Catherine Dorton for her precise attention to language. When I signed the contract with Penguin, neither robocalls nor the Senate scandal had appeared on the national radar, and both stories have unfolded at the snail's pace of the legal calendar. I thank my editors at Penguin for their support and patience in keeping the book as current as possible.

Two former colleagues from my radio years, Ms. Ronnie Roberts and Dean Staff, smoothed the logistics of arranging countless interviews with people spread out across the country. Without their cheerful assistance, the job would have been much harder.

Suzanne Norman, who teaches a publishing course at Simon Fraser University, was my tutor in how best to reach the widest audience in social media. Her knowledge, perspicacity, and friendship lightened the load.

Special thanks to Jan Reatherford and Jane Fordham, who contributed their energy and ideas to the project. Tragically, Jane passed away before she could see the book come to fruition. She is sorely missed by her family, friends, and by me.

This book also benefitted from the superb reporting of various news agencies and individual reporters covering the Harper government. Heather Schoffield's reporting team at Canadian Press produced a string of original and important stories on the conduct of the federal government.

Robert Fife of CTV News and Stephen Maher and Glen McGregor of Postmedia News broke major stories that changed the political landscape in Ottawa. They were generous in sharing their observations with me. Elizabeth Thompson, my colleague at iPolitics.ca, contributed many original stories on the modus operandi of the government, often employing her gift for computer-assisted journalism.

I also carefully followed the work of CBC reporters Laura Payton and Hannah Thibedeau in their excellent daily coverage of happenings on the Hill. Veteran Ottawa reporter Tim Naumetz of the *Hill Times* contributed more than his share of important investigative pieces. I also learned a lot from inspired reporting across Canada, some of the best of it written in *The Tyee* by author and journalist Andrew Nikiforuk.

It goes without saying that I am grateful to the hundreds of people who talked to me, formally and informally, for this book. Sheila Fraser, Robert Marleau, and Peter Milliken shared their learned insights about the state of our parliamentary democracy. Lifelong diplomat Paul Heinbecker offered badly needly context for the current revolution in Canada's foreign policy. Major-General Lewis MacKenzie, Alan Williams, and Winslow Wheeler debunked some of the more obvious falsehoods about the disastrous F-35 program. Preston Manning, the dean of Canadian conservatism, provided invaluable insights into Stephen Harper's career from the earliest days. Individuals like Linda Keen and Helena Guergis, who have felt the full, power of the Harper government's displeasure, shared the details of their stories, despite the obvious pain in so doing.

Deepening my gratitude to so many people is the fact that there was a fear factor involved in participating in this project that I have never encountered before. Some very prominent Canadians decided not to go on the record with their full stories because they feared official reprisals might be the price of frankness—a favourite charity losing its charitable status, the loss of a pension, or even charges under national security legislation. I respect their decision but regret the loss of their personal accounts, which I hope will one day be told. I should add, Stephen Harper respectfully declined an interview for this book.

Finally, thanks to my wife, Lynda Harris. Without her prodigious work ethic, keen editorial judgment, and dogged determination to see this project through to completion, there would be no book.

INDEX